MW01610092

THE COMPLETE
AIR FRYER
COOKBOOK

1000 Recipes for Flavorful, Quick & Easy
Homemade Meals

Sarah Jones

© Copyright 2022 - All rights reserved. -

Sarah Jones

The content contained within this book may not be reproduced, duplicated, or transmitted without direct written permission from the author or the publisher. Under no circumstances will any blame or legal responsibility be held against the publisher, or author, for any damages, reparation, or monetary loss due to the information contained within this book. Either directly or indirectly.

Legal Notice:

This book is copyright protected. This book is only for personal use. You cannot amend, distribute, sell, use, quote or paraphrase any part, or the content within this book, without the consent of the author or publisher.

Disclaimer Notice:

Please note the information contained within this document is for educational and entertainment purposes only. All effort has been executed to present accurate, up to date, and reliable, complete information. No warranties of any kind are declared or implied. Readers acknowledge that the author is not engaging in the rendering of legal, financial, medical, or professional advice. The content within this book has been derived from various sources. Please consult a licensed professional before attempting any techniques outlined in this book.

By reading this document, the reader agrees that under no circumstances is the author responsible for any losses, direct or indirect, which are incurred because of the use of information contained within this document, including, but not limited to, errors, omissions, or inaccuracies.

Table Of Contents

INTRODUCTION..11

  WHAT IS AN AIR FRYER? 11

  HOW DOES IT WORK? 11

  BENEFITS OF USING AN AIR FRYER 11

  TOP 10 MISTAKES TO AVOID WHEN COOKING 12

  COMMON Q&A 12

CHAPTER 1: BREAKFAST 14

  HERB TOMATO EGG CUPS 14

  TASTY EGG BITES 14

  CHEESE SANDWICH 14

  EASY FRENCH TOAST 14

  FLAVORFUL BANANA MUFFINS 14

  QUICK & EASY GRANOLA 15

  BREAKFAST HUSH PUPPIES.....................15

  TASTY BREAKFAST POTATOES 15

  BLUEBERRY OATMEAL 15

  BANANA BREAD 15

  AIR FRYER BRUSSELS SPROUTS 16

  AIR FRYER ROASTED ASPARAGUS 16

  AIR-FRYER ROASTED VEGGIES 16

  AIR FRYER APPLE PIES 16

  AIR FRYER CORN NUTS............................16

  AIR FRYER COCONUT SHRIMP..................17

  AIR FRYER BREAKFAST FRITTATA 17

  AIR FRYER WIENER SCHNITZEL...............17

  AIR FRYER PLANTAIN CHIPS 17

  AIR FRYER POTATO CHIPS 18

  AIR FRYER CALAMARI 18

  AIR FRYER RANCH-STUFFED OLIVES 18

  AIR FRYER SPICY BAY SCALLOPS 18

  "EVERYTHING" SEASONING AIR FRYER ASPARAGUS....18

  AIR FRYER FINGERLING POTATOES WITH DIP 19

  KETO AIR FRYER JALAPENO POPPERS......19

  AIR FRYER SHORTBREAD COOKIE FRIES ...19

  AIR FRYER KETO THUMBPRINT COOKIES...19

  AIR FRYER SPICY ROASTED PEANUTS........20

  AIR FRYER ROASTED SALSA VERDE 20

  AIR FRYER PERI PERI FRIES 20

  AIR FRYER CHILE VERDE BURRITOS.........20

  AIR FRYER BOURSIN-STUFFED WONTONS 20

  AIR FRYER SPINACH AND FETA CASSEROLE 21

  AIR FRYER SUGARED PECANS 21

  AIR FRYER PIZZA DOGS 21

AIR FRYER ZUCCHINI CHIPS.............................21

AIR FRYER SAUSAGE PATTIES..........................21

LEMON-GARLIC AIR FRYER SALMON.................22

AIR FRYER STEAK AND MUSHROOMS 22

AIR FRYER SWEET POTATO HASH 22

AIR FRYER TOFU 22

AIR FRYER ROASTED BANANAS 22

AIR FRYER APPLE CRUMBLE 22

AIR FRYER CRAB RANGOON 23

AIR FRYER FISH STICKS 23

AIR FRYER HASSELBACK POTATOES 23

AIR-FRYER ASPARAGUS FRIES.........................23

BASIC AIR FRYER HOT DOGS............................24

AIR FRYER MEATLOAF 24

AIR-FRYER TEMPURA VEGGIES 24

AIR FRYER CELERY ROOT FRIES 24

AIR FRYER FRIED OKRA 25

LUMPIA IN THE AIR FRYER 25

AIR FRYER PASTA CHIPS 25

AIR FRYER PORTOBELLO PIZZAS FOR TWO 25

EASY AIR FRYER APPLE PIES 25

AIR FRYER AVOCADO FRIES 26

AIR FRYER RANCH PORK CHOPS 26

AIR FRYER MAC AND CHEESE BALLS 26

CHAPTER 2: SNACKS & APPETIZERS 28

  ROSEMARY POTATO WEDGES 28

  HEALTHY MIXED NUTS 28

  STUFF MUSHROOMS................................28

  CRISPY BROCCOLI POPCORN 28

  ZUCCHINI BITES 28

  AIR FRYER ALMONDS 29

  TASTY BROCCOLI NUGGETS 29

  CURRIED SWEET POTATO FRIES 29

  ASPARAGUS FRIES 29

  SAVORY WALNUTS 29

  AIR FRYER ZUCCHINI CURLY FRIES 29

  AIR FRYER RIB-EYE STEAK 30

  AIR FRYER ROASTED BROCCOLI AND CAULIFLOWER ..30

  AIR FRYER ROASTED CAULIFLOWER 30

  AIR FRYER LEMON PEPPER SHRIMP 30

  AIR FRYER BABY BACK RIBS 30

  ROASTED RAINBOW VEGETABLES IN THE AIR FRYER..31

  AIR FRYER FLOUR TORTILLA BOWLS 31

  AIR FRYER STEAK AND CHEESE MELTS 31

AIR FRYER MINI PIZZA CALZONES 31
AIR FRYER SPANISH POTATO WEDGES 32
AIR FRYER BACON 32
AIR FRYER PUMPKIN SEEDS 32
STUFFED AIR FRYER POTATOES 32
AIR FRYER OREOS 32
AIR FRYER BLUEBERRY MUFFINS 32
AIR FRYER SOURDOUGH BREAD 33
AIR FRYER ASPARAGUS TOTS...............................33
AIR FRYER CINNAMON-SUGAR DOUGHNUTS 33
ROSEMARY POTATO WEDGES FOR THE AIR FRYER.....33
AIR FRYER FRIED GREEN TOMATOES 33
AIR FRYER TO STONES 34
AIR FRYER FRENCH TOAST STICKS 34
AIR FRYER ZESTY CHEDDAR BISCUITS 34
TEX-MEX AIR FRYER HASH BROWNS 34
PERFECT TURKEY BREAST ROAST IN THE AIR FRYER ..35
AIR FRYER TRIPLE-CHOCOLATE OATMEAL COOKIES...35
AIR FRYER MINI PEPPERS STUFFED WITH CHEESE AND
SAUSAGE 35
AIR FRYER CHEESE-STUFFED MINI ITALIAN
MEATLOAVES..36
AIR FRYER BLACK GARLIC-CAULIFLOWER PATTIES 36
AIR FRYER MAHI MAHI WITH BROWN BUTTER..........36
AIR FRYER BANG BANG TOFU 36
AIR FRYER SRIRACHA-HONEY SHRIMP 37
AIR FRYER LOBSTER TAILS WITH LEMON-GARLIC
BUTTER 37
AIR FRYER DRY-RUBBED PORK TENDERLOIN WITH
BROCCOLI 37
AIR FRYER APPLE FRITTERS 37
AIR FRYER ROSEMARY GARLIC BABY POTATOES 38
AIR FRYER ROSEMARY GARLIC BABY POTATOES 38
AIR FRYER BACON-WRAPPED SCALLOPS WITH
SRIRACHA MAYO 38
AIR FRYER BEIGNETS 38
AIR FRYER BUTTERNUT SQUASH HOME FRIES 39
AIR FRYER TERIYAKI SNAP PEAS AND MUSHROOMS ...39
SPICY HOMEMADE BREAKFAST SAUSAGE IN THE AIR
FRYER 39
AIR FRYER PROSCIUTTO AND MOZZARELLA GRILLED
CHEESE 39
AIR FRYER SWEET AND SPICY ROASTED CARROTS 39
AIR-FRYER POTATO-SKIN WEDGES 40
AIR FRYER SALT AND VINEGAR CHICKPEAS 40
FRIED GREEN TOMATOES IN THE AIR FRYER 40
AIR FRYER TAJIN APPLE CHIPS 40
AIR FRYER CAJUN CRAB CAKES 40

CHAPTER 3: VEGETABLES & SIDES 42

AIR FRYER MIXED VEGGIES 42
CRISPY CARROT & SWEET POTATOES 42
BALSAMIC TOMATOES 42
HERB MUSHROOMS 42
AIR FRYER GREEN BEANS 42
TASTY RADISH HASH BROWNS 43
CURRIED CAULIFLOWER 43
LEMON GARLIC BROCCOLI 43
HERB CARROTS SLICES 43
AIR FRYER ASPARAGUS 43
EASY ROASTED VEGETABLES 43
DICED POTATO CASSEROLE WITH VEGETABLES 44
BEEF WITH VEGETABLES 44
GRILLED VEGETABLES WITH BALSAMIC VINEGAR 44
QUICK MEDITERRANEAN VEGETABLES....................44
EASY GRILLED VEGETABLES 45
CURRIED VEGETABLES 45
OVEN ROASTED VEGETABLES 45
BEER BATTERED FRIED VEGETABLES 45
ROASTED VEGETABLES 45
IMPERIAL VEGETABLES AND NOODLES 46
HEARTY TURKEY STEW WITH VEGETABLES 46
MEDITERRANEAN ROAST VEGETABLES 46
ROASTED BALSAMIC VEGETABLES 46
ROASTED INDIAN-SPICED VEGETABLES....................47
SPICY ROASTED VEGETABLES 47
MARINATED BARBEQUED VEGETABLES 47
MIXED GREEK VEGETABLES IN TOMATO SAUCE 47
CREOLE VEGETABLES 48
HALIBUT WITH VEGETABLES 48
VEGETARIAN MEATLOAF WITH VEGETABLES 48
VEGETABLE DIP 48
VEGETABLE WHIP 48
CHEESY VEGETABLES AND NOODLES......................49
ONE POT EASY CHEESY VEGETABLES AND RICE 49
GREAT GRILLED SMOKY VEGETABLES WITH AVOCADO
AND GOAT CHEESE CRUMBLES............................49
FROZEN VEGETABLE STIR-FRY...........................49
ROASTED ROOT VEGETABLES WITH APPLE JUICE 49
GRANDPA'S GRILLED VEGETABLES IN FOIL 50
PASTA WITH VEGETABLES 50
SAVORY ROASTED ROOT VEGETABLES.....................50
ROASTED VEGETABLES AND PUFF PASTRY.................50
MEDITERRANEAN GRILLED VEGETABLES 51
BALSAMIC-ROASTED VEGETABLES 51
RAMEN NOODLE STIR-FRY WITH CHICKEN AND
VEGETABLES 51
SHEET PAN ROASTED VEGETABLES 51
SMOKY GRILLED VEGETABLES............................52

STIR-FRIED SWEET AND SOUR VEGETABLES 52
STIR-FRIED VEGETABLES.................................52
AIR-FRIED MEDITERRANEAN VEGETABLE MEDLEY 52
MARINATED VEGETABLE SALAD 53
SHRIMP AND VEGETABLE SHEET PAN DINNER 53
HERB GRILLED VEGETABLES 53
BROWNED BUTTER VEGETABLES WITH ALMONDS.......53
CHRISTMAS ROASTED VEGETABLES 53
ROASTED VEGETABLE AND KALE LASAGNA 54
ROASTED AUTUMN ROOT VEGETABLES.....................54
POT ROAST, VEGETABLES, AND BEER........................54
STIR-FRIED SESAME VEGETABLES WITH RICE 55
CREAMY CHEESE FALL VEGETABLE CASSEROLE...........55

CHAPTER 4: POULTRY...57

CRISPY CHICKEN WINGS...............................57
FLAVORFUL TURKEY PATTIES 57
EASY CHICKEN TENDERS 57
JERK CHICKEN WINGS..................................57
CHEESY CHICKEN FRITTERS 57
JUICY TURKEY BREAST 58
FLAVORS CHICKEN THIGHS 58
DELICIOUS CHICKEN BREASTS 58
CHICKEN KEBAB 58
MARINATED CHICKEN THIGHS 58
AIR FRYER BUTTERMILK FRIED CHICKEN 59
AIR FRYER BLACKENED CHICKEN BREAST 59
SPICY AIR FRYER WINGS 59
AIR FRYER STUFFING BALLS 59
AIR FRYER CHICKEN FAJITAS 60
AIR FRYER CHIMICHANGAS 60
AIR FRYER BUFFALO CHICKEN WINGS.....................60
AIR FRYER CHICKEN NUGGETS 60
AIR FRYER POPCORN CHICKEN 61
CORNFLAKE-CRUSTED CHICKEN DRUMSTICKS IN THE
AIR FRYER 61
HEALTHIER BANG BANG CHICKEN IN THE AIR FRYER.61
MEXICAN-STYLE AIR FRYER STUFFED CHICKEN
BREASTS 61
AIR FRYER CHICKEN THIGH SCHNITZEL 62
HONEY-SRIRACHA AIR FRYER WINGS 62
AIR FRYER COCONUT CHICKEN 62
AIR FRYER CHICKEN KIEV 63
SPICY CHICKEN JERKY IN THE AIR FRYER 63
CRISPY KETO FRIED CHICKEN IN THE AIR FRYER........63
AIR FRYER STUFFED CHICKEN BREASTS 63
AIR FRYER GENERAL TSO'S CHICKEN.........................64
AIR FRYER CHICKEN KATSU...........................64
AIR FRYER OLD BAY® CHICKEN WINGS..................64

AIR FRYER CHICKEN TAQUITOS.........................65
AIR FRYER CHICKEN THIGHS 65
AIR FRYER KETO CHICKEN WINGS 65
AIR FRYER CORNFLAKE CHICKEN FINGERS 65
AIR FRYER CHICKEN FAJITA TAQUITOS 65
AIR FRIED MAPLE CHICKEN THIGHS 66
CRISPY RANCH AIR FRYER NUGGETS.....................66
AIR FRYER BANG-BANG CHICKEN 66
AIR FRYER CHICKEN CORDON BLEU.....................66
AIR FRYER HONEY-CAJUN CHICKEN THIGHS 67
BACON-WRAPPED STUFFED CHICKEN BREASTS IN THE
AIR FRYER 67
AIR FRYER HERB-SEASONED CHICKEN WINGS 67
AIR FRYER BALSAMIC-GLAZED CHICKEN WINGS........68
AIR FRYER CHICKEN STRIPS 68
KETO LEMON-GARLIC CHICKEN THIGHS IN THE AIR
FRYER 68
AIR FRYER BACON-WRAPPED CHICKEN THIGHS 68
AIR FRYER SESAME CHICKEN THIGHS 69
AIR FRYER CORNFLAKE-CRUSTED CHICKEN TENDERS69
AIR FRYER CHICKEN KATSU WITH HOMEMADE KATSU
SAUCE 69
AIR FRYER CHICKEN KYIV BALLS 69
AIR FRYER SWEET AND SOUR CHICKEN WINGS 70
AIR FRYER BBQ CHEDDAR-STUFFED CHICKEN BREASTS
....70
AIR FRYER APRICOT-GLAZED CHICKEN BREASTS 70
AIR FRYER PIZZA-STUFFED CHICKEN BREASTS 71
AIR FRIED VEGETARIAN "CHICKEN TENDERS." 71
AIR-FRIED KOREAN CHICKEN WINGS 71
CRISPY AIR-FRIED CHICKEN 71
AIR-FRIED BUFFALO CHICKEN 72

CHAPTER 5: BEEF, PORK & LAMB.........................74

JUICY TENDER PORK CHOPS 74
MEATBALLS...74
MOIST & TENDER HAM 74
JUICY PORK TENDERLOIN 74
STEAK KEBAB 74
ONION GARLIC PORK CHOPS 75
EASY BEEF ROAST 75
MEATBALLS...75
FLAVORFUL PORK PATTIES 75
LEMON HERB LAMB CHOPS...........................75
DUTCH OVEN BEEF STEW 76
BEEF STROGANOFF SAUCE WITH MEATBALLS.............76
DRIED BEEF BALL 76
SIMPLE BEEF STEW 76
CONFETTI BEEF TACOS 76
BEEF TACO NOODLE BAKE 77

FILIPINO CORNED BEEF AND CABBAGE 77
SLOW COOKER BARBECUE BEEF 77
BLUE CHEESE BEEF TENDERLOIN............................ 77
MUSHROOM BEEF BURGERS.................................. 78
CORNED BEEF HASH 78
SMOTHERED BEEF SHORT RIBS 78
CORNED BEEF AND SWISS DIP 78
HOT BEEF DIP 78
CHEF JOHN'S BEEF GOULASH.............................. 79
SLOW COOKER ROAST BEEF 79
BEEF KEBABS WITH POMEGRANATE COUSCOUS 79
PATSY'S BEST BARBEQUE BEEF 79
EASY GINGER BEEF 80
GLAZED CORNED BEEF 80
DSF'S SHREDDED BEEF.. 80
LENGUA (BEEF TONGUE) 80
BIBIMBAP WITH BEEF 80
BEEF MARTINI.. 81
HAWAIIAN BEEF STEW 81
SLOW COOKER BEEF BARBACOA 81
GREEK-STYLE BEEF PITA...................................... 81
BACKYARD BOURBON BEEF MARINADE 82
ASIAN BEEF WITH SNOW PEAS.............................. 82
GRILLED BEEF FAJITAS 82
BUTTER BEEF 82
BEEF BOURGUIGNON WITHOUT THE BURGUNDY........ 82
BAKED SPANISH RICE AND BEEF........................... 83
BEEF AND CHEESE BALL...................................... 83
SIMPLE BEEF STROGANOFF 83
CORNED BEEF AND CABBAGE................................ 83
CORNED BEEF AND CABBAGE................................ 84
EASY VEGETABLE BEEF SOUP 84
ROASTED LAMB BREAST 84
SIMPLE GRILLED LAMB CHOPS 84
STUFFED GREEK LEG OF LAMB 85
CHEF JOHN'S GRILLED LAMB WITH MINT ORANGE
SAUCE 85
JINX-PROOF BRAISED LAMB SHANKS 85
CHILE PORK 85
PORK MARINADE.. 86
BASIC PORK BRINE 86
HONEY-GRILLED PORK CHOPS.............................. 86
TIM'S SMOKED PORK BUTT.................................. 86
SIMPLY THE EASIEST BEEF BRISKET 86
BEST EVER BEEF MARINADE 87

CHAPTER 6: FISH & SEAFOOD...............................89

TENDER & FLAKY SALMON 89
SPICY PRAWNS... 89

SHRIMP SKEWERS 89
CHIPOTLE LIME SHRIMP 89
LEMON GARLIC SHRIMP 89
CREOLE SHRIMP 90
LEMON SCALLOPS 90
ASIAN SALMON 90
HERB SALMON 90
HONEY GARLIC SALMON 90
WONDERFUL FRIED FISH TACOS........................... 90
MARINATED FRIED FISH 91
BAKED FISH FILLETS 91
EASY BAKED FISH WITH LEMON 91
AIR FRYER BLACKENED FISH TACOS 91
TAMARIND SAUCE FISH CURRY 92
POACHED FISH WITH CUCUMBERS 92
AIR-FRIED CRUMBED FISH 92
SEASONED SWAI FISH FILLET 92
WHOLE FISH FRIED WITH BASIL AND CHILES 93
BAJA SAUCE FOR FISH OR SHRIMP TACOS 93
INDIAN FISH CURRY.. 93
PORTUGUESE COD FISH CASSEROLE 93
CRISPY BEER BATTER FISH & CHIPS....................... 94
PARCHMENT-COOKED FISH WITH MORELS, SPRING
GARLIC, AND THYME 94
SMOKED FISH DIP 94
EASY ELEGANT BAKED FISH 94
CRUNCHY FISH TACOS 95
BETH'S BAKED FISH 95
CHICKEN-CHEESE-FISH....................................... 95
MEXICAN BAKED FISH 95
CLASSIC FISH AND CHIPS 95
FISH AND THINGS TERIYAKI MARINADE.................. 96
FISH TACOS FROM REYNOLDS WRAP 96
CERVEZA AND LIME MARINADE FOR SHRIMP AND FISH
.... 96
CORN CRUSTED RED FISH................................... 96
HALIBUT FISH TACOS... 96
BEER BATTER FOR FISH 97
TWICE FRIED FISH 97
QUICK AND EASY BAKED FISH FILLET 97
BAKED FISH CROQUETTES 97
GRILLED TUNA FISH STEAKS................................ 98
FISH BATTER WITH NEWCASTLE™ BROWN ALE......... 98
ACCIDENTAL FISH 98
EASY-BAKE FISH 98
COCONUT FISH CURRY....................................... 98
LEMONY STEAMED FISH...................................... 99
FREDA'S FABULOUS FISH 99
FIERY FISH TACOS WITH CRUNCHY CORN SALSA........ 99

SPICY FISH SOUP 99

AIR FRYER FISH STICKS 99

EASY BAKED FISH 100

FISH ON A PLANK 100

PRETZEL COATED FRIED FISH1-QUART OIL FOR FRYING
....100

EASY MEDITERRANEAN FISH 101

HOMEMADE FISH STOCK 101

SEXY FISH STEW 101

FISH AND CHIPS SLIDERS.....................................101

FORT WORTH FISH TACOS 102

COD FISH CAKES..102

CHAPTER 7: RICE & GRAINS..........................104

RICE STUFFED PEPPERS.......................................104

APPLE OATS..104

PEANUT BUTTER OATMEAL 104

OATS GRANOLA 104

BERRY OATMEAL 105

CHOCOLATE OATS 105

CURRIED CHICKPEAS 105

CHOCOLATE CHIP OATS 105

RANCH CHICKPEAS 105

COCONUT OATS 105

MANGO GINGER RICE 106

CARROT RICE..106

PERSIAN RICE WITH POTATO TAHDIG 106

EASY CILANTRO-LIME RICE 106

JASMINE RICE 106

BETTER SPANISH RICE..107

BLACK RICE..107

DIRTY RICE...107

YELLOW RICE WITH VEGETABLES1 TEASPOON
VEGETABLE OIL 107

ALMOND WILD RICE..108

BASMATI RICE 108

THAI FRIED RICE 108

BROWN RICE PUDDING 108

CHERRY WILD RICE 109

THE PERFECT EGYPTIAN RICE WITH VERMICELLI 109

BAKED "FRIED" RICE 109

RICE PATTIES 109

MUSHROOM RICE 110

SARAH'S RICE PILAF 110

ISLAND-STYLE FRIED RICE 110

VEGAN KOREAN KIMCHI FRIED RICE....................110

GARLIC RICE...110

CINDY'S YELLOW RICE..111

SWEET COCONUT RICE 111

QUINOA FRIED RICE 111

ONE-POT RICE AND BEEF PILAF............................111

CINNAMON RICE 112

CAULIFLOWER RICE (BIRYANI-STYLE) 112

MOREL MUSHROOM AND WILD RICE RISOTTO 112

CLASSIC FRIED RICE 112

PARMESAN ASPARAGUS RICE 112

EASY OVEN BROWN RICE 113

YELLOW RICE WITH MEAT 113

PERFECT WHITE RICE 113

JEERA RICE 113

SOUTH INDIAN-STYLE LEMON RICE 113

CAJUN WILD RICE...114

LINNIE'S SPANISH RICE.......................................114

KHEER (RICE PUDDING) 114

DELICATE JASMINE RICE 114

SPENT GRAIN WHEAT BREAD 114

CHICKEN AND MULTI-GRAIN STIR FRY 115

CRANBERRY PECAN MULTI-GRAIN STUFFING 115

WHOLE GRAIN PANCAKES WITH FRESH FRUIT 115

WHOLE GRAIN PANCAKES 115

EASTER GRAIN PIE 115

GRAIN AND NUT WHOLE WHEAT PANCAKES 116

RUSTIC GRAIN CEREAL 116

WHOLE GRAIN CARROT PEACH MUFFINS................116

ZUCCHINI BANANA MULTI-GRAIN BREAD 117

CHAPTER 8: VEGAN 119

VEGETABLE SKEWERS 119

HEALTHY JICAMA & GREEN BEANS 119

CRISPY BRUSSELS SPROUTS 119

FLAVORFUL GREEN BEANS 119

EASY RATATOUILLE 119

TASTY ZUCCHINI CHIPS 120

CRISPY CAULIFLOWER TOTS 120

CRISPY TOFU CUBES 120

TASTY CARROTS CHIPS 120

HERB OLIVES 120

AIR FRYER BURGERS 120

AIR FRYER VEGAN BUFFALO TOFU BITES 121

AIR FRYER VEGAN BUFFALO CAULIFLOWER 121

AIR FRYER VEGAN SWEET POTATO FRITTERS..........121

VEGAN AIR FRYER TAQUITOS 121

VEGAN JALAPENO CORNBREAD IN THE AIR FRYER ...122

AIR FRYER DONUT STICKS 122

AIR FRYER ROOT VEGETABLES WITH VEGAN AIOLI ..122

AIR FRYER APPLE DUMPLINGS 123

AIR FRYER EGG ROLLS 123

AIR FRYER PAKORAS 123

AIR FRYER STEAK FOR FAJITAS.....................123

HASSELBACK AIR FRYER POTATOES........................124

AIR FRYER SALMON NUGGETS 124

AIR FRYER MINI MEATLOAVES 124

AIR FRYER TOFU MILANESE 124

SPICY AIR FRYER SALMON 124

AIR FRYER SHRIMP AND POLENTA 125

AIR FRYER TURKEY FAJITAS 125

AIR FRYER SALMON FOR ONE 125

AIR FRYER BROILED GRAPEFRUIT 125

AIR FRYER TURKEY FAJITAS 126

AIR FRYER LATKES 126

SPICY AIR FRYER SALMON 126

AIR FRYER SALMON PATTIES 127

AIR FRYER STUFFED MUSHROOMS 127

AIR FRYER CORN ON THE COB 127

AIR FRYER FRITTATA 127

AIR FRYER FINGERLING POTATOES 127

AIR FRYER BAKED POTATOES 128

AIR FRYER EGGPLANT FRIES 128

AIR FRYER MUSHROOMS 128

AIR FRYER TURKEY BREAST 128

AIR FRYER FRENCH FRIES 128

AIR FRYER BABA GHANOUSH.................................129

AIR FRYER ROASTED GARLIC.................................129

AIR FRYER EGGPLANT PARMESAN 129

AIR FRYER POPCORN SHRIMP.................................129

AIR FRYER SHRIMP FAJITAS 130

AIR FRYER POTATO WEDGES 130

AIR FRYER SCOTCH EGGS 130

AIR-FRYER FRIES 130

AIR FRYER BLUEBERRY CHIMICHANGAS 131

CAJUN AIR FRYER SALMON 131

AIR FRYER FALAFEL 131

AIR FRYER ROASTED OKRA 131

AIR FRYER ARANCINI 131

AIR FRYER ROASTED PINEAPPLE 132

AIR FRYER BISON BURGERS 132

AIR FRYER POLENTA FRIES 132

CHAPTER 9: SPECIAL EVENTS....................134

FLAVORFUL CHICKEN SKEWERS 134

TURKEY MEATBALLS.................................134

TANDOORI CHICKEN DRUMSTICKS 134

CHICKEN BURGER PATTIES.................................134

FLAVORFUL STEW MEAT 135

CHEESY LAMB PATTIES 135

CHIPOTLE RIB-EYE STEAK 135

YOGURT BEEF KEBABS.................................135

ASIAN PORK CHOPS 135

CHEESE BALLS.................................136

CRUMBED CHICKEN TENDERLOINS 136

AIR-FRIED SWEET AND SOUR CHICKEN WINGS........136

AMAZING BUTTERMILK AIR FRIED CHICKEN...........136

AIR-FRIED PERUVIAN CHICKEN DRUMSTICKS WITH
GREEN CREMA 136

DRY-RUB AIR-FRIED CHICKEN WINGS 137

MUSTARD FRIED CHICKEN 137

BEER CAN CHICKEN TEXAS STYLE 137

GARLIC AND PARMESAN CHICKEN WINGS 138

GLUTEN-FREE ALMOND FLOUR CHICKEN NUGGETS 138

AIR-FRIED POPCORN CHICKEN GIZZARDS 138

RESTAURANT-STYLE EXTRA CRISPY CHICKEN..........139

AIRLINE CHICKEN BREAST 139

CRISPY FLAUTAS 139

CRISPY BAKED MOROCCAN CHICKEN WINGS WITH
YOGURT DIP 140

BAKED PANKO-CRUSTED CHICKEN TENDERS 140

CRISPY HONEY SRIRACHA CHICKEN WINGS 140

ZESTY BROILED CHICKEN THIGHS 141

PAPER-WRAPPED CHICKEN.................................141

CHICKEN FAJITA EGG ROLLS 141

GRANDMA EGAN'S CHICKEN STOCK 141

SMOKED CHICKEN DRUMSTICKS 142

CHICKEN AND WAFFLE SANDWICH 142

HOT BEAN AND BACON DIP WITH AIR FRYER TORTILLA
CHIPS.................................142

AIR FRYER ROTISSERIE CHICKEN.................................142

AIR FRYER STUFFED CHICKEN THIGHS 143

AIR-FRIED BREADED CHICKEN THIGHS 143

AIR-FRIED CHICKEN CALZONE.................................143

CRISPY CHICKEN SALAD WITH YUMMY HONEY
MUSTARD DRESSING.................................144

AIR FRYER GLUTEN-FREE FRIED CHICKEN 144

AIR FRYER CHICKEN THIGHS AND POTATOES..........144

CRISPY AIR-FRIED CHICKEN 145

GREEK-INSPIRED AIR FRYER CORNISH HEN 145

AIR FRYER CORNISH HEN 145

CRISPY SMOKED CHICKEN WINGS.................................145

GREEK-INSPIRED AIR FRYER CORNISH HEN 146

AIR FRYER CHICKEN PICCATA 146

AIR FRYER CHICKEN PICCATA WITH LEMON-CAPER
SAUCE.................................146

AIR FRYER HONEY CHICKEN 147

CHICKEN CORDON IN THE AIR FRYER 147

AIR-FRIED CHICKEN STRIPS 147

AIR FRYER CORNFLAKE CHICKEN 147

AIR FRYER CHICKEN SATAY WITH DIPPING SAUCE... 148

AIR FRYER CHICKEN FAJITAS FOR TWO 148

AIR FRYER FRIED CHICKEN 148

AIR FRYER BBQ CHICKEN TENDERS 149

GOLDEN AIR-FRIED CHICKEN TENDERS 149

AIR FRYER CORNISH HEN 149

AIR FRYER CHICKEN PICCATA 149

CHICKEN CORDON BLEU IN THE AIR FRYER 150

EASY AIR-FRIED CHICKEN BREAST 150

CHAPTER 10: DESSERTS 152

DELICIOUS APPLE CRISPS 152

MOIST ORANGE MUFFINS 152

SLICED APPLES 152

BAKED PEARS 152

GOOEY CHOCOLATE CAKE 152

CHOCOLATE BROWNIES 153

SWEET CARAMEL PINEAPPLE 153

BLUEBERRY COBBLER 153

APPLE PECAN CARROT MUFFINS 153

BLUEBERRY MUFFINS 153

AIR FRYER KALE CHIPS WITH PARMESAN 154

AIR FRYER PEAR CRISP FOR TWO 154

AIR FRYER MINI BLUEBERRY SCONES 154

AIR FRYER TURKEY BREAKFAST SAUSAGE LINKS 154

AIR FRYER GARLIC AND PARSLEY BABY POTATOES ...154

AIR FRYER SALMON CAKES WITH SRIRACHA MAYO...155

AIR FRYER SPICY DILL PICKLE FRIES 155

AIR FRYER BROWN SUGAR AND PECAN ROASTED
APPLES 155

AIR FRYER HARD-BOILED EGGS 155

AIR FRYER SOY-GINGER SHISHITO PEPPERS 155

AIR FRYER TILAPIA WITH FRESH LEMON PEPPER 156

AIR FRYER BREADED SEA SCALLOPS 156

EASY AIR FRYER FRENCH TOAST STICKS 156

AIR FRYER PULL-APART PEPPERONI-CHEESE BREAD
........................156

AIR FRYER ASIAN-INSPIRED DEVILED EGGS 157

AIR FRYER CHOCOLATE CHIP COOKIE BITES 157

AIR FRYER STEAK TIPS AND PORTOBELLO MUSHROOMS
........................157

CRISPY AIR FRYER COD 157

AIR FRYER FRIED MUSHROOMS 157

AIR FRYER ONE-BITE ROASTED POTATOES 158

AIR FRYER KETO GARLIC CHEESE 'BREAD.' 158

CHOCOLATE CAKE IN AN AIR FRYER 158

AIR FRYER ITALIAN SAUSAGES, PEPPERS, AND ONIONS
........................158

AIR FRYER SHRIMP A LA BANG BANG 159

AIR FRYER FRIED PICKLES 159

AIR FRYER SWEET POTATO TOTS 159

AIR FRYER CAULIFLOWER TOTS 159

AIR FRYER SOUFFLE EGG CUPS 159

AIR FRYER BBQ BABY BACK RIBS 160

AIR FRYER JERK PORK SKEWERS WITH BLACK BEAN
AND MANGO SALSA 160

AIR FRYER PEANUT BUTTER & JELLY S'MORES 160

AIR FRYER MINI BEAN AND CHEESE TACOS 160

SWEET POTATO CHIPS IN THE AIR FRYER 161

SKINNY AIR FRYER FUNNEL CAKES 161

AIR-FRIED JALAPENO POPPERS 161

AIR FRYER FROG LEGS 161

AIR FRYER HUSH PUPPIES 161

AIR-FRIED RATATOUILLE, ITALIAN-STYLE 162

AIR FRYER EGGPLANT PARMESAN MINI PIZZAS 162

AIR FRYER CORN DOGS 162

AIR FRYER MUSTARD-CRUSTED PORK TENDERLOIN
WITH POTATOES AND GREEN BEANS 163

CHINESE FIVE-SPICE AIR FRYER BUTTERNUT SQUASH
FRIES 163

AIR FRYER CHURROS 163

AIR FRYER SALT AND VINEGAR FRIES FOR ONE........163

AIR-FRIED CAULIFLOWER WITH ALMONDS AND
PARMESAN 163

AIR FRYER BREAKFAST TOAD-IN-THE-HOLE TARTS. 164

AIR FRYER ROASTED BRUSSELS SPROUTS WITH MAPLE-
MUSTARD MAYO 164

AIR FRYER ONION BHAJI 164

EASY SPRING ROLLS (AIR FRIED) 164

AIR-FRIED ITALIAN STUFFED TOMATOES 165

CONCLUSION 166

Introduction

An air fryer is one of the versatile kitchen appliances that work like a convection oven. It comes in a compact size and easily fits on your kitchen countertop. As compared with the traditional deep frying method air fryer cooks your food by circulating hot air around the food basket. It requires 90% less fat and oil while air frying your favorite food. The air fryer makes your food crispy crunchy from the outside and juicy tenders from the inside. During the cooking process, the air fryer cooks without producing harmful compounds and gives you healthy air-fried food without changing the taste and texture like deep-fried food. Using little fats and oil you can make your favorite snacks effortlessly. The air fryer one of the safest appliances comes with auto-shutoff options. When the countdown timer reaches zero the air fryer goes shut off itself to avoid overcooking or burning your food.

This cookbook contains healthy and delicious air fryer recipes that come from different categories like breakfast to desserts. The recipes written in this cookbook are simple to make and written into an easy and understandable format. All the recipes start with their preparation and cooking time information with the step-by-step instruction set. All the recipes written in this cookbook come with their nutritional values which will help you to keep track of daily calorie consumption. There are various types of cookbooks available in the market on this topic thanks for choosing my cookbook. I hope you love and enjoy all the healthy and delicious air fryer recipes written in this cookbook.

What Is an Air Fryer?

An air fryer is one of the most popular healthy cooking appliances that allows you to fry your favorite food without submerging it into the oil. It works similarly to a convection oven. The air fryer works on a rapid hot air circulation technique to cook your food by circulating hot air around the food with the help of a convection fan. It equally distributes the hot air into a cooking chamber which ensures faster and even cooking results every time.

The air fryer is not only used for air frying your food but also used to grill, bake, and roast your food by using very few fats and oils. It is one of the multifunctional cooking appliances. If you love to eat fried food but are worried about extra calories intake, then an air fryer is one of the healthy cooking options available for you. It allows you to cook French fries, mozzarella sticks, onion rings, chicken wings, and more without compromising the taste and texture of deep-fried food.

The structure of an air fryer contains

> - **Cooking Chamber:** A cooking chamber is nothing but a place where food is placed for the cooking process. The cooking chamber comes with non-stick coatings. There are two types of cooking chamber one is a single tray, and another is multi tray all is depending on the brand you choose.
> - **Heating Elements:** Heating elements are fixed exactly at the top of the cooking chamber. They are capable to produce up to 400°F temperature to cook your food faster and evenly. The heating elements automatically turn on and off to maintain desired cooking temperature.
> - **Convection Fan:** The convection fan is situated at the top of the heating coil. It helps to distribute the heat equally into the cooking chamber to cook your food fast and evenly.
> - **Exhaust system:** The exhaust system starts working when there is enough hot air present in the cooking chamber. It helps to maintain the inside air pressure by releasing a small amount of air into the atmosphere.
> - **Removable food basket:** The removable food basket is used to place your food; it comes with non-stick coatings. Depending upon the air fryer model the food basket comes with a divider and layers. The food basket has a universal handle to hold and slide the food basket in and out of the cooking chamber.

How Does It Work?

The air fryer works on rapid hot air circulation technology. The heating mechanism of the air fryer with a convection fan is situated at the top section of the air fryer. Place your food into the air fryer basket when you turn on your air fryer. Very hot air circulates the food basket. The force of the hot air produces the convection effect around the food to make it crisp like deep frying food without using oil and fats. Compare with the traditional deep frying method air fryer cooks your food by using 90% less oil and fats.

When you cook your food into an air fryer triggers one chemical reaction called as Maillard effect. This reaction happens in between reduced sugar and amino acids. This improves the flavor and gives nice brown color to your favorite chicken, fish, veggies, snacks, and potatoes without overcooking them from inside.

Benefits Of Using an Air Fryer

An air fryer is one of the advanced and innovative cooking appliances. It allows you to cook a variety of healthy and tasty food in your kitchen. The air fryer comes with various kinds of benefits. These benefits include,

1. **Air Fryer is a healthy cooking appliance:** An air fryer is one of the healthy cooking appliances that allows you to air fry your food with very little fats and oils sometimes no oil. Compared with the traditional deep-frying method air fryer cooks your food by using 90% fewer fats and oils. Less oil and fats mean less calorie consumption helps you to keep fit and healthy. Most people's love to eat fried food but are worried due to extra calories consumption for those people air fryer is one of the best appliances available in the market. Using an air fryer, you can make tasty food at home without compromising the taste and texture like deep-fried food.
2. **Saves nutritional values:** Most of the essential nutrients are lost in the traditional deep-frying method. The deep-frying method not only adds extra calories to your food but is also responsible to increase the bad cholesterol level in your body. An air fryer cooks your food by using a rapid hot air circulation technique to circulate hot air around the food basket. You can air fry your favourite food by using 5 to 10 % of oil and fats. The nutritional values are kept in food in the air frying method. It looks like healthy and nutritional balanced food for you without adding extra calories.

3. **Faster and even cooking:** The air fryer cooks your food by circulating hot air into the cooking chamber. The internal temperature of the cooking chamber reaches up to 400°F to cook your favorite food faster. As compared with another oven the air fryer cooks your food 65 % faster. It is one of the perfect cooking appliances for those people who have a busy schedule and do not spend more time preparing their food at home. An air fryer is capable to makes crispy crunchy French fries within 12 minutes due to high-speed hot air movement into the cooking chamber.

4. **Reduce the formation of toxic compounds:** In the deep-frying method of cooking due to high heat, some harmful toxic compounds are added to your food. These compounds are responsible for the development of some types of cancer like oesophageal, ovarian, and breast cancer. The air fryer cooks your food into very little oil or sometimes no oil. It cooks your favourite food by circulating hot air into the cooking chamber. Air frying your food is one of the healthy methods of cooking your food without the formation of toxic compounds during the air frying process.

5. **Protects nutritional values:** In the traditional deep-frying method, most of the essential vitamins, minerals, and nutrients are destroyed due to high heat. The air fryer cooks your food by circulating hot air into the cooking chamber. This method of cooking helps to protect the nutritional values that remain in the food.

6. **Safe to use:** In the traditional deep-frying method there are lots of chances to splatter hot oil on your skin during deep-frying your food. On the other hand, an air fryer frying your favorite food into the cooking chamber is closed from all the sides while you air fries your food. So, there is no chance of accidental splatter and burns during the air frying process. The most modern air fryer comes with an auto-shutoff feature. This feature allows your air fryer goes automatically shut off when the cooking countdown timer reaches zero. This feature never overcooks or burns your food after finishing cooking time.

7. **It can promote weight loss:** The traditional deep-frying method adds lots of calories and fats to your food. The consumption of such deep-fried food increases the risk of obesity. The air fryer cooks your food into very few fats and oils. Less fat and oil mean low-calorie intake which promotes weight loss and helps to maintain healthy body weight.

Top 10 Mistakes to Avoid When Cooking

1. **Putting your food into the unheated food basket**
   Always preheat your air fryer before placing your food into a food basket to get faster and even cooking results every time. If you put your food into an unheated food basket then it takes a longer time to cook your food, or you will get uneven cooking results.

2. **Overcrowding food basket**
   If you overcrowd the food into the cooking basket the hot air never passes properly so you could not get perfect crispiness into your food and get uneven cooking results. Some of the recipes need to be cooked into batches for perfect crispiness and even cooking results.

3. **Not using enough fats and oils in your recipe**
   Your air fryer cooks your food without oil but still, you need a little oil sprinkled over your food to get perfect crunchiness and texture over your food. You need to spray 1 to 2 tablespoons of oil-air frying bowl of French fries or roasting veggies.

4. **Forgot to shake the food basket**
   It is recommended to shake your food basket periodically to prevent overcooking your food on one side. Shake your food basket at least once or twice during the cooking cycle. Reheat your leftover food into an air fryer gives you original food taste and texture even if you reheat them.

5. **Keeping your air fryer into bad ventilation area**
   To function properly air fryer needs proper ventilation from all the sides to move the air in and out. Due to improper ventilation, your air fryer overheats and stops functioning. Keep your air fryer in a proper ventilation area.

6. **You are not patting your protein dry before placing it into the food basket**
   To avoid soggy food, make sure your food is properly dry before frying it into the air fryer. Dry food browns quickly as compared with wet food. So always dry your meat and veggies with the help of a paper towel before placing them into the air fryer.

7. **Use too much oil while air frying**
   If you use excess oil while air frying your food, it may result in your food is not cooked properly. You can use one or two tablespoons of oil to get better cooking results.

8. **When the food is too light**
   The air fryer cooks your food by circulating hot air into the cooking chamber. If you use too light food like spinach it starts to fry and ends in a heating coil.

9. **Purchasing the wrong air fryer**
   Before adding an air fryer into your shopping cart make sure how much food we cook into the air fryer. We have made the mistake when we buy our first air fryer and then realize that to upgrade or purchase a larger one.

10. **Using low smoke point spray**
    The use of low smoke point sprays such as coconut oil or canola oil fills your air fryer with smoke. So, it is better to use high smoke point oil sprays such as avocado oil.

Common Q&A

- **Is it compulsory to preheat the air fryer?**
  ➤ It is optional and uses it when it is necessary. Preheating your air fryer gives you faster and even cooking results.
- **How much food can the air fryer hold?**
  ➤ The standard air fryer can hold 2 to 4 servings of food. Don't overcrowd the food into the air fryer basket to avoid uneven cooking. I cook a large quantity of food then cook it into batches.
- **How do I prevent food to stick my air fryer?**
  ➤ To avoid this, you can coat your food basket with a little vegetable oil spray before placing your food into it.
- **Can I bake in the air fryer?**
  ➤ Yes, you can bake your favourite cake and cookies into the air fryer. Baking into an air fryer not only saves your time but also saves energy.
- **Can I use an oven-proof bowl or dish in my air fryer?**
  ➤ Yes, you can use an oven-proof bowl or dish in your air fryer. The dish which is safe for your oven is also safe for your air fryer.

CHAPTER 1:

Breakfast

Herb Tomato Egg Cups
Preparation Time: 10 minutes
Cooking Time: 12 minutes
Serve: 6
Ingredients:
- 5 eggs
- 1 medium onion, chopped
- ½ cup tomatoes, chopped
- 2 tbsp fresh parsley, chopped
- 2 tbsp fresh basil, chopped
- Pepper
- Salt

Directions:
- Preheat the air fryer to 300 F.
- In a mixing bowl, whisk eggs with pepper and salt. Add onion, basil, parsley, and tomatoes and stir well.
- Pour egg mixture into the silicone muffin molds.
- Place muffin molds into the air fryer basket and cook for 10-12 minutes.
- Serve and enjoy.

Tasty Egg Bites
Preparation Time: 10 minutes
Cooking Time: 12 minutes
Serve: 6
Ingredients:
- 6 eggs
- ¼ tsp mustard powder
- 2 green onions, sliced
- 1 tbsp milk
- 2 bacon slices, cooked & chopped
- ¼ cup cheddar cheese, shredded
- 1 tbsp heavy cream
- Pepper
- Salt

Directions:
- Preheat the air fryer to 350 F.
- In a bowl, whisk eggs with mustard powder, cream, pepper, and salt until fluffy.
- Add green onions, cheese, and bacon and stir well.
- Pour egg mixture into the silicone muffin molds.
- Place muffin molds into the air fryer basket and cook for 10-12 minutes or until eggs are set.
- Serve and enjoy.

Cheese Sandwich
Preparation Time: 10 minutes
Cooking Time: 5 minutes
Serve: 2
Ingredients:
- 4 bread slices
- ¼ tsp garlic powder
- 2 tbsp butter
- 4 oz cheddar cheese slices
- 1 tomato, cut into slices

Directions:
- Preheat the air fryer to 350 F.
- Spread butter on one side of each bread slice.
- Take two bread slices and top with cheddar cheese slices and tomato slices.
- Cover with remaining bread slices. Make sure buttered side up.
- Sprinkle garlic powder on top of sandwiches.
- Place sandwiches into the air fryer basket and cook for 4-5 minutes.
- Serve and enjoy.

Easy French Toast
Preparation Time: 10 minutes
Cooking Time: 10 minutes
Serve: 2
Ingredients:
- 2 eggs
- 4 bread slices
- ¼ tsp cinnamon
- 1 tsp vanilla
- 1 tbsp sugar
- ½ cup milk

Directions:
- Preheat the air fryer to 380 F.
- In a shallow bowl, whisk eggs with milk, sugar, vanilla, and cinnamon.
- Dip bread slices in egg mixture from both sides.
- Place bread slices into the air fryer basket and cook for 4 minutes.
- Turn bread slices and cook for 6 minutes more.
- Serve and enjoy.

Flavorful Banana Muffins
Preparation Time: 10 minutes
Cooking Time: 15 minutes
Serve: 10
Ingredients:

- 1 egg
- ¾ cup self-rising flour
- 1 tsp cinnamon
- 1 tsp vanilla
- ½ cup brown sugar
- 1/3 cup olive oil
- 2 ripe bananas

Directions:

- Preheat the air fryer to 320 F.
- In a mixing bowl, add ripe bananas and mash using a fork. Add oil, brown sugar, vanilla, and egg and stir until well combined.
- Add cinnamon and flour and mix until just combined.
- Spoon batter into the silicone muffin molds.
- Place muffin molds into the air fryer basket and cook for 15 minutes.
- Serve and enjoy.

Quick & Easy Granola

Preparation Time: 10 minutes
Cooking Time: 10 minutes
Serve: 4
Ingredients:

- 1 cup rolled oats
- 1 tsp vanilla
- 2 tbsp butter, melted
- 3 tbsp honey
- 1 tsp cinnamon
- ½ cup almonds, sliced
- Pinch of salt

Directions:

- In a mixing bowl, mix together oats, vanilla, butter, honey, cinnamon, almonds, and salt.
- Add granola mixture into the parchment-lined air fryer basket and cook for 10 minutes. Stir after every 2-3 minutes.
- Serve and enjoy.

Breakfast Hush Puppies

Preparation Time: 10 minutes
Cooking Time: 10 minutes
Serve: 4
Ingredients:

- 1 egg
- ¼ cup onion, chopped
- ¾ cup milk
- ½ tsp garlic powder
- ½ tsp onion powder
- ¼ tsp sugar
- 1 ½ tsp baking powder
- ¾ cup all-purpose flour
- 1 cup yellow cornmeal
- ½ tsp salt

Directions:

- In a mixing bowl, mix together cornmeal, flour, baking powder, sugar, onion, garlic powder, onion powder, and salt
- Add milk and egg and mix until well combined.
- Make small balls from the cornmeal mixture and place into the parchment-lined air fryer basket and cook for 10 minutes. Turn halfway through.
- Serve and enjoy.

Tasty Breakfast Potatoes

Preparation Time: 10 minutes
Cooking Time: 25 minutes
Serve: 4
Ingredients:

- 1 ½ lbs. potatoes, diced
- ¼ tsp fennel seed
- ¼ tsp garlic powder
- 2 bell peppers, sliced
- ¼ cup onion, diced
- Pepper
- Salt

Directions:

- Preheat the air fryer to 360 F.
- In a mixing bowl, toss potatoes with remaining ingredients.
- Add potato mixture into the air fryer basket and cook for 20-25 minutes. Stir after every 5 minutes.
- Serve and enjoy.

Blueberry Oatmeal

Preparation Time: 10 minutes
Cooking Time: 15 minutes
Serve: 2
Ingredients:

- 1 egg
- ¼ cup blueberries
- 1/3 cup milk
- 2 tbsp maple syrup
- 2 tbsp butter, melted
- ¼ tsp baking powder
- ½ tsp vanilla
- ½ tsp cinnamon
- ¾ cup rolled oats
- ¼ tsp salt

Directions:

- In a mixing bowl, mix together oats, egg, cinnamon, vanilla, baking powder, maple syrup, milk, and salt.
- Add blueberries and fold well.
- Pour oat mixture into the two greased ramekins.
- Place ramekins into the air fryer basket and cook at 300 F for 12-15 minutes.
- Serve and enjoy.

Banana Bread

Preparation Time: 10 minutes
Cooking Time: 15 minutes
Serve: 6
Ingredients:

- 1 egg
- ¼ cup butter, melted
- 1/3 cup walnuts, chopped
- 1 cup sugar
- 3 bananas, overripe & mashed
- 1 tsp baking soda
- 1 ½ cups all-purpose flour
- ½ tsp salt

Directions:

- In a mixing bowl, mix together flour, baking soda, sugar, walnuts, and salt.

- Add melted butter, egg, and mashed bananas and mix until well combined.
- Pour batter into the greased loaf pan.
- Place loaf pan into the air fryer basket and cook at 350 F for 12-15 minutes.
- Slice and serve.

Air Fryer Brussels Sprouts
Preparation Time: 15 minutes
Cooking Time: 25 minutes
Serve: 1
Ingredients:

- 1 teaspoon avocado oil
- ½ teaspoon salt
- ½ teaspoon ground black pepper
- 10 ounces Brussels sprouts
- 1 teaspoon balsamic vinegar
- 2 teaspoons crumbled cooked bacon

Directions:

- Preheat an air fryer carefully to 350°F (175 degrees C).
- In a mixing dish, combine the oil, salt, and pepper. Turn the Brussels sprouts to coat.
- Cook for 5 minutes in the air fryer, then shake the sprouts and cook for another 5 minutes.
- Place the sprouts in a serving dish, drizzle with balsamic vinegar; toss to coat. Garnish with bacon.

Air Fryer Roasted Asparagus
Preparation Time: 20 minutes
Cooking Time: 20 minutes
Serve: 1
Ingredients:

- 1 bunch fresh asparagus, trimmed
- avocado oil cooking spray
- ½ teaspoon garlic powder
- ½ teaspoon Himalayan pink salt
- ¼ teaspoon ground multi-colored peppercorns
- ¼ teaspoon red pepper flakes
- ¼ cup freshly grated Parmesan cheese

Directions:

- Preheat the air fryer carefully to 375°F (190 degrees C). Using parchment paper, line the basket.
- Mist the asparagus stalks with avocado oil and place them in the air fryer basket. Garlic powder, pink Himalayan salt, pepper, and red pepper flakes are optional. Garnish with Parmesan cheese.
- 7 to 9 minutes in the air fryer until asparagus spears brown.

Air-Fryer Roasted Veggies
Preparation Time: 15 minutes
Cooking Time: 25 minutes
Serve: 1
Ingredients:

- ½ cup diced zucchini
- ½ cup diced sweet red pepper
- 2 teaspoons vegetable oil
- ¼ teaspoon salt
- ¼ teaspoon ground black pepper
- ½ cup diced summer squash
- ½ cup diced mushrooms
- ½ cup diced cauliflower
- ½ cup diced asparagus
- 1/4 teaspoon seasoning

Directions:

- Preheat the air fryer carefully to 360°F (180 degrees C).
- Combine the veggies, oil, salt, pepper, and preferred spice in a mixing dish. Toss to coat and place in a frying basket.
- Cook for 10 minutes, stirring every 5 minutes.

Air Fryer Apple Pies
Preparation Time: 15 minutes
Cooking Time: 20 minutes
Serve: 1
Ingredients:

- 4 tablespoons butter
- 6 tablespoons brown sugar
- 1 teaspoon ground cinnamon
- 2 medium Granny Smith apples, diced
- 1 teaspoon cornstarch
- 2 teaspoons cold water
- 14 ounces pastry for a 9-inch double-crust pie
- cooking spray
- ½ tablespoon grapeseed oil
- ¼ cup powdered sugar
- 1 teaspoon milk, or more as needed

Directions:

- Combine the brown sugar, apples, butter, and cinnamon in a nonstick pan. Cook for 5 minutes over medium heat or until the apples are softened.
- Coldwater should be used to dissolve cornstarch. Cook, constantly stirring, until the sauce thickens, approximately 2 minutes. Remove the apple pie filling from the heat and leave it aside to cool while preparing the crust.
- On a lightly floured board, roll out the pie crust carefully to smooth the surface of the dough. Next, cut the dough into rectangles small enough to fit in your air fryer simultaneously. Repeat with the remaining crust, re-rolling any scraps of dough as needed until you have 8 equal rectangles.
- Wet the edges of four rectangles and place some apple filling in the center, about 1/2-inch from the edges. Roll out the remaining four rectangles, making them somewhat larger than the filled ones. Place these rectangles on the filling and use a fork to seal the edges. Make four little slits on the tops of the pies.
- Cooking spray should be sprayed on the air fryer basket. Brush the tops of two pies with grapeseed oil and arrange them, spatula-style, in the air fryer basket.
- Set the temperature to 385°F after inserting the basket (195 degrees C). 8 minutes in the oven or until golden brown. Remove the pies from the basket and repeat with the other two pies.
- In a small mixing dish, combine powdered sugar and milk. Allow the glaze to dry on the heated pies. Pies can be served warm or at room temperature.

Air Fryer Corn Nuts
Preparation Time: 20 minutes
Cooking Time: 25 minutes
Serve: 1
Ingredients:

- 14 ounces giant white corn
- 3 tablespoons vegetable oil
- 1 ½ teaspoons salt

Directions:

- Place the corn in a big bowl, cover with water, and set aside to rehydrate for 8 hours overnight.
- Drain the corn and put it out on a wide baking sheet in an equal layer. Using paper towels, pat dry. Allow for a 20-minute air-drying period.
- Preheat the air fryer carefully to 400°F (200 degrees C).
- Put the corn in a large mixing dish. Mix in the oil and salt. Stir until everything is uniformly covered.
- Place the corn in a uniform layer in the air fryer basket in batches. The cooking time is 10 minutes. Cook for another 10 minutes after shaking the basket. Shake the basket and cook for 5 minutes more before transferring to a paper towel-lined dish. Rep with the leftover corn. Allow corn nuts to cool for about 20 minutes or until crisp.

Air Fryer Coconut Shrimp

Preparation Time: 15 minutes
Cooking Time: 20 minutes
Serve: 1
Ingredients:

- ½ cup all-purpose flour
- 1 ½ teaspoon ground black pepper
- 2 large eggs
- ⅓ cup panko breadcrumbs
- ⅔ cup unsweetened flaked coconut
- 12 ounces uncooked medium shrimp
- cooking spray
- ½ teaspoon kosher salt, divided
- ¼ cup honey
- ¼ cup lime juice
- 1 serrano chili, thinly sliced
- 2 teaspoons chopped fresh cilantro

Directions:

- In a shallow bowl, combine the flour and pepper. In a second shallow dish, lightly beat the eggs. In a third shallow dish, combine the coconut and panko. Holding each shrimp by the tail, dredge it in the flour mixture and shake off the excess. Then, immerse the floured shrimp in the egg, allowing any excess to fall off. Finally, dredge in the coconut mixture and push down to adhere. Serve on a platter. Coat the shrimp well with cooking spray.
- Preheat the air fryer carefully to 400°F (200 degrees C). Cook for 3 minutes with half of the shrimp in the air fryer. Turn the shrimp over and cook for another 3 minutes or golden. Season with a quarter teaspoon of salt. Rep with the remaining shrimp.
- Meanwhile, make the dip by whisking together honey, lime juice, and serrano chili in a small dish.
- Garnish fried shrimp with cilantro and serve with dipping sauce.

Air Fryer Breakfast Frittata

Preparation Time: 15 minutes
Cooking Time: 18 minutes
Serve: 1
Ingredients:

- ¼ pound breakfast sausage fully cooked and crumbled
- 4 eggs, lightly beaten

- ½ cup shredded Cheddar-Monterey Jack cheese blend
- 2 tablespoons red bell pepper, diced
- 1 green onion, chopped
- 1 pinch cayenne pepper (Optional)
- cooking spray

Directions:

- Combine sausage, eggs, and Cheddar-Monterey cheese. Combine the Jack cheese, bell pepper, onion, and cayenne in a mixing dish.
- Preheat the air fryer carefully to 360°F (180 degrees C). Coat a 6x2 inch nonstick cake pan with cooking spray.
- Fill the prepared cake pan halfway with the egg mixture.
- Cook in the air fryer for 18 to 20 minutes, or until the frittata is set.

Air Fryer Wiener Schnitzel

Preparation Time: 15 minutes
Cooking Time: 22 minutes
Serve: 1
Ingredients:

- 1 pound veal, scallopini cut
- 2 tablespoons lemon juice
- salt and ground black pepper to taste
- ¼ cup all-purpose flour, 1 egg
- 1 tablespoon chopped fresh parsley
- 1 cup panko breadcrumbs
- nonstick cooking spray
- 1 lemon, cut into wedges

Directions:

- Preheat an air fryer carefully to 400°F (200 degrees C).
- Sprinkle lemon juice, salt, and pepper over the veal in a clean work area.
- Fill a flat plate halfway with flour. In a separate dish, combine the egg and parsley. In a third dish, place the breadcrumbs. Dredge each veal cutlet in flour, then in the egg-parsley mixture, and last in breadcrumbs, pressing down to ensure that the breadcrumbs adhere.
- Spray the air fryer basket properly with nonstick cooking spray. Place the breaded veal cutlets in the basket, being careful not to overcrowd it. Nonstick cooking spray should be sprayed on the tops.
- 5 minutes in the oven Cook for 5 minutes more after flipping, spraying any chalky parts with nonstick cooking spray. Rep with the leftover veal. With lemon slices, serve.

Air Fryer Plantain Chips

Preparation Time: 10 minutes
Cooking Time: 18 minutes
Serve: 1
Ingredients:

- 1 green plantain
- avocado oil spray
- 1 pinch salt

Directions:

- Preheat an air fryer carefully to 350°F (175 degrees C).
- Plantain should be cut on both ends and scored along the side only through the skin. Remove the peel from the plantain and chop it in half. Then, using a vegetable peeler, cut the peel into strips.

- Avocado oil should be sprayed on the air fryer basket. Fill the basket with plantain strips, ensuring sure they don't touch. Oil the tops of the plantain slices.
- Cook for 7 to 9 minutes in a preheated air fryer. Turn each strip over with tongs and continue frying until crispy, 3 to 5 minutes more. Sprinkle with salt right away.

Air Fryer Potato Chips
Preparation Time: 18 minutes
Cooking Time: 20 minutes
Serve: 1
Ingredients:
- 1 large russet potato, peeled
- cooking spray
- 1 teaspoon smoked Cheddar salt (such as Batterman)

Directions:
- Set a man doline to the thinnest setting and cut the potato into thin slices.
- Soak sliced potatoes in a dish of water for 15 minutes. Then, pour off the water, cover the potatoes with new water and soak for 15 minutes.
- Meanwhile, prepare the air fryer to 400°F (200°C) for 10 minutes. Cooking spray should be sprayed on the air fryer basket.
- Remove the potatoes from the water and carefully dry them. Sprinkle with smoked Cheddar salt and place it in the air fryer basket, avoiding overcrowding. Cooking spray should be sprayed on the potatoes.
- 8 minutes in the air fryer. Shake the potatoes in the air fryer. Cook for another 7 minutes, or until the potatoes are golden brown. Check to see if they're not becoming too hot and starting to burn.

Air Fryer Calamari
Preparation Time: 15 minutes
Cooking Time: 25 minutes
Serve: 1
Ingredients:
- ½ cup all-purpose flour
- 1 large egg
- ¼ cup milk
- 2 cups panko breadcrumbs
- 1 teaspoon sea salt
- 1 teaspoon ground black pepper
- 1-pound calamari rings, patted dry
- nonstick cooking spray

Directions:
- Preheat an air fryer carefully to 400°F (200 degrees C).
- In a mixing dish, combine the flour and baking powder. In a separate dish, whisk together the egg and milk. In a third bowl, combine panko, salt, and pepper.
- Coat the calamari rings in flour first, then in the egg mixture, and then in the panko mixture.
- Place the rings in the air fryer basket to not overlap. If necessary, work in bunches. Nonstick cooking spray should be sprayed on the tops.
- 4 minutes in the air fryer. Cook for 3 minutes more after flipping rings and spraying with nonstick cooking spray.
-

Air Fryer Ranch-Stuffed Olives
Preparation Time: 20 minutes
Cooking Time: 20 minutes
Serve: 1
Ingredients:
- 3 ounces cream cheese, softened
- 2 teaspoons dry ranch dressing mix
- 1 (5.75 ounces) can jumbo pitted black olives, drained
- ½ cup all-purpose flour
- 1 large egg, beaten
- 1 cup panko breadcrumbs
- nonstick cooking spray

Directions:
- Preheat an air fryer carefully to 400°F (200 degrees C).
- In a mixing bowl, blend cream cheese and ranch powder until well incorporated. Fill a resealable plastic bag halfway with the mixture. Snip a tiny piece of the cheese mixture with scissors and pipe it into the olives.
- In a mixing dish, combine the flour and baking powder. Place the egg in a second bowl and the breadcrumbs in a third. Coat the olives in flour first, then in egg, then in flour again, then in egg again, and finally in breadcrumbs. Spray the tops of the olives with cooking spray before placing them in the air fryer basket.
- Cook for 8 minutes in a hot air fryer, shaking halfway through.

Air Fryer Spicy Bay Scallops
Preparation Time: 15 minutes
Cooking Time: 25 minutes
Serve: 1
Ingredients:
- 1 pound bay scallops, rinsed and patted dry
- 2 teaspoons smoked paprika
- 2 teaspoons chili powder
- 2 teaspoons olive oil
- 1 teaspoon garlic powder
- ¼ teaspoon ground black pepper
- ⅛ teaspoon cayenne red pepper

Directions:
- Preheat an air fryer carefully to 400°F (200 degrees C).
- Add bay scallops, smoked paprika, chili powder, olive oil, garlic powder, pepper, and cayenne pepper in a mixing bowl. Place in the air fryer basket.
- Cook until the scallops are cooked through, about 8 minutes, shaking the basket halfway through.

"Everything" Seasoning Air Fryer Asparagus
Preparation Time: 15 minutes
Cooking Time: 20 minutes
Serve: 1
Ingredients:
- 1-pound thin asparagus
- 1 tablespoon olive oil
- 1 tablespoon everything bagel seasoning
- 1 pinch salt to taste
- 4 wedge (blank)s lemon wedges

Directions:

- Rinse and trim the asparagus, removing any woody ends. Drizzle olive oil over asparagus on a platter. Toss with the bagel seasoning until well blended. Arrange the asparagus in a single layer in the air fryer basket. If necessary, work in bunches.
- Preheat the air fryer carefully carefully to 390°F (200 degrees C).
- 5–6 minutes, flipping with tongs halfway through, until slightly soft. If necessary, season with salt. With lemon slices, serve.

Air Fryer Fingerling Potatoes with Dip
Preparation Time: 20 minutes
Cooking Time: 25 minutes
Serve: 1
Ingredients:

- 12 ounces fingerling potatoes, halved lengthwise
- 1 tablespoon olive oil
- 1 teaspoon garlic powder, ¼ teaspoon paprika
- salt and ground black pepper to taste
- ⅓ cup reduced-fat sour cream, 2 tablespoons mayonnaise
- 2 tablespoons finely grated Parmesan cheese
- 1 ½ tablespoons ranch dressing mix (such as Hidden Valley Ranch®)
- 1 tablespoon white vinegar
- 1 tablespoon chopped fresh parsley

Directions:

- Preheat an air fryer carefully for 5 minutes at 390 degrees F (200 degrees C).
- Combine the potatoes, olive oil, garlic powder, paprika, salt, and pepper in a mixing bowl. Transfer the potatoes to the air fryer basket after tossing until coated.
- Cook, shaking the basket halfway through until the potatoes are cooked through and crispy, 15 to 17 minutes in a preheated air fryer.
- In a separate bowl, combine sour cream, mayonnaise, Parmesan cheese, ranch dressing mix, and vinegar while the potatoes are boiling.
- Transfer the cooked potatoes to a platter and sprinkle with parsley. Serve right away with dipping sauce.

Keto Air Fryer Jalapeno Poppers
Preparation Time: 15 minutes
Cooking Time: 20 minutes
Serve: 1
Ingredients:

- 6 jalapeno peppers, halved and seeded
- 7 ½ ounces garden vegetable cream cheese (such as Philadelphia®)
- 6 bacon strips, halved lengthwise

Directions:

- Preheat the air fryer carefully to 390°F (200 degrees C).
- Fill each half of jalapeño with cream cheese and wrap a split bacon strip. To secure, tuck in the bacon ends or use toothpicks.
- Place the jalapeno poppers in the air fryer basket, working in batches as necessary to minimize congestion.
- Cook in a preheated air fryer for 10 to 12 minutes, or until the bacon is done to your preference.

Air Fryer Shortbread Cookie Fries
Preparation Time: 15 minutes
Cooking Time: 18 minutes
Serve: 1
Ingredients:

- 1 ¼ cups all-purpose flour
- 3 tablespoons white sugar
- ½ cup butter
- ⅓ cup strawberry jam
- ⅛ teaspoon ground dried chipotle pepper (Optional)
- ⅓ cup lemon curd

Directions:

- In a medium mixing bowl, combine the flour and sugar. Using a pastry blender, cut in the butter until the mixture resembles fine crumbs and begins to cling. Make a ball out of the ingredients and knead it until smooth.
- Preheat an air fryer carefully to 350°F (190 degrees C).
- On a lightly floured surface, roll out the dough to 1/4-inch thickness. Cut into 3- to 4-inch-long 1/2-inch-wide "fries." Sprinkle with more sugar if desired.
- Arrange the fries in the air fryer basket in a single layer. Cook for 3 to 4 minutes, or until gently browned. Allow cooling in the basket until hard enough to transfer to a wire rack to finish cooling. Rep with the remaining dough.
- To make strawberry "ketchup," use the back of a spoon to push jam through a fine-mesh sieve. Next, stir in the chipotle powder. Next, whip the lemon curd until it is dippable for the "mustard."
- Serve the strawberry ketchup and lemon curd mustard with the sugar cookie fries.

Air Fryer Keto Thumbprint Cookies
Preparation Time: 15 minutes
Cooking Time: 22 minutes
Serve: 1
Ingredients:

- 1 cup almond flour
- 2 ounces cream cheese, softened
- 3 tablespoons low-calorie natural sweetener (such as Swerve®)
- 1 egg
- 1 teaspoon baking powder
- 3 ½ tablespoons reduced-sugar raspberry preserves

Directions:

- In a mixing bowl, combine the flour, cream cheese, sweetener, egg, and baking powder until a moist dough forms.
- Place the bowl in the freezer for 20 minutes or until the dough is cold enough to shape into balls.
- According to the manufacturer's instructions, preheat an air fryer carefully to 400°F (200°C). Then, using parchment paper, line the basket.
- Roll the dough into ten balls and set them in the prepared basket. In the center of each cookie, make a thumbprint. Fill each indentation with 1 spoonful of preserves.
- Cook for 7 minutes in a warm air fryer until the edges are golden brown.
- Cool the cookies entirely before removing them from the parchment paper, about 15 minutes, or they will crumble.

Air Fryer Spicy Roasted Peanuts
Preparation Time: 10 minutes
Cooking Time: 18 minutes
Serve: 1
Ingredients:
- 2 tablespoons olive oil
- 3 teaspoons seafood seasoning (such as Old Bay®)
- ½ teaspoon cayenne pepper
- 8 ounces raw Spanish peanuts
- salt to taste

Directions:
- Preheat an air fryer carefully to 320°F (160 degrees C).
- Combine olive oil, seafood seasoning, and cayenne pepper in a large mixing bowl. Stir in the peanuts until they are equally coated. Place the peanuts in the air fryer basket.
- Cook the peanuts for 10 minutes in the air fryer. Cook for a further 10 minutes, tossing occasionally.
- Remove the air fryer basket and season the peanuts to taste. Cook for 5 minutes more after tossing the peanuts one last time. Allow the peanuts to cool on a dish lined with paper towels

Air Fryer Roasted Salsa Verde
Preparation Time: 18 minutes
Cooking Time: 20 minutes
Serve: 1
Ingredients:
- 1-pound tomatillos
- 1 serrano pepper, halved and seeded
- 1 jalapeno pepper, halved and seeded
- ½ large white onion, cut into 2 wedges
- 1 serving cooking spray
- 4 cloves garlic, peeled
- ½ cup chopped cilantro
- ½ lime, juiced, or more to taste
- 1 pinch salt to taste

Directions:
- Preheat the air fryer carefully to 390°F (200 degrees C).
- Remove the husks from the tomatillos and rinse them; cut the tomatillos in half. Place the tomatillos and peppers in the air fryer basket, skin side down. Add the onion. To aid in the roasting process, lightly coat veggies with cooking spray.
- 5 minutes in the air fryer. Open the basket and place the garlic cloves inside. Spray lightly with cooking spray and continue to air fry for 5 minutes.
- Allow 10 minutes for the veggies to cool. Transfer to a food processor bowl. Combine the cilantro, lime juice, and salt in a mixing bowl. Pulse several times until the veggies are finely chopped, reaching the ideal consistency. Refrigerate or serve at room temperature to let flavors mingle.

Air Fryer Peri Peri Fries
Preparation Time: 15 minutes
Cooking Time: 25 minutes
Serve: 1
Ingredients:
- 2 pounds russet potatoes
- ¼ teaspoon smoked paprika
- ¼ teaspoon chili powder
- ¼ teaspoon garlic granules
- ⅛ teaspoon ground white pepper
- ½ teaspoon salt
- 2 tablespoons grapeseed oil

Directions:
- Feel the potatoes and cut them into 3/8-inch slices. Place for 15 minutes in a water basin to remove most of the starch. Remove to a clean kitchen towel to dry.
- Preheat the air fryer carefully for 5 minutes at 350 degrees F (180 degrees C).
- Combine paprika, chili powder, garlic, white pepper, and salt in a small bowl.
- Mix the potatoes with the grapeseed oil in a medium basin. Fill the air fryer basket halfway with the mixture.
- Cook for 10 minutes in an air fryer, shaking periodically. Raise the temperature to 400°F (200°C) and continue to air fry for 12 to 15 minutes, or until golden brown.
- Four the fries into a bowl, sprinkle with the seasoning mix, and shake to coat evenly. If necessary, taste and adjust the salt. Serve right away.

Air Fryer Chile Verde Burritos
Preparation Time: 20 minutes
Cooking Time: 20 minutes
Serve: 1
Ingredients:
- 2 cups finely chopped leftover pulled pork
- 1 cup salsa Verde
- 2 tablespoons cotija cheese
- 10 (6 inches) flour tortillas
- cooking spray

Directions:
- According to the manufacturer's instructions, preheat an air fryer carefully to 400°F (200°C).
- Combine the pulled pork, salsa Verde, and cotija cheese in a mixing bowl. Stir until everything is well blended.
- Fill the bottom half of a tortilla with a heaping scoop of filling. Make two folds on either side of the big fold to form an envelope. Roll it up, tucking the filling in with the tips of your fingers as you go. Rep with the remaining tortillas.
- Spray the air fryer basket with nonstick cooking spray. Place several burritos in the basket, seam side down, being careful not to overcrowd them. Coat the burritos' tops with cooking spray.
- 6 minutes in the air fryer Rep with the leftover burritos. If preferred, serve with more salsa Verde for dipping.

Air Fryer Boursin-Stuffed Wontons
Preparation Time: 15 minutes
Cooking Time: 25 minutes
Serve: 1
Ingredients:
- 18 wonton wrappers
- 6 tablespoons garlic and herb cheese spread (such as Boursin®)
- water, as needed
- cooking spray

Directions:
- Preheat the air fryer carefully to 325°F (160 degrees C).
- Place the wonton wrappers on a clean work area and separate them. 1 teaspoon garlic and herb cheese should be placed in the center of each wonton. Wet the sides of each

- wonton with a pastry brush or your finger and fold in half, pressing carefully to make a perfect seal. Wet the wrapper tips and push them together. Spray generously with cooking spray and place on a clean platter.
- Coat the inside basket with cooking spray and arrange half of the packed wontons inside.
- 4 minutes in the air fryer until lightly browned. Rep with the remaining wontons. Allow cooling for a few minutes before serving.

Air Fryer Spinach and Feta Casserole
Preparation Time: 15 minutes
Cooking Time: 20 minutes
Serve: 1
Ingredients:
- cooking spray
- 1 (13.5 ounces) can of spinach
- 1 cup cottage cheese
- 2 eggs, beaten
- 2 tablespoons butter, melted
- ¼ cup crumbled feta cheese
- 2 tablespoons all-purpose flour
- 1 clove garlic, minced, or more to taste
- 1 ½ teaspoons onion powder
- ⅛ teaspoon ground nutmeg

Directions:
- Preheat an air fryer carefully to 375°F (190 degrees C). Set aside an 8-inch pie tin sprayed with cooking spray.
- In a mixing bowl, combine spinach, feta cheese, flour, butter, cottage cheese, eggs, garlic, onion powder, and nutmeg. Stir until all of the ingredients are properly combined. Pour into the pie pan that has been prepared.
- Air fry until the center is set, 15 to 20 minutes.

Air Fryer Sugared Pecans
Preparation Time: 20 minutes
Cooking Time: 25 minutes
Serve: 1
Ingredients:
- 2 tablespoons salted butter, melted
- 1 egg white
- ¼ cup white sugar
- ¼ teaspoon ground cinnamon
- 1 cup pecan halves

Directions:
- Preheat an air fryer carefully to 300°F (150 degrees C). Aluminum foil should be used to line the air fryer basket.
- Melt the butter and pour it into the prepared basket. Combine the egg white, sugar, and cinnamon in a mixing dish. Toss in the pecans until evenly coated. Spread the contents of the lined basket out.
- 5 minutes in the air fryer. Shake the basket and continue to air fry for 5 minutes. Shake the basket again and continue to air fry for 2 to 4 minutes.

Air Fryer Pizza Dogs
Preparation Time: 15 minutes
Cooking Time: 20 minutes
Serve: 1
Ingredients:

- 2 hot dogs
- 4 slices pepperoni, halved
- ½ cup pizza sauce
- 2 hot dog buns
- ¼ cup shredded mozzarella cheese
- 2 teaspoons sliced olives

Directions:
- Preheat an air fryer carefully to 390°F (200 degrees C).
- Make four slits down the center of each hot dog. Cook the hot dogs in the air fryer basket for 3 minutes. Using tongs, transfer to a chopping board.
- Insert a pepperoni half into each hot dog slit. Fill the buns with the pizza sauce, hot dogs, mozzarella cheese, and olives.
- Return the hot dogs to the air fryer basket and cook for 2 minutes, or until the buns are crisp and the cheese has melted.

Air Fryer Zucchini Chips
Preparation Time: 15 minutes
Cooking Time: 18 minutes
Serve: 1
Ingredients:
- 1 cup panko breadcrumbs
- ¾ cup grated Parmesan cheese
- 1 medium zucchini, thinly sliced
- 1 large egg, beaten
- cooking spray

Directions:
- Before prepping the zucchini, Preheat an air fryer carefully to 350 degrees F (175 degrees C).
- On a plate, combine panko and Parmesan cheese. Dip 1 zucchini slice into the beaten egg, then into the panko mixture, pressing down to coat. Repeat with the remaining zucchini slices on a wire baking rack. Coat the zucchini slices lightly with cooking spray.
- Place as many zucchini slices as you can in the air fryer basket without overlapping them.
- The cooking time is 10 minutes. Toss with tongs. Cook for another 2 minutes. Remove from the air fryer and continue with the remaining zucchini slices.

Air Fryer Sausage Patties
Preparation Time: 15 minutes
Cooking Time: 22 minutes
Serve: 1
Ingredients:
- 1 (12 ounces) package sausage patties (such as Johnsonville®)
- 1 serving nonstick cooking spray

Directions:
- Preheat an air fryer carefully to 400°F (200 degrees C).
- Place the sausage patties in a single layer in the basket, working in batches if required.
- Cook for 5 minutes in a hot air fryer. Remove the basket, flip the sausage, and cook for another 3 minutes, or until an instant-read thermometer placed into the middle of a patty registers 160 degrees F (70 degrees C).

Lemon-Garlic Air Fryer Salmon

Preparation Time: 10 minutes
Cooking Time: 18 minutes
Serve: 1
Ingredients:

- 1 tablespoon melted butter
- ½ teaspoon minced garlic
- 2 (6 ounce) fillets center-cut salmon fillets with skin
- ¼ teaspoon lemon-pepper seasoning
- ⅛ teaspoon dried parsley
- cooking spray
- 3 thin slices lemon, cut in half

Directions:

- Preheat the air fryer carefully to 390°F (200 degrees C).
- In a small bowl, combine melted butter and chopped garlic.
- Salmon fillets should be rinsed and dried with a paper towel. Brush with the butter mixture and top with the lemon-pepper spice and parsley.
- Coat the air fryer basket with cooking spray. Place the salmon fillets in the basket, skin side down, and top with 3 lemon halves each.
- Cook for 8 to 10 minutes in a preheated air fryer. Remove from the air fryer and set aside for 2 minutes to rest before serving.

Air Fryer Steak and Mushrooms

Preparation Time: 18 minutes
Cooking Time: 20 minutes
Serve: 1
Ingredients:

- ¼ cup Worcestershire sauce
- 1 tablespoon olive oil
- 1 pound beef sirloin steak, cut into 1-inch cubes
- 8 ounces button mushrooms, sliced
- 1 teaspoon parsley flakes
- 1 teaspoon paprika
- 1 teaspoon crushed chili flakes

Directions:

- Combine the steak, mushrooms, Worcestershire sauce, olive oil, parsley, paprika, and chili flakes in a mixing bowl. Refrigerate for at least 4 hours or overnight. 30 minutes before cooking, remove from refrigerator.
- Preheat an air fryer carefully to 400°F (200 degrees C).
- Remove the steak mixture from the marinade and set it aside. Place the steak and mushrooms in the air fryer basket.
- Cook for 5 minutes in a hot air fryer. Cook for 5 minutes more after tossing. Transfer the steak and mushrooms to a serving platter and set aside for 5 minutes to rest.

Air Fryer Sweet Potato Hash

Preparation Time: 15 minutes
Cooking Time: 25 minutes
Serve: 1
Ingredients:

- 2 large, sweet potatoes
- 2 slices bacon, cut into small pieces
- 2 tablespoons olive oil
- 1 tablespoon smoked paprika
- 1 teaspoon sea salt
- 1 teaspoon ground black pepper
- 1 teaspoon dried dill weed

Directions:

- Preheat an air fryer carefully to 400°F (200 degrees C).
- Combine sweet potato, bacon, olive oil, paprika, salt, pepper, and dill in a large mixing bowl. Place the mixture in the air fryer that has been warmed. Cook for 12 to 16 minutes, depending on the size of your pan. After 10 minutes, check and stir, then every 3 minutes until crispy and golden.

Air Fryer Tofu

Preparation Time: 20 minutes
Cooking Time: 20 minutes
Serve: 1
Ingredients:

- 8 ounces firm tofu
- 1 large clove garlic, finely chopped
- 1 tablespoon low-sodium soy sauce
- 1 tablespoon olive oil
- ½ teaspoon sesame oil

Directions:

- Place the tofu on a dish lined with paper towels. Cover with additional paper towels and a second plate. Set a 4- to 5-pound weight on top and press the tofu for 30 minutes; drain and discard any excess liquid before cutting the tofu into 1/2-inch cubes.
- Whisk together the soy sauce, olive oil, garlic, and sesame oil in a small bowl. Marinate the tofu cubes for 15 to 20 minutes.
- Preheat an air fryer carefully to 350°F (180 degrees C).
- Place the tofu in the air fryer basket in a single layer.
- Without shaking the fryer, air-fried for 5 minutes. Continue air frying, tossing periodically, for about 10 minutes more, or until browned.

Air Fryer Roasted Bananas

Preparation Time: 15 minutes
Cooking Time: 25 minutes
Serve: 1
Ingredients:

- 1 banana, sliced into 1/8-inch-thick diagonals
- avocado oil cooking spray

Directions:

- The parchment paper should be used to line the air fryer basket.
- Preheat an air fryer carefully to 375°F (190 degrees C).
- Place the banana slices in the basket, ensuring they don't touch; cook in batches if required. Avocado oil should be sprayed on banana slices.
- Cook for 5 minutes in the air fryer. Remove the basket and carefully turn the banana slices (soft). Cook for another 2 to 3 minutes, or until the banana slices are browning and caramelized. Remove from the basket with caution.

Air Fryer Apple Crumble

Preparation Time: 15 minutes
Cooking Time: 20 minutes
Serve: 1
Ingredients:

- 1 cup all-purpose flour
- ½ cup white sugar

- ¼ cup cold salted butter, cubed
- ½ teaspoon ground cinnamon
- ½ teaspoon baking powder
- ¼ teaspoon ground nutmeg
- cooking spray
- 2 ½ cups peeled, cored, and diced apples

Directions:

- Preheat an air fryer carefully to 350°F (175 degrees C).
- Combine the flour, sugar, and butter in a medium mixing bowl. Mix with your hands until the mixture is crumbly. Next, combine the cinnamon, baking powder, and nutmeg in a mixing bowl.
- Nonstick cooking spray should be sprayed into two 4 1/2-inch ramekins. Fill ramekins halfway with crumble and top with apples. Repeat twice more, finishing with a mounded crumble on top.
- Wrap the ramekins with big strips of foil, tucking the ends beneath to keep them from flying away. Cook until the apples are soft, about 16 to 20 minutes in the air fryer. Remove the foil and continue to air fry until the crumble is golden brown, 2 to 4 minutes more.

Air Fryer Crab Rangoon

Preparation Time: 20 minutes
Cooking Time: 25 minutes
Serve: 1
Ingredients:

- 1 (8 ounces) package cream cheese
- 1 serving nonstick cooking spray
- 4 ounces lump crab meat
- 2 tablespoons chopped scallions
- 1 teaspoon soy sauce
- 1 teaspoon Worcestershire sauce
- 24 each wonton wrappers
- 2 tablespoons Asian sweet chili sauce for dipping

Directions:

- In a mixing bowl, add cream cheese, crab meat, scallions, soy sauce, and Worcestershire sauce, whisk until well blended.
- Preheat an air fryer carefully to 350°F (175 degrees C). Coat the air fryer basket with cooking spray. Warm water should be placed in a small dish.
- On a clean work area, arrange 12 wonton wrappers. 1 teaspoon cream cheese mixture should be placed in the center of each wonton wrapper. Wet the sides of each wonton wrapper with your index finger after dipping it into the warm water. Crimp the wrapper corners upwards until they meet in the middle to make dumplings.
- Spray the tops of the dumplings with cooking spray and place them in the prepared basket.
- Cook dumplings for 8 to 10 minutes, or until desired crispness is achieved. Transfer to a plate lined with paper towels.
- While the first dumplings are cooking, construct the remaining dumplings using the leftover wrappers and filling.
- Serve with sweet chili sauce as a dipping sauce.

Air Fryer Fish Sticks

Preparation Time: 15 minutes
Cooking Time: 20 minutes
Serve: 1
Ingredients:

- 1 pound cod fillets
- ¼ cup all-purpose flour
- 1 egg
- ½ cup panko breadcrumbs
- ¼ cup grated Parmesan cheese
- 1 tablespoon parsley flakes, 1 teaspoon paprika
- ½ teaspoon black pepper
- cooking spray

Directions:

- Preheat an air fryer carefully to 400°F (200 degrees C).
- Pat the fish dry using paper towels before slicing it into 1x3-inch pieces.
- In a small bowl, combine the flour and salt. In a separate shallow dish, beat the egg. In a third shallow dish, combine panko, Parmesan cheese, parsley, paprika, and pepper.
- Each fish stick should be coated in flour, then dipped in beaten egg, and then coated in seasoned panko mixture.
- Spray the air fryer basket with nonstick cooking spray. Arrange half of the sticks in the basket, ensuring none of them is a contact. Cooking spray should be sprayed on the top of each stick.
- Cook for 5 minutes in a hot air fryer. Cook for a further 5 minutes after flipping the fish sticks. Rep with the rest of the fish sticks.

Air Fryer Hasselback Potatoes

Preparation Time: 15 minutes
Cooking Time: 18 minutes
Serve: 1
Ingredients:

- 4 medium Yukon Gold potatoes
- 3 tablespoons melted butter
- 1 tablespoon olive oil
- 3 cloves garlic, crushed
- ½ teaspoon ground paprika
- salt and ground black pepper to taste
- 1 tablespoon chopped fresh parsley

Directions:

- Preheat an air fryer carefully to 350°F (175 degrees C).
- Make 1/4-inch or 1/2-inch slices across the full length of each potato, making sure the knife only cuts through to the bottom 1/2-inch, leaving the bottom of the potato intact.
- Combine the butter, olive oil, garlic, and paprika in a small mixing bowl. Brush some of the mixtures into the slits of each potato. Season with salt and pepper to taste.
- Cook the potatoes in the air fryer basket for 15 minutes. Brushing the potatoes with the butter mixture again, being careful to get it all the way down into the fanned-out slices to prevent them from drying out. Cook for another 15 minutes, or until the potatoes are tender.
- Remove the potatoes from the basket and brush with any leftover butter mixture. Serve immediately garnished with chopped parsley.

Air-Fryer Asparagus Fries

Preparation Time: 15 minutes
Cooking Time: 22 minutes
Serve: 1
Ingredients:

- 1 large egg
- 1 teaspoon honey

- 1 cup panko breadcrumbs
- ½ cup grated Parmesan cheese
- 12 asparagus spears, trimmed
- ¼ cup stone-ground mustard
- ¼ cup Greek yogurt
- 1 pinch cayenne pepper (Optional)

Directions:
- Preheat an air fryer carefully to 400°F (200 degrees C).
- In a long, thin bowl, whisk together the egg and honey. In a separate dish, combine panko and Parmesan cheese. Coat each asparagus stalk in the egg mixture before rolling in the panko mixture to coat.
- Cook 6 spears in the air fryer for 4 to 6 minutes, or until desired brownness is achieved. Rep with the remaining spears.
- Combine the mustard, yogurt, and cayenne pepper in a small bowl. Serve with asparagus spears and dipping sauce.

Basic Air Fryer Hot Dogs
Preparation Time: 10 minutes
Cooking Time: 18 minutes
Serve: 1
Ingredients:
- 4 hot dog buns
- 4 hot dogs

Directions:
- Preheat the air fryer carefully to 390°F (200 degrees C).
- Place the buns in the air fryer basket and cook for 2 minutes. Then, place the buns on a platter.
- Cook the hot dogs in the air fryer basket for 3 minutes. Place hot dogs in buns.

Air Fryer Meatloaf
Preparation Time: 18 minutes
Cooking Time: 20 minutes
Serve: 1
Ingredients:
- 1-pound lean ground beef
- 1 egg, lightly beaten
- 3 tablespoons dry breadcrumbs
- 1 small onion, finely chopped
- 1 tablespoon chopped fresh thyme
- 1 teaspoon salt
- ground black pepper to taste
- 2 mushrooms, thickly sliced
- 1 tablespoon olive oil, or as needed

Directions:
- Preheat an air fryer carefully at 392°F (200 degrees C).
- Combine ground beef, egg, breadcrumbs, onion, thyme, salt, and pepper in a mixing bowl. Knead and completely combine.
- Smooth the top of the beef mixture in a baking pan. Coat the mushrooms in olive oil and press them into the top. Insert the pan into the air fryer basket and place it in it.
- Set the air fryer to 25 minutes and roast the meatloaf until it is well browned.
- Allow the meatloaf to rest for at least 10 minutes before slicing it into wedges and serving it.

Air-Fryer Tempura Veggies
Preparation Time: 15 minutes
Cooking Time: 25 minutes
Serve: 1
Ingredients:
- ½ cup all-purpose flour
- ½ teaspoon salt, divided, or more to taste
- ½ teaspoon ground black pepper
- 2 eggs
- 2 tablespoons water
- 1 cup panko breadcrumbs
- 2 teaspoons vegetable oil
- ½ cup whole green beans
- ½ cup whole asparagus spears
- ½ cup red onion rings
- ½ cup sweet pepper rings
- ½ cup avocado wedges
- ½ cup zucchini slices

Directions:
- Combine the flour, 1/4 teaspoon salt, and pepper in a small bowl. In a separate shallow bowl, properly whisk together the eggs and water. In a third shallow dish, combine panko and oil. Season the panko and flour mixture as desired.
- Sprinkle the remaining 1/4 teaspoon salt over the veggies. To coat, dip in the flour mixture, then the egg mixture, and finally the panko mixture.
- Preheat the air fryer carefully to 400 degrees Fahrenheit (200 degrees Celsius) and the oven to 200 degrees Fahrenheit (95 degrees C).
- Place half of the veggies in the air fryer basket in a single layer. Cook for about 10 minutes, or until golden brown. If desired, season with more salt. Place the veggies in the oven to remain warm. Rep with the remaining veggies.

Air Fryer Celery Root Fries
Preparation Time: 20 minutes
Cooking Time: 20 minutes
Serve: 1
Ingredients:
- ½ celeriac (celery root), peeled and cut into 1/2-inch sticks
- 3 cups water, 1 tablespoon lime juice
- ⅓ cup vegan mayonnaise
- 1 tablespoon brown mustard
- 1 teaspoon powdered horseradish
- 1 pinch salt and ground black pepper
- 1 tablespoon olive oil

Directions:
- Place the celery root in a basin. Pour in the lime juice and water. Allow resting for 20 minutes after mixing.
- Preheat the air fryer carefully to 400°F (200 degrees C).
- Make the mayonnaise sauce. Combine vegan mayonnaise, mustard, and horseradish powder in a mixing bowl. Store in the refrigerator, covered, until required.
- Drain and dry the celery root sticks before reserving them in a basin. Season the fries with salt and pepper after drizzling them with oil. To coat evenly, toss everything together.
- Place the celery root in the air fryer basket. Cook for about 10 minutes, testing for doneness halfway through. Shake the basket and cook for another 8 minutes, or until the fries are crisp and golden.

- Serve the fries right away, with vegan mayo on the side.

cook in batches as needed. Fry for 4 minutes, then turn and cook for another 4 minutes, or until the crispy skins.

Air Fryer Fried Okra
Preparation Time: 15 minutes
Cooking Time: 25 minutes
Serve: 1
Ingredients:

- 1 large egg
- ½ pound okra pods, cut into 1/2-inch slices
- 1 cup cornmeal
- ¼ cup all-purpose flour
- cooking spray
- salt to taste

Directions:

- In a shallow bowl, beat the egg; carefully fold in the cut okra.
- In a gallon-size resealable plastic bag, combine cornmeal and flour. Place 5 okra slices in the cornmeal mixture, seal the bag, and shake. Transfer the breaded okra to a dish. Repeat with the rest of the okra slices.
- Preheat the air fryer carefully to 400°F (200 degrees C). Spray half of the breaded okra pieces with cooking spray in the air fryer basket. Cook for 4 minutes. Shake the basket and respray the okra with frying spray. Cook for another 4 minutes. Cook for 2 minutes after shaking the basket one more. Remove the okra from the basket and season with salt and pepper to taste.
- Repeat with the rest of the okra slices.

Lumpia in the Air Fryer
Preparation Time: 15 minutes
Cooking Time: 20 minutes
Serve: 1
Ingredients:

- 1-pound Italian hot sausage links
- ½ cup finely sliced green onions
- ¼ cup diced onions
- ½ cup finely chopped carrots
- ½ cup finely chopped water chestnuts
- 2 cloves garlic, minced
- 2 tablespoons soy sauce
- ½ teaspoon salt
- ¼ teaspoon ground ginger
- 16 spring roll wrappers
- avocado oil cooking spray

Directions:

- Remove the casing from the sausage and cook it in a pan over medium heat for 4 to 5 minutes, or until slightly browned. Combine the green onions, onions, carrots, and water chestnuts in a mixing bowl. Cook and stir for 5 to 7 minutes, or until the onions are tender and transparent. Cook for 1 to 2 minutes after adding the garlic. Soy sauce, salt, and ginger to taste. Remove from heat after stirring until the filling is fully mixed.
- Place a spring roll wrapper at an angle on a plate. Fill the wrapper with a scant 1/4 cup of the filling. Fold the bottom corner over the filling and tuck in the edges to construct a roll. Wet your finger and softly wet the edges. Rep with the rest of the wrappers and filling. Each roll should be sprayed with avocado oil spray.
- Preheat an air fryer carefully to 390°F (198 degrees C). Place the lumpia rolls in the basket, making sure they don't touch;

Air Fryer Pasta Chips
Preparation Time: 20 minutes
Cooking Time: 25 minutes
Serve: 1
Ingredients:

- 2 cups farfalle pasta
- 1 tablespoon olive oil
- ½ cup grated Parmesan cheese
- 1 teaspoon garlic powder
- 1 teaspoon Italian seasoning
- ½ teaspoon salt

Directions:

- A big saucepan of lightly salted water should be brought to a boil. Cook farfalle pasta at a boil, tossing periodically, for 8 minutes, or until soft yet firm to the biting. Rinse, but do not drain. Allow for a 2-minute rest.
- Preheat an air fryer carefully to 400°F (200 degrees C).
- Drizzle olive oil over the spaghetti in a large mixing basin. Combine the Parmesan cheese, garlic powder, Italian seasoning, and salt in a mixing bowl. Gently combine all of the ingredients in a mixing bowl.
- Cook the pasta in batches in the air fryer basket for 5 minutes. Cook for 2 to 3 minutes more after flipping with a spatula. Transfer to a plate lined with paper towels. Separate any spaghetti chips that have been glued together. Rep with the remaining spaghetti. Allow cooling completely before crisping the last time.

Air Fryer Portobello Pizzas for Two
Preparation Time: 15 minutes
Cooking Time: 20 minutes
Serve: 1
Ingredients:

- 2 tablespoons olive oil
- 2 portobello mushroom caps, gills removed
- 1 teaspoon Italian seasoning
- 6 tablespoons pizza sauce
- 5 tablespoons shredded mozzarella cheese, divided
- 2 tablespoons sliced black olives
- 8 pepperoni slices

Directions:

- Preheat an air fryer carefully to 350°F (175 degrees C).
- 1 tablespoon olive oil, rubbed on each mushroom. Fill each with 1/2 teaspoon Italian spice. Place the mushrooms, cap sides up, in the air fryer basket. 3 minutes in the air fryer
- Turn the mushrooms over in the basket so that the cap is facing down. Divide the pizza sauce evenly between the two mushrooms. 2 tablespoons shredded mozzarella and 1 tablespoon chopped olives on top 3 minutes in the air fryer
- Cover each pizza with 4 pepperoni pieces and the remaining mozzarella cheese. The pepperoni must be weighed down with cheese, or the fan will blow them off the pie.
- Air fried for 2 minutes, or until the cheese is melted and the pepperoni is browned.

Easy Air Fryer Apple Pies
Preparation Time: 15 minutes
Cooking Time: 18 minutes

Serve: 1
Ingredients:

- 1 (14.1 ounces) package refrigerated pie crusts (2 pie crusts)
- 1 (21 ounces) can apple pie filling
- 1 egg, beaten
- 2 tablespoons cinnamon sugar, or to taste
- 1 serving cooking spray

Directions:

- Roll out 1 pie crust using a rolling pin on a lightly floured board. Cut the pie dough into 10 circles with a 2-1/4-inch round biscuit or cookie cutter. Repeat with the remaining pie dough to make 20 pie crust circles.
- Fill approximately half of each circle with apple pie filling. Make a tiny pie by adding a second pie crust circle on top. Don't overfill the container. Crimp the edges of the tiny pies with a fork to seal them. Tops should be brushed with beaten egg and sprinkled with cinnamon sugar.
- Preheat the air fryer carefully to 360°F (175 degrees C).
- Coat the air fryer basket lightly with cooking spray. Place a batch of mini pies in the air fryer basket, leaving room for air circulation around each.
- 5 to 7 minutes, or until golden brown. Remove the pies from the basket and bake the remaining pies. Warm or at room temperature, serve.

Air Fryer Avocado Fries

Preparation Time: 15 minutes
Cooking Time: 22 minutes
Serve: 1
Ingredients:

- ¼ cup all-purpose flour
- ½ teaspoon ground black pepper
- ¼ teaspoon salt
- 1 egg
- 1 teaspoon water
- 1 ripe avocado, halved, seeded, peeled, and cut into 8 slices
- ½ cup panko breadcrumbs
- cooking spray

Directions:

- Preheat the air fryer carefully to 400°F (200 degrees C).
- In a small bowl, combine the flour, pepper, and salt. In a second shallow dish, whisk together the egg and water. Finally, in a third shallow dish, place the panko.
- Dredge an avocado slice in flour, brushing off any excess. Allow the extra egg to drip out before dipping. Finally, coat both sides of the slice with panko. Repeat with the remaining slices on a dish.
- Spray avocado slices liberally with cooking spray and place sprayed side down in the air fryer bowl. Also, spray the tops of the avocado slices.
- Cook for 4 minutes in a hot air fryer. Cook until the avocado slices are browned, about 3 minutes more.

Air Fryer Ranch Pork Chops

Preparation Time: 10 minutes
Cooking Time: 18 minutes
Serve: 1

Ingredients:

- 4 boneless
- cooking spray
- 2 teaspoons dry ranch salad dressing mix
- aluminum foil

Directions:

- Place the pork chops on a dish and coat both sides lightly with cooking spray. Allow both sides to remain at room temperature for 10 minutes after sprinkling with ranch seasoning mix.
- Preheat an air fryer carefully to 390 degrees F and coat the basket with cooking spray (200 degrees C).
- Place the chops in the preheated air fryer, working in batches if required to avoid overcrowding.
- 5 minutes in the oven Cook for another 5 minutes on the other side. Allow it to rest for 5 minutes on a foil-covered dish before serving.

Air Fryer Mac and Cheese Balls

Preparation Time: 18 minutes
Cooking Time: 20 minutes
Serve: 1
Ingredients:

- 6 cups water
- 1 (7.25 ounce) package macaroni and cheese dinner mix (such as Kraft®)
- ¼ cup milk
- 4 tablespoons margarine
- ¾ cup shredded sharp Cheddar cheese
- nonstick cooking spray
- ½ cup panko breadcrumbs
- ½ cup seasoned breadcrumbs
- ½ teaspoon salt
- ½ teaspoon garlic powder
- 2 eggs, beaten

Directions:

- Fill a bowl halfway with water and bring to a boil over high heat. Mix in the macaroni noodles from the supper packet. Cook, occasionally stirring, for 7 to 8 minutes, or until the vegetables are soft. Do not rinse after draining. Return to the saucepan and toss in the cheese sauce, milk, and margarine, if using. Stir in the Cheddar cheese until fully blended and melted.
- Refrigerate the macaroni and cheese for at least 2 hours and up to overnight.
- Scoop macaroni and cheese into a 1 1/2-inch ball and set on a baking sheet lined with parchment paper. 1 hour in the freezer
- Preheat an air fryer carefully to 350°F (175°C) according to the manufacturer's instructions. Nonstick cooking spray should be sprayed on the basket.
- Combine panko, breadcrumbs, salt, and garlic powder in a medium mixing bowl. Each ball should be dipped in beaten eggs and then in the panko mixture.
- Place the mac and cheese balls in a single layer in the air fryer basket, ensuring they don't touch; cook in batches if required.
- Cook for 6 to 8 minutes in a preheated air fryer. Fry until golden brown on the other side, 3 to 4 minutes more.

CHAPTER 2:

Snacks & Appetizers

Rosemary Potato Wedges
Preparation Time: 10 minutes
Cooking Time: 25 minutes
Serve: 4
Ingredients:
- 3 potatoes, cut into wedges
- 1 tbsp parsley, chopped
- 3 tbsp olive oil
- 1 tsp garlic powder
- 1 tbsp fresh rosemary, chopped
- Pepper
- Salt

Directions:
- Preheat the air fryer to 390 F.
- Soak potato wedges into the water for 30 minutes. Drain well and pat dry with paper towels.
- In a mixing bowl, toss potato wedges with parsley, oil, garlic powder, rosemary, pepper, and salt.
- Place potato wedges into the air fryer basket and cook for 15 minutes.
- Stir well and cook for 10 minutes more.
- Serve and enjoy.

Healthy Mixed Nuts
Preparation Time: 10 minutes
Cooking Time: 9 minutes
Serve: 4
Ingredients:
- 1/4 cup hazelnuts
- 1/2 cup pecans
- 1/2 cup macadamia nuts
- 1 tbsp olive oil
- 1/4 cup walnuts
- 1 tsp salt

Directions:
- Preheat the air fryer to 320 F.
- In a bowl, toss nuts with oil and salt.
- Add nuts into the air fryer basket and cook for 9 minutes. Stir halfway through.
- Serve and enjoy.

Stuff Mushrooms
Preparation Time: 10 minutes
Cooking Time: 5 minutes
Serve: 6
Ingredients:
- 9 oz mushrooms, cut stems
- 1 tbsp butter
- 1 tsp dried parsley

- 6 oz mozzarella cheese, shredded
- 1/2 tsp salt

Directions:
- Preheat the air fryer to 400 F.
- In a small bowl, mix together cheese, butter, parsley, and salt until well combined.
- Stuff cheese mixture into the mushroom caps and place in the air fryer basket and cook for 5 minutes.
- Serve and enjoy.

Crispy Broccoli Popcorn
Preparation Time: 10 minutes
Cooking Time: 6 minutes
Serve: 4
Ingredients:
- 4 eggs yolks
- 2 cups broccoli florets
- 1/4 cup butter, melted
- 2 cups coconut flour
- Pepper
- Salt

Directions:
- Preheat the air fryer to 400 F.
- In a small bowl, whisk egg yolks with butter, pepper, and salt.
- In a separate bowl, add coconut flour.
- Dip each broccoli floret with egg mixture and coat with coconut flour.
- Place coated broccoli florets into the air fryer basket and cook for 6 minutes.
- Serve and enjoy.

Zucchini Bites
Preparation Time: 10 minutes
Cooking Time: 10 minutes
Serve: 6
Ingredients:
- 1 egg, lightly beaten
- 1 tsp Italian seasoning
- 4 zucchinis, grated and squeezed
- 1 cup shredded coconut
- 1/2 cup parmesan cheese, grated
- Pepper
- Salt

Directions:
- Preheat the air fryer to 400 F.
- Add all ingredients into the bowl and mix until well combined.

- Make small balls from the zucchini mixture and place into the air fryer basket and cook for 10 minutes. Turn halfway through.
- Serve and enjoy.

Air Fryer Almonds
Preparation Time: 5 minutes
Cooking Time: 6 minutes
Serve: 6
Ingredients:
- 1 cup almonds
- 2 tsp olive oil
- 1/4 tsp cumin
- 1 tsp chili powder
- 1/4 tsp paprika
- Salt

Directions:
- Preheat the air fryer to 320 F.
- Add almond and remaining ingredients into the bowl and toss to coat.
- Transfer almonds into the air fryer basket and cook for 6 minutes.
- Serve and enjoy.

Tasty Broccoli Nuggets
Preparation Time: 10 minutes
Cooking Time: 15 minutes
Serve: 4
Ingredients:
- 2 egg whites
- 2 cups broccoli florets, cooked & mashed
- 1/4 cup almond flour
- 1 cup mozzarella cheese, shredded
- 1/8 tsp salt

Directions:
- Preheat the air fryer to 325 F.
- Add all ingredients to the bowl and mix well to combine.
- Make nuggets from broccoli mixture and place into the air fryer basket and cook for 15 minutes.
- Serve and enjoy.

Curried Sweet Potato Fries
Preparation Time: 10 minutes
Cooking Time: 20 minutes
Serve: 2
Ingredients:
- 2 small, sweet potatoes, peel and cut into fry's shape
- 2 tbsp olive oil
- 1/2 tsp curry powder
- 1/4 tsp coriander
- Pepper
- Salt

Directions:
- Preheat the air fryer to 370 F.
- Add sweet potato slices and remaining ingredients into the mixing bowl and toss well.
- Transfer sweet potato slices into the air fryer basket and cook for 20 minutes. Stir after every 5 minutes.
- Serve and enjoy.

Asparagus Fries
Preparation Time: 10 minutes
Cooking Time: 10 minutes
Serve: 6
Ingredients:
- 4 eggs, lightly beaten
- 1 lb. asparagus, trimmed & poke using a fork
- 1/4 tsp baking powder
- 1 cup parmesan cheese, grated
- 1/4 tsp cayenne
- 3/4 cup almond flour
- Pepper
- Salt

Directions:
- Preheat the air fryer to 400 F.
- Season asparagus spears with pepper and salt.
- In a shallow dish, mix together parmesan cheese, almond flour, and cayenne.
- In a separate shallow dish, add eggs and whisk well.
- Dip each asparagus spear in eggs then coat with cheese mixture.
- Place coated asparagus spears into the air fryer basket and cook for 10 minutes. Turn halfway through.
- Serve and enjoy.

Savory Walnuts
Preparation Time: 10 minutes
Cooking Time: 5 minutes
Serve: 6
Ingredients:
- 2 cups walnuts
- 1 tsp olive oil
- 1/4 tsp garlic powder
- 1/8 tsp paprika
- Pepper
- Salt

Directions:
- Preheat the air fryer to 350 F.
- In a bowl, add walnuts, oil, paprika, garlic powder, pepper, and salt and toss well.
- Add walnuts into the air fryer basket and cook for 4-5 minutes.
- Serve and enjoy.

Air Fryer Zucchini Curly Fries
Preparation Time: 15 minutes
Cooking Time: 25 minutes
Serve: 1
Ingredients:
- 1 zucchini
- 1 egg, beaten
- 1 cup panko breadcrumbs
- ½ cup grated Parmesan cheese
- 1 teaspoon Italian seasoning
- nonstick cooking spray

Directions:
- Preheat an air fryer carefully to 400°F (200 degrees C).
- Spiralize zucchini with a spiralizer fitted with the big shredding blade.

- In a shallow dish, place the egg. In a large resealable plastic bag, combine breadcrumbs, Parmesan cheese, and Italian seasoning. 1/2 of the spiralized zucchini should be dipped in the beaten egg before being placed in the bag to be coated with the bread crumb mixture.
- Coat the air fryer basket with cooking spray. Arrange the breaded zucchini fries in the prepared basket, being careful not to overcrowd them. Coat the tops in cooking spray.
- Cook for about 10 minutes, turning halfway during the cooking time. Place the fries on a dish lined with paper towels. Repeat the breading and frying with the remaining zucchini spirals.

Air Fryer Rib-Eye Steak

Preparation Time: 20 minutes
Cooking Time: 20 minutes
Serve: 1
Ingredients:

- 2 rib-eye steaks, cut 1 1/2- inch thick
- 4 teaspoons grill seasoning (such as Montreal Steak Seasoning®)
- ¼ cup olive oil
- ½ cup reduced-sodium soy sauce

Directions:

- Combine the steaks, soy sauce, olive oil, and spice in a large resealable bag. Marinate the meat for at least 2 hours before cooking.
- Take the steaks out of the bag and discard the marinade. Next, remove any extra oil from the steaks.
- To prevent the air fryer pan from smoking throughout the cooking process, add roughly 1 tablespoon of water to the bottom.
- Preheat the air fryer carefully to 400°F (200 degrees C).
- Cook the steaks in the air fryer for 7 minutes. Cook for another 7 minutes, or until the steaks are medium-rare. Increase the overall cook time to 16 minutes for a medium steak, turning after 8 minutes.
- Remove the steaks from the pan, keep warm, and set aside for 4 minutes before serving.

Air Fryer Roasted Broccoli and Cauliflower

Preparation Time: 15 minutes
Cooking Time: 25 minutes
Serve: 1
Ingredients:

- 3 cups broccoli florets
- 3 cups cauliflower florets
- 2 tablespoons olive oil
- ½ teaspoon garlic powder
- ¼ teaspoon sea salt
- ¼ teaspoon paprika
- ⅛ teaspoon ground black pepper

Directions:

- Heat an air fryer to 400°F (200°C) according to the manufacturer's instructions.
- In a large microwave-safe dish, combine broccoli florets. Cook for 3 minutes on high power in the microwave. Any collected liquid should be drained.
- Combine the cauliflower, olive oil, garlic powder, sea salt, paprika, and black pepper in the same bowl as the broccoli. To blend, mix everything thoroughly. Fill the air fryer basket

halfway with the mixture. Cook for 12 minutes, turning the veggies halfway through to ensure equal browning.

Air Fryer Roasted Cauliflower

Preparation Time: 15 minutes
Cooking Time: 20 minutes
Serve: 1
Ingredients:

- 3 cloves garlic
- 1 tablespoon peanut oil
- ½ teaspoon salt
- ½ teaspoon smoked paprika
- 4 cups cauliflower florets

Directions:

- Preheat an air fryer carefully to 400°F (200 degrees C).
- Cut the garlic in half and pound it with a knife blade. Combine in a mixing dish with the oil, salt, and paprika. Pour in the cauliflower and toss to coat.
- Place the coated cauliflower in the air fryer dish and cook until crisp, about 15 minutes total, shaking every 5 minutes.

Air Fryer Lemon Pepper Shrimp

Preparation Time: 20 minutes
Cooking Time: 25 minutes
Serve: 1
Ingredients:

- 1 tablespoon olive oil
- 1 lemon, juiced
- 1 teaspoon lemon pepper
- ¼ teaspoon paprika
- ¼ teaspoon garlic powder
- 12 ounces uncooked medium shrimp, peeled and deveined
- 1 lemon, sliced

Directions:

- Preheat an air fryer carefully to 400 degrees F. (200 degrees C).
- Cut the garlic in half and smash it with the blade of a knife. Combine in a bowl with the oil, salt, and paprika. Add the cauliflower and toss to coat.
- Place the coated cauliflower in the air fryer bowl and cook until crisp, about 15 minutes total, shaking every 5 minutes.

Air Fryer Baby Back Ribs

Preparation Time: 15 minutes
Cooking Time: 20 minutes
Serve: 1
Ingredients:

- 1 rack baby back ribs
- 1 tablespoon olive oil
- 1 tablespoon liquid smoke flavoring
- 1 tablespoon brown sugar
- ½ teaspoon salt
- ½ teaspoon ground black pepper
- ½ teaspoon garlic powder
- ½ teaspoon onion powder
- ½ teaspoon chili powder
- 1 cup BBQ sauce

Directions:

- Remove the membrane off the back of the ribs and pat dry with a paper towel. Cut the rack into four parts. In a small dish, combine the olive oil and liquid smoke and apply them on both sides of the ribs.

- Combine brown sugar, garlic powder, onion powder, salt, pepper, and chili powder in a mixing bowl. Season both sides of the ribs well with the seasoning mixture. Allow the ribs to rest for 30 minutes to allow the taste to develop.
- Preheat an air fryer carefully to 375°F (190 degrees C).
- Place the ribs in the air fryer basket, bone side down, ensure they don't touch; cook in batches if required.
- The cooking time is 15 minutes. Cook for 10 minutes more after flipping the ribs (meat-side down). Remove the ribs from the air fryer and brush the bone-side with 1/2 cup BBQ sauce. Return the basket to the air fryer and cook for 5 minutes. Cook for a further 5 minutes, or until desired char is obtained, after flipping the ribs over and brushing the meat side with the remaining 1/2 cup BBQ sauce.

Roasted Rainbow Vegetables in the Air Fryer
Preparation Time: 15 minutes
Cooking Time: 18 minutes
Serve: 1
Ingredients:
- 1 red bell pepper
- 1 yellow summer squash, cut into 1-inch pieces
- 1 zucchini, cut into 1-inch pieces
- 4 ounces fresh mushrooms, cleaned and halved
- ½ sweet onion, cut into 1-inch wedges
- 1 tablespoon extra-virgin olive oil
- salt and pepper to taste

Directions:
- Preheat an air fryer carefully according to the manufacturer's instructions.
- Combine the red bell pepper, summer squash, zucchini, mushrooms, and onion in a large bowl. Toss in the olive oil, salt, and black pepper to taste.
- In the air fryer basket, arrange the vegetables in an even layer. Cook until the veggies are roasted, approximately 20 minutes, stirring halfway through.

Air Fryer Flour Tortilla Bowls
Preparation Time: 15 minutes
Cooking Time: 22 minutes
Serve: 1
Ingredients:
- 1 (8 inches) flour tortilla
- 1 (4 1/2-inch) souffle dish

Directions:
- Preheat the air fryer carefully to 375°F (190 degrees C).
- Heat the tortilla in a big pan or directly on the gas stove grates until warm and malleable. Place the tortilla in the souffle dish, smoothing it down and fluting it up the sides.
- 4 to 5 minutes in the air fryer until the tortilla becomes golden brown.
- Place the tortilla bowl upside down in the basket after removing it from the souffle dish. 1 to 2 minutes more air fry until golden brown.

Air Fryer Steak and Cheese Melts
Preparation Time: 10 minutes
Cooking Time: 18 minutes

Serve: 1
Ingredients:
- 1 pound beef rib-eye steak, thinly sliced
- 2 tablespoons Worcestershire sauce
- 1 tablespoon reduced-sodium soy sauce
- 1 medium onion, sliced into petals
- 4 ounces sliced baby portobello mushrooms
- ½ green bell pepper, thinly sliced
- 1 tablespoon olive oil
- ½ teaspoon salt
- ½ teaspoon ground mustard
- ¼ teaspoon ground black pepper
- 4 hoagie rolls
- 4 slices Provolone cheese

Directions:
- Combine the steak, Worcestershire sauce, and soy sauce in a mixing bowl. Refrigerate for 4 hours to overnight. Remove from the refrigerator and set aside for 30 minutes to come to room temperature.
- Preheat the air fryer carefully to 380°F (190 degrees C).
- Combine the onion, mushrooms, and bell pepper in a large mixing basin. Stir in the olive oil, salt, ground mustard, and pepper to coat.
- Place the hoagie rolls in the air fryer basket and toast for about 2 minutes. Then, place the rolls on a platter.
- Place the steak in the air fryer basket and cook for 3 minutes. Cook for 1 minute more after stirring. Place on a platter.
- Cook for 5 minutes in the air fryer basket with the veggie mix. Cook until softened, approximately 5 minutes more.
- Incorporate the meat into the veggie mixture. Place somewhat overlapping cheese slices on top. Cook for 3 minutes, or until the cheese is melted and bubbling. Serve immediately on toasted buns with the mixture.

Air Fryer Mini Pizza Calzones
Preparation Time: 18 minutes
Cooking Time: 20 minutes
Serve: 1
Ingredients:
- 1 (13.8 ounces) package refrigerated pizza dough (such as Pillsbury®)
- 9 teaspoons pizza sauce
- 1 (1.75 ounces) package pepperoni (such as Hormel®)
- 4 ½ tablespoons shredded mozzarella cheese
- avocado oil cooking spray

Directions:
- On a lightly floured board, roll out the pizza dough. Then, using a 2 1/8-inch biscuit cutter, cut out 9 circles. Each circular should be rolled into a 4 1/2-inch disc. 1 teaspoon pizza sauce, 3 slices pepperoni, and 1/2 tablespoon mozzarella cheese in each disc. Fold over, seal the edges by folding, and crimp with fork tines.
- Preheat an air fryer carefully to 375°F (190 degrees C). Spray the air fryer basket with avocado oil after lining it with parchment paper. Mist a batch of calzones with avocado oil and place them in the basket.
- Cook for 6 to 8 minutes in an air fryer. Turn the calzones over, spritz with avocado oil, and air fry for another 2 to 3 minutes, or until golden brown. Rep with the leftover calzones.

Air Fryer Spanish Potato Wedges

Preparation Time: 15 minutes
Cooking Time: 25 minutes
Serve: 1
Ingredients:

- 1 ½ pounds russet potatoes, unpeeled
- cooking spray, 2 tablespoons vegetable oil
- 1 teaspoon chili powder, 1 teaspoon ground cumin
- ½ teaspoon paprika
- ½ teaspoon ground coriander
- ¼ teaspoon garlic powder
- ⅛ teaspoon ground cinnamon
- salt to taste

Directions:

- To avoid breaking, cut potatoes into 8 equal wedges less than 5 inches long.
- Soak potato wedges in a dish of boiling tap water for about 10 minutes. Take the potatoes out of the water, rinse them, and wipe them dry with a paper towel.
- Preheat an air fryer carefully to 375°F (190 degrees C). Cooking oil spray should be sprayed on the air fryer basket.
- Drizzle oil over the potatoes in a large mixing basin. Combine chili powder, cumin, paprika, coriander, garlic powder, and cinnamon; sprinkle over potatoes and mix thoroughly. Place the potatoes in the air fryer basket without crowding them. If necessary, cook in two batches.
- 10 minutes in the air fryer. Open the air fryer and delicately turn the wedges with tongs. Cook for another 10 to 15 minutes, or until crispy and golden brown. Season with salt and pepper and serve immediately.

Air Fryer Bacon

Preparation Time: 20 minutes
Cooking Time: 20 minutes
Serve: 1
Ingredients:

- ½ (16 ounces) package bacon

Directions:

- Preheat an air fryer carefully to 390°F (200 degrees C).
- Lay the bacon in a single layer in the air fryer basket; little overlap is OK.
- Cook for 8 minutes. Cook for another 7 minutes, or until the bacon is crisp. Place fried bacon on a dish lined with paper towels to absorb extra fat.

Air Fryer Pumpkin Seeds

Preparation Time: 15 minutes
Cooking Time: 25 minutes
Serve: 1
Ingredients:

- 1 ¾ cups pumpkin seeds
- 2 teaspoons avocado oil
- 1 teaspoon smoked paprika
- 1 teaspoon salt

Directions:

- Rinse the pumpkin seeds well in a small colander.
- On a plate, place two sheets of paper towels. Cover two additional paper towels after placing the pumpkin seeds on the towels. Press down to get rid of the majority of the water. Allow at least 15 minutes for drying.
- Preheat the air fryer carefully to 350°F (180 degrees C).
- Place the seeds in a medium mixing basin. Mix in the avocado oil, paprika, and salt. Mix with a medium spoon. Cook for 35 minutes, stirring the basket periodically, in the air fryer basket with the seeds. Keep an eye on the pumpkin seeds for the last 5 minutes; they may easily go from nicely cooked to burnt.

Stuffed Air Fryer Potatoes

Preparation Time: 15 minutes
Cooking Time: 20 minutes
Serve: 1
Ingredients:

- 4 baking potatoes, peeled and halved
- 3 teaspoons olive oil, divided
- ½ cup Cheddar cheese, divided
- ½ yellow onion diced fine
- 2 slices bacon

Directions:

- Preheat the air fryer carefully to 350°F (175 degrees C).
- Brush potatoes lightly with 1 teaspoon oil; place in the air fryer basket and cook for 10 minutes.
- Brush potatoes with 1 teaspoon more oil and cook in the air fryer for 10 minutes. Cook until soft, approximately 10 minutes more, after coating with the remaining oil.
- Cooked potatoes should be cut in half. Spoon the insides into a mixing basin; stir in 1/4 cup Cheddar cheese.
- In a pan, sauté the onion and bacon over medium-high heat, rotating periodically until the bacon is uniformly browned, about 10 minutes.
- Stuff the potato-Cheddar cheese mixture, onion, and bacon into the skins. Top with the remaining cheese.
- Return the filled potatoes to the air fryer and cook for 6 minutes, or until the cheese has melted.

Air Fryer Oreos

Preparation Time: 20 minutes
Cooking Time: 25 minutes
Serve: 1
Ingredients:

- ½ cup complete pancake mix
- ⅓ cup water
- cooking spray
- 9 chocolate sandwich cookies (such as Oreo®)
- 1 tablespoon confectioners' sugar, or to taste

Directions:

- In a mixing bowl, combine the pancake mix and water.
- Line an air fryer basket with parchment paper. On parchment paper, apply the nonstick cooking spray. After dipping each cookie in the pancake mixture, place it in the basket. Make sure they don't touch and, if necessary, cook in batches.
- Preheat the air fryer to 400°F on a low setting (200 degrees C). Cook for 4 to 5 minutes on one side, then turn and cook for another 2 to 3 minutes on the other side, or until golden brown. On top, confectioners' sugar is strewn.

Air Fryer Blueberry Muffins

Preparation Time: 15 minutes
Cooking Time: 20 minutes
Serve: 1

Ingredients:

- 1 cup self-rising flour
- 2 ½ tablespoons white sugar
- ¼ teaspoon ground cinnamon
- ⅓ cup milk
- 3 tablespoons melted butter
- 1 egg
- 2 teaspoons vanilla extract
- ½ cup blueberries

Directions:

- Preheat the air fryer carefully for 5 minutes at 340 degrees F (170 degrees C).
- In a mixing basin, combine the flour, sugar, and cinnamon. Combine the milk, melted butter, egg, and vanilla essence in a mixing bowl. Blend until everything is properly incorporated. Blueberries should be folded in. Fill silicone cupcake liners 3/4 full of the mixture, using a tiny scoop. Carefully place in the air fryer basket.
- Muffins should be cooked in the oven for 14 minutes.

Air Fryer Sourdough Bread

Preparation Time: 15 minutes
Cooking Time: 18 minutes
Serve: 1
Ingredients:

- 1 cup bread flour
- ½ cup spelled flour
- ½ cup sourdough starter
- 1 tablespoon extra-virgin olive oil
- ½ teaspoon fine sea salt
- ½ cup water

Directions:

- In the bowl of a stand mixer, combine bread flour, spelled flour, sourdough starter, oil, and salt. Begin kneading with the dough hook. Add water until all ingredients come together and start to pull together; you may not need all of the water. Knead for 5 minutes at low speed.
- Form the dough into a ball by folding it in half. Place in a baking dish that can be used in an air fryer. Cover with plastic wrap and set aside for 5 hours to overnight to double in volume.
- Preheat the air fryer carefully to 390°F (200 degrees C). Remove the plastic wrap off the bread and score it.
- Place the baking dish in the air fryer and cook for 20 minutes, or until the loaf is golden. In the middle, an instant-read thermometer should read at least 190 degrees F. (88 degrees C). Allow cooling completely before slicing.

Air Fryer Asparagus Tots

Preparation Time: 15 minutes
Cooking Time: 22 minutes
Serve: 1
Ingredients:

- 12 ounces asparagus, trimmed and diced
- ½ cup panko breadcrumbs
- ¼ cup finely shredded Parmesan cheese
- 1 serving cooking spray

Directions:

- Over medium-high heat, bring a saucepan of salted water to a boil. Cook the asparagus for 5 minutes. Drain in a colander and set aside to cool for 5 minutes, or until easily handled.

- Combine the asparagus, breadcrumbs, and Parmesan cheese in a large mixing dish. Knead the ingredients with your hands until it resembles dough. 1 tablespoon of the mixture should be formed into a tot. Serve on a platter. Repeat with the rest of the mixture. Freeze the tater tots for 30 minutes.
- Preheat the air fryer carefully to 400°F (200 degrees C).
- Spray the air fryer basket with nonstick cooking spray. Next, spray the tops of the tots with cooking spray before placing them in the basket. Fry for 10 minutes, shaking once halfway through.

Air Fryer Cinnamon-Sugar Doughnuts

Preparation Time: 10 minutes
Cooking Time: 18 minutes
Serve: 1
Ingredients:

- ¼ cup butter, melted
- ½ cup white sugar
- ¼ cup brown sugar
- 1 teaspoon ground cinnamon
- ¼ teaspoon ground nutmeg (optional)
- 1 (16.3 ounces) package refrigerated flaky biscuit dough (such as Pillsbury™ Grands! ™ Flaky Layers)

Directions:

- Melt the butter in a basin. Combine the white sugar, brown sugar, cinnamon, and nutmeg in a separate dish.
- Separate the biscuit dough into individual biscuits and use a biscuit cutter to cut out the centers to make a doughnut shape. Fill the air fryer basket halfway with doughnuts.
- 4 to 6 minutes in an air fryer at 350°F (175°C) until golden brown. Cook for a further 1 to 3 minutes after flipping the doughnuts.
- Take the doughnuts out of the air fryer. Dip each doughnut into melted butter (coating top, bottom, and sides), then into the sugar-cinnamon mixture until completely coated. Serve right away.

Rosemary Potato Wedges for the Air Fryer

Preparation Time: 18 minutes
Cooking Time: 20 minutes
Serve: 1
Ingredients:

- 2 russet potatoes, sliced into 12 wedges, each with skin on
- 1 tablespoon extra-virgin olive oil
- 2 teaspoons seasoned salt
- 1 tablespoon finely chopped fresh rosemary

Directions:

- Preheat an air fryer carefully to 380°F (190 degrees C).
- Toss the potatoes with the olive oil in a large mixing basin. Toss with the seasoned salt and rosemary to mix.
- Once the air fryer is heated, place the potatoes in a uniform layer in the fryer basket; you may need to cook them in batches.
- Air fried the potatoes for 10 minutes before flipping them with tongs. Continue air frying until the potato wedges are done to your liking, about 10 minutes longer.

Air Fryer Fried Green Tomatoes

Preparation Time: 15 minutes
Cooking Time: 25 minutes
Serve: 1

Ingredients:

- 2 green tomatoes, cut into 1/4-inch slices
- salt and freshly ground black pepper
- ⅓ cup all-purpose flour
- ½ cup buttermilk
- 2 eggs, lightly beaten
- 1 cup plain panko breadcrumbs
- 1 cup yellow cornmeal
- 1 teaspoon garlic powder
- ½ teaspoon paprika
- 1 tablespoon olive oil, or as needed

Directions:

- Season the tomato slices properly with salt and pepper to taste.
- Set up a breading station with three shallow dishes: flour in the first, buttermilk and eggs in the second, and breadcrumbs, cornmeal, garlic powder, and paprika in the third.
- Dredge tomato slices in flour and shake off excess. Dip the tomatoes into the egg mixture, then the bread crumb mixture, coating both sides.
- Preheat the air fryer carefully to 400°F (200 degrees C). Brush olive oil into the frying basket. Place the breaded tomato slices in the fryer basket, making sure they don't touch; cook in batches if required. Brush olive oil over the tops of the tomatoes.
- Cook for 12 minutes, then turn the tomatoes and spray with olive oil one more. 3 to 5 minutes more, or until crisp and golden brown. To keep the tomatoes crisp, place them on a rack lined with paper towels. Rep with the remaining tomatoes.

Air Fryer To stones

Preparation Time: 20 minutes
Cooking Time: 20 minutes
Serve: 1
Ingredients:

- 2 green (unripe) plantains
- olive oil cooking spray
- 3 cups water, or as needed, salt to taste

Directions:

- Preheat an air fryer carefully to 400°F (200 degrees C).
- Remove the plantain tips. Make a vertical cut from end to end in the skin, careful not to cut through the thick skin and into the plantain flesh. Plantain, still in its peel, should be cut into 1-inch segments. Peel the skin off each portion, beginning with the slit you formed.
- Spray the plantain pieces with olive oil spray and place them in the air fryer basket. 5 minutes in the air fryer. Prepare a dish of salted water in the meantime.
- Using tongs, remove the plantain pieces from the air fryer. Using a Costanera, pound to a thickness of about 1/2-inch (plantain smasher). While the remainder of the two stones is being broken, soak them in a dish of salted water.
- After removing the two stones from the salted water, blot them dry using a paper towel.
- Return to stones to the air fryer in batches, each time filling the basket with a single layer. Season the tops with salt and coat with olive oil spray; air fry for 5 minutes. With tongs, flip the pan over and coat the opposite side with olive oil spray. Season with salt and pepper. 4 to 5 minutes longer air fry until golden brown and crunchy.

Air Fryer French Toast Sticks

Preparation Time: 15 minutes
Cooking Time: 25 minutes
Serve: 1
Ingredients:

- 2 large eggs
- ⅓ cup milk
- 1 tablespoon butter, melted
- 1 teaspoon vanilla extract
- 1 teaspoon ground cinnamon
- 4 slices of day-old bread, cut into thirds
- 1 teaspoon confectioners' sugar, or to taste

Directions:

- Combine the eggs, milk, butter, vanilla essence, and cinnamon in a mixing dish.
- Using parchment paper, line an air fryer basket. Place each slice of bread in the basket after dipping it in the milk mixture. Make sure they are not touching and, if required, cook in batches.
- Preheat the air fryer carefully to 370°F (188 degrees C). Fry the bread for 6 minutes in the basket, then flips and cook for another 3 minutes. Confectioners' sugar should be sprinkled on each stick.

Air Fryer Zesty Cheddar Biscuits

Preparation Time: 15 minutes
Cooking Time: 20 minutes
Serve: 1
Ingredients:

- 1 cup self-rising flour
- ¾ cup freshly shredded sharp Cheddar cheese
- ½ cup milk, 2 tablespoons canned chopped green chili peppers
- ¾ teaspoon taco seasoning mix
- ¾ teaspoon garlic powder
- ¼ teaspoon ground cumin
- 1 pinch white sugar
- 1 serving cooking spray
- ¼ cup salted butter, melted
- 2 teaspoons taco seasoning mix

Directions:

- Preheat an air fryer carefully for 5 minutes at 350 degrees F (175 degrees C).
- Combine the flour, Cheddar cheese, milk, green chili peppers, taco seasoning, garlic powder, cumin, and sugar in a medium mixing bowl. Combine all of the ingredients in a mixing bowl until a dough forms.
- Line the air fryer basket with a ring of parchment paper. Coat the pan with nonstick cooking spray. Using a spring-hinged scoop, place dough in the basket. 12 minutes in the air fryer
- Meanwhile, make the taco spice topping by combining melted butter and seasoning mix. Brush biscuits with taco-seasoned butter after separating them. Serve right away.

Tex-Mex Air Fryer Hash Browns

Preparation Time: 20 minutes
Cooking Time: 25 minutes
Serve: 1
Ingredients:

- 1 ½ pounds potatoes
- 1 tablespoon olive oil
- ½ teaspoon olive oil
- ½ teaspoon taco seasoning mix
- ½ teaspoon ground cumin
- 1 red bell pepper, seeded and cut into 1-inch pieces
- 1 small onion, cut into 1-inch pieces
- 1 jalapeno, seeded and cut into 1-inch rings
- 1 pinch salt and ground black pepper to taste

Directions:

- Soak potatoes for 20 minutes in cold water.
- Preheat the air fryer carefully to 320°F (160 degrees C). Drain the potatoes, dry them with a clean towel, and place them in a large mixing basin. Toss the potatoes with 1 tablespoon olive oil to coat. Place them in the air fryer basket that has been warmed. Make a timer for 18 minutes.
- In the previously used basin for the potatoes, combine bell pepper, onion, and jalapeño. Add 1/2 teaspoon olive oil, taco seasoning, ground cumin, salt, and pepper to taste. To coat, toss everything together.
- Remove the potatoes from the air fryer and place them in the bowl with the veggie mixture. Return the empty basket to the air fryer and heat it to 356 degrees F. (180 degrees C).
- Toss the dish's contents quickly to combine the potatoes, veggies, and spices evenly. Place the mixture in the basket. Cook for 6 minutes, then shake the basket and cook for another 5 minutes, or until the potatoes are browned and crispy. Serve right away.

Perfect Turkey Breast Roast in the Air Fryer

Preparation Time: 15 minutes
Cooking Time: 20 minutes
Serve: 1
Ingredients:

- 1 (3 pounds) frozen turkey breast roast
- 2 cups water
- ⅓ cup kosher salt
- ⅓ cup brown sugar
- ground black pepper to taste
- 2 tablespoons butter, or as needed
- 1 seasoned pinch salt, or to taste (such as Texas Roadhouse®)

Directions:

- Refrigerate frozen turkey breast for roughly 24 hours to thaw.
- Bring the water to a boil, then add the kosher salt, brown sugar, and pepper. Remove the brine from the heat and set it aside for 30 minutes to cool fully. Remove the turkey breast from the wrapping, leaving the netting in place if feasible. Place the turkey in a container and cover with the cooled brine; add extra water as needed to completely cover, stirring to ensure the brine is combined with the water. Allow the turkey to brine in the refrigerator for 8 hours or overnight.
- Preheat an air fryer carefully to 390°F (200°C) according to the manufacturer's instructions.
- Remove the turkey from the brine and set it aside. Pat the turkey dry. Rub with butter and season with salt and pepper.
- Cook the turkey for 15 minutes in a preheated air fryer; flip, remove the netting, and season again. Next, reduce the temperature to 360°F (182 degrees C). Cook for another 20 minutes, rotating after 15 minutes. Then, raise the

temperature to 390°F (200°C), flip, and cook until the center is no longer pink, about 15 minutes more. Finally, remove the turkey from the oven and set it aside for 5 minutes before slicing and serving.

Air Fryer Triple-Chocolate Oatmeal Cookies

Preparation Time: 15 minutes
Cooking Time: 18 minutes
Serve: 1
Ingredients:

- 3 cups quick-cooking oatmeal
- 1 ½ cups all-purpose flour
- ¼ cup cocoa powder
- 1 (3.4 ounces) package instant chocolate pudding mix
- 1 teaspoon baking soda
- 1 teaspoon salt
- 1 cup butter, softened
- ¾ cup brown sugar
- ¾ cup white sugar
- 2 eggs
- 1 teaspoon vanilla extract
- 2 cups chocolate chips
- 1 cup chopped walnuts (optional)
- nonstick cooking spray

Directions:

- Preheat an air fryer carefully to 350°F (175°C) according to the manufacturer's instructions. Nonstick cooking spray should be sprayed on the air fryer basket.
- Combine the oats, flour, cocoa powder, pudding mix, baking soda, and salt in a mixing dish. Place aside.
- Cream together the butter, brown sugar, and white sugar in a separate dish using an electric mixer. Combine the eggs and vanilla essence in a mixing bowl. Mix in the oatmeal mixture well. Finally, combine the chocolate chips and walnuts in a mixing bowl.
- Place dough in the air fryer; level out and allow approximately 1 inch between each cookie.
- Cook for 6 to 10 minutes, or until gently browned. Allow cooling on a wire rack before serving.

Air Fryer Mini Peppers Stuffed with Cheese and Sausage

Preparation Time: 15 minutes
Cooking Time: 22 minutes
Serve: 1
Ingredients:

- 8 ounces bulk Italian sausage
- 1 (16 ounces) package miniature multi-colored sweet peppers
- 2 tablespoons olive oil, divided
- 1 (8 ounces) package cream cheese, softened
- ½ cup shredded Cheddar cheese
- 2 tablespoons crumbled blue cheese (Optional)
- 1 tablespoon finely chopped fresh chives
- 1 clove garlic, minced
- ¼ teaspoon ground black pepper
- 2 tablespoons panko breadcrumbs

Directions:

- Melt the butter in a large nonstick pan over medium-high heat. Cook and stir sausage in a heated pan for 5 to 7

- minutes or browned and crumbled. Set away grease after draining and discarding it.
- Preheat an air fryer carefully to 350°F (175 degrees C).
- Cut a slit in one side of each sweet pepper, from stem to tip, lengthwise. Place the peppers in the air fryer basket and brush with 1 tablespoon olive oil.
- Cook for 3 minutes in a hot air fryer. Shake the basket and continue to cook until the peppers begin to brown and soften, about 3 minutes longer. Remove the peppers from the air fryer and set aside until cool enough to handle.
- While the peppers are cooling, combine the sausage, cream cheese, Cheddar cheese, blue cheese, chives, garlic, and black pepper in a medium mixing bowl. Combine the breadcrumbs and the remaining 1 tablespoon olive oil in a separate dish.
- Fill each pepper with cheese mixture and top with bread crumb mixture. Place the filled peppers in the air fryer basket, working in batches if required, and cook for 4 to 5 minutes, or until the filling is cooked through and the breadcrumbs are toasted. Allow cooling slightly before serving.

Air Fryer Cheese-Stuffed Mini Italian Meatloaves

Preparation Time: 10 minutes
Cooking Time: 18 minutes
Serve: 1
Ingredients:

- ⅓ cup milk
- ⅓ cup Italian-seasoned panko breadcrumbs
- 8 slices pepperoni
- 2 ounces small fresh mozzarella balls
- ½ cup marinara sauce, warmed
- 2 tablespoons purchased basil pesto
- 1 egg, lightly beaten
- 1 clove garlic, minced
- ¼ teaspoon ground black pepper
- 1 pound 90% lean ground beef
- 1 tablespoon chopped fresh basil

Directions:

- Combine the milk, pesto, egg, garlic, and pepper in a medium mixing bowl. Next, combine the ground beef and breadcrumbs, being careful not to overmix.
- Divide the meat mixture into four equal halves. Make a well in the center of each section, leaving a 1/2-inch border around the edge. Fill each well with 2 slices of pepperoni, overlapping to span the whole length of the well. Top with a quarter of the mozzarella balls. Enclose the filling by pressing the meat mixture around it; shape each chunk into an oblong loaf shape. Loaves should be placed in the air fryer basket in batches.
- Cook in the air fryer at 370°F (190°C) for 15 minutes, or until an instant-read thermometer inserted into the thickest part of the meat registers 165°F (75°C). Serve the meatloaves with warm marinara sauce and fresh basil on top.

Air Fryer Black Garlic-Cauliflower Patties

Preparation Time: 18 minutes
Cooking Time: 20 minutes
Serve: 1
Ingredients:

- 1 medium head cauliflower, cut into florets
- 2 solo black garlic bulbs
- ½ cup all-purpose flour
- 2 eggs, beaten
- ¼ cup Italian-seasoned breadcrumbs
- 2 teaspoons baking powder
- 1 teaspoon salt
- ½ teaspoon ground black pepper to taste
- ½ teaspoon dried basil
- ½ teaspoon dried parsley
- ½ teaspoon dried oregano
- ½ teaspoon dried rosemary
- ½ teaspoon red pepper flakes
- ½ teaspoon onion powder
- cooking spray
- 4 slices Swiss cheese, torn into 4 pieces each

Directions:

- Combine cauliflower and black garlic; process until finely "riced." Transfer to a mixing basin. In a large mixing bowl, combine the flour, eggs, breadcrumbs, baking powder, salt, black pepper, basil, parsley, oregano, rosemary, red pepper flakes, and onion powder. Stir until everything is completely blended.
- Preheat an air fryer carefully to 400°F (200 degrees C). Spray the air fryer basket with cooking spray and line it with parchment paper.
- Using a big cookie scoop, drop the cauliflower mixture onto the parchment paper and flatten gently with your fingertips.
- Cook for 4 to 6 minutes in the air fryer, turn with a spatula, and continue cooking until patties are set, about 1 minute more. Remove each burger from the air fryer and top with 1/4 slice Swiss cheese. Return to the air fryer and cook for 30 to 40 seconds more, or until the cheese is melted.

Air Fryer Mahi Mahi with Brown Butter

Preparation Time: 15 minutes
Cooking Time: 25 minutes
Serve: 1
Ingredients:

- 4 (5 ounces) mahi-mahi fillets
- salt and ground black pepper to taste
- cooking spray
- ⅔ cup butter

Directions:

- Preheat an air fryer carefully to 350°F (175 degrees C).
- Season the mahi-mahi fillets with salt and pepper and coat both sides with cooking spray. Place the fillets in the air fryer basket, leaving space between them.
- Cook for 12 minutes, or until the fish flakes easily with a fork and has a golden tint.
- Melt butter in a small saucepan over medium-low heat while the fish cooks. Bring the butter to a boil and cook for 3 to 5 minutes, or until it becomes foamy and deep brown. Turn off the heat.
- Place the fish fillets on a platter and top with brown butter.

Air Fryer Bang Bang Tofu

Preparation Time: 20 minutes
Cooking Time: 20 minutes
Serve: 1

Ingredients:

- 1 (14 ounces) package extra-firm tofu
- 2 tablespoons toasted sesame oil
- 1 cup mayonnaise
- ½ cup sweet chili sauce
- 1 ½ tablespoons Sriracha sauce
- 1 ½ cups panko breadcrumbs
- 1 green onion, chopped

Directions:

- Place the tofu on a dish lined with paper towels. Cover with additional paper towels and a second plate. Press the tofu for 30 minutes with a 3- to 5-pound weight on top. Drain and discard any remaining liquid, then cut the tofu into 1/2-inch pieces.
- Toss the cubed tofu in a dish with the sesame oil. Allow for a 20-minute resting period after gently stirring.
- Meanwhile, create the bang bang sauce by whisking together the mayonnaise, sweet chili sauce, and Sriracha sauce until smooth. Then, in a separate dish, combine the panko.
- Preheat the air fryer carefully to 400°F (200 degrees C).
- Tofu should be mixed with 1/2 cup bang bang sauce until evenly incorporated. Coat the tofu in the panko breadcrumbs and set it in the air fryer basket, ensuring the tofu pieces do not overlap. You may need to perform this in batches depending on the size of your air fryer.
- 5 minutes in the oven. Cook for 3 minutes more after shaking. Serve with the leftover bang bang sauce and garnished with green onion.

Air Fryer Sriracha-Honey Shrimp

Preparation Time: 15 minutes
Cooking Time: 25 minutes
Serve: 1
Ingredients:

- 1 tablespoon Sriracha sauce
- 1 tablespoon honey
- ½ tablespoon lime juice
- ½ tablespoon soy sauce
- ½ teaspoon minced garlic
- ½ pound large raw tail-on shrimp
- 2 green onions, chopped

Directions:

- According to the manufacturer's instructions, preheat the air fryer carefully to 400°F (200°C).
- Combine the Sriracha, honey, lime juice, soy sauce, and garlic in a large mixing bowl. Stir in the shrimp until evenly coated.
- Place the shrimp in the air fryer basket with tongs and cook for 3 minutes. Return the shrimp to the sauce and toss to combine. Return the shrimp to the basket and cook for 3 minutes more. Garnish with green onions, if desired.

Air Fryer Lobster Tails with Lemon-Garlic Butter

Preparation Time: 15 minutes
Cooking Time: 20 minutes
Serve: 1
Ingredients:

- 2 (4 ounces) lobster tails
- 4 tablespoons butter
- 1 teaspoon lemon zest
- 1 clove garlic, grated
- salt and ground black pepper to taste
- 1 teaspoon chopped fresh parsley
- 2 wedges lemon

Directions:

- Butterfly lobster tails by using kitchen shears to cut longitudinally through the hard upper shells and flesh. Cut to the bottoms of the shells, but not all the way through. Separate the tail halves. Place the lobster tails in the air fryer basket, lobster flesh facing up.
- In a small saucepan over medium heat, melt the butter. Heat the lemon zest and garlic for 30 seconds, or until the garlic is soft. Brush 2 tablespoons of the butter mixture onto the lobster tails; remove any excess brushed butter to avoid contamination with raw lobster. Season the lobster with salt and pepper to taste.
- Cook for 5 to 7 minutes in an air fryer at 380°F (195°C) until lobster flesh is opaque. Reserved butter from the pot should be spooned over lobster flesh. Serve with lemon wedges and garnished with parsley.

Air Fryer Dry-Rubbed Pork Tenderloin with Broccoli

Preparation Time: 20 minutes
Cooking Time: 25 minutes
Serve: 1
Ingredients:

- 2 tablespoons brown sugar
- 1 tablespoon smoked paprika
- 1 teaspoon ground mustard
- 1 teaspoon salt
- ½ teaspoon ground black pepper
- ¼ teaspoon garlic powder
- ¼ teaspoon ground cayenne pepper (Optional)
- 1 tablespoon olive oil
- 1 (1 1/2 pound) pork tenderloin
- 4 cups chopped broccoli florets
- 1 tablespoon olive oil
- salt and ground black pepper to taste

Directions:

- In a small mixing bowl, add brown sugar, paprika, ground mustard, salt, black pepper, garlic powder, and cayenne pepper until equally blended.
- Brush the pork tenderloin with olive oil until it is evenly covered. Rub the spice mixture all over the tenderloin and set aside for 5 minutes.
- Preheat an air fryer carefully to 400°F (200 degrees C).
- Place the tenderloin in the air fryer basket and cook for 20 minutes, undisturbed, in the preheated air fryer.
- In the meantime, arrange the broccoli in a microwave-safe bowl. Microwave on high for 3 minutes, or until tender. Season with salt and pepper after adding the olive oil.
- Place the tenderloin on a cutting board and set it aside for 10 minutes before slicing.
- Place the broccoli in the air fryer basket while the tenderloin is resting. Cook for 10 minutes, shaking the basket halfway during the cooking time.

Air Fryer Apple Fritters

Preparation Time: 15 minutes
Cooking Time: 20 minutes

Serve: 1
Ingredients:

- cooking spray
- 1 cup all-purpose flour
- ¼ cup white sugar
- ¼ cup milk
- 1 egg
- 1 ½ teaspoons baking powder
- 1 pinch salt
- 2 tablespoons white sugar
- ½ teaspoon ground cinnamon
- 1 apple - peeled, cored, and chopped
- ½ cup confectioners' sugar
- 1 tablespoon milk
- ½ teaspoon caramel extract (such as Watkins™)
- ¼ teaspoon ground cinnamon

Directions:

- Preheat an air fryer carefully to 350°F (175 degrees C). Insert a round of parchment paper into the bottom of the air fryer. Coat the pan with nonstick cooking spray.
- Combine the flour, 1/4 cup sugar, milk, egg, baking powder, and salt in a small mixing bowl. Stir until everything is mixed.
- Combine 2 tablespoons sugar and cinnamon; sprinkle over apples until evenly covered. Combine the apples and flour in a mixing bowl.
- Place the cakes in the bottom of the air fryer basket using a cookie scoop.
- Air-fry for 5 minutes in a preheated fryer. Cook until the cakes are golden brown, approximately 5 minutes more.
- Meanwhile, combine the confectioners' sugar, milk, caramel essence, and cinnamon in a mixing dish. Drizzle the glaze over the cakes and set them aside to cool.

Air Fryer Rosemary Garlic Baby Potatoes

Preparation Time: 15 minutes
Cooking Time: 18 minutes
Serve: 1
Ingredients:

- 1 ½ pounds multi-colored new potatoes, halved
- 2 tablespoons olive oil
- 2 cloves garlic, minced
- 1 teaspoon finely chopped fresh rosemary
- ½ teaspoon kosher salt
- ½ teaspoon lemon zest

Directions:

- Preheat the air fryer carefully to 400°F (200 degrees C).
- Combine the potatoes, oil, garlic, rosemary, and salt in a large mixing basin. Arrange the potatoes in the air fryer basket in a single layer, not overcrowded; work in batches if required. Cook for 20 minutes, or until potatoes are golden brown and soft. Before serving, sprinkle with lemon zest.

Air Fryer Rosemary Garlic Baby Potatoes

Preparation Time: 15 minutes
Cooking Time: 22 minutes
Serve: 1
Ingredients:

- 1 ½ pounds multi-colored new potatoes, halved
- 2 tablespoons olive oil

- 2 cloves garlic, minced
- 1 teaspoon finely chopped fresh rosemary
- ½ teaspoon kosher salt
- ½ teaspoon lemon zest

Directions:

- Preheat the air fryer carefully to 400 degrees F. (200 degrees C).
- In a large mixing basin, combine potatoes, oil, garlic, rosemary, and salt. Arrange the potatoes in a single layer in the air fryer basket, not overcrowded; work in batches if required. Cook until the potatoes are golden brown and soft, about 20 minutes. Before serving, top with lemon zest.

Air Fryer Bacon-Wrapped Scallops with Sriracha Mayo

Preparation Time: 10 minutes
Cooking Time: 18 minutes
Serve: 1
Ingredients:

- ½ cup mayonnaise
- 2 tablespoons Sriracha sauce
- 1 pound bay scallops (about 36 small scallops), 1 pinch coarse salt
- 1 pinch freshly cracked black pepper
- 12 slices bacon, cut into thirds
- 1 serving olive oil cooking spray

Directions:

- In a small bowl, combine mayonnaise and Sriracha sauce. Refrigerate the Sriracha mayonnaise until ready to use.
- Preheat the air fryer carefully to 390°F (200 degrees C).
- Spread the scallops on a plate or cutting board and wipe dry with a paper towel. Season with salt and pepper to taste. Wrap a third of a slice of bacon around each scallop and fasten with a toothpick.
- Cooking spray should be sprayed on the air fryer basket. Place the bacon-wrapped scallops in a single layer in the basket; if required, divide them into two groups.
- Cook for 7 minutes in the air fryer. Check for doneness; the scallops should be opaque and the bacon crispy. Cook for an additional 1 to 2 minutes, checking every minute. With tongs, carefully remove the scallops and lay them on a paper towel-lined dish to soak any extra oil from the bacon. Toss with Sriracha mayonnaise and serve.

Air Fryer Beignets

Preparation Time: 18 minutes
Cooking Time: 20 minutes
Serve: 1
Ingredients:

- cooking spray
- ½ cup all-purpose flour
- ¼ cup white sugar
- ⅛ cup water
- 1 large egg, separated
- 1 ½ teaspoon melted butter
- ½ teaspoon baking powder
- ½ teaspoon vanilla extract
- 1 pinch salt
- 2 tablespoons confectioners' sugar, or to taste

Directions:

- Preheat the air fryer carefully to 370°F (185 degrees C). Nonstick cooking sprays a silicone egg-bite mold.
- Combine the flour, sugar, water, egg yolk, butter, baking powder, vanilla extract, and salt in a large mixing basin. To blend, stir everything together.
- In a small mixing basin, beat the egg white with an electric hand mixer on medium speed until soft peaks form. Incorporate into the batter. Transfer the batter to the prepared mold using a tiny, hinged ice cream scoop.
- Fill the silicone mold and place it in the air fryer basket.
- Fry for 10 minutes in a hot air fryer. Carefully remove the mold from the basket; pop the beignets out and flip them onto a parchment paper circle.
- Return the parchment round containing the beignets to the air fryer basket. Cook for another 4 minutes. Remove the beignets from the air fryer basket and sprinkle them with confectioners' sugar.

Air Fryer Butternut Squash Home Fries
Preparation Time: 15 minutes
Cooking Time: 25 minutes
Serve: 1
Ingredients:
- 1 pound butternut squash
- 1 tablespoon extra-virgin olive oil
- 2 teaspoons bagel seasoning (such as Trader Joe's Everything but the Bagel Sesame Seasoning Blend)
- 1 teaspoon chopped fresh rosemary

Directions:
- Preheat an air fryer carefully to 400°F (200 degrees C).
- Toss the butternut squash with the olive oil in a large mixing basin. Place the squash pieces in the air fryer basket. Cook until gently browned, approximately 22 minutes total, stirring every 3 to 4 minutes.
- Transfer to a dish or serving plate and evenly sprinkle with the spice blend. Garnish with fresh rosemary if desired.

Air Fryer Teriyaki Snap Peas and Mushrooms
Preparation Time: 20 minutes
Cooking Time: 20 minutes
Serve: 1
Ingredients:
- 1 (8 ounces) package fresh sugar snap peas
- ½ (8 ounces) package mushrooms, sliced
- 3 tablespoons teriyaki sauce
- 2 teaspoons olive oil

Directions:
- Preheat an air fryer carefully to 400°F (200 degrees C).
- Add snap peas, mushrooms, teriyaki sauce, and olive oil; toss until equally mixed. Fill the air fryer basket halfway with the veggie mixture. Cook for 12 minutes in an air fryer, shaking halfway through.

Spicy Homemade Breakfast Sausage in the Air Fryer
Preparation Time: 15 minutes
Cooking Time: 25 minutes
Serve: 1
Ingredients:

- 1 pound ground pork
- 1 teaspoon sea salt
- 1 teaspoon rubbed sage
- 1 teaspoon crushed red pepper
- ½ teaspoon dried marjoram
- ½ teaspoon onion powder
- ½ teaspoon ground black pepper
- ¼ teaspoon dried thyme

Directions:
- Preheat an air fryer carefully to 400°F (200 degrees C).
- In a large mixing bowl, combine ground pork, sea salt, sage, red pepper, marjoram, onion powder, pepper, and thyme. Mix thoroughly with your hands until everything is equally incorporated. Make 8 patties out of the mixture.
- Cook for 5 minutes with 4 patties in the air fryer basket. Cook for 5 minutes longer after carefully flipping the burgers. Repeat with the remaining patties on a plate lined with paper towels.

Air Fryer Prosciutto and Mozzarella Grilled Cheese
Preparation Time: 15 minutes
Cooking Time: 20 minutes
Serve: 1
Ingredients:
- 2 tablespoons unsalted butter
- 3 ounces fresh mozzarella
- 2 slices sourdough bread
- 2 ounces prosciutto

Directions:
- Preheat the oven to 360° F. (180 degrees C).
- Butter one side of a slice of bread and set it greased side down on a platter. Top with prosciutto and mozzarella slices in an even layer. Butter the second slice of bread and set it on top, buttered side out.
- Place in the air fryer and cook for 8 minutes, or until gently browned and toasted.

Air Fryer Sweet and Spicy Roasted Carrots
Preparation Time: 20 minutes
Cooking Time: 25 minutes
Serve: 1
Ingredients:
- 1 serving cooking spray
- 1 tablespoon butter, melted
- 1 tablespoon hot honey (such as Mike's Hot Honey®)
- 1 teaspoon grated orange zest
- ½ teaspoon ground cardamom
- ½ pound baby carrots
- 1 tablespoon freshly squeezed orange juice
- 1 pinch salt and ground black pepper

Directions:
- Preheat an air fryer carefully to 400°F (200 degrees C). Nonstick cooking spray should be sprayed on the basket.
- Combine the butter, honey, orange zest, and cardamom in a mixing dish. Set aside 1 tablespoon of the sauce in a separate dish. Toss the carrots in the remaining sauce until evenly covered. Place the carrots in the air fryer basket.
- Toss carrots every 7 minutes for 15 to 22 minutes, or until roasted and fork tender. Combine orange juice and reserved

honey-butter sauce in a mixing bowl. Toss with carrots until well blended. Season with salt and pepper to taste.

Air-Fryer Potato-Skin Wedges

Preparation Time: 15 minutes
Cooking Time: 20 minutes
Serve: 1
Ingredients:

- 4 medium russet potatoes
- 1 cup water
- 3 tablespoons canola oil
- 1 teaspoon paprika
- ¼ teaspoon ground black pepper
- ¼ teaspoon salt

Directions:

- Fill a big saucepan halfway with salted water and bring to a boil. Reduce the heat to medium-low and cook until the potatoes are fork-tender, about 20 minutes. Drain. Refrigerate in a bowl for 30 minutes or until totally cold.
- Combine the oil, paprika, black pepper, and salt in a mixing dish. Toss the quartered cold potatoes into the mixture.
- Preheat an air fryer carefully to 400°F (200 degrees C).
- Place half of the potato wedges in the air fryer basket, skin side down, being careful not to overcrowd.
- 13 to 15 minutes, or until golden brown. Rep with the remaining wedges.

Air Fryer Salt and Vinegar Chickpeas

Preparation Time: 15 minutes
Cooking Time: 18 minutes
Serve: 1
Ingredients:

- 1 (15 ounces) can of chickpeas
- 1 cup white vinegar
- 1 tablespoon olive oil
- ½ teaspoon sea salt

Directions:

- In a small saucepan, combine the chickpeas and vinegar and bring to a boil. Turn off the heat. Allow for a 30-minute resting period.
- Remove any loose skins from the chickpeas before draining.
- Preheat an air fryer carefully to 390°F (198 degrees C). In the basket, distribute the chickpeas equally. Cook for 4 minutes or until the mixture is dry.
- Place chickpeas in a heat-resistant bowl and drizzle with oil and sea salt. To coat, toss everything together. Return chickpeas to air fryer and cook for 8 minutes, shaking basket every 2 to 3 minutes, until gently toasted. Serve right away.

Fried Green Tomatoes in the Air Fryer

Preparation Time: 15 minutes
Cooking Time: 22 minutes
Serve: 1
Ingredients:

- cooking spray
- 1 egg, beaten
- ½ cup cornmeal
- ⅓ cup self-rising flour
- ⅓ cup panko breadcrumbs
- 1 teaspoon salt

- ½ teaspoon ground black pepper
- 2 green tomatoes, sliced

Directions:

- Preheat an air fryer carefully to 400°F (200 degrees C). Coat the air fryer basket with cooking spray.
- Place the egg in a small dish. Combine cornmeal, flour, panko, salt, and pepper in a second shallow dish. Dip each tomato slice in the egg, then in the cornmeal mixture on both sides.
- Place the tomato slices in the prepared basket in a single layer and gently sprinkle the tops with cooking spray.
- Cook for 8 minutes in a hot air fryer. Cooking spray should be sprayed on any dry parts after flipping the tomatoes. Cook for 4 minutes more before transferring to a dish lined with paper towels. Repeat with the rest of the tomato slices.

Air Fryer Tajin Apple Chips

Preparation Time: 10 minutes
Cooking Time: 18 minutes
Serve: 1
Ingredients:

- 1 apple, cored
- ½ tablespoon chili-lime seasoning (such as Tajin®), or more to taste

Directions:

- Preheat the air fryer carefully to 180°F (82 degrees C).
- Using a mandolin, thinly slice the apple.
- Place as many apple slices as you can in the air fryer basket, ensuring they don't touch.
- Cook for 12 minutes in the air fryer, working in batches as required. Remove the basket and heat until the apple slices are gently browned on the other side, 8 to 12 minutes longer. Sprinkle with chili-lime seasoning right away.

Air Fryer Cajun Crab Cakes

Preparation Time: 18 minutes
Cooking Time: 20 minutes
Serve: 1
Ingredients:

- ¾ cup panko breadcrumbs
- ¼ cup mayonnaise
- 1 egg
- 2 teaspoons Worcestershire sauce
- 1 teaspoon Dijon mustard
- ¾ teaspoon Cajun seasoning
- ½ teaspoon salt
- ¼ teaspoon cayenne pepper
- ¼ teaspoon ground white pepper (Optional)
- 4 ounces fresh lump crabmeat
- 3 tablespoons remoulade sauce, or to taste
- 3 brioche slider buns (Optional)

Directions:

- According to the manufacturer's instructions, preheat an air fryer carefully to 370°F (188°C).
- In a small mixing bowl, combine breadcrumbs, mayonnaise, egg, Worcestershire sauce, mustard, Cajun spice, salt, cayenne pepper, and pepper. Gently fold in the crabmeat.
- Using a biscuit cutter, cut out three equal-sized crab cakes. Place the cakes on a parchment-lined baking sheet and place them in the air fryer basket.

- Cook for 6 minutes in a hot air fryer. Cook until browned on the other side, approximately 6 minutes longer. Serve on slider buns with remoulade sauce.

CHAPTER 3:

Vegetables & Sides

Air Fryer Mixed Veggies
Preparation Time: 10 minutes
Cooking Time: 10 minutes
Serve: 4
Ingredients:
- 1 small zucchini, cut into ½-inch sliced
- 1 cup mushrooms, sliced
- 1 bell pepper, chopped
- 1 tbsp parmesan cheese, grated
- ½ tsp Italian seasoning
- 1 tbsp olive oil
- 1 tsp garlic, minced
- Pepper
- Salt

Directions:
- Preheat the air fryer to 390 F.
- In a mixing bowl, toss together zucchini, mushrooms, bell pepper, Italian seasoning, oil, garlic, pepper, and salt.
- Pour veggie mixture into the air fryer basket and cook for 6 minutes.
- Sprinkle parmesan cheese on top of veggie and cook for 4 minutes more.
- Serve and enjoy.

Crispy Carrot & Sweet Potatoes
Preparation Time: 10 minutes
Cooking Time: 15 minutes
Serve: 6
Ingredients:
- 3 large carrots, peeled & sliced
- 3 cups sweet potatoes, peeled & diced
- 1 tbsp butter, melted
- 1 tbsp brown sugar
- 1 tbsp olive oil
- 1/8 tsp ground ginger
- ¼ tsp cinnamon
- Pepper
- Salt

Directions:
- Preheat the air fryer to 400 F.
- In a mixing bowl, toss carrots, sweet potatoes, cinnamon, ginger, oil, sugar, butter, pepper, and salt.
- Add carrot and sweet potato mixture into the air fryer basket and cook for10 minutes.
- Stir well and cook for 5 minutes more.
- Serve and enjoy.

Balsamic Tomatoes
Preparation Time: 10 minutes
Cooking Time: 8 minutes
Serve: 4
Ingredients:
- 2 large tomatoes, cut into 4 slices
- 1/4 cup balsamic vinegar
- 1 tsp red pepper flakes, crushed
- 1 tbsp oregano, dried
- 1/4 tsp black pepper
- 1/2 tsp sea salt

Directions:
- Preheat the air fryer to 360 F.
- In a bowl, mix together vinegar, red pepper flakes, oregano, pepper, and salt.
- Dip each tomato slice into the vinegar mixture and place into the air fryer basket and cook for 5-8 minutes.
- Serve and enjoy.

Herb Mushrooms
Preparation Time: 10 minutes
Cooking Time: 14 minutes
Serve: 4
Ingredients:
- 1 lb. mushrooms
- 1 tsp thyme, chopped
- 2 garlic cloves, minced
- 1 tbsp basil, minced
- 1 tsp rosemary, chopped
- 1/2 tbsp vinegar
- Pepper
- Salt

Directions:
- Preheat the air fryer to 350 F.
- Add mushrooms and remaining ingredients into the large bowl and toss well.
- Spread mushrooms into the air fryer basket and cook for 14 minutes.
- Serve and enjoy.

Air Fryer Green Beans
Preparation Time: 10 minutes
Cooking Time: 10 minutes
Serve: 2
Ingredients:
- 2 cups green beans, cut in half
- 2 tbsp canola oil

- 1 tbsp shawarma spice
- 1/2 tsp salt

Directions:
- Preheat the air fryer to 370 F.
- In a bowl, toss green beans with shawarma spice, oil, and salt.
- Add beans into the air fryer basket and cook for 10 minutes. Turn halfway through.
- Serve and enjoy.

Tasty Radish Hash Browns
Preparation Time: 10 minutes
Cooking Time: 13 minutes
Serve: 4
Ingredients:
- 15 oz radishes, sliced
- 1 onion, sliced
- 1 tsp garlic powder
- 1 tbsp canola oil
- 1 tsp onion powder
- 1/2 tsp paprika
- 1/4 tsp black pepper
- 3/4 tsp sea salt

Directions:
- Preheat the air fryer to 360 F.
- In a bowl, toss onion and radishes with oil.
- Add onion and radishes into the air fryer basket and cook for 8 minutes.
- Transfer radishes and onion in a mixing bowl. Add seasonings and mix well and cook for 5 minutes more.
- Serve and enjoy.

Curried Cauliflower
Preparation Time: 10 minutes
Cooking Time: 10 minutes
Serve: 4
Ingredients:
- 1 medium cauliflower, cut into florets
- ¼ tsp paprika
- 1 tbsp canola oil
- 1 tsp curry powder
- 1/4 tsp pepper
- 1/4 tsp salt

Directions:
- Preheat the air fryer to 390 F.
- Add cauliflower florets and remaining ingredients into the mixing bowl and toss well.
- Place cauliflower florets into the air fryer basket and cook for 10 minutes. Stir halfway through.
- Serve and enjoy.

Lemon Garlic Broccoli
Preparation Time: 10 minutes
Cooking Time: 8 minutes
Serve: 4
Ingredients:
- 3 cups broccoli florets
- 1 tbsp canola oil
- 3 garlic cloves, chopped

- 2 tbsp fresh lemon juice
- Pepper
- Salt

Directions:
- Preheat the air fryer to 375 F.
- In a bowl, toss broccoli florets with olive oil.
- Add broccoli florets into the air fryer basket and cook for 8 minutes.
- Transfer cooked broccoli into the bowl. Add lemon juice, garlic, pepper, and salt and toss well.
- Serve and enjoy.

Herb Carrots Slices
Preparation Time: 10 minutes
Cooking Time: 14 minutes
Serve: 4
Ingredients:
- 6 carrots peel and slice into thick chips
- 1 tbsp oregano
- 2 tbsp canola oil
- 1 tbsp fresh parsley, chopped
- Pepper
- Salt

Directions:
- Preheat the air fryer to 360 F.
- In a bowl, toss carrots with oil.
- Add carrots slices into the air fryer basket and cook for 12 minutes.
- Add pepper, oregano, and salt and stir well and cook for 2 minutes more.
- Garnish with parsley and serve.

Air Fryer Asparagus
Preparation Time: 10 minutes
Cooking Time: 8 minutes
Serve: 4
Ingredients:
- 1 lb. asparagus, ends trimmed
- 1/8 tsp garlic powder
- 1 tsp canola oil
- 1/8 tsp onion powder
- 1/8 tsp pepper
- 1/8 tsp kosher salt

Directions:
- Preheat the air fryer to 360 F.
- Toss asparagus with oil and season with onion powder, garlic powder, pepper, and salt.
- Place asparagus into the air fryer basket and cook for 8 minutes.
- Serve and enjoy.

Easy Roasted Vegetables
Preparation Time: 15 minutes
Cooking Time: 25 minutes
Serve: 1
Ingredients:
- 5 cups cauliflower florets
- 5 cups broccoli florets
- 1-pound fresh asparagus, trimmed and halved

- 4 medium carrots, cut into matchsticks, 1 medium red bell pepper
- 1 medium red onion, sliced and separated into rings, ½ cup olive oil
- 3 tablespoons lemon juice
- 3 cloves garlic, minced
- 1 tablespoon dried rosemary, crushed
- 1 teaspoon salt
- 1 teaspoon ground black pepper

Directions:

- Preheat the oven carefully to 400 degrees Fahrenheit (200 degrees C).
- In a large mixing basin, combine cauliflower, broccoli, asparagus, carrots, bell pepper, and onion.
- Combine the olive oil, lemon juice, garlic, rosemary, salt, and pepper in a small mixing bowl. Drizzle the dressing over the veggies and toss to coat. Place on two rimmed baking sheets.
- Roast, stirring periodically, in a preheated oven for 20 to 25 minutes, or until tender.

Diced Potato Casserole with Vegetables

Preparation Time: 20 minutes
Cooking Time: 20 minutes
Serve: 1
Ingredients:

- 1-pound potatoes, peeled and cubed
- ¼ cup butter, divided
- 1 onion, chopped
- 1 pound zucchini, cut into large chunks
- 1 teaspoon herbs de Provence
- salt and ground black pepper to taste
- 1 tomato, cut into large chunks
- 1 ¼ cups grated Parmesan cheese
- 1 cup coarsely shredded Gruyere cheese
- 1 cup dry breadcrumbs

Directions:

- Fill a big saucepan halfway with salted water and bring to a boil. Reduce the heat to medium-low and cook for approximately 15 minutes, or until they are almost tender. Drain through a colander.
- Preheat the oven carefully to 350°F (175 degrees C). Grease a large baking dish with cooking spray.
- While the potatoes are boiling, melt 2 tablespoons of butter in a large pan and sauté the onion until soft and translucent, about 5 minutes. Cook until the zucchini is softened, about 5 minutes. Cook for 1 minute more after seasoning with herbs de Provence, salt, and pepper. Cook for 2 minutes after adding the drained potatoes and tomato.
- In a mixing dish, combine the Parmesan and Gruyere cheeses. Transfer half of the cheese mixture to the potato-vegetable mixture and place it in a baking dish.
- Melt the remaining 2 tablespoons of butter and combine it with the cheese mixture and breadcrumbs. Spread equally over the potato-vegetable mixture in the baking dish.
- Bake for 15 to 25 minutes, or until the cheese is browned and crusty.

Beef with Vegetables

Preparation Time: 15 minutes
Cooking Time: 25 minutes
Serve: 1
Ingredients:

- 8 ounces beef filet, cut into 1/2-inch strips
- 2 tablespoons vegetable oil
- 1 onion, chopped, 1 clove garlic, minced
- 1 teaspoon chopped fresh ginger root, 1 green bell pepper, chopped
- 1 carrot, chopped
- 1 (10.5 ounces) can of beef broth
- 1 tablespoon cornstarch
- 1 teaspoon white sugar, 1 tablespoon soy sauce
- 1 tablespoon oyster sauce
- salt and pepper to taste

Directions:

- Sauté the beef slices in the oil in a large pan over medium-high heat for 5 minutes or until nicely browned. Cook for 5 minutes more after adding the onion, garlic, and ginger. Then add the carrot, green bell pepper, and beef broth. Reduce the heat to low and allow to simmer.
- Meanwhile, mix the corn flour, sugar, soy sauce, and oyster sauce, if used, in a separate small bowl. Stir until a smooth paste is formed. Slowly add this to the cooking meat and veggies, stirring constantly, and allow it to cook until desired thickness is reached. Season to taste with salt and pepper.

Grilled Vegetables with Balsamic Vinegar

Preparation Time: 15 minutes
Cooking Time: 20 minutes
Serve: 1
Ingredients:

- ½ cup olive oil
- 2 medium eggplants
- 3 medium zucchinis
- 2 tablespoons soy sauce
- 2 tablespoons balsamic vinegar
- ½ teaspoon salt
- ½ teaspoon ground black pepper
- 2 medium green bell peppers

Directions:

- Combine the olive oil, soy sauce, balsamic vinegar, salt, and pepper in a large mixing bowl. Marinate eggplant, zucchini, and bell peppers in soy sauce. Marinate for approximately 45 minutes.
- Preheat the grill to medium-high heat and liberally oil the grill grate. Shake off any extra marinade from the veggies.
- Grill veggies on a hot grill for 10 to 15 minutes, coating with marinade. Serve the cooked veggies with any residual marinade on a plate.

Quick Mediterranean Vegetables

Preparation Time: 20 minutes
Cooking Time: 25 minutes
Serve: 1
Ingredients:

- 1 tablespoon olive oil
- ½ onion, chopped
- 2 carrots, sliced
- 1 green bell pepper, cubed
- 1 red bell pepper, cubed
- 1 fennel bulb, thinly sliced
- 2 teaspoons dried Italian herb mix, or to taste
- salt and freshly ground black pepper

Directions:

- Heat the olive oil and sauté the onion until tender and transparent in a large pan, about 5 minutes. Cook, occasionally turning, until carrots, bell peppers, and fennel are cooked but still firm to the bite, 5 to 10 minutes. Season with salt, pepper, and Italian herbs.

Easy Grilled Vegetables

Preparation Time: 15 minutes
Cooking Time: 20 minutes
Serve: 1
Ingredients:

- 2 yellow squashes, sliced
- 2 zucchinis, sliced
- 1 medium yellow bell pepper, chopped
- 1 medium red bell pepper, chopped
- 1 medium orange bell pepper, chopped
- 1 medium green bell pepper, chopped
- 1 cup sliced sweet onion
- 1 cup sliced portobello mushrooms
- 3 tablespoons olive oil
- 2 tablespoons garlic and herb seasoning blend
- 1 tablespoon balsamic vinegar
- ½ teaspoon sea salt
- ½ teaspoon cracked black pepper
- 1 teaspoon olive oil, or as needed

Directions:

- Preheat the grill to medium-high heat.
- Combine yellow squash, zucchini, bell peppers, onion, and mushrooms in a large mixing dish. 3 tablespoons olive oil, garlic, and herb spice combination, balsamic vinegar, salt, and pepper
- Heat 1 teaspoon olive oil on a preheated grill in a grill-safe pan. Grill the vegetables, often tossing, for 8 to 10 minutes, or until the squash and zucchini are opaque and the peppers are still somewhat crisp.

Curried Vegetables

Preparation Time: 15 minutes
Cooking Time: 18 minutes
Serve: 1
Ingredients:

- 3 tablespoons olive oil
- 1 tablespoon curry powder
- ½ teaspoon cumin seeds
- 1 eggplant, cubed
- 3 jalapeno peppers, seeded and minced
- 4 Yukon Gold potatoes, cubed
- 3 tomatoes, diced
- ½ teaspoon salt
- ½ teaspoon chili powder
- ½ teaspoon ground turmeric
- ¼ cup chopped fresh cilantro

Directions:

- Heat oil, curry powder, and cumin in a Dutch oven or big saucepan over medium heat until fragrant. Combine the eggplant, jalapenos, potatoes, tomatoes, salt, chili powder, and turmeric in a mixing bowl. Cook, covered, for 30 to 45 minutes, adding water as needed to maintain a stew-like consistency.
- Before serving, top with cilantro.

Oven Roasted Vegetables

Preparation Time: 15 minutes
Cooking Time: 22 minutes
Serve: 1
Ingredients:

- cooking spray
- ½ cup olive oil
- 1-ounce dry onion soup mix
- 2 pounds potatoes, cut into 1-inch pieces
- 1 pound baby carrots
- 2 large bell peppers
- 1 large onion

Directions:

- Preheat the oven carefully to 450°F (230 degrees C). Coat a baking sheet with cooking spray.
- In a mixing dish, combine the olive oil and onion soup mix. In a large mixing bowl, combine potatoes, baby carrots, bell peppers, and onion; add oil mixture and toss to coat evenly.
- Cook until the veggies are cooked, 15 to 30 minutes in a preheated oven.

Beer Battered Fried Vegetables

Preparation Time: 10 minutes
Cooking Time: 18 minutes
Serve: 1
Ingredients:

- 2 cups all-purpose flour
- 1 ½ cups beer
- 2 eggs
- 1 cup milk
- salt and pepper to taste
- 2 cups vegetable oil for frying
- 1 carrot, cut into thick strips
- 1 onion, sliced into rings
- 6 fresh mushrooms, stems removed
- 1 green bell pepper, sliced in rings

Directions:

- Combine 1 1/2 cup flour and beer with a wooden spoon in a medium mixing basin; set aside for at least 3 hours at room temperature.
- In a small mixing dish, combine the eggs and milk. Next, combine 1/2 cup flour, salt, and pepper in a separate basin.
- Preheat the oil to 375°F (190 degrees C).
- Each veggie should be dipped in the egg and milk mixture. Next, dip the veggie in the flour and spice mixture, followed by the beer and flour combination. Fry the veggies in the oil until golden brown.

Roasted Vegetables

Preparation Time: 18 minutes
Cooking Time: 20 minutes
Serve: 1
Ingredients:

- 1 small butternut squash, cubed
- 2 red bell peppers, seeded and diced
- 1 sweet potato, peeled and cubed
- 3 Yukon Gold potatoes, cubed
- 1 red onion, quartered
- 1 tablespoon chopped fresh thyme

- 2 tablespoons chopped fresh rosemary
- ¼ cup olive oil
- 2 tablespoons balsamic vinegar
- salt and freshly ground black pepper

Directions:
- Preheat the oven carefully to 475°F (245 degrees C).
- Combine the squash, red bell peppers, sweet potato, and Yukon Gold potatoes in a large mixing basin. Divide the red onion quarters into pieces and add to the mixture.
- Combine the thyme, rosemary, olive oil, vinegar, salt, and pepper in a small mixing dish. Toss the veggies in the dressing until evenly covered. Distribute equally in a large roasting pan.
- Roast for 35 to 40 minutes, tossing every 10 minutes, or until veggies are cooked through and browned in a preheated oven.

Imperial Vegetables and Noodles
Preparation Time: 15 minutes
Cooking Time: 25 minutes
Serve: 1
Ingredients:
- 1 (500 gram) package Europe's Best® Imperial Blend vegetables
- 1 (12 ounces) package Cantonese-style steamed chow Mein noodles
- 1 ½ cups Imagine® Organic Vegetable Broth
- 2 tablespoons naturally brewed soy sauce
- 2 tablespoons cornstarch
- 1 ½ teaspoon sesame oil
- 1 tablespoon Spectrum Naturals® Canola Oil
- 1 (170 gram) package Yves Veggie Cuisine® Chicken or Beef Veggie Tenders
- 1 tablespoon grated fresh ginger
- 1 teaspoon minced garlic
- ¼ cup chopped green onion

Directions:
- Thaw the veggies and thoroughly drain. Place aside.
- Noodles should be cooked according to package recommendations. Keep heated and set aside.
- Make the sauce: Combine broth and soy sauce in a small mixing dish. Stir in the cornstarch. Mix with the sesame oil. Place aside.
- Heat the oil in a large nonstick skillet over medium-high heat. Stir in the vegetable chicken tenders, ginger, and garlic for 1 minute. Stir-fry the veggies for 2 minutes. Stir in the sauce; lower to low heat and continue to cook for approximately 2 minutes or thickened.
- Distribute the veggie mixture over the noodles. Garnish with green onion. Grab a pair of chopsticks and dive in!

Hearty Turkey Stew with Vegetables
Preparation Time: 20 minutes
Cooking Time: 20 minutes
Serve: 1
Ingredients:
- 2 tablespoons butter
- 2 onions, chopped
- 1 stalk celery, cut into 1-inch pieces
- 2 carrots, peeled and sliced into 1-inch pieces
- 2 potatoes, peeled and cubed

- 3 tablespoons all-purpose flour
- 3 cups chicken stock
- ¼ teaspoon dried marjoram
- 2 skinless, boneless turkey breast halves, cubed
- 1 green bell pepper, diced

Directions:
- Melt the butter in a small saucepan over medium heat. Cook until the onions are soft in the pot. Cook until celery and carrots are soft. Combine the potatoes and flour in a mixing bowl. Season the soup with marjoram after adding the chicken stock. Bring the turkey to a boil in the pot. Reduce the heat to low, cover, and leave to simmer for 30 minutes.
- Cook for another 10 minutes, or until the green bell pepper is soft, in the soup.

Mediterranean Roast Vegetables
Preparation Time: 15 minutes
Cooking Time: 25 minutes
Serve: 1
Ingredients:
- 6 large potatoes, diced
- 2 red bell peppers, diced
- 1 fennel bulb, diced
- 1 zucchini, diced
- 6 cloves garlic
- 6 tablespoons olive oil
- 2 teaspoons salt
- 2 teaspoons vegetable bouillon powder
- ¼ cup chopped fresh rosemary
- ½ cup balsamic vinegar

Directions:
- Preheat the oven carefully to 400°F (200 degrees C).
- Combine the potatoes, peppers, fennel, zucchini, and garlic in a large baking dish. Drizzle the olive oil over the veggies in an equal layer. Sprinkle the top with salt, bouillon powder, and rosemary. Stir the mixture until the veggies are completely covered.
- Bake for 1 hour, stirring regularly, in a preheated oven until soft. Toss the veggies with balsamic vinegar and serve immediately.

Roasted Balsamic Vegetables
Preparation Time: 15 minutes
Cooking Time: 20 minutes
Serve: 1
Ingredients:
- ¼ cup olive oil
- 2 tablespoons balsamic vinegar
- 1 teaspoon chopped fresh thyme
- 1 teaspoon chopped fresh rosemary
- 1 clove garlic, minced
- salt and freshly ground black pepper
- 2 potatoes
- ½ small pumpkin
- 2 onions, peeled and quartered
- 1 red chili pepper
- 1 clove garlic

Directions:
- Combine olive oil, balsamic vinegar, thyme, rosemary, minced garlic, salt, and pepper in a mixing bowl. Set aside for 40 minutes to allow flavors to combine.

- Preheat the oven carefully to 475°F (245 degrees C).
- In a large mixing bowl, combine potatoes, pumpkin, onions, red chili pepper, and entire garlic clove; drizzle olive oil mixture over veggies and toss to cover. Arrange the veggies in a single layer in a roasting pan.
- 1 hour 10 minutes in a preheated oven, stirring once or twice, until veggies are soft.
-

Roasted Indian-Spiced Vegetables

Preparation Time: 20 minutes
Cooking Time: 25 minutes
Serve: 1
Ingredients:

- 3 tablespoons olive oil
- 2 teaspoons garam masala
- 1 teaspoon salt
- 2 medium potatoes, peeled
- 2 cups cauliflower florets
- 1 medium yellow onion, cut into 1/2-inch wedges
- 2 tablespoons minced cilantro

Directions:

- Preheat the oven carefully to 425° F. (220 degrees C). Next, preheat the oven carefully to 350°F. Line a baking sheet with parchment paper.
- Combine the olive oil, garam masala, and salt in a small bowl. In a large mixing basin, combine the potatoes, cauliflower, and onion. Toss with the oil mixture to coat. Arrange the veggies on the baking sheet that has been prepared.
- 30 to 35 minutes in a preheated oven, stirring every 10 minutes until veggies are soft and edges are browned. Remove from the oven and top with the cilantro.

Spicy Roasted Vegetables

Preparation Time: 15 minutes
Cooking Time: 20 minutes
Serve: 1
Ingredients:

- 1 cup broccoli florets
- ½ cup cauliflower florets
- ½ cup julienned green bell pepper
- ½ cup julienned red bell pepper
- ½ cup diced eggplant
- 1 ⅓ tablespoon olive oil
- 1 teaspoon garlic powder
- 1 teaspoon paprika
- 1 teaspoon minced onion
- ½ teaspoon cayenne pepper
- ½ teaspoon ground black pepper
- ½ teaspoon salt

Directions:

- Preheat the oven carefully to 450 degrees Fahrenheit (230 degrees C). Aluminum foil should be used to line a baking pan.
- Combine broccoli, cauliflower, bell peppers, eggplant, olive oil, garlic powder, paprika, onion, cayenne pepper, black pepper, and salt in a mixing bowl.
- Roast for 10 minutes in a preheated oven until tender.

Marinated Barbequed Vegetables

Preparation Time: 15 minutes

Cooking Time: 18 minutes
Serve: 1
Ingredients:

- 1 small eggplant
- 6 fresh mushrooms, stems removed
- ¼ cup olive oil
- 2 small red bell peppers
- 3 zucchinis, sliced
- ¼ cup lemon juice
- ¼ cup coarsely chopped fresh basil
- 2 cloves garlic, peeled and minced

Directions:

- Combine the eggplant, red bell peppers, zucchini, and fresh mushrooms in a medium mixing dish.
- Combine the olive oil, lemon juice, basil, and garlic in a medium mixing bowl. Pour the mixture over the veggies, cover, and refrigerate for at least 1 hour.
- Preheat a high heat outside grill.
- Vegetables can be grilled directly on the grill or skewers. Cook for 2 to 3 minutes on each side on a preheated grill, brushing regularly with the marinade, or until done to preference.

Mixed Greek Vegetables in Tomato Sauce

Preparation Time: 15 minutes
Cooking Time: 22 minutes
Serve: 1
Ingredients:

- 4 tomatoes
- ½ cup olive oil
- 2 tablespoons red wine vinegar
- 2 tablespoons white sugar
- ⅓ cup chopped fresh parsley
- ⅓ cup chopped fresh mint
- ⅓ cup chopped fresh basil
- 2 tablespoons fresh oregano
- ¼ cup capers
- 2 cloves garlic
- salt and ground black pepper to taste
- 2 tablespoons olive oil
- 2 onions, sliced
- 2 potatoes, sliced
- 2 eggplants, sliced
- 3 zucchinis, sliced
- 3 green bell peppers, sliced
- 2 cups okra

Directions:

- Preheat the oven carefully to 350°F (175 degrees C). In a food processor, combine three tomatoes, 1/2 cup olive oil, red wine vinegar, sugar, parsley, mint, basil, oregano, capers, and garlic to make a fresh tomato sauce. Set aside and season with salt and black pepper. Set aside the leftover tomato.
- In a pan over medium heat, heat the 2 tablespoons olive oil and sauté and toss the onions until slightly brown, about 10 minutes.
- In a large baking pan, combine the onions, potatoes, eggplant, zucchini, bell peppers, okra, the saved diced tomato, and the fresh tomato sauce. If necessary, add a little water to ensure that the veggies are just coated in sauce.
- Bake it in a preheated oven for 1 hour or until all veggies are soft.

Creole Vegetables

Preparation Time: 10 minutes
Cooking Time: 18 minutes
Serve: 1
Ingredients:

- ½ pound bacon
- 2 tablespoons bacon grease
- ½ cup finely chopped onion
- ½ cup finely chopped green bell pepper
- 2 cups chopped peeled tomatoes
- 2 cups chopped fresh green beans
- ¾ teaspoon salt
- ⅛ teaspoon pepper
- 1 ½ cups fresh corn kernels, cut from the cob
- 3 tablespoons all-purpose flour
- 3 tablespoons water
- 1 cup evaporated milk

Directions:

- Cook bacon in a large skillet over medium heat until evenly browned. Set aside, leaving 2 tablespoons bacon fat aside. In bacon grease, sauté the onion and green pepper until soft. Add the tomatoes, green beans, salt, and pepper to taste. Simmer for 15 minutes, covered. Stir in the corn, cover, and simmer until the veggies are soft, approximately 20 minutes.
- In a small mixing dish, combine the flour and water. Cook until the veggies are thickened, approximately 2 minutes. Take the pan off the heat and whisk in the evaporated milk. Top with crumbled bacon. Serve right away.

Halibut with Vegetables

Preparation Time: 18 minutes
Cooking Time: 20 minutes
Serve: 1
Ingredients:

- 2 pounds halibut fillets
- salt and pepper to taste
- ¼ cup olive oil
- ½ cup chopped fresh parsley
- 1 yellow onion, thinly sliced
- 2 stalks celery, chopped
- 1 green bell pepper, chopped
- 1 (16 ounces) can diced tomatoes
- 2 tablespoons capers
- 4 cloves garlic, minced

Directions:

- Preheat the oven carefully to 425°F (220 degrees C).
- Wash and pat dry the halibut. Place in a 9x13 inch baking pan, cut into serving-size pieces. Season with salt and pepper to taste. Pour over the halibut olive oil, parsley, onion, celery, bell pepper, tomatoes, capers, and garlic mixture.
- Bake for 20 minutes or until the halibut is slightly opaque in the center. Remove from the oven and set aside for 10 minutes before serving.

Vegetarian Meatloaf with Vegetables

Preparation Time: 15 minutes
Cooking Time: 25 minutes
Serve: 1
Ingredients:

- ½ (14 ounces) package vegetarian ground beef (e.g., Gimme Lean TM)
- 1 (12 ounces) package vegetarian burger crumbles
- 1 onion, chopped
- 2 eggs, beaten
- 2 tablespoons vegetarian Worcestershire sauce
- 1 teaspoon salt
- ⅓ teaspoon pepper
- 1 teaspoon ground sage
- ½ teaspoon garlic powder
- 2 teaspoons prepared mustard
- 1 tablespoon vegetable oil
- 3 ½ slices bread, cubed
- ⅓ cup milk
- 1 (8 ounces) can tomato sauce
- 4 carrots, cut into 1-inch pieces
- 4 potatoes, cubed
- 1 cooking spray

Directions:

- Preheat the oven carefully to 350°F (175 degrees C).
- Combine vegetarian ground beef, crumbled vegetarian ground beef, onion, eggs, Worcestershire sauce, salt, pepper, sage, garlic powder, mustard, oil, bread cubes, and milk in a large mixing bowl. Form the mixture into a loaf in a 9 x 13-inch baking dish. Top with tomato sauce.
- Spray carrots and potatoes with cooking spray and arrange them around the bread.
- Bake for 30 to 45 minutes, turning veggies halfway through. Bake for a further 30 to 45 minutes. Allow standing for 15 minutes before slicing.

Vegetable Dip

Preparation Time: 20 minutes
Cooking Time: 20 minutes
Serve: 1
Ingredients:

- ⅔ cup mayonnaise
- ⅔ cup sour cream
- 2 teaspoons Beau Monde ™ seasoning
- 1 tablespoon dried dill weed
- 1 tablespoon dried parsley
- 1 tablespoon minced onion

Directions:

- In a mixing bowl, combine mayonnaise, sour cream, Beau Monde spice, dill, parsley, and chopped onion. Blend well. Refrigerate for at least four hours before serving.

Vegetable Whip

Preparation Time: 15 minutes
Cooking Time: 25 minutes
Serve: 1
Ingredients:

- 1 turnip, peeled and diced
- 4 carrots - peeled and diced
- 1 large onion, chopped
- 6 medium potatoes - peeled and cubed
- ¼ cup butter
- ½ cup milk
- salt and pepper to taste

Directions:

- Cover the turnip, carrots, onion, and potatoes with water in a saucepan. Bring to a boil over medium-high heat and simmer until the potatoes are fork-tender.
- Drain the veggies and toss in the butter until it has melted. Using an electric mixer, beat until light and fluffy, gradually adding milk. Beat for a short period, just until smooth. Season with salt and pepper to taste and serve immediately.

Cheesy Vegetables and Noodles

Preparation Time: 15 minutes
Cooking Time: 20 minutes
Serve: 1
Ingredients:

- 1 (8 ounces) package rigatoni pasta
- 1 (10 ounces) package frozen mixed vegetables
- 2 cups cubed processed cheese
- ½ teaspoon soy sauce
- ½ teaspoon garlic salt

Directions:

- A big saucepan of lightly salted water should be brought to a boil. Cook for 5 to 10 minutes, or until pasta is al dente; drain.
- Cook frozen veggies as directed on the box.
- Combine processed cheese, soy sauce, and garlic salt in a small pot. Over medium heat, stir until the cheese is melted.
- Combine the pasta, veggies, and cheese sauce in a mixing bowl.

One Pot Easy Cheesy Vegetables and Rice

Preparation Time: 20 minutes
Cooking Time: 25 minutes
Serve: 1
Ingredients:

- 1 ½ tablespoon vegetable or canola oil
- ½ teaspoon Morton® Fine Sea Salt
- 1 cup extra-long grain rice (15 minutes)
- 2 cups frozen mixed vegetables
- 3 cups chicken stock
- 1 ½ cups shredded Cheddar cheese

Directions:

- In a medium saucepan over medium-high heat, heat the oil.
- Except for the cheese, combine the remaining ingredients.
- 1 minute after bringing to a boil
- Reduce the heat to low, cover, and leave to simmer for 10 minutes, or until the liquid has been absorbed.
- Serve immediately after adding the cheese and stirring it in until it melts.

Great Grilled Smoky Vegetables with Avocado and Goat Cheese Crumbles

Preparation Time: 15 minutes
Cooking Time: 20 minutes
Serve: 1
Ingredients:

- 6 portobello mushroom caps
- 4 red bell peppers, cored and quartered
- 1 red onion, thickly sliced
- ½ cup olive oil
- 2 limes, juiced
- 2 tablespoons grill seasoning
- 2 cloves garlic, minced
- 1 pinch cayenne pepper, or to taste
- 2 tablespoons balsamic vinegar
- 1 avocado - peeled, pitted, and cubed
- ½ cup crumbled goat cheese
- salt to taste
- freshly ground black pepper to taste
- 2 tablespoons finely chopped fresh basil

Directions:

- In a 9x13-inch baking dish, combine the mushrooms, red bell peppers, and red onion. Combine olive oil, lime juice, grill seasoning, garlic, and cayenne pepper, drizzle over veggies. Allow veggies to marinate for at least 30 minutes after tossing to coat.
- Preheat the grill to medium-high heat and liberally oil the grill grate.
- Shake off any extra marinade from the veggies. Save any leftover marinade.
- Grill the veggies until tender, about 5 minutes, over a hot grill. Place the grilled veggies on a wide plate. Pour the remaining marinade and balsamic vinegar over the veggies. Season with salt and pepper and top with avocado and goat cheese. To serve, sprinkle with basil.

Frozen Vegetable Stir-Fry

Preparation Time: 15 minutes
Cooking Time: 18 minutes
Serve: 1
Ingredients:

- 2 tablespoons soy sauce
- 1 tablespoon brown sugar
- 2 teaspoons garlic powder
- 2 teaspoons peanut butter
- 2 teaspoons olive oil
- 1 (16 ounces) package frozen mixed vegetables

Directions:

- Combine the soy sauce, brown sugar, garlic powder, and peanut butter in a small mixing bowl.
- In a large pan over medium heat, heat the oil and sauté and toss the frozen veggies until they are just soft, 5 to 7 minutes. Remove from the fire and stir in the soy sauce mixture.

Roasted Root Vegetables with Apple Juice

Preparation Time: 15 minutes
Cooking Time: 22 minutes
Serve: 1
Ingredients:

- 3 tablespoons butter
- 3 cups apple juice
- 1 cup dry white wine
- 1 ¼ pounds turnips
- 1 ¼ pounds parsnip
- 1 ¼ pounds carrots
- 1 ¼ pounds sweet potatoes
- 1 ¼ pounds rutabagas
- salt and pepper to taste

Directions:

- In a large saucepan, bring apple juice and wine to a boil for 30 minutes, or until reduced to 3/4 cup. Incorporate the butter or margarine.
- Preheat the oven carefully to 425°F (220 degrees C).

- Vegetables should be peeled and chopped into 2-inch pieces. Divide the mixture into two roasting pans. Pour the combination of apple juice and water over the veggies. Season with salt and pepper to taste. To coat, toss everything together.
- Cook, occasionally stirring, until the veggies are soft and brown, approximately 40 minutes.

Grandpa's Grilled Vegetables in Foil

Preparation Time: 10 minutes
Cooking Time: 18 minutes
Serve: 1
Ingredients:

- aluminum foil
- 3 medium potatoes, peeled and cubed
- 1 onion, sliced
- 2 fresh beets, peeled and cubed
- 2 peeled carrots, cut in half crosswise, then quartered lengthwise
- 1 bell pepper, sliced
- 3 cloves garlic, minced
- salt and ground black pepper to taste
- ¼ cup extra virgin olive oil
- 1 teaspoon balsamic vinegar, or to taste

Directions:

- Preheat a medium-sized outside grill. Arrange many pieces of aluminum foil on a flat surface.
- In a large mixing basin, combine the potatoes, onion, beets, carrots, bell pepper, and garlic. Season with salt and pepper to taste. Drizzle with olive oil liberally. Mix in the balsamic vinegar.
- Arrange the veggies on the aluminum foil. Wrap tightly with at least two layers of foil to prevent the liquid from leaking out.
- Place the skewers on the prepared grill. The cooking time is 15 minutes. Cook for another 15 minutes on the opposite side. Cook for 10 to 15 minutes, or until the veggies are fork tender.

Pasta with Vegetables

Preparation Time: 18 minutes
Cooking Time: 20 minutes
Serve: 1
Ingredients:

- ⅓ cup olive oil
- 2 tablespoons red wine vinegar, 1 teaspoon dried basil
- 1 teaspoon dried oregano
- salt and pepper to taste
- 1 red bell pepper, chopped, 1 green bell pepper, chopped
- 2 cloves garlic, minced, 2 carrots
- 1 ½ cups broccoli florets, lightly steamed or blanched
- 4 cups uncooked rotini pasta

Directions:

- Combine the oil, vinegar, basil, oregano, salt, and pepper in a mixing bowl. Place aside.
- Bring a large saucepan of salted water to a boil; add the rotini and return to a boil. Cook until the rotini is al dente; drain thoroughly. Put the rotini back in the saucepan.
- While the rotini is cooking, heat the oil in a frying pan and sauté the red and green bell peppers, garlic, and carrots. Cook until the veggies are tender. Cook for another 2 minutes with the broccoli in the frying pan.

- Place the cooked veggies in the same pot as the pasta. Dress the spaghetti and veggies with the vinaigrette. Toss to mix the veggies and vinaigrette properly.

Savory Roasted Root Vegetables

Preparation Time: 15 minutes
Cooking Time: 25 minutes
Serve: 1
Ingredients:

- 1 cup diced, raw beet
- 4 carrots, diced, 1 onion, diced
- 2 cups diced potatoes
- 4 cloves garlic, minced
- ¼ cup canned garbanzo beans (chickpeas), drained
- 2 tablespoons olive oil
- 1 tablespoon dried thyme leaves
- salt and pepper to taste
- ⅓ cup dry white wine
- 1 cup torn beet greens

Directions:

- Preheat the oven carefully to 400°F (200 degrees C).
- In a 9x13 inch baking dish, combine the beet, carrot, onion, potatoes, garlic, and garbanzo beans. Drizzle with olive oil and season with thyme, salt, and pepper to taste. Combine thoroughly.
- Bake for 30 minutes, uncovered, in a preheated oven, stirring once halfway through. After baking, remove the baking dish from the oven and whisk in the wine. Return to the oven and bake for another 15 minutes, or until the wine has almost evaporated and the soft veggies. Allow the beet greens to wilt from the heat of the veggies before adding them. Before serving, season with salt and pepper to taste.

Roasted Vegetables and Puff Pastry

Preparation Time: 20 minutes
Cooking Time: 20 minutes
Serve: 1
Ingredients:

- 1 onion, chopped
- 1 green bell pepper, chopped
- 1 red bell pepper, chopped
- 1 green chili pepper, chopped
- 1 clove garlic, chopped
- freshly ground black pepper to taste
- 1 tablespoon extra-virgin olive oil
- 1 (14.5 ounces) can diced tomatoes, drained
- 1 (4 ounces) package feta cheese, crumbled
- ½ (17.5 ounces) package frozen puff pastry (1 sheet), thawed

Directions:

- Preheat the oven carefully to 400°F (200 degrees C). Lightly grease a small baking dish or pie plate.
- In a preheated pan, combine the onion, peppers, and garlic. Season with freshly ground pepper, then drizzle with olive oil. Roast in a preheated oven for about 10 minutes or until the vegetables appear to be done.
- Remove the veggies from the oven when they are tender. Distribute the tomatoes equally over the veggies and top with feta cheese. Roll out the puff pastry and arrange it on top of the veggies.

- Bake the pastry for 20 minutes, or until golden brown. Remove the dish from the oven, set a tray over it, and then flip it upside down to create a puff pastry foundation with the veggies on top. While the puff pastry is still crisp, serve immediately.

Mediterranean Grilled Vegetables
Preparation Time: 15 minutes
Cooking Time: 25 minutes
Serve: 1
Ingredients:
- 2 tablespoons olive oil
- 8 large mushrooms, quartered
- 1 teaspoon balsamic vinegar
- 1 teaspoon lemon juice
- ½ teaspoon dried rosemary
- ½ teaspoon dried oregano
- 1 large zucchini, quartered
- 1 large green bell pepper, cut into pieces
- 1 large red onion

Directions:
- Preheat a high heat outside grill.
- Combine the olive oil, balsamic vinegar, lemon juice, rosemary, and oregano in a mixing bowl.
- Brush the mushrooms, zucchini, bell pepper, and onion with the oil mixture in a large grill-safe pan.
- Place the pan on a hot grill and cook for 10 to 15 minutes, flipping once.

Balsamic-Roasted Vegetables
Preparation Time: 15 minutes
Cooking Time: 20 minutes
Serve: 1
Ingredients:
- cooking spray
- ⅓ cup balsamic vinegar
- ¼ cup unsalted butter, melted
- 10 medium potatoes
- 4 large carrots
- 1 medium onion
- 8 sprigs of fresh thyme
- 1 teaspoon minced garlic
- 1 teaspoon salt
- ½ teaspoon ground black pepper

Directions:
- Preheat the oven carefully to 425° F. (220 degrees C). Coat a 9x13-inch baking pan with nonstick cooking spray.
- Combine the potatoes, carrots, onion, balsamic vinegar, butter, thyme, garlic, salt, and pepper in a large glass bowl. Spread the mixture evenly in the prepared pan. Wrap with foil.
- Cook for 45 minutes in a preheated oven, shaking the pan every 15 minutes to achieve equal cooking.
- Remove the foil and continue to roast, uncovered, for another 30 minutes, stirring periodically.

Ramen Noodle Stir-Fry with Chicken and Vegetables
Preparation Time: 20 minutes
Cooking Time: 25 minutes

Serve: 1
Ingredients:
- 1 ½ cups hot water
- 1 (3 ounces) package Oriental-flavor ramen noodle soup mix
- 2 teaspoons vegetable oil, divided
- 8 ounces skinless, boneless chicken breast halves
- 2 cups broccoli florets
- 1 cup sliced onion wedges
- 2 cloves garlic, minced
- 1 cup fresh bean sprouts
- ½ cup water
- ½ cup sliced water chestnuts
- 1 teaspoon soy sauce
- 1 teaspoon oyster sauce
- ¼ teaspoon chili-garlic sauce
- 1 Roma tomato, cut into wedges

Directions:
- In a small saucepan, bring 1 1/2 cups water to a boil. Reserving the spice package for later use, add the ramen noodles. Boil the noodles for 2 minutes, then drain and put aside.
- In a large skillet over medium heat, heat 1 teaspoon oil. Cook and toss the chicken in the skillet for 5 minutes, or until it is thoroughly browned. Remove the chicken from the skillet with a slotted spoon and set aside, retaining the drippings in the skillet. Cover the bowl with a plate to keep the chicken warm.
- Turn the heat beneath the skillet up to high. In a skillet, cook and stir broccoli, onion, and garlic until just tender, 3 to 5 minutes. Mix in the drained noodles, reserved ramen noodle seasoning, bean sprouts, water, water chestnuts, soy sauce, oyster sauce, and chili-garlic sauce; simmer and stir until heated, 3 to 5 minutes. Cook until the tomato wedges are heated, 2 to 3 minutes.

Sheet Pan Roasted Vegetables
Preparation Time: 15 minutes
Cooking Time: 20 minutes
Serve: 1
Ingredients:
- 8 zucchinis, peeled and chopped
- 1 eggplant, peeled and diced
- 8 carrots, diced
- 16 cherry tomatoes
- 2 red onions, sliced
- 1 red bell pepper, sliced
- 1 yellow bell pepper, sliced
- ½ cup olive oil
- 1 teaspoon dried rosemary
- 1 teaspoon dried thyme
- 2 bay leaves, crushed
- 1 teaspoon dried oregano
- 2 cloves garlic, minced
- 2 tablespoons fresh lemon juice
- 1 teaspoon grated lemon zest
- salt and pepper to taste

Directions:
- Combine the zucchini, eggplant, carrots, tomatoes, onions, and peppers in a large mixing bowl with the oil, rosemary, garlic, lemon juice, lemon zest, thyme, bay leaves, oregano,

salt, and pepper. Refrigerate for at least 2 hours, ideally overnight.

- Preheat the oven carefully to 400°F (200 degrees C).
- Roast the veggies, uncovered, in a large roasting pan for 25 minutes. Return to the oven for another 20 minutes after removing from the oven and stirring. Reduce the heat to 200°F (95°C) and continue cooking until the veggies are cooked, turning every 20 minutes.

Smoky Grilled Vegetables
Preparation Time: 15 minutes
Cooking Time: 18 minutes
Serve: 1
Ingredients:

- 1 eggplant, sliced into 1/2-inch rounds
- 2 red bell peppers, halved and seeded
- 2 yellow bell peppers, halved and seeded
- 2 zucchinis, sliced
- 2 large onions
- 4 tablespoons vegetable oil
- 1 cup teriyaki sauce

Directions:

- Brush the veggies with oil to coat them.
- Prepare the smoker according to the manufacturer's directions, using either alder or apple chips. Arrange the vegetables in single layers on the smoker racks. Allow around 30 minutes to smoke.
- Preheat the grill to high.
- Grates should be oiled. Arrange the veggies on the grill, peppers out from the center. Cook for 10 to 15 minutes, turning halfway through. Frequently baste with teriyaki sauce. Vegetables cook at varying speeds; take tender sections from the grill and continue to cook until all are done.

Stir-Fried Sweet and Sour Vegetables
Preparation Time: 15 minutes
Cooking Time: 22 minutes
Serve: 1
Ingredients:

- 3 tablespoons palm sugar
- 2 tablespoons lime juice
- 1 tablespoon fish sauce
- 1 tablespoon oyster sauce
- 1 tablespoon light soy sauce
- 2 tablespoons vegetable oil
- 4 cloves garlic, minced
- 1 onion, cut into thin slivers
- ½ head cauliflower, chopped into bite-size pieces
- 1 carrot, peeled and sliced
- 1 cucumber, cut into bite-size pieces
- 8 baby corn, sliced
- 1 cup peas
- 1 large red bell pepper, sliced
- 1 tomato, cut into bite-size pieces
- ¼ fresh pineapple, cut into bite-size chunks

Directions:

- In a small saucepan over medium-low heat, combine the palm sugar, lime juice, fish sauce, oyster sauce, and soy sauce until the sugar is fully dissolved; bring to a boil. Place aside.

- In a large pan, heat the oil; cook the garlic in the heated oil until browned, 7 to 10 minutes. Cook for 1 minute after adding the onion. Cook and toss the cauliflower and carrot into the mixture for 1 minute. Cook for 1 minute more after adding the cucumber, corn, and peas. Cook for 1 minute after adding the bell pepper and tomato to the mixture. Pour the sauce over the mixture, add the pineapple, and toss to coat evenly, simmer for another minute. Serve immediately.

Stir-Fried Vegetables
Preparation Time: 10 minutes
Cooking Time: 18 minutes
Serve: 1
Ingredients:

- 2 tablespoons light soy sauce
- 1 teaspoon ground ginger
- 2 tablespoons all-purpose flour
- 1 cup low-sodium chicken broth
- ¼ cup cold water
- 3 tablespoons vegetable oil
- 4 green bell peppers, cut into matchsticks
- 4 carrots, cut into matchsticks
- 2 cups broccoli florets
- 8 mushrooms, sliced

Directions:

- In a small bowl, combine the soy sauce and ginger. Next, combine the flour, chicken broth, and water in a separate basin.
- In a large pan or wok, heat the oil over high heat and sauté and toss the peppers, carrots, broccoli, and mushrooms until just tender, approximately 3 minutes.
- Cook and stir for 1 minute after tossing veggies with soy sauce mixture. Gradually incorporate the flour mixture into the veggies; bring to a boil and simmer for 3 minutes, or until thickened.

Air-Fried Mediterranean Vegetable Medley
Preparation Time: 18 minutes
Cooking Time: 20 minutes
Serve: 1
Ingredients:

- ½ small eggplant, cut into 1/4-inch slices
- 1 small zucchini
- 1 small summer squash, cut into 1/4-inch slices
- 1 cup shiitake mushrooms, stemmed and sliced
- 1 cup grape tomatoes
- 2 tablespoons olive oil
- 2 cloves garlic, minced
- ½ teaspoon dried oregano
- ½ teaspoon kosher salt
- 1 teaspoon lemon zest

Directions:

- Preheat the oven carefully to 200 degrees Fahrenheit (95 degrees C).
- Place the eggplant slices in a large mixing basin and cut them into wedges. Toss in the zucchini, summer squash, mushrooms, tomatoes, olive oil, garlic, oregano, and salt. Place the veggies in the air fryer basket in a single layer, working in small batches if required.

- Cook the veggies in the air fryer for 5 minutes at 360°F (182°C). Cook, occasionally stirring, until the vegetables are soft, and the rims are golden brown, approximately 5 minutes longer. Transfer veggies to a baking sheet and keep warm in a preheated oven while preparing the remaining vegetables.
- Before serving, sprinkle the veggies with lemon zest.

Marinated Vegetable Salad

Preparation Time: 15 minutes
Cooking Time: 25 minutes
Serve: 1
Ingredients:

- ¾ cup white sugar
- 1 teaspoon celery seed
- ½ teaspoon ground black pepper
- 1 cup distilled white vinegar
- ¼ cup canola oil
- 1 teaspoon salt
- 2 cups cucumbers, peeled and thinly sliced
- 1 onion, sliced into thin rings
- 2 cups thinly sliced carrots
- ½ cup chopped celery

Directions:

- Combine sugar, celery seeds, black pepper, vinegar, oil, and salt in a screw-top jar. Shake vigorously to combine.
- In a large mixing bowl, combine the veggies. Gently mix the dressing into the veggies. Refrigerate for several hours or overnight.

Shrimp and Vegetable Sheet Pan Dinner

Preparation Time: 20 minutes
Cooking Time: 20 minutes
Serve: 1
Ingredients:

- 1 red onion, coarsely chopped
- 1 red bell pepper, chopped
- 1 cup sliced fresh mushrooms
- 1 zucchini, chopped
- 3 tablespoons olive oil, divided
- salt and freshly ground black pepper
- ¼ teaspoon paprika
- 1-pound fresh shrimp, peeled and deveined
- 1 teaspoon lemon zest
- ½ teaspoon garlic powder

Directions:

- Preheat the oven carefully to 425° F. (220 degrees C).
- Toss together the red onion, bell pepper, mushrooms, zucchini, 2 tablespoons olive oil, salt, pepper, and paprika on a sheet pan.
- Cook until the veggies are softened, about 15 minutes in a preheated oven.
- While the veggies are roasting, add the shrimp, 1 tablespoon olive oil, lemon zest, garlic powder, salt, and pepper in a mixing dish. To mix, toss everything together.
- Remove the roasted veggies from the oven and add the shrimp to the sheet pan, laying them out evenly in a single layer. Return to the oven and then bake for 5 to 7 minutes, or until the shrimp are pink and cooked through.

Herb Grilled Vegetables

Preparation Time: 15 minutes
Cooking Time: 25 minutes
Serve: 1
Ingredients:

- ½ cup Swanson® Chicken Broth or Swanson® Certified Organic Chicken Broth or Swanson® Natural Goodness® Chicken Broth
- ½ teaspoon dried thyme leaves, crushed
- ⅛ teaspoon ground black pepper
- 1 large red onion, thickly sliced
- 1 large red or green pepper
- 1 medium zucchini
- 2 cups large mushrooms

Directions:

- Combine the broth, thyme, and black pepper in a small bowl. Brush the broth mixture over the veggies.
- Heat the grill to medium and lightly oil the grill rack. Grill the veggies for 10 minutes, or until tender-crisp, turning once and often brushing with the broth mixture.

Browned Butter Vegetables with Almonds

Preparation Time: 15 minutes
Cooking Time: 20 minutes
Serve: 1
Ingredients:

- ½ cup butter
- 1 teaspoon garlic salt
- 1 teaspoon garlic pepper
- 2 tablespoons sliced almonds
- 2 tablespoons white wine
- 1 medium onion, chopped
- 1 medium red bell pepper, chopped
- 2 cups chopped broccoli
- 2 cups chopped cauliflower

Directions:

- In a pan over medium-low heat, melt the butter. Garlic salt and garlic pepper to taste. Cook until the almonds are golden brown. Combine the wine, onion, red bell pepper, broccoli, and cauliflower in a mixing bowl. Cook for another 5 minutes, or until the veggies are soft.

Christmas Roasted Vegetables

Preparation Time: 20 minutes
Cooking Time: 25 minutes
Serve: 1
Ingredients:

- 1 large butternut squash
- 1 large delicate squash
- 3 sweet potatoes
- 1 (2 pounds) rutabaga, peeled
- 2 red potatoes, peeled
- 6 dried bay leaves
- 1 dash lemon juice
- 2 carrots, sliced
- 1 large onion, sliced
- 2 tablespoons dried rosemary
- 2 tablespoons dried thyme
- 1 teaspoon dried oregano

- 2 tablespoons extra-virgin olive oil
- 1 dash red wine vinegar
- 1 pinch salt
- 1 pinch ground black pepper

Directions:

- Preheat the oven carefully to 400°F (200 degrees C).
- In a large roasting pan, combine butternut squash, delicate squash, sweet potato, rutabaga, red potato chunks, carrots, and onion. In a small bowl, combine rosemary, thyme, and oregano.
- Drizzle olive oil over the veggies and top with herb mixture; toss to coat with oil and herbs. Scatter bay leaves over the veggies and drizzle with lemon juice and red wine vinegar.
- Cook until the veggies are soft, about 1 hour and 30 minutes, stirring every 30 minutes in a preheated oven. Season with salt and black pepper to taste.

Roasted Vegetable and Kale Lasagna

Preparation Time: 15 minutes
Cooking Time: 20 minutes
Serve: 1
Ingredients:

- 1 red bell pepper, thinly sliced
- 1 yellow bell pepper, thinly sliced
- 1 zucchini, thinly sliced
- 6 large mushrooms, thinly sliced
- 6 tablespoons extra-virgin olive oil, divided
- 1 tablespoon salt
- 2 teaspoons ground black pepper
- 1 cup water
- 1 bunch kale, torn into bite-sized pieces
- 2 cloves garlic, chopped
- 2 (26 ounce) cans pasta sauce
- 1 (12 ounces) box no-boil lasagna noodles
- 9 cups grated mozzarella cheese
- 1 (8 ounces) package bocconcini cheese, thinly sliced

Directions:

- Preheat the oven carefully to 450 degrees Fahrenheit (230 degrees C). Aluminum foil should be used to line a baking pan.
- Combine red bell pepper, yellow bell pepper, zucchini, mushrooms, and 4 tablespoons olive oil in a mixing dish. Season with salt and pepper to taste. Place the veggies in a single layer on the prepared baking sheet.
- Cook for roughly 10 minutes in a preheated oven. Cook for another 10 to 15 minutes after turning the veggies.
- Meanwhile, bring a pot of water to a boil. Cook until the kale is barely darkened in color, about 1 minute. Drain.
- In a frying pan over medium heat, heat the remaining olive oil. Cook for 1 minute after adding the garlic. Cook until the kale is wilted, 3 to 5 minutes. Turn off the heat.
- Remove the bell peppers from the oven and raise the temperature to 375°F (190 degrees C).
- In a 9x13-inch baking dish, layer pasta sauce, lasagna noodles, roasted bell pepper mixture, and shredded mozzarella cheese. Place another layer of noodles, spaghetti sauce, greens, and bocconcini cheese slices on top. Continue layering until all of the ingredients are used up, making sure to keep the noodle layers and sauce close together to avoid dried noodles.
- Bake lasagna in a hot oven for 45 minutes or until the noodles are tender. Allow 20 to 30 minutes to cool before serving.

Roasted Autumn Root Vegetables

Preparation Time: 15 minutes
Cooking Time: 18 minutes
Serve: 1
Ingredients:

- cooking spray
- 4 beets, peeled
- 2 new potatoes, peeled
- 2 parsnips, peeled
- 2 turnips, peeled
- 1 rutabaga, peeled
- 2 tablespoons olive oil
- 2 tablespoons balsamic vinegar
- salt and ground black pepper to taste
- ⅓ cup vegetable broth
- 1 pinch Italian seasoning
- 1 (4 ounces) package goat cheese

Directions:

- Preheat the oven carefully to 450°F (230 degrees C).
- Coat a baking sheet with nonstick cooking spray.
- In a large mixing bowl, combine beets, potatoes, parsnips, turnips, and rutabaga with olive oil, salt, and pepper.
- Spread the seasoned veggies evenly in the prepared baking dish.
- Roast veggies in a preheated oven for 40 minutes or until beets can be easily punctured with a fork.
- Combine the veggie broth, balsamic vinegar, and Italian spice in a small bowl.
- Pour broth mixture over veggies and continue roasting for another 10 minutes, or until liquid has evaporated.
- Toss the roasted veggies with the goat cheese in a mixing basin.

Pot Roast, Vegetables, and Beer

Preparation Time: 15 minutes
Cooking Time: 22 minutes
Serve: 1
Ingredients:

- 2 tablespoons olive oil
- 1 (3 pounds) beef pot roast
- 1 onion, chopped
- 5 cloves garlic, minced
- 1-pound carrots, cut into chunks
- 1 (8 ounces) package sliced fresh mushrooms
- 1 ½ pounds potatoes, peeled and cut into chunks
- 2 tablespoons all-purpose flour
- 2 cups beef stock
- 1 can or bottle of dark beer
- 1 bay leaf
- 3 tablespoons chopped fresh thyme
- 1 teaspoon brown sugar
- 2 tablespoons whole-grain Dijon mustard
- 1 tablespoon tomato paste
- salt and ground black pepper to taste

Directions:

- Preheat the oven carefully to 350°F (175 degrees C).
- In a Dutch oven, heat the olive oil. In the heated oil, brown the pot roast on both sides; remove from pan and put aside. Cook the onion and garlic in the heated oil for 5 minutes, or until they soften and turn brown. Cook and stir the carrots,

mushrooms, and potatoes in the saucepan for 2 to 3 minutes, or until they brown. Mix the flour into the veggies for 1 minute, stirring constantly. Pour in the beef stock and beer and heat to a boil, stirring constantly. Combine the Bay leaf, thyme, brown sugar, mustard, tomato paste, salt, and pepper in a mixing bowl. Place the pot roast on top of everything. Put the cover on the saucepan.

- Bake in a preheated oven for 2 1/2 hours or until the meat and veggies are thoroughly soft.

Stir-Fried Sesame Vegetables with Rice
Preparation Time: 10 minutes
Cooking Time: 18 minutes
Serve: 1
Ingredients:
- 1 ½ cups vegetable broth
- ¾ cup uncooked long-grain white rice
- 1 tablespoon margarine
- 1 tablespoon sesame seeds
- 2 tablespoons peanut oil
- ½ pound fresh asparagus
- 1 large red bell pepper, cut into 1-inch pieces
- 1 large yellow onion, sliced
- 2 cups sliced mushrooms
- 2 teaspoons minced fresh ginger root
- 1 teaspoon minced garlic
- 3 tablespoons soy sauce
- 1 tablespoon sesame oil

Directions:
- Preheat the oven carefully to 350°F (175 degrees C). Combine the broth, rice, and margarine in a saucepan. Bring to a boil, covered, over high heat. Reduce the heat to low and continue to cook for 15 minutes, or until all of the liquid has been absorbed.
- Place sesame seeds on a small baking sheet and toast for 5 to 6 minutes, or until golden brown; set aside. Meanwhile, heat the peanut oil until it is extremely hot in a large pan or wok over medium-high heat. Stir in the asparagus, bell pepper, onion, mushrooms, ginger, and garlic for 4 to 5 minutes, or until the veggies are soft but crisp. Cook for 30 seconds after adding the soy sauce. Take the pan off the heat

and toss in the sesame oil and toasted sesame seeds. Serve with rice.

Creamy Cheese Fall Vegetable Casserole
Preparation Time: 18 minutes
Cooking Time: 20 minutes
Serve: 1
Ingredients:
- 3 cups milk
- 3 carrots, peeled and diced
- 2 sweet potatoes, peeled and diced
- 2 leeks, finely chopped (white part only)
- 2 parsnips, peeled and diced
- 2 stalks celery, diced
- 1 butternut squash, peeled and diced
- 1 small turnip, peeled and diced
- 1 (8 ounces) package cream cheese, cubed
- 1 cup shredded Parmesan cheese
- 1 pinch ground nutmeg
- salt and ground black pepper to taste
- 1 cup fine breadcrumbs
- 2 tablespoons melted butter, or as needed

Directions:
- Preheat the oven carefully to 350°F (175 degrees C). Grease a 3-quart casserole dish with cooking spray.
- Bring milk, carrots, sweet potatoes, leeks, parsnips, celery, butternut squash, and turnip to a boil in a large saucepan. Reduce heat to medium-low and cook veggies until soft, approximately 15 minutes, stirring occasionally.
- Melt the cream cheese into the veggie mixture. Mix in the Parmesan cheese and nutmeg. Season the vegetable mixture with salt and pepper before pouring it into the prepared casserole dish.
- Combine breadcrumbs and melted butter, sprinkle crumb mixture over casserole.
- Bake, covered, in a preheated oven for 30 minutes, or until bubbling. Cook until the top is gently browned, approximately 5 minutes more. Allow the dish to cool for 2 minutes before serving.

SARAH JONES

CHAPTER 4:

Poultry

Crispy Chicken Wings
Preparation Time: 10 minutes
Cooking Time: 22 minutes
Serve: 4
Ingredients:
- 1 ½ lbs. chicken wings
- 3 tbsp everything seasoning
- 2 tbsp butter, melted
- 1 tbsp olive oil
- ¼ tsp garlic powder
- Pepper
- Salt

Directions:
- Preheat the air fryer to 400 F.
- In a mixing bowl, toss chicken wings with oil, garlic powder, pepper, and salt.
- Place chicken wings into the air fryer basket and cook for 20 minutes.
- Transfer chicken wings into the mixing bowl and toss with everything seasoning and melted butter.
- Return chicken wings into the air fryer basket and cook for 2 minutes more.
- Serve and enjoy.

Flavorful Turkey Patties
Preparation Time: 10 minutes
Cooking Time: 20 minutes
Serve: 4
Ingredients:
- 1 lb. ground turkey
- 1 tsp Italian seasoning
- 1 tbsp olive oil
- 1 tbsp garlic, minced
- 4 oz feta cheese, crumbled
- 1 1/4 cup spinach, chopped
- Pepper
- Salt

Directions:
- Preheat the air fryer to 390 F.
- Add ground turkey and remaining ingredients into the bowl and mix until well combined.
- Make equal shapes of patties from the mixture and place into the air fryer basket and cook for 20 minutes. Turn halfway through.
- Serve and enjoy.

Easy Chicken Tenders
Preparation Time: 10 minutes

Cooking Time: 16 minutes
Serve: 4
Ingredients:
- 1 lb. chicken tenders
- 1 tbsp smoked paprika
- 1/2 tbsp onion powder
- 1/2 tsp cayenne
- 1/2 tbsp dried thyme
- 1 tbsp garlic powder
- Pepper
- Salt

Directions:
- Preheat the air fryer to 370 F.
- Add chicken tenders and remaining ingredients into the mixing bowl and mix until well coated.
- Place chicken tenders into the air fryer basket and cook for 16 minutes. Turn halfway through.
- Serve and enjoy.

Jerk Chicken Wings
Preparation Time: 10 minutes
Cooking Time: 20 minutes
Serve: 2
Ingredients:
- 1 lb. chicken wings
- 1 tsp canola oil
- 1 tbsp jerk seasoning
- 1 tbsp arrowroot
- Pepper
- Salt

Directions:
- Preheat the air fryer to 380 F.
- Add chicken wings and remaining ingredients into the mixing bowl and toss well.
- Arrange chicken wings into the air fryer basket and cook for 20 minutes. Turn halfway through.
- Serve and enjoy.

Cheesy Chicken Fritters
Preparation Time: 10 minutes
Cooking Time: 10 minutes
Serve: 4
Ingredients:
- 1 lb. ground chicken
- 2 tbsp green onions, chopped
- 1/2 tsp garlic powder
- 1/2 cup parmesan cheese, shredded
- 1/2 tsp onion powder
- 1/2 tbsp dill, chopped

THE COMPLETE AIR FRYER COOKBOOK

- 1/2 cup almond flour
- Pepper
- Salt

Directions:
- Preheat the air fryer to 350 F.
- Add chicken and remaining ingredients into the large bowl and mix until well combined.
- Make small patties from the mixture and place into the air fryer basket and cook for 10 minutes. Turn halfway through.
- Serve and enjoy.

Juicy Turkey Breast
Preparation Time: 10 minutes
Cooking Time: 60 minutes
Serve: 8
Ingredients:
- 4 lbs. turkey breast, boneless
- 1 tbsp canola oil
- 1/2 tsp cinnamon
- 1 1/2 tsp paprika
- 1 1/2 tsp garlic powder
- 1/2 tsp pepper
- 2 tsp salt

Directions:
- Preheat the air fryer to 350 F.
- In a small bowl, mix together paprika, garlic powder, cinnamon, pepper, and salt.
- Brush turkey breast with oil and rub with spice mixture.
- Place turkey breast into the air fryer basket and cook for 60 minutes. Turn after 25 minutes.
- Slice and serve.

Flavors Chicken Thighs
Preparation Time: 10 minutes
Cooking Time: 20 minutes
Serve: 4
Ingredients:
- 4 chicken thighs, bone-in & skin-on
- 1 tsp smoked paprika
- 1/2 tsp oregano
- 3/4 tsp onion powder
- 1 tbsp canola oil
- 3/4 tsp garlic powder
- 1/2 tsp kosher salt

Directions:
- Preheat the air fryer to 380 F.
- Add chicken thighs and remaining ingredients into the large zip-lock bag. Seal bag and shake well.
- Add marinated chicken into the air fryer basket and cook for 20 minutes. Turn halfway through.
- Serve and enjoy.

Delicious Chicken Breasts
Preparation Time: 10 minutes
Cooking Time: 10 minutes
Serve: 3
Ingredients:
- 1/2 cup almond flour
- 1 egg, beaten

- ¼ tsp paprika
- 12 oz chicken breasts, skinless and boneless
- 1/2 tsp pepper
- 1/2 tsp salt

Directions:
- Preheat the air fryer to 330 F.
- In a bowl, add egg and whisk well.
- In a shallow dish, mix almond flour, paprika, pepper, and salt.
- Dip chicken breasts in egg and coat with almond flour mixture.
- Place the coated chicken into the air fryer basket and cook for 10 minutes. Turn halfway through.
- Serve and enjoy.

Chicken Kebab
Preparation Time: 10 minutes
Cooking Time: 15 minutes
Serve: 4
Ingredients:
- 1 lb. chicken thighs, skinless, boneless, and cut into 4 pieces
- 1/2 tsp cayenne
- 1/2 tsp cinnamon
- 1 tbsp canola oil
- 1 tbsp tomato paste
- 1 tbsp garlic, minced
- 1/4 cup lemon juice
- 1 tsp paprika
- 1 tsp ground cumin
- 1/2 tsp pepper
- 1 tsp salt

Directions:
- Preheat the air fryer to 370 F.
- Add chicken and remaining ingredients into the zip-lock bag. Seal bag and place in the refrigerator for 2 hours.
- Arrange marinated chicken into the air fryer basket and cook for 15 minutes. Turn halfway through.
- Serve and enjoy.

Marinated Chicken Thighs
Preparation Time: 10 minutes
Cooking Time: 20 minutes
Serve: 4
Ingredients:
- 1 lb. chicken thighs, boneless and skinless
- 2 tbsp curry paste
- 2 tsp ginger, minced
- 1/2 cup coconut milk
- 1 tbsp garlic, chopped
- Pepper
- Salt

Directions:
- Preheat the air fryer to 350 F.
- Add chicken and remaining ingredients into the zip-lock bag. Seal bag and place in the refrigerator for 1 hour.
- Arrange marinated chicken into the air fryer basket and cook for 20 minutes. Turn halfway through.
- Serve and enjoy.

Air Fryer Buttermilk Fried Chicken

Preparation Time: 15 minutes
Cooking Time: 25 minutes
Serve: 1
Ingredients:

- 1 ½ pound boneless, skinless chicken thighs
- 2 cups buttermilk
- 1 cup all-purpose flour
- 1 tablespoon seasoned salt
- ½ tablespoon ground black pepper
- 1 cup panko breadcrumbs
- 1 serving cooking spray

Directions:

- In a shallow casserole dish, place the chicken thighs. Refrigerate the chicken for 4 hours or overnight in the buttermilk.
- Preheat the air fryer carefully to 380°F (190 degrees C).
- In a large gallon-sized resealable bag, combine the flour, seasoned salt, and pepper. Chicken thighs should be dredged in seasoned flour. Return to the buttermilk and coat with panko breadcrumbs.
- Spray the air fryer basket with nonstick cooking spray. Place half of the chicken thighs in the basket, ensuring no contact. Cooking spray should be sprayed on the top of each chicken thigh.
- Cook for 15 minutes in a preheated air fryer. Flip. Spray the tops of the birds once more. Cook for another 15 minutes. In the middle, an instant-read thermometer should read at least 165 degrees F. Rep with the remaining chicken.

Air Fryer Blackened Chicken Breast

Preparation Time: 20 minutes
Cooking Time: 20 minutes
Serve: 1
Ingredients:

- 2 teaspoons paprika
- 1 teaspoon ground thyme
- 2 teaspoons vegetable oil
- 1 teaspoon cumin
- ½ teaspoon cayenne pepper
- ½ teaspoon onion powder
- ½ teaspoon black pepper
- ¼ teaspoon salt
- 2 (12 ounces) skinless, boneless chicken breast halves

Directions:

- Combine paprika, onion powder, black pepper, thyme, cumin, cayenne pepper, and salt in a mixing bowl. Place the spice mixture on a flat dish.
- Rub the oil all over each chicken breast until it is well covered. Roll each piece of chicken in the blackening spice mixture, pressing down, so the spice adheres to both sides. Allow resting for 5 minutes while the air fryer heats up.
- Preheat the air fryer carefully for 5 minutes at 360 degrees F (175 degrees C).
- Cook the chicken in the air fryer basket for 10 minutes. Cook it for another 10 minutes on the other side. Place the chicken on a platter and let it aside for 5 minutes before serving.

Spicy Air Fryer Wings

Preparation Time: 15 minutes

Cooking Time: 25 minutes
Serve: 1
Ingredients:

- 1 ½ pounds chicken wings and drumettes
- 2 teaspoons olive oil
- 1 tablespoon smoked paprika
- 1 tablespoon chili powder
- 1 ½ teaspoon garlic powder
- 1 ½ teaspoon ground cumin, 1 ½ teaspoons onion powder
- 1 ½ teaspoon kosher salt
- 1 ½ teaspoon ground black pepper
- 1 teaspoon cayenne pepper

Directions:

- Rinse and pat dry the chicken. Toss in a large mixing basin with the oil to coat.
- In a small bowl, combine paprika, garlic powder, black pepper, salt, chili powder, cumin, onion powder, and cayenne. Sprinkle over chicken and toss to coat evenly.
- According to the manufacturer's instructions, preheat the air fryer carefully to 375°F (190°C).
- Arrange the chicken in a single layer in the preheated air fryer basket, not touching. Cook, rotating halfway through until the meat is no longer pink at the bone and the juices run clear about 12 minutes. A thermometer near the bone should read 165 degrees F. (74 degrees C). Cook for an additional 2 to 3 minutes at 400 degrees F (200 degrees C) for crispier wings.
- Allow for a few minutes of rest before serving.

Air Fryer Stuffing Balls

Preparation Time: 15 minutes
Cooking Time: 20 minutes
Serve: 1
Ingredients:

- 1 tablespoon butter
- ¼ cup finely chopped onion
- ½ cup finely chopped celery
- 5 cups stale bread, cut into cubes
- 1 teaspoon dried parsley
- ½ teaspoon poultry seasoning
- ½ teaspoon salt
- ¼ teaspoon ground black pepper
- 1 egg, well beaten
- ¼ cup no-salt-added chicken broth
- cooking spray

Directions:

- In a small pan over medium heat, melt the butter. Cook until the celery and onion are cooked, about 5 minutes.
- Combine the bread, parsley, poultry seasoning, salt, and pepper in a mixing bowl. Incorporate the sautéed onion and celery. With one hand, slowly pour the egg into the bowl while mixing to ensure that the mixture is equally covered. Repeat with the chicken broth and stir everything together until fully blended. Divide the filling mixture into 8 equal amounts and roll it into balls on a platter. Refrigerate for at least 15 minutes before serving.
- Preheat the air fryer carefully to 350°F (180 degrees C).
- Remove the stuffing balls from the refrigerator and gently coat them with cooking spray. Place the stuffing balls in the air fryer, sprayed side down, without touching. Lightly spray the opposite side.
- Cook for 5 minutes in a hot air fryer, then turn and cook for 2 minutes.

Air Fryer Chicken Fajitas

Preparation Time: 20 minutes
Cooking Time: 25 minutes
Serve: 1

Ingredients:

- 1 medium red bell pepper
- 1 medium green bell pepper, cut into thin strips
- 1 large onion, sliced into petals
- 3 teaspoons olive oil, divided
- salt and pepper to taste
- 1 pound chicken tenders, cut into strips
- 2 teaspoons fajita seasoning
- 8 (6 inches) flour tortillas, warmed

Directions:

- Combine the bell pepper strips and onion petals in a large mixing basin. Drizzle with 2 tablespoons olive oil and season with salt and pepper. Stir until everything is well blended.
- In a separate dish, toss the chicken strips with the fajita spice. Drizzle with the remaining 1 teaspoon olive oil and stir with your fingertips until evenly incorporated.
- Preheat the air fryer carefully to 350 degrees Fahrenheit (175 degrees C). Cook for 12 minutes, shaking halfway through, with the chicken in the basket. Transfer to a platter and set aside while you prepare the veggies.
- Cook for 14 minutes, shaking halfway through, in the air fryer basket with the vegetable mixture.
- Distribute the chicken and veggie mixture among the tortillas.

Air Fryer Chimichangas

Preparation Time: 15 minutes
Cooking Time: 20 minutes
Serve: 1

Ingredients:

- 1 tablespoon vegetable oil
- ½ cup diced onion
- 2 cups shredded cooked chicken
- ½ (8 ounces) package Neufchatel cheese, softened
- 1 (4 ounces) can hot fire-roasted diced green chiles
- ¼ cup chicken broth
- 1 ½ tablespoons chicken taco seasoning mix
- ½ teaspoon salt
- ¼ teaspoon ground black pepper
- 6 (10 inches) flour tortillas
- 1 cup shredded Mexican cheese blend
- avocado oil cooking spray

Directions:

- In a medium skillet, heat the oil. Cook until the onion is tender and transparent, 4 to 6 minutes. Combine the chicken, Neufchatel cheese, diced chiles, chicken broth, taco seasoning, salt, and pepper in a mixing bowl. Cook and stir until the mixture is fully mixed and the Neufchatel has softened.
- Heat tortillas until soft and malleable in a big pan or directly on the grates of a gas burner. Fill each tortilla with a third of the chicken mixture and a heaping spoonful of Mexican cheese. Fold the top and bottom of the tortillas over the filling, then wrap each tortilla into a burrito form. Spray with cooking spray and set in an air fryer basket.

- 4 to 6 minutes in an air fryer at 400 degrees F (200 degrees C). Flip each chimichanga over, sprinkle with cooking spray, and air-fried for 2 to 4 minutes more, or until lightly browned.

Air Fryer Buffalo Chicken Wings

Preparation Time: 15 minutes
Cooking Time: 18 minutes
Serve: 1

Ingredients:

- 2 ½ pounds chicken wings
- 1 tablespoon olive oil
- ⅔ cup cayenne pepper sauce
- ½ cup butter
- 2 tablespoons vinegar
- 1 teaspoon garlic powder
- ¼ teaspoon cayenne pepper

Directions:

- Preheat the air fryer carefully to 360°F (182 degrees C).
- Place the wings in a large mixing basin. Drizzle oil over the wings and massage until evenly covered.
- Cook for 25 minutes with half of the wings in the air fryer basket. Flip the wings with tongs and cook for another 5 minutes. Place the cooked wings in a large mixing dish. Rep with the remaining wings.
- In a small saucepan over medium heat, mix hot pepper sauce, butter, vinegar, garlic powder, and cayenne pepper while the second batch is cooking. Keep stirring and heating until the wings are done.
- Toss cooked wings with sauce to coat.

Air Fryer Chicken Nuggets

Preparation Time: 15 minutes
Cooking Time: 22 minutes
Serve: 1

Ingredients:

- 1 cup buttermilk
- 2 pounds chicken tenderloins, cut into nugget size
- 1 cup flour
- 3 tablespoons grated Parmesan cheese
- 1 tablespoon paprika
- 1 tablespoon parsley flakes
- 1 teaspoon salt
- 1 teaspoon ground black pepper
- 2 eggs
- 2 cups panko breadcrumbs
- cooking spray

Directions:

- In a large mixing basin, combine the buttermilk and chicken and set aside while you make the seasoned flour.
- Combine the flour, Parmesan cheese, paprika, parsley, salt, and pepper in a large mixing bowl. Separately, beat the eggs. On a flat dish, spread out the breadcrumbs.
- Each chicken nugget should be dredged in flour, then in beaten egg, and finally in breadcrumbs.
- Preheat the air fryer carefully to 400°F (200 degrees C). Cooking spray should be sprayed on the basket. Fill the basket with as many nuggets as you can without overflowing it. Spray the tops of the nuggets lightly with cooking spray.

- The cooking time is 10 minutes. Cook for a further 2 minutes after flipping the chicken nuggets. Repeat with the remaining nuggets.

Air Fryer Popcorn Chicken

Preparation Time: 10 minutes
Cooking Time: 18 minutes
Serve: 1
Ingredients:

- 1-pound boneless, skinless chicken breast halves
- ¾ teaspoon salt
- ½ teaspoon paprika
- ¼ teaspoon black pepper
- ¼ teaspoon ground mustard
- ¼ teaspoon garlic powder
- ¼ teaspoon onion powder
- ⅛ teaspoon ground thyme
- ⅛ teaspoon dried basil
- ⅛ teaspoon dried oregano
- ⅛ teaspoon dried sage
- 3 tablespoons cornstarch
- cooking spray (such as Misto®)

Directions:

- In a medium mixing dish, combine the chicken pieces.
- Combine salt, paprika, black pepper, mustard, garlic powder, onion powder, thyme, basil, oregano, and sage in a small bowl. 1 teaspoon of the spice combination should be set aside, and the remaining seasoning should be sprinkled on the chicken. To coat evenly, toss everything together.
- In a resealable plastic bag, add cornstarch and reserved 1 teaspoon seasoning; shake to incorporate. Place the chicken in the bag, close it, and shake to coat evenly. Next, shake the chicken in a fine-mesh sieve to remove extra cornstarch. Allow to rest for 5 to 10 minutes, or until the cornstarch has begun to seep into the chicken.
- Preheat the air fryer carefully to 390°F (200 degrees C).
- Spray the air fryer basket with oil and arrange the chicken pieces inside, ensuring they do not overlap. Depending on the size of your air fryer, you may need to prepare two batches. Cooking spray should be sprayed on the chicken.
- 4 minutes in the oven. Shake the air fryer basket and re-spray the chicken with oil to ensure no dry or powdery parts. Cook until the chicken is no longer pink on the interior, 4 to 5 minutes more. Serve right away.

Cornflake-Crusted Chicken Drumsticks in the Air Fryer

Preparation Time: 18 minutes
Cooking Time: 20 minutes
Serve: 1
Ingredients:

- 1 egg
- 1 tablespoon water
- ½ cup cornflake crumbs
- ½ teaspoon garlic powder
- ½ teaspoon onion powder
- ½ teaspoon salt
- ¼ teaspoon Cajun seasoning
- ¼ teaspoon chili powder
- ¼ teaspoon paprika
- 6 large chicken drumsticks

- salt to taste
- 1 serving no-stick cooking spray

Directions:

- In a small dish, combine the egg and water. In a separate shallow dish, combine cornflake crumbs, garlic powder, onion powder, 1/2 teaspoon salt, Cajun spice, chili powder, and paprika.
- Preheat the air fryer carefully to 400°F (200 degrees C).
- Season both sides of the drumsticks gently with salt. Dip each drumstick into the egg mixture, then into the cornflake mixture, rolling and pushing down to cover all sides.
- Cooking sprays the top of the chicken and lays it, sprayed side down, in the air fryer basket. Next, spray the tops of the drumsticks; depending on their size, you may need to turn them on their side.
- Air-fry for 10 minutes, then carefully flip them. Reduce the temperature to 325°F (160 degrees C). Cook for another 10 minutes, or until the internal temperature of the chicken reaches 165 degrees F. (74 degrees C). After 5 minutes, check for doneness because the size of the drumsticks determines the time.

Healthier Bang Bang Chicken in the Air Fryer

Preparation Time: 15 minutes
Cooking Time: 25 minutes
Serve: 1
Ingredients:

- 1 egg
- ½ cup milk
- 1 tablespoon hot pepper sauce
- ½ cup flour
- ½ cup tapioca starch
- 1 ½ teaspoon seasoned salt
- 1 teaspoon garlic granules
- ½ teaspoon cumin
- 1-pound boneless, skinless chicken breasts
- cooking spray
- ¼ cup plain Greek yogurt
- 3 tablespoons sweet chili sauce
- 1 teaspoon hot sauce

Directions:

- Preheat the air fryer carefully to 380°F (190 degrees C).
- Whisk together the egg, milk, and spicy sauce in a small bowl. Combine the flour, tapioca starch, salt, garlic, and cumin in a separate bowl. Dredge the chicken pieces in the dry mix first, then in the egg mixture, brushing off excess. Place the chicken in the air fryer basket in batches, be careful not to overcrowd it, and lightly spritz with oil.
- Cook for about 10 minutes per batch, shaking the basket every 5 minutes until the chicken is no longer pink in the middle and the juices flow clear.
- Combine Greek yogurt, sweet chili sauce, and spicy sauce in a small bowl. Serve the sauce beside the chicken.

Mexican-Style Air Fryer Stuffed Chicken Breasts

Preparation Time: 20 minutes
Cooking Time: 20 minutes
Serve: 1
Ingredients:

- 4 extra-long toothpicks
- 2 teaspoons Mexican oregano
- salt and ground black pepper to taste
- ½ red bell pepper, sliced into thin strips
- 4 teaspoons chili powder, divided
- 4 teaspoons ground cumin, divided
- 1 skinless, boneless chicken breast
- 2 teaspoons chipotle flakes
- ½ onion, sliced into thin strips
- 1 fresh jalapeno pepper, sliced into thin strips
- 2 teaspoons corn oil
- ½ lime, juiced

Directions:
- Fill a small basin halfway with water and soak toothpicks to protect them from burning during cooking.
- In a small dish, combine 2 teaspoons of chili powder and 2 tablespoons of cumin.
- Preheat the air fryer carefully to 400°F (200 degrees C).
- Place the chicken breast on a flat work surface. Cut horizontally through the center. Using a kitchen mallet or rolling pin, pound each half until it is approximately 1/4-inch thick.
- Sprinkle the remaining chili powder, cumin, chipotle flakes, oregano, salt, and pepper evenly over each breast half. In the middle of 1 breast half, place 1/2 of the bell pepper, onion, and jalapeño. Roll the chicken from the tapered end up and fasten with two toothpicks. Repeat with the remaining breast, spices, veggies, and fasten with toothpicks. Roll each roll-up in the chili-cumin mixture in the shallow dish while drizzling with olive oil until equally coated.
- Place the roll-ups in the air fryer basket, toothpick side up. Set a 6-minute timer.
- Flip the roll-ups over. Cook for another 5 minutes in the air fryer, or until the juices flow clear and an instant-read thermometer put into the middle reads at least 165 degrees F (74 degrees C).
- Before serving, evenly drizzle the roll-ups with lime juice.

Air Fryer Chicken Thigh Schnitzel
Preparation Time: 15 minutes
Cooking Time: 25 minutes
Serve: 1
Ingredients:
- 1-pound skinless, boneless chicken thighs, trimmed of fat
- ¼ cup flour
- ½ cup seasoned breadcrumbs
- 1 teaspoon salt
- ½ teaspoon ground black pepper
- 1 egg, beaten
- avocado oil cooking spray

Directions:
- Place one chicken thigh between two pieces of parchment paper and flatten with a mallet.
- Combine breadcrumbs, salt, and black pepper in a small dish. In a separate shallow bowl, place the flour, and in a third shallow bowl, place the beaten egg. Dip the chicken thighs in flour, then in the beaten egg, and finally in the bread crumb mixture.
- Preheat the air fryer carefully to 375°F (190 degrees C).
- Place the breaded thighs in the air fryer basket, not touching; work in batches if required. Cook for 6 minutes after misting

with avocado oil. Cook for another 3 to 4 minutes after flipping each thigh.

Honey-Sriracha Air Fryer Wings
Preparation Time: 15 minutes
Cooking Time: 20 minutes
Serve: 1
Ingredients:
- 12 fresh chicken wing drumettes
- ½ teaspoon salt
- ½ teaspoon garlic powder
- 1 tablespoon butter
- ¼ cup honey
- 2 teaspoons rice vinegar
- 1 tablespoon sriracha sauce

Directions:
- Preheat the air fryer carefully to 360°F (182 degrees C).
- Toss the chicken wings in a basin with the salt and garlic powder to coat.
- Fill the air fryer basket halfway with wings. Cook the wings for 25 minutes, shaking the basket every 7 to 8 minutes. When the timer goes off, switch off the air fryer and leave the wings in the basket for another 5 minutes.
- Meanwhile, in a small saucepan over medium heat, melt the butter. Bring butter, honey, rice vinegar, and sriracha sauce to a boil. Reduce the heat to medium-low and cook the sauce for 8 to 10 minutes, stirring regularly. Remove from fire and set aside; the sauce will thicken as it cools.
- In a mixing dish, combine the cooked wings and the sauce. Next, make the extra sauce to serve with the wings.

Air Fryer Coconut Chicken
Preparation Time: 20 minutes
Cooking Time: 25 minutes
Serve: 1
Ingredients:
- ½ cup canned coconut milk
- ½ cup pineapple juice
- 2 tablespoons brown sugar
- 1 tablespoon soy sauce
- 1-pound boneless skinless chicken breasts
- 2 teaspoons Sriracha sauce
- 1 teaspoon ground ginger
- 2 eggs
- 1 cup sweetened shredded coconut
- 1 cup panko breadcrumbs
- 1 ½ teaspoons salt
- ½ teaspoon ground black pepper
- nonstick cooking spray

Directions:
- Combine the coconut milk, pineapple juice, brown sugar, soy sauce, Sriracha sauce, and ginger in a medium mixing bowl. Toss in the chicken strips to coat. Refrigerate for 2 hours or overnight, covered with plastic wrap.
- Preheat the air fryer carefully to 375°F (190 degrees C).
- In a mixing dish, whisk together the eggs. Next, combine the shredded coconut, panko, salt, and pepper in a separate dish.
- Shake off any excess marinade from the chicken strips. Remove and discard the leftover marinade. Next, dip chicken strips in beaten egg, then in the coconut-panko

mixture, then back in egg mixture, and finally in the coconut-panko mixture, dipping and coating each strip twice.
- Cooking spray should be sprayed on the air fryer basket.
- Place the breaded chicken strips in the air fryer basket, not touching; work in batches if required.
- Cook for 6 minutes, rotate the strips, and cook for another 4 to 6 minutes, or gently browned and toasted.

Air Fryer Chicken Kiev
Preparation Time: 15 minutes
Cooking Time: 20 minutes
Serve: 1
Ingredients:
- 4 tablespoons butter, softened
- 2 tablespoons chopped fresh flat-leaf parsley
- 1 clove garlic, minced
- 1 teaspoon salt
- salt and ground black pepper to taste
- 2 sheets plastic wrap
- 2 (8 ounces) skinless, boneless chicken breast halves
- ½ cup all-purpose flour
- 1 egg, beaten
- 1 cup panko breadcrumbs
- 1 teaspoon paprika
- nonstick cooking spray

Directions:
- Combine the butter, parsley, garlic, and salt in a mixing dish until well blended. Place half of the herbed butter on a baking sheet. 10 minutes in the freezer
- Season the chicken in a clean work area with salt and pepper. In the center of each pounded chicken breast, place 1/2 of the herbed butter. Gather the chicken's sides up around the butter mixture. Wrap each chicken ball in plastic wrap and twist to seal. Return to the baking sheet and place in the freezer for 30 minutes.
- Meanwhile, prepare an air fryer to 400°F (200 degrees C).
- Combine the flour, the beaten egg, and the panko and paprika in one bowl. Remove the plastic from the chicken. Dredge each chicken breast in flour, then in beaten egg, and finally in panko breadcrumbs.
- Place the breaded chicken in the air fryer basket. Coat the tops in cooking spray.
- 5 minutes in the air fryer. Cook for 5 minutes more after respraying with nonstick spray. Transfer to a chopping board and let aside for 5 minutes to rest.

Spicy Chicken Jerky in the Air Fryer
Preparation Time: 15 minutes
Cooking Time: 18 minutes
Serve: 1
Ingredients:
2 (5 ounces) boneless chicken breasts, cut into strips
½ cup mojo criollo marinade (such as Goya®)
2 teaspoons Cajun seasoning
wooden skewers
Directions:
- Combine the chicken strips, marinade, and Cajun spice in a resealable plastic bag. Refrigerate for at least 8 hours and up to overnight.

- Skewers should be measured to fit across the air fryer basket, barely overlapping the edge. Remove any surplus length.
- Preheat the air fryer carefully for 10 minutes at 180 degrees F (80 degrees C).
- While the air fryer is heating, thread chicken strips onto skewers, allowing space between each piece.
- 1 hour 15 minutes in the air fryer cooking time should be adjusted because most air fryers have a maximum of 32 minutes. During the reset time, rearrange the skewers.
- Increase the temperature to 200°F (95°C) and air fry for 15 minutes.
- Transfer the strips to a storage container lined with paper towels. Seal. Allow resting for at least an overnight before serving.

Crispy Keto Fried Chicken in the Air Fryer
Preparation Time: 15 minutes
Cooking Time: 22 minutes
Serve: 1
Ingredients:
- ½ cup whole-milk plain kefir (such as Lifeway®)
- 1 tablespoon hot sauce
- 1 ½ pounds chicken tenders
- 2 (3.25 ounce) packages pork rinds, crushed
- 3 ounces finely grated Parmesan cheese
- 1 ½ teaspoon garlic powder
- ¾ teaspoon Catanzaro herbs (such as Savory Spice Shop®) or Italian seasoning
- ½ teaspoon sweet smoked paprika

Directions:
- In a small bowl, combine the kefir and spicy sauce. Marinate the chicken tenders for 30 minutes to an hour, or longer if desired.
- Fill a small resealable container halfway with crumbled pork rinds. Combine the Parmesan cheese, garlic powder, Catanzaro herbs, and paprika in a mixing bowl.
- Preheat the air fryer carefully to 390°F (200°C) for about 3 minutes.
- Remove the chicken from the kefir mixture and dredge it in the pork rind mixture.
- Air fried the chicken for 17 minutes in a preheated fryer, flipping halfway through.

Air Fryer Stuffed Chicken Breasts
Preparation Time: 10 minutes
Cooking Time: 18 minutes
Serve: 1
Ingredients:
- 2 tablespoons extra-virgin olive oil
- ½ cup diced red onion
- ½ cup crumbled feta cheese
- 4 boneless, skinless chicken breasts
- ½ cup diced red bell pepper
- ½ cup diced fresh mushrooms
- 1 teaspoon minced garlic
- ½ cup chopped fresh spinach
- ½ teaspoon dried Italian seasoning
- 1 pinch salt and ground black pepper
- 4 slices prosciutto
- 12 toothpicks

- ¾ cup grated Parmesan cheese
- ¾ cup fine dry breadcrumbs
- 1 teaspoon dried parsley
- 1 egg, beaten
- 1 serving avocado oil cooking spray

Directions:

- In a small pan over medium heat, heat the olive oil until hot. Cook and stir for 3 minutes, or until the onion is softened. Cook, stirring periodically, for 3 minutes more after adding the red bell pepper and mushrooms. Remove the skillet from the heat and toss in the chopped spinach and garlic. Continue to stir until the spinach has wilted somewhat. Allow cooling for 10 minutes after seasoning with Italian seasoning, salt, and pepper.
- Mix in the feta cheese crumbles, breaking up any large pieces as you go.
- Place the chicken pieces on a secure cutting board and pat dry. Insert a knife into the thickest section of each breast and slice parallel to the cutting board, leaving about 1 inch at each tip. Be cautious not to cut through the breast's thinnest edge.
- If the manufacturer recommends it, preheat the air fryer carefully to 370 degrees F (190 degrees C).
- Place the prosciutto slices on a clean prep surface. Place 2 tablespoons of the vegetable-feta mixture on top and twist up into an oblong bundle. Tuck one prosciutto-wrapped bundle into each cut chicken breast and secure with toothpicks.
- Combine the Parmesan cheese, breadcrumbs, parsley, salt, and pepper on a dish. Dredge each filled chicken breast in the breadcrumb mixture after dipping it in the beaten egg. Use avocado oil spray to coat the pan.
- Cook until browned in the air fryer basket, about 15 minutes on each side. In the middle, an instant-read thermometer should read at least 165 degrees F. (74 degrees C).

Air Fryer General Tso's Chicken

Preparation Time: 18 minutes
Cooking Time: 20 minutes
Serve: 1
Ingredients:

- ½ cup chicken broth
- 1 tablespoon sesame oil
- 1 tablespoon soy sauce
- 1 tablespoon hoisin sauce
- 1 tablespoon cornstarch
- 1 teaspoon minced garlic
- 1 teaspoon Sriracha
- 1-pound skinless, boneless chicken breasts
- 2 tablespoons cornstarch
- 1 tablespoon soy sauce
- cooking spray
- 1 teaspoon chopped scallions, or to taste
- 1 teaspoon toasted sesame seeds

Directions:

- In a medium saucepan, combine broth, sesame oil, soy sauce, hoisin sauce, cornstarch, garlic, and Sriracha for the sauce. Whisk until the cornstarch is completely dissolved. Bring the water to a boil over medium-high heat. Turn down the heat to low.
- Preheat the air fryer carefully to 400°F (200°C) according to the manufacturer's instructions.

- Stir together the chicken, cornstarch, and soy sauce in a mixing dish until the chicken is equally covered. Place the chicken in the air fryer basket. Coat the pan with cooking spray.
- Cook for 8 minutes in a hot air fryer. Shake the basket, breaking up any stuck-together bits, then respray with cooking spray. Cook for another 8 minutes, or until the chicken is no longer pink in the center.
- Place the chicken in a large mixing basin. Toss the chicken in the sauce to coat. Garnish with onions and sesame seeds if desired.

Air Fryer Chicken Katsu

Preparation Time: 15 minutes
Cooking Time: 25 minutes
Serve: 1
Ingredients:

- 1 large egg
- salt to taste
- 1 cup panko breadcrumbs
- ¾ pound chicken breast cutlets
- avocado oil cooking spray
- 1 tablespoon barbecue sauce (Optional)
- 1 tablespoon chopped green onions (Optional)

Directions:

- Preheat the air fryer carefully to 400°F (200°C) according to the manufacturer's instructions.
- Softly beat the egg and season with salt in a shallow bowl or small casserole dish. On a dish, spread out the panko breadcrumbs.
- Allow extra egg mixture to drop back into the bowl as you dip each cutlet. Turn the cutlets in the panko breadcrumbs to cover both sides well, carefully pushing the cutlets into the crumbs. Place on a sheet of parchment paper. Spray each side with cooking spray and set in an air fryer basket.
- Air-fry for 5 minutes, then turn and air-fry for another 4 minutes. Garnish with green onions and serve with barbecue sauce.

Air Fryer Old Bay® Chicken Wings

Preparation Time: 20 minutes
Cooking Time: 20 minutes
Serve: 1
Ingredients:

- 2 pounds chicken wings
- 2 tablespoons seafood seasoning
- ½ cup cornstarch
- ¼ teaspoon freshly cracked black pepper
- 4 tablespoons butter
- 1 teaspoon seafood seasoning

Directions:

- Preheat the air fryer carefully to 400°F (200 degrees C).
- Toss the chicken wings with 2 tablespoons Old Bay® seasoning and black pepper in a large mixing dish. Toss the wings in the cornstarch until well covered. Shake each wing before placing it in the air fryer basket, making sure they don't contact; cook in batches if necessary.
- Fry for 10 minutes in a hot air fryer, then shake the basket and cook for another 8 minutes. Fry the wings for 5 to 6 minutes longer, or until the chicken is cooked through and the juices flow clear.

- Meanwhile, add butter and 1 teaspoon Old Bay® in seasoning for the sauce in a small saucepan. Bring to a boil, frequently stirring, over medium heat.
- Each wing should be dipped in the sauce. Serve with any leftover sauce on the side.

Air Fryer Chicken Taquitos

Preparation Time: 15 minutes
Cooking Time: 25 minutes
Serve: 1
Ingredients:

- 1 teaspoon vegetable oil
- 2 tablespoons diced onion
- 1 pinch salt and ground black pepper to taste
- 6 each corn tortillas
- ½ cup shredded Mexican cheese blend
- 1 clove garlic, minced
- 2 tablespoons chopped green chiles
- 2 tablespoons Mexican-style hot tomato sauce
- 1 cup shredded rotisserie chicken
- 2 tablespoons Neufchatel cheese
- 1 serving avocado oil cooking spray

Directions:

- In a skillet, heat the oil. Cook until the onion is tender and transparent, 3 to 5 minutes. Cook until the garlic is aromatic, approximately 1 minute. Stir in the green chilies and Mexican tomato sauce. Combine the chicken, Neufchatel cheese, and Mexican cheese mixture in a bowl. Cook and stir for 3 minutes, or until the cheeses have melted and the mixture is well warmed. Season with salt and pepper to taste.
- Heat tortillas in a pan or directly on the gas stove grates till warm and flexible. Fill each tortilla with 3 tablespoons of the chicken mixture. Roll into taquitos after folding over.
- Preheat the air fryer carefully to 400°F (200 degrees C).
- Place the taquitos in the air fryer basket without touching and spritz with avocado oil. If necessary, cook in batches. Cook for 6 to 9 minutes, or until golden brown and crispy. Turn the taquitos over, spray with avocado oil, and continue to air fry for 3 to 5 minutes.

Air Fryer Chicken Thighs

Preparation Time: 15 minutes
Cooking Time: 20 minutes
Serve: 1
Ingredients:

- 4 skin-on, boneless chicken thighs
- 2 teaspoons extra-virgin olive oil
- 1 teaspoon smoked paprika
- ¾ teaspoon garlic powder
- ½ teaspoon salt
- ½ teaspoon ground black pepper

Directions:

- Preheat the air fryer carefully to 400°F (200 degrees C).
- Dry the chicken thighs with a paper towel and brush the skin side with olive oil. Arrange the chicken thighs in a single layer on a platter, skin side down.
- Combine the smoked paprika, garlic powder, salt, and pepper in a mixing dish. Sprinkle half of the seasoning mixture equally over the 4 chicken thighs. Turn the thighs over and equally sprinkle with the remaining spice mixture. Place the chicken thighs in a single layer in the air fryer basket, skin side up.

- Fry in a preheated air fryer for 18 minutes, or until the chicken is brown and the juices flow clear. In the middle, an instant-read thermometer should read at least 165 degrees F. (74 degrees C).

Air Fryer Keto Chicken Wings

Preparation Time: 20 minutes
Cooking Time: 25 minutes
Serve: 1
Ingredients:

- 3 pounds chicken wings
- 1 tablespoon taco seasoning mix
- 2 teaspoons olive oil

Directions:

- Combine the chicken wings, taco seasoning, and oil in a resealable plastic bag. Shake well to coat.
- Preheat the air fryer carefully for 2 minutes at 350 degrees F (175 degrees C).
- Cook the wings in the air fryer for 12 minutes, flipping after 6 minutes. Serve right away.

Air Fryer Cornflake Chicken Fingers

Preparation Time: 15 minutes
Cooking Time: 20 minutes
Serve: 1
Ingredients:

- 1 pound chicken tenders
- 1 teaspoon poultry seasoning
- 1 teaspoon salt
- ½ teaspoon ground black pepper
- 1 large egg, beaten
- 1 cup corn flakes, crushed
- 1 serving avocado oil cooking spray

Directions:

- Preheat the air fryer carefully to 375°F (190 degrees C).
- Chicken tenders should be seasoned with poultry seasoning, salt, and black pepper. Dip in the egg, then in the crumbled cornflakes. Spray with avocado oil and place in the air fryer basket.
- Cook for 7 to 8 minutes in an air fryer. Flip the chicken tenders, spritz with avocado oil again, and air fry for 3 to 5 minutes more. In the middle, an instant-read thermometer should read at least 165 degrees F. (74 degrees C).

Air Fryer Chicken Fajita Taquitos

Preparation Time: 15 minutes
Cooking Time: 18 minutes
Serve: 1
Ingredients:

- 2 (4 ounces) boneless, skinless chicken breasts, cut into strips
- 1 ¼ cups mojo criollo marinade
- 1 pound corn tortillas
- 1 (14 ounces) package fire-roasted peppers and onion blend (such as Trader Joe's®), thawed
- 1 cup shredded Mexican cheese blend
- cooking spray

Directions:

- Add the marinade to the chicken strips in a sealable container. Allow to marinade for 2 hours after sealing.

- Drain and discard marinade. Cook the chicken strips in a pan over medium-high heat until browned, 6 to 7 minutes. Cook for 2 to 3 minutes more after adding the thawed peppers and onions.
- Place the chicken strips on a chopping board and cut them into smaller pieces. Return the chopped chicken to the peppers and onions and stir to mix.
- Preheat the air fryer carefully to 370 degrees Fahrenheit (187 degrees Celsius) for 5 minutes.
- Fill a tortilla bag halfway with tortillas. Microwave 5 tortillas for 30 seconds at a time.
- Place warmed tortillas on a cutting board and spray each side with about 1/2 teaspoon of oil. 1 to 2 tablespoons chicken filling on top, followed by 1 tablespoon cheese mixture. Taquitos should be firmly rolled.
- Place the taquitos in the air fryer basket, seam side down, and cook for 5 minutes. Then, increase the temperature of the air fryer to 400 degrees F (200 degrees C) and continue to air fry for 5 minutes.

Air Fried Maple Chicken Thighs
Preparation Time: 15 minutes
Cooking Time: 22 minutes
Serve: 1
Ingredients:

- 1 cup buttermilk
- ½ cup maple syrup
- 1 egg
- 1 teaspoon granulated garlic
- 4 skin-on, bone-in chicken thighs
- ½ cup all-purpose flour
- ¼ cup tapioca flour
- 1 tablespoon salt
- 1 teaspoon sweet paprika
- ½ teaspoon smoked paprika
- 1 teaspoon granulated onion
- ¼ teaspoon ground black pepper
- ¼ teaspoon cayenne pepper
- ½ teaspoon granulated garlic
- ½ teaspoon honey powder (such as Savory Spice®)

Directions:

- In a resealable bag, combine buttermilk, maple syrup, egg, and 1 teaspoon granulated garlic. Marinate the chicken thighs for at least 1 hour or overnight in the refrigerator.
- In a shallow bowl, combine flour, granulated onion, pepper, tapioca flour, salt, sweet paprika, smoked paprika, cayenne pepper, 1/2 teaspoon granulated garlic, and honey powder.
- Preheat the air fryer carefully to 380°F (190 degrees C).
- Remove the chicken thighs from the marinade and set them aside. Dredge the chicken in the flour mixture and brush off any excess. Cook the chicken for 12 minutes, skin side down, in a preheated air fryer. Fry the thighs for a further 13 minutes on the other side.

Crispy Ranch Air Fryer Nuggets
Preparation Time: 10 minutes
Cooking Time: 18 minutes
Serve: 1
Ingredients:

- 1 pound chicken tenders, cut into 1.5 to 2-inch pieces
- 1 package dry ranch salad dressing mix

- 2 tablespoons flour
- 1 egg, lightly beaten
- 1 cup panko breadcrumbs
- 1 serving olive oil cooking spray

Directions:

- Toss the chicken in a bowl with the ranch seasoning to mix. Allow for 5-10 minutes of resting time.
- Fill a resealable bag halfway with flour. Place the panko breadcrumbs on a dish and the egg in a small bowl. Preheat the air fryer carefully to 390°F (200 degrees C).
- Toss the chicken in the bag to coat. Dip the chicken in the egg mixture lightly, allowing excess to drain off. Roll the chicken in panko, pushing the crumbs into the meat.
- Spray the air fryer basket with oil and arrange the chicken pieces inside, ensuring no overlap. Depending on the size of your air fryer, you may need to prepare two batches. Next, spray the chicken lightly with cooking spray.
- 4 minutes in the oven. Cook for 4 minutes more, or until the chicken is no longer pink on the inside. Serve right away.

Air Fryer Bang-Bang Chicken
Preparation Time: 18 minutes
Cooking Time: 20 minutes
Serve: 1
Ingredients:

- 1 cup mayonnaise
- ½ cup sweet chili sauce
- 2 tablespoons Sriracha sauce
- ⅓ cup flour
- 1 pound chicken breast tenderloins, cut into bite-size pieces
- 1 ½ cups panko breadcrumbs
- 2 green onions, chopped

Directions:

- Combine the mayonnaise, sweet chili sauce, and Sriracha in a large mixing bowl. Set aside a third of a cup of the mixture.
- Fill a big resealable plastic bag halfway with flour. Close the bag and shake to coat the chicken. Stir the coated chicken pieces into the large mixing bowl with the mayonnaise mixture.
- In a separate big plastic resealable bag, place the panko breadcrumbs. Drop chicken pieces into breadcrumbs in batches, close, and shake to coat.
- Preheat the air fryer carefully to 400°F (200 degrees C).
- Fill the air fryer basket with as many chicken pieces as you can without overflowing it. Cook for 10 minutes in a hot air fryer. Cook for 5 minutes more on the other side. Rep with the remaining chicken.
- Pour the saved sauce over the fried chicken in a large mixing bowl. Stir in the green onions and toss to coat. Serve right away.

Air Fryer Chicken Cordon Bleu
Preparation Time: 15 minutes
Cooking Time: 25 minutes
Serve: 1
Ingredients:

- 2 boneless, skinless chicken breasts
- salt and ground black pepper to taste
- 1 tablespoon Dijon mustard
- 4 slices deli Swiss cheese
- 4 slices of deli ham

- 2 toothpicks
- ¼ cup all-purpose flour
- 1 egg, beaten
- 1 cup panko breadcrumbs
- ⅓ cup grated Parmesan cheese
- cooking spray

Directions:

- 1 chicken breast should be placed on a chopping board. Holding a sharp knife parallel to the cutting board and down one long edge of the chicken breast, cut it almost in half, leaving one side connected. Cover the breast with plastic wrap once it has been opened flat like a book. Lightly pound to 1/4-inch thickness with the flat side of a meat mallet. Rep with the remaining chicken breasts.
- Season both sides of each chicken breast with salt and pepper. On top, smear Dijon mustard. 1 piece of cheese on each breast, 2 slices of ham, and 1 slice of cheese on top of each. Each breast should be rolled up and secured with a toothpick.
- In a small basin, combine the flour and salt. In a separate bowl, crack the egg. In a third bowl, combine panko breadcrumbs and grated Parmesan.
- Preheat the air fryer carefully to 350°F (175 degrees C).
- Dip the chicken in flour first, then in egg, and then in the bread crumb mixture. Spray the chicken rolls with nonstick cooking spray and set aside for 5 minutes while the air fryer warms up.
- Cook the chicken for 10 minutes in the prepared air fryer basket. Reapply nonstick spray to any chalky areas. Cook for 8 minutes more, or until the chicken is no longer pink in the center.

Air Fryer Honey-Cajun Chicken Thighs

Preparation Time: 20 minutes
Cooking Time: 20 minutes
Serve: 1
Ingredients:

- ½ cup buttermilk
- 1 teaspoon hot sauce
- 1 ½ pound skinless, boneless chicken thighs
- ¼ cup all-purpose flour
- ⅓ cup tapioca flour
- 2 ½ teaspoons Cajun seasoning
- ½ teaspoon garlic salt
- ½ teaspoon honey powder (such as Savory Spice®)
- ¼ teaspoon ground paprika
- ⅛ teaspoon cayenne pepper
- 4 teaspoons honey

Directions:

- In a resealable plastic bag, combine buttermilk and spicy sauce. Marinate the chicken thighs for 30 minutes.
- Combine the flour, tapioca flour, Cajun spice, garlic salt, honey powder, paprika, and cayenne pepper in a small mixing bowl. Remove the thighs from the buttermilk mixture and coat them in the flour mixture. Excess flour should be shaken off.
- Preheat the air fryer carefully to 360°F (175 degrees C).
- Cook the chicken thighs in the air fryer basket for around 15 minutes. Cook until the chicken thighs are no longer pink in the middle and the juices run clear, about 10 minutes more. In the middle, an instant-read thermometer should read at least 165 degrees F. (74 degrees C).

- Remove the chicken thighs from the air fryer and sprinkle with 1 teaspoon honey on each thigh
.

Bacon-Wrapped Stuffed Chicken Breasts in the Air Fryer

Preparation Time: 15 minutes
Cooking Time: 25 minutes
Serve: 1
Ingredients:

- 3 breast half, bone, and skin removed
- 3 slices Monterey Jack cheese
- 1 teaspoon lemon-pepper seasoning, 6 spears of fresh asparagus
- 9 slices bacon
- 12 each wooden toothpick

Directions:

- If the manufacturer recommends it, preheat the air fryer carefully to 350°F (175°C).
- Using paper towels, pat the chicken pieces dry. Slice horizontally down the center, starting at the thickest area and being cautious not to cut through to the other side with a sharp knife. Spread the two sides out as if they were a book.
- Both sides should be seasoned with lemon-pepper spice. Next, 1 piece of cheese for each chicken breast Cut the asparagus spears in half and arrange four halves on top of the cheese. Then roll the chicken up and over the cheese and asparagus, maintaining the filling within each roll. Next, wrap three slices of bacon around each chicken breast, using wooden toothpicks to bind the bacon where it overlaps.
- Place each bacon-wrapped breast in the air fryer basket and cook for 15 minutes on high. Cook for another 15 minutes on the opposite side. Check the doneness of the chicken; an instant-read thermometer placed into the center should read 165 degrees F. (74 degrees C).

Air Fryer Herb-Seasoned Chicken Wings

Preparation Time: 15 minutes
Cooking Time: 20 minutes
Serve: 1
Ingredients:

- 1 cooking spray (such as Pam®)
- 8 chicken wings
- 1 teaspoon ground black pepper
- 1 teaspoon Hungarian paprika
- 1 teaspoon ground cumin
- 1 teaspoon garlic powder
- 1 teaspoon onion powder
- 1 teaspoon herbs de Provence
- ½ teaspoon kosher salt

Directions:

- Preheat the air fryer carefully to 390°F (200°C) according to the manufacturer's instructions. Cooking spray should be sprayed on the basket.
- Rinse and pat dry the chicken wings. Combine black pepper, paprika, cumin, garlic powder, onion powder, herbs de Provence, and kosher salt in a mixing bowl. On both sides of the wings, sprinkle with the seasoning.
- Place the wings in the fryer basket in a single layer, ensuring they don't touch. Fry for about 9 minutes per side, or until browned and no longer pink in the middle.

Air Fryer Balsamic-Glazed Chicken Wings
Preparation Time: 20 minutes
Cooking Time: 25 minutes
Serve: 1
Ingredients:

- cooking spray
- 3 tablespoons baking powder
- 1 ½ teaspoons salt
- 1 ½ teaspoon freshly ground black pepper
- 1 teaspoon paprika
- 2 pounds chicken wings
- ⅓ cup water
- ⅓ cup balsamic vinegar
- 2 tablespoons soy sauce
- 2 tablespoons honey
- 2 tablespoons chili sauce (such as Heinz®)
- 2 cloves garlic, minced
- 1 teaspoon water
- ¼ teaspoon cornstarch
- 1 green onion, thinly sliced
- ¼ teaspoon toasted sesame seeds

Directions:

- Preheat the air fryer carefully to 380°F (190 degrees C). Cooking spray should be sprayed on the fryer basket.
- Combine the baking powder, salt, pepper, and paprika in a small mixing bowl. Place some chicken wings in a bag with the baking powder mixture and shake to coat. Remove the wings from the bag, shake off any excess powder, and continue until all of the wings have been coated with the baking powder mixture.
- Cook for 20 minutes, shaking and rotating the wings midway through, after lightly spraying them with frying spray and placing them in the preheated air fryer basket. Next, raise the heat to 400°F (200°C) and cook until the bacon is crispy, about 5 minutes longer. You may need to cook the wings in batches depending on the size of your air fryer.
- Meanwhile, add 1/3 cup water, balsamic vinegar, soy sauce, honey, chili sauce, and garlic in a saucepan over medium heat. Bring to a low boil and simmer for 15 minutes, or until the sauce has reduced. Whisk together 1 teaspoon water and cornstarch; pour into the sauce and stir until thickened.
- Toss crispy wings in a large mixing basin with sauce until fully covered. Serve immediately, garnished with chopped green onion and sesame seeds.

Air Fryer Chicken Strips
Preparation Time: 15 minutes
Cooking Time: 20 minutes
Serve: 1
Ingredients:

- 1 cup all-purpose flour
- 1 tablespoon paprika
- 1 tablespoon parsley flakes
- 1 teaspoon seasoned salt
- ½ teaspoon ground black pepper
- 1 large egg
- 1 ½ pounds chicken tenderloins
- cooking spray

Directions:

- Preheat the air fryer carefully to 400°F (200°C) according to the manufacturer's instructions.
- Combine the flour, paprika, parsley, seasoned salt, and pepper in a large mixing bowl. In a separate dish, beat the egg.
- Dredge each chicken strip in seasoned flour, then in beaten egg, and last in seasoned flour.
- Fill the basket with as many strips as you can without overflowing it. Spray the tops of the strips lightly with cooking spray. 8 minutes in the oven, turn the strips over, and sprinkle the tops gently with additional cooking spray. Cook for an additional 8 minutes. Rep with the rest of the strips.

Keto Lemon-Garlic Chicken Thighs in the Air Fryer
Preparation Time: 15 minutes
Cooking Time: 18 minutes
Serve: 1
Ingredients:

- ¼ cup lemon juice
- 2 tablespoons olive oil
- 1 teaspoon Dijon mustard
- 2 cloves garlic, minced
- ¼ teaspoon salt
- ⅛ teaspoon ground black pepper
- 4 skin-on, bone-in chicken thighs
- 4 lemon wedges

Directions:

- Combine the lemon juice, olive oil, Dijon mustard, garlic, salt, and pepper in a mixing bowl. Set aside the marinade.
- Fill a large resealable plastic bag halfway with chicken thighs. Pour marinade over chicken and close bag, ensuring that all chicken portions are covered. Refrigerate for at least 2 hours before serving.
- Preheat the air fryer carefully to 360°F (175 degrees C).
- Take the chicken out of the marinade and blot it dry with paper towels. Cook the chicken in batches if required in the air fryer basket.
- Fry for 22 to 24 minutes, or until the chicken is no longer pink at the bone and the juices flow clear. A thermometer near the bone should read 165 degrees F. (74 degrees C). When serving, squeeze a lemon slice over each piece.

Air Fryer Bacon-Wrapped Chicken Thighs
Preparation Time: 15 minutes
Cooking Time: 22 minutes
Serve: 1
Ingredients:

- ½ stick butter softened
- ½ clove minced garlic
- ¼ teaspoon dried thyme, ¼ teaspoon dried basil
- ⅛ teaspoon coarse salt
- freshly ground black pepper
- ⅓ pound thick-cut bacon
- 1 ½ pounds boneless skinless chicken thighs
- 2 teaspoons minced garlic

Directions:

- Combine melted butter, garlic, thyme, basil, salt, and pepper in a mixing bowl. Place the butter on wax paper and roll it up tightly to produce a butter log. Refrigerate for 2 hours, or until firm.

- One bacon strip should be placed flat on a sheet of wax paper. Sprinkle with garlic and place the chicken thigh on top of the bacon. Remove the chicken thigh. Place 1-2 tablespoons of the cool finishing butter in the center of each chicken thigh. Insert one end of the bacon into the center of the chicken thigh. Fold the bacon over the chicken thigh and wrap it around it. Repeat with the rest of the thighs and bacon.
- Preheat the air fryer carefully to 370°F (190 degrees C).
- Place the chicken thighs in the air fryer basket and cook for 25 minutes. A thermometer near the bone should read 165 degrees F. (74 degrees C).

Air Fryer Sesame Chicken Thighs
Preparation Time: 10 minutes
Cooking Time: 18 minutes
Serve: 1
Ingredients:
- 2 tablespoons sesame oil
- 2 tablespoons soy sauce
- 1 tablespoon honey
- 1 tablespoon sriracha sauce
- 1 teaspoon rice vinegar
- 2 pounds chicken thighs
- 1 green onion, chopped
- 2 tablespoons toasted sesame seeds

Directions:
- Combine sesame oil, soy sauce, honey, sriracha, and vinegar in a large mixing bowl. Stir in the chicken to mix. Refrigerate for at least 30 minutes, covered.
- Preheat the air fryer carefully to 400°F (200 degrees C). Remove the chicken from the marinade.
- Place them skin-side up chicken thighs in the air fryer basket. 5 minutes in the oven Cook for another 10 minutes on the other side.
- Place the chicken on a platter and set it aside for 5 minutes before serving. Garnish with green onion and sesame seeds if desired.

Air Fryer Cornflake-Crusted Chicken Tenders
Preparation Time: 18 minutes
Cooking Time: 20 minutes
Serve: 1
Ingredients:
- 1 egg
- 1 tablespoon pesto
- 1 pinch salt
- 1 cup crushed cornflakes
- 1 ounce finely shredded Parmesan cheese
- ½ teaspoon Catanzaro herbs (such as Savory Spice Shop®)
- ½ teaspoon granulated garlic
- 1 pinch salt
- 1 pound chicken tenders

Directions:
- Preheat the air fryer carefully to 400°F (200 degrees C).
- In a shallow bowl, combine the egg, pesto, and salt. Separately, combine cornflake crumbs, Parmesan cheese, Catanzaro herbs, garlic, and salt in a separate dish.

- Dip each piece of chicken in the egg wash first, then in the cornflake mixture, brushing off excess breading. Finally, place the chicken in the air fryer basket.
- After 5 minutes, rotate the chicken pieces and air fry until the center is no longer pink and the juices run clear, about 5 minutes more.

Air Fryer Chicken Katsu with Homemade Katsu Sauce
Preparation Time: 15 minutes
Cooking Time: 25 minutes
Serve: 1
Ingredients:
- ½ cup ketchup
- 2 tablespoons soy sauce
- 1 tablespoon brown sugar
- 1 tablespoon sherry
- 2 teaspoons Worcestershire sauce
- 1 teaspoon minced garlic
- 1-pound boneless skinless chicken breast
- 1 pinch salt and ground black pepper
- 2 large eggs, beaten
- 1 ½ cups panko breadcrumbs
- 1 serving cooking spray

Directions:
- In a mixing bowl, combine ketchup, soy sauce, brown sugar, sherry, Worcestershire sauce, and garlic until the sugar is dissolved. Set aside the katsu sauce.
- Preheat the air fryer carefully to 350°F (175 degrees C).
- In the meantime, arrange the chicken pieces in a clean work area. Season with salt and pepper to taste.
- On a flat plate, place the beaten eggs. Fill a second flat plate halfway with breadcrumbs. Dredge the chicken in the egg, then in the breadcrumbs. Repeat by dredging the chicken in egg and then breadcrumbs, pressing down to ensure that the breadcrumbs adhere to the chicken.
- Place the chicken pieces in the air fryer basket that has been preheated. Nonstick cooking spray should be sprayed on the tops.
- 10 minutes in the air fryer. Flip the chicken pieces over and coat the tops with nonstick cooking spray using a spatula. Cook for an additional 8 minutes. Slice the chicken on a chopping board. Toss with katsu sauce and serve.

Air Fryer Chicken Kyiv Balls
Preparation Time: 20 minutes
Cooking Time: 20 minutes
Serve: 1
Ingredients:
- ½ cup unsalted butter softened
- 2 tablespoons chopped fresh flat-leaf parsley
- 2 cloves garlic, crushed
- 1 (19.1 ounces) package ground chicken breast
- 2 eggs, beaten
- 1 cup panko breadcrumbs
- 1 teaspoon paprika
- 1 teaspoon salt
- ½ teaspoon ground black pepper
- cooking spray

Directions:

- Blend the butter, parsley, and garlic until well incorporated into a mixing dish. On a baking sheet, divide the mixture into 12 equal sections. Freeze for approximately 20 minutes or until solid.
- Make 12 balls out of the ground chicken. In the middle of each ball, make a deep imprint. Place a slice of frozen herbed butter in the indentation and wrap the meat around it until it is completely enclosed. Rep with the remaining balls.
- In a mixing dish, combine the beaten eggs. Next, combine panko, paprika, salt, and pepper in a separate bowl.
- 1 ground chicken ball should be dipped in the beaten eggs first, then in the seasoned breadcrumbs. Re-dunk the ball in the egg and then in the seasoned breadcrumbs. Rep with the remaining balls. Place on a baking sheet and place in the freezer for 10 minutes.
- Preheat the air fryer carefully to 400°F (200 degrees C). Spray half of the balls with nonstick cooking spray and place them in the air fryer.
- 5 minutes in the oven with tongs, turn the balls over and re-spray with nonstick cooking spray. Cook for another 5 minutes. Repeat with the rest of the chicken balls.

Air Fryer Sweet and Sour Chicken Wings

Preparation Time: 15 minutes
Cooking Time: 25 minutes
Serve: 1
Ingredients:

- 1 ½ pounds chicken wings, tips discarded
- 2 tablespoons baking powder
- 1 teaspoon salt
- 1 teaspoon ground black pepper
- 1 teaspoon paprika
- ½ cup white vinegar
- ¼ cup pineapple juice
- ¼ cup ketchup
- 1 tablespoon brown sugar
- 1 tablespoon reduced-sodium soy sauce
- 1 teaspoon Sriracha sauce
- 1 teaspoon sesame oil
- 1 tablespoon cornstarch
- 1 tablespoon water
- ¾ teaspoon sesame seeds
- 1 stalk green onion, sliced

Directions:

- Preheat the air fryer carefully to 380°F (190 degrees C). Coat the basket with cooking spray.
- Using a paper towel, pat dries the chicken wings. Combine baking powder, salt, pepper, and paprika in a resealable plastic bag. Place some chicken wings in the bag and shake vigorously until the wings are fully covered. Shake off any extra baking powder mixture, then repeat with the remaining wings until all of them are covered.
- Cook the chicken wings in the air fryer basket for 22 to 23 minutes, turning halfway through.
- Meanwhile, add vinegar, pineapple juice, ketchup, brown sugar, soy sauce, Sriracha, and sesame oil in a small saucepan over medium heat. Bring to a boil, stirring constantly. For around 2 minutes, bring the water to a boil. Then, reduce the heat to a low simmer. In a small bowl, mix the cornstarch and water. Pour into the pot and stir vigorously until the sauce thickens about 1 minute. Thin the sauce with a little water if it's too thick.

- Increase the temperature of the air fryer to 400 degrees F (200 degrees C) and cook the wings for another 2 minutes, or until they are cooked through and crispy brown.
- Pour the sauce into a large mixing dish and toss in the cooked wings. Toss well to coat. Serve immediately, garnished with sesame seeds and green onion.

Air Fryer BBQ Cheddar-Stuffed Chicken Breasts

Preparation Time: 15 minutes
Cooking Time: 20 minutes
Serve: 1
Ingredients:

- 3 strips bacon, divided
- 2 ounces Cheddar cheese, cubed, divided
- ¼ cup barbeque sauce, divided
- 2 (4 ounces) skinless, boneless chicken breasts
- salt and ground black pepper to taste

Directions:

- Preheat the air fryer carefully to 380°F (190 degrees C). Cook 1 strip of bacon in the air fryer for 2 minutes. Remove from the air fryer and slice into small pieces. Preheat the air fryer basket to 400°F and line it with parchment paper (200 degrees C).
- Combine cooked bacon, Cheddar cheese, and 1 tablespoon barbeque sauce in a mixing bowl.
- To make a little internal pouch, make a horizontal 1-inch cut at the top of each chicken breast using a long, sharp knife. Stuff each breast evenly with the bacon-cheese mixture. Wrap each chicken breast with the remaining bacon pieces. Coat the chicken breast with the remaining barbecue sauce before placing it in the air fryer basket.
- Cook in the air fryer for 10 minutes, then flip and cook for another 10 minutes, or until the chicken is no longer pink in the middle and the juices run clear. An instant-read thermometer should read at least 165 degrees F in the center (74 degrees C).

Air Fryer Apricot-Glazed Chicken Breasts

Preparation Time: 20 minutes
Cooking Time: 25 minutes
Serve: 1
Ingredients:

- 3 tablespoons apricot preserves
- 1 teaspoon fresh ginger paste
- 2 (8 ounces) boneless, skinless chicken breasts
- ½ teaspoon minced fresh rosemary
- 1 teaspoon vegetable oil
- salt and ground black pepper to taste

Directions:

- Combine the apricot preserves, ginger paste, and rosemary in a small mixing dish. To make preserves easier to distribute, microwave for around 20 seconds.
- Pound the chicken breasts to a consistent thickness and blot dry with a paper towel. Season with salt and pepper after rubbing with oil.
- Preheat the air fryer carefully to 400°F (200 degrees C). Cooking sprays the basket and arranges the chicken breasts in a single layer.
- 4 minutes in the air fryer. The chicken breasts should be flipped and rotated. Brush the apricot mixture over the top. Return the basket to the air fryer for 8 to 12 minutes, or

until the chicken is no longer pink in the center and the juices flow clear. An instant-read thermometer should read at least 165 degrees F in the center (74 degrees C).

- Cover the chicken loosely with aluminum foil and set aside for 5 minutes. Serve the chicken breasts sliced.

Air Fryer Pizza-Stuffed Chicken Breasts
Preparation Time: 15 minutes
Cooking Time: 20 minutes
Serve: 1
Ingredients:
- 2 (6 ounces) chicken breasts
- 2 teaspoons olive oil
- 2 teaspoons Italian seasoning
- 1 teaspoon garlic salt
- 2 ounces fresh mozzarella cheese
- ¼ cup sliced pepperoni
- 2 tablespoons minced onion
- 2 tablespoons pizza sauce

Directions:
- Preheat the air fryer carefully to 380°F (190 degrees C).
- Make a shallow slice lengthwise through the center of each chicken breast. Fold the chicken breasts in half and cut two additional shallow horizontal slices. The pocket will look like an upside-down "T."
- Rub 1 teaspoon oil over each chicken breast and season with Italian seasoning and garlic salt.
- Stuff half of the fresh mozzarella, pepperoni, onion, and pizza sauce into each chicken breast. Place in the air fryer basket.
- Air fried for 18 minutes, or until the chicken is no longer pink in the middle and the juices flow clear. In the middle, an instant-read thermometer should read at least 165 degrees F. (74 degrees C).

Air Fried Vegetarian "Chicken Tenders."
Preparation Time: 15 minutes
Cooking Time: 18 minutes
Serve: 1
Ingredients:
- 1 cup all-purpose flour
- 3 eggs, beaten
- 2 cups panko breadcrumbs
- 1 teaspoon garlic powder
- ¾ teaspoon paprika
- ½ teaspoon cayenne pepper
- ½ teaspoon ground black pepper
- ½ teaspoon chili powder
- ¼ teaspoon salt
- 2 (16 ounce) packages imitation chicken breast halves (seitan), cut into 1-inch-wide strips
- cooking spray

Directions:
- On a big dish, pour the flour. In a small dish, place the eggs. Combine the breadcrumbs, garlic powder, paprika, cayenne pepper, black pepper, chili powder, and salt in a separate shallow bowl.
- Coat the fake chicken strips in flour, then dip them in eggs, the bread crumb mixture, and set them on a platter.
- Preheat the air fryer carefully to 500°F (260 degrees C).

- In the air fryer basket, arrange a row of coated strips. Next, apply a light layer of cooking spray to the pan.
- Cook the strips for 6 minutes in the air fryer. To turn the strips using tongs, open the fryer. Cook for another 4 to 6 minutes, or until golden brown.

Air-Fried Korean Chicken Wings
Preparation Time: 15 minutes
Cooking Time: 22 minutes
Serve: 1
Ingredients:
- ¼ cup hot honey
- 3 tablespoons gochujang
- 2 teaspoons minced garlic
- 1 teaspoon minced fresh ginger root
- 1 tablespoon brown sugar
- 1 tablespoon soy sauce
- 1 teaspoon lemon juice
- 1 teaspoon sesame seeds
- 2 pounds chicken wings
- 1 teaspoon salt
- 1 teaspoon garlic powder
- 1 teaspoon onion powder
- ½ teaspoon black pepper
- ½ teaspoon salt
- ¼ teaspoon black pepper
- ¼ cup finely chopped green onions (green part only)
- 2 tablespoons chopped green onions
- ½ cup cornstarch

Directions:
- Combine heated honey, lemon juice, garlic, ginger, salt, gochujang, brown sugar, soy sauce, and black pepper in a saucepan. Bring sauce to a boil over medium heat, lower to low heat, and continue to cook for 5 minutes. Stir in the green onions.
- Preheat the air fryer carefully to 400°F (200 degrees C).
- Toss the wings with salt, garlic powder, onion powder, and black pepper in a large mixing basin. Toss the wings in the cornstarch until well covered. Shake each wing before placing it in the air fryer basket, making sure they don't contact; cook in batches if necessary.
- Cook in the preheated air fryer for 15 minutes, shake the basket and fry for an additional 15 minutes. Flip wings over and fry until chicken is cooked through and juices run clear 5 to 8 more minutes.
- Dip each wing in the sauce and top with chopped green onions and sesame seeds. Serve with any leftover sauce on the side.

Crispy Air-Fried Chicken
Preparation Time: 10 minutes
Cooking Time: 18 minutes
Serve: 1
Ingredients:
- 1 tablespoon ground paprika
- 1 teaspoon salt
- 1 teaspoon onion powder
- 1 teaspoon garlic powder
- ½ teaspoon dried marjoram
- ½ teaspoon ground sage
- ½ teaspoon ground black pepper

- ⅛ teaspoon ground nutmeg
- 2 (8 ounces) bone-in, skin-on chicken breast halves
- ¼ cup coconut oil, at room temperature
- 2 tablespoons dry sherry
- 2 tablespoons lime juice

Directions:
- Combine paprika, salt, onion powder, garlic powder, marjoram, sage, pepper, and nutmeg in a small bowl. Rub the spice rub all over the chicken breasts, including beneath the skin.
- Preheat the air fryer carefully to 400°F (200°C) according to the manufacturer's instructions. In a small dish, combine the coconut oil, sherry, and lime juice; put aside.
- Cook for 15 minutes with the chicken breast side down in the air fryer basket. Brush the saved basting oil over the chicken. Cook for another 15 minutes after flipping the chicken and lowering the heat to 360 degrees F (182 degrees C). Cook until the chicken is no longer pink at the bone and the juices run clear, about 6 to 12 minutes more. A thermometer near the bone should read 165 degrees F. (74 degrees C).

Air-Fried Buffalo Chicken
Preparation Time: 18 minutes

Cooking Time: 20 minutes
Serve: 1
Ingredients:
- ½ cup plain fat-free Greek yogurt
- ¼ cup egg substitute
- 1 tablespoon hot sauce
- 1 tablespoon sweet paprika
- 1 tablespoon garlic pepper seasoning
- 1 tablespoon cayenne pepper
- 1 teaspoon hot sauce
- 1 cup panko breadcrumbs
- 1-pound skinless, boneless chicken breasts

Directions:
- Combine Greek yogurt, egg replacement, and 1 tablespoon + 1 teaspoon spicy sauce in a mixing dish.
- Combine the panko breadcrumbs, paprika, garlic pepper, and cayenne pepper in a separate bowl.
- Coat chicken strips with panko bread crumb mixture after dipping them in the yogurt mixture.
- In an air fryer, arrange coated chicken strips in a single layer. Cook for 10 minutes per side or until uniformly browned.

CHAPTER 5:

Beef, Pork & Lamb

Juicy Tender Pork Chops
Preparation Time: 10 minutes
Cooking Time: 12 minutes
Serve: 4
Ingredients:

- 4 pork chops, boneless
- ½ tsp garlic powder
- 1 tsp chili powder
- 2 tbsp brown sugar
- Pepper
- Salt

Directions:

- Preheat the air fryer to 400 F.
- In a small bowl, mix together brown sugar, chili powder, garlic powder, pepper, and salt and rub all over pork chops.
- Place pork chops into the air fryer basket and cook for 12 minutes. Turn halfway through.
- Serve and enjoy.

Meatballs
Preparation Time: 10 minutes
Cooking Time: 12 minutes
Serve: 6
Ingredients:

- 1 egg
- ½ lb. ground pork
- 1 lb. ground beef
- ½ tsp onion powder
- ½ tsp Italian seasoning
- 1 tbsp parmesan cheese, grated
- 2 tbsp fresh parsley, chopped
- 2 tbsp fresh mint, chopped
- 2 tbsp milk
- 1/3 cup breadcrumbs
- Pepper
- Salt

Directions:

- Preheat the air fryer to 380 F.
- Add ground meat and remaining ingredients into the mixing bowl and mix until well combined.
- Make small balls from the meat mixture and place into the air fryer basket and cook for 10-12 minutes.
- Serve and enjoy.

Moist & Tender Ham
Preparation Time: 10 minutes
Cooking Time: 35 minutes

Serve: 4
Ingredients:

- 3 lbs. cooked ham
- For glaze:
- 1 tsp dry mustard
- 1 tbsp pineapple juice
- 1 tbsp honey
- 2 tbsp brown sugar

Directions:

- Preheat the air fryer to 320 F.
- Wrap ham in aluminum foil and place into the air fryer basket and cook for 25 minutes.
- In a small bowl, mix together pineapple juice, brown sugar, honey, and mustard.
- After 25 minutes brush ham with glaze and cook for 10-15 minutes more.
- Slice and serve.

Juicy Pork Tenderloin
Preparation Time: 10 minutes
Cooking Time: 18 minutes
Serve: 4
Ingredients:

- 1 ½ lbs. pork tenderloin
- ½ tsp Italian seasoning
- 1 tsp olive oil
- 1 tbsp balsamic vinegar
- 1 tsp Dijon mustard
- Pepper
- Salt

Directions:

- Preheat the air fryer to 400 F.
- In a small bowl, mix together mustard, vinegar, Italian seasoning, pepper, and salt.
- Brush pork tenderloin with oil and rub with mustard mixture.
- Place pork tenderloin into the air fryer basket and cook for 16-18 minutes.
- Slice and serve.

Steak Kebab
Preparation Time: 10 minutes
Cooking Time: 10 minutes
Serve: 4
Ingredients:

- 1 lb. sirloin steak, cut into 1-inch pieces
- 1 onion, cut into 1-inch pieces
- 1 bell pepper, cut into 1-inch pieces
- **For marinade:**

- 2 tbsp vinegar
- 1 tsp ginger garlic paste
- 2 tbsp olive oil
- 1/4 cup soy sauce
- 1 tsp pepper

Directions:
- Preheat the air fryer to 350 F.
- Add meat pieces and remaining ingredients into the zip-lock bag. Seal bag and place in the refrigerator overnight.
- Thread marinated meat pieces, onion, and bell pepper onto the skewers.
- Place skewers into the air fryer basket and cook for 10 minutes. Turn halfway through.
- Serve and enjoy.

Onion Garlic Pork Chops

Preparation Time: 10 minutes
Cooking Time: 12 minutes
Serve: 4
Ingredients:
- 4 pork chops, boneless
- 1/2 tsp granulated onion
- 1/2 tsp celery seeds, crushed
- 1/2 tsp granulated garlic
- 2 tsp canola oil
- 1/2 tsp parsley
- 1/2 tsp salt

Directions:
- Preheat the air fryer to 350 F.
- In a small bowl, mix together garlic, celery seeds, onion, parsley, and salt.
- Brush pork chops with oil and rub with spice mixture.
- Place pork chops into the air fryer basket and cook for 12 minutes. Turn halfway through.
- Serve and enjoy.

Easy Beef Roast

Preparation Time: 10 minutes
Cooking Time: 45 minutes
Serve: 8
Ingredients:
- 2 1/2 lbs. beef roast
- 1/2 tsp garlic powder
- 1 tsp rosemary
- 1/2 tsp onion powder
- 2 tbsp canola oil
- 1 tsp dill
- 1/2 tsp pepper
- Salt

Directions:
- Preheat the air fryer to 360 F.
- In a small bowl, mix together rosemary, pepper, garlic powder, onion powder, dill, and oil and rub all over the beef roast.
- Place beef roast into the air fryer basket and cook for 45 minutes.
- Serve and enjoy.

Meatballs

Preparation Time: 10 minutes
Cooking Time: 20 minutes
Serve: 12
Ingredients:
- 1 lb. ground beef
- 1/4 cup onion, chopped
- 2 tbsp mushrooms, chopped
- 2 tbsp fresh parsley, chopped
- 1/2 cup almond flour
- 1/2 tsp pepper
- 1 tsp salt

Directions:
- Preheat the air fryer to 350 F.
- In a mixing bowl, mix together meat and remaining ingredients until well combined.
- Make small balls from the meat mixture and place into the air fryer basket and cook for 20 minutes. Turn halfway through.
- Serve and enjoy.

Flavorful Pork Patties

Preparation Time: 10 minutes
Cooking Time: 35 minutes
Serve: 6
Ingredients:
- 1 egg, lightly beaten
- 2 lbs. ground pork
- 1 tsp garlic powder
- 1 tsp smoked paprika
- 1 onion, minced
- 1 carrot, minced
- 1/2 cup almond flour
- Pepper
- Salt

Directions:
- Preheat the air fryer to 375 F.
- Add meat and remaining ingredients into the large bowl and mix until well combined.
- Make patties from the meat mixture and place into the air fryer basket and cook for 35 minutes. Turn patties after 20 minutes.
- Serve and enjoy.

Lemon Herb Lamb Chops

Preparation Time: 10 minutes
Cooking Time: 8 minutes
Serve: 4
Ingredients:
- 1 lb. lamb chops
- 1 tsp rosemary
- 2 tbsp fresh lemon juice
- 2 tbsp canola oil
- 1 tsp oregano
- 1 tsp thyme
- 1 tsp coriander
- 1 tsp salt

Directions:
- Preheat the air fryer to 390 F.

- Add lamb chops and remaining ingredients into the zip-lock bag. Seal bag and place in the refrigerator for 1 hour.
- Place marinated lamb chops into the air fryer basket and cook for 8 minutes. Turn lamb chops halfway through.
- Serve and enjoy.

Dutch Oven Beef Stew

Preparation Time: 15 minutes
Cooking Time: 25 minutes
Serve: 1
Ingredients:

- ½ cup all-purpose flour
- 1 tablespoon ground paprika
- salt and ground black pepper to taste
- 1 ½ tablespoon Worcestershire sauce
- 2 pounds cubed beef stew meat
- 2 tablespoons extra-virgin olive oil
- 4 cups beef broth
- 2 large potatoes, cubed
- 1 (8 ounces) package mushrooms
- 3 medium carrots, sliced
- 1 medium onion, chopped
- 1 stalk celery, chopped
- 2 cloves garlic, minced
- 2 bay leaves

Directions:

- Combine the flour, paprika, salt, and pepper in a medium mixing bowl. Toss the steak in the flour mixture until evenly covered.
- Heat the oil over medium-high heat in a cast-iron Dutch oven or big saucepan. Sear the meat for 2 to 3 minutes per side, or until nicely browned. Cover and stir in the broth, potatoes, mushrooms, carrots, onion, celery, Worcestershire sauce, garlic, and bay leaves.
- Reduce heat to medium and simmer, stirring periodically, for 2 1/2 hours, or until soft meat and veggies.

Beef Stroganoff Sauce with Meatballs

Preparation Time: 20 minutes
Cooking Time: 20 minutes
Serve: 1
Ingredients:

- ½ teaspoon vegetable oil, or as needed
- 1 pound ground sirloin
- 3 tablespoons Worcestershire sauce
- 1 egg
- ⅓ cup dry breadcrumbs
- ½ small onion, chopped
- salt and ground black pepper to taste
- ¼ cup butter, divided
- 1 (16 ounces) package mushrooms, sliced
- 2 tablespoons all-purpose flour
- 1 (10.5 ounces) can of beef broth
- 1 teaspoon ground mustard
- ⅓ cup sour cream

Directions:

- Preheat the oven carefully to 350 degrees Fahrenheit (175 degrees C). Coat a baking sheet with cooking spray.
- Combine the ground sirloin, Worcestershire sauce, egg, breadcrumbs, onion, salt, and pepper in a mixing bowl. Combine thoroughly. Make meatballs the size of golf balls. Place on the baking sheet that has been prepared.

- Bake for 15 minutes, or until the meatballs are no longer pink in the center.
- In a large pan over medium heat, melt 2 tablespoons of butter. Cook and stir until the mushrooms are tender about 10 minutes. Push the mushrooms to the pan's side.
- Melt the remaining 2 tablespoons of butter in the skillet and mix in the flour. Bring the broth and mustard to a boil. Cook for 10 to 15 minutes, or until some of the sauce has been absorbed by the meatballs. Turn off the heat. Stir in the sour cream until well combined.

Dried Beef Ball

Preparation Time: 15 minutes
Cooking Time: 25 minutes
Serve: 1
Ingredients:

- 5 ounces dried beef, chopped
- 2 (8 ounces) packages cream cheese, softened
- 6 green onions, chopped
- 1 tablespoon Worcestershire sauce
- ½ teaspoon seasoned salt

Directions:

- Set aside approximately a half cup of the chopped dry beef.
- Combine the remaining meat, cream cheese, green onions, Worcestershire sauce, and seasoned salt in a separate medium bowl. Roll into a ball after thoroughly mixing.
- Roll the ball in the reserved beef, covering it all the way around.

Simple Beef Stew

Preparation Time: 15 minutes
Cooking Time: 20 minutes
Serve: 1
Ingredients:

- 3 tablespoons vegetable oil
- 2 pounds room temperature beef stew meat, cut into 1 1/2-inch cube
- ½ cup all-purpose flour
- 1 yellow onion, roughly chopped
- 1 teaspoon minced garlic
- 1 (32 ounces) carton low-sodium beef broth
- 1 (15 ounces) can have crushed tomatoes
- 3 yellow potatoes, or more to taste, cubed
- 3 stalks celery, chopped
- 1 cup baby carrots
- 1 teaspoon Creole seasoning
- 1 teaspoon dried basil

Directions:

- In a big saucepan, heat the oil over medium-high heat. Cook and stir for 10 to 15 minutes, or until the meat, flour, onion, and garlic are browned.
- Stir in the broth, tomatoes, potatoes, celery, and carrots, followed by the Creole spice and basil. Bring to a boil. Reduce heat to maintain a simmer and cook, uncovered, for 1 hour, or until potatoes are soft, meat is cooked, and gravy is thick.

Confetti Beef Tacos

Preparation Time: 20 minutes
Cooking Time: 25 minutes

Serve: 1

Ingredients:

- 1 pound ground beef
- 2 teaspoons chili powder
- ½ teaspoon salt
- 1 (11 ounces) can corn, drained
- 1 cup prepared chunky salsa
- 12 taco shells, warmed

Directions:

- Warm-up a big nonstick skillet over medium heat. Cook for 8 to 10 minutes, breaking up the ground beef into small crumbles and stirring regularly. Drain drippings and season with chili powder and salt.
- Heat through the corn and salsa. Serve in taco shells with your choice of toppings.

Beef Taco Noodle Bake

Preparation Time: 15 minutes
Cooking Time: 20 minutes
Serve: 1
Ingredients:

- PAM® Original No-Stick Cooking Spray
- 6 ounces dry extra-wide egg noodles, uncooked
- 1 pound ground chuck beef (80% lean)
- 2 cups frozen Southwest mixed vegetables (corn, black beans, red peppers)
- 1 (10 ounces) can Ro*Tel® Original Diced Tomatoes & Green Chilies, undrained
- 1 (10 ounces) can red enchilada sauce
- 1 ¼ cups water
- 1 ¼ cups shredded Mexican blend cheese
- ¼ cup thinly sliced green onions
- 1 teaspoon Sour cream

Directions:

- Preheat the oven carefully to 400°F.
- Coat a 13x9 inch glass baking dish with nonstick cooking spray. In a baking dish, place uncooked noodles.
- Melt butter in a large pan over medium-high heat. Cook it for 5 to 7 minutes, or until the beef is crumbled and no longer pink. Drain. Stir in the veggies, undrained tomatoes, enchilada sauce, and water. Bring the water to a boil. Pour the mixture over the noodles.
- Cover securely with foil and bake for 15 minutes. Cover with foil after stirring and sprinkling with cheese. Bake for another 10 minutes or until the noodles are soft. Garnish with green onions. If desired, top with sour cream.

Filipino Corned Beef and Cabbage

Preparation Time: 15 minutes
Cooking Time: 18 minutes
Serve: 1
Ingredients:

- ⅓ cup butter
- 1 teaspoon olive oil
- ½ onion, chopped
- ⅓ small head cabbage, cored and cut into strips
- 3 cloves garlic, minced
- 4 Roma tomatoes, cubed
- ¼ cup chicken stock
- 1 (12 ounces) can corned beef

Directions:

- In a large saucepan over medium heat, melt the butter and oil. Cook until the onion and garlic are tender and transparent, about 5 minutes. Heat through the tomatoes, approximately 3 minutes.
- Cook until the cabbage is tender, about 5 minutes. Heat through with a splash of chicken stock, about 3 minutes.
- Cook until the corned beef is cooked through, and the flavors have blended for about 10 minutes.

Slow Cooker Barbecue Beef

Preparation Time: 15 minutes
Cooking Time: 22 minutes
Serve: 1
Ingredients:

- 3 tablespoons all-purpose flour
- 3 pounds chuck roast
- 15 ounces tomato sauce
- ½ cup chopped onion
- ⅓ cup brown sugar
- 2 cubes beef bouillon
- 1 ½ teaspoon chili powder
- 1 clove garlic, minced
- 1 teaspoon mustard powder

Directions:

- The flour should be rubbed into the roast. Place the roast in the bottom of the slow cooker. Combine the tomato sauce, onion, brown sugar, bouillon, chili powder, garlic powder, and mustard powder in a mixing bowl. Combine thoroughly.
- Cover the slow cooker and cook on high for 8 hours or low for 14 to 16 hours.

Blue Cheese Beef Tenderloin

Preparation Time: 10 minutes
Cooking Time: 18 minutes
Serve: 1
Ingredients:

- 1 (3 pounds) whole beef tenderloin
- ½ cup teriyaki sauce
- ½ cup red wine
- 2 cloves garlic, chopped
- 4 ounces blue cheese, crumbled
- ⅓ cup mayonnaise
- ⅔ cup sour cream
- 1 ½ teaspoon Worcestershire sauce

Directions:

- In a shallow dish, place the meat. Pour teriyaki sauce, red wine, and garlic over the steak. Allow beef to marinate for 30 minutes in the refrigerator.
- Preheat the oven carefully to 450°F (230 degrees C).
- Place the tenderloin on a broiler pan and cook for 15 minutes in a preheated oven. Reduce the heat to 375 degrees F (190 degrees C) and continue to cook for 30 to 40 minutes, or until done to preference. Allow for a 10-minute rest before slicing.
- Combine blue cheese, mayonnaise, sour cream, and Worcestershire sauce in a skillet over low heat. Stir until smooth and serve over tenderloin slices.

Mushroom Beef Burgers

Preparation Time: 18 minutes
Cooking Time: 20 minutes
Serve: 1
Ingredients:

- 2 pounds ground beef
- 1 (8 ounces) package mushrooms, chopped, or more to taste
- 1 onion, chopped
- 3 cloves garlic, minced
- 1 teaspoon Italian seasoning
- 1 teaspoon salt
- ½ teaspoon ground black pepper
- cooking spray

Directions:

- Remove the ground beef from the refrigerator and set it aside for 20 minutes to come to room temperature.
- Combine mushrooms, onion, garlic, Italian seasoning, salt, and pepper in a large mixing bowl. Add in the meat. Make 1/2-inch-thick patties out of the meat mixture.
- Cooking spray should be sprayed on an indoor grill pan. Cook patties in batches for approximately 10 minutes on each side or browned and no longer pink in the center.

Corned Beef Hash

Preparation Time: 15 minutes
Cooking Time: 25 minutes
Serve: 1
Ingredients:

- 6 large potatoes, peeled and diced
- 1 (12 ounces) can corned beef, cut into chunks
- 1 medium onion, chopped
- 1 cup beef broth

Directions:

- Combine the potatoes, corned beef, onion, and beef stock in a large deep pan over medium heat.
- Cover and cook until the potatoes are mashed, and the liquid has almost evaporated.
- Serve with a well-mixed sauce.

Smothered Beef Short Ribs

Preparation Time: 20 minutes
Cooking Time: 20 minutes
Serve: 1
Ingredients:

- ½ cup olive oil
- 4 pounds beef short ribs
- salt and pepper to taste
- 1 cup all-purpose flour
- 2 cups chopped onions
- 1 cup chopped celery
- 1 cup chopped carrots
- 2 tablespoons minced garlic
- 3 bay leaves
- 1 tablespoon dried thyme
- 1 cup red wine
- 8 cups beef stock
- ¼ cup chopped fresh parsley

Directions:

- In a big saucepan, heat the oil over medium-high heat. Season the ribs with salt and pepper to taste, then coat them in flour. Fry the ribs in small batches in the oil, adding oil as required to sear the meat. This should take between 2 and 3 minutes for each batch. Set aside the ribs.
- Sauté the onions in the same saucepan for 2 minutes. Cook for 1 minute more after adding the celery and carrots. Season to taste with salt and pepper, then toss in the garlic, bay leaves, and thyme and cook for 1 minute longer.
- Deglaze the saucepan with the red wine, scraping away any particles accumulated on the bottom. Bring the stock to a boil, then lower to low heat and simmer. Continue to boil for 2 hours, or until the sauce thickens. Serve with the parsley stirred in.

Corned Beef and Swiss Dip

Preparation Time: 15 minutes
Cooking Time: 25 minutes
Serve: 1
Ingredients:

- 1 tablespoon vegetable oil
- ¾ onion, chopped
- 3 (2.5 ounces) packages deli-sliced corned beef (such as Budding ®), diced
- 2 (8 ounces) packages cream cheese, softened
- 1 ½ cups mayonnaise
- 1 (8 ounces) carton sour cream
- 1 cup shredded Swiss cheese
- 1 teaspoon garlic powder
- 1 (1 pound) loaf unsliced Italian bread

Directions:

- Preheat the oven carefully to 350°F (175 degrees C).
- In a pan over medium heat, heat the vegetable oil. Cook and stir onion for 5 to 7 minutes, or until tender.
- Place the onion in a large mixing basin.
- Combine corned beef, cream cheese, mayonnaise, sour cream, Swiss cheese, and garlic powder in a mixing bowl. Mix until everything is well blended.
- Slice a slice of bread off the top of the loaf and hollow out the center of the loaf to make a long bread bowl. At least 1/2 inch of bread should be left on the sides. If desired, save bread chunks from the center of the loaf for dipping.
- Fill the bread dish halfway with the corned beef mixture.
- Place the full bread dish on a baking sheet wrapped in aluminum foil.
- 1 to 1 1/2 hours in a preheated oven until the dip is thoroughly cooked and bubbling.

Hot Beef Dip

Preparation Time: 15 minutes
Cooking Time: 20 minutes
Serve: 1
Ingredients:

- 2 (8 ounces) jars dried chipped beef
- 1 green bell pepper, finely chopped
- 1 onion, finely chopped
- 2 (8 ounces) packages cream cheese, softened
- 1 (8 ounces) package shredded Cheddar cheese

Directions:

- Preheat the oven carefully to 350°F (175 degrees C).
- In a small baking dish, combine the dry chipped beef, green bell pepper, onion, cream cheese, and Cheddar cheese.

- Bake for 45 minutes, uncovered, in a preheated oven, or until the center is bubbling and the sides are gently browned.

Chef John's Beef Goulash
Preparation Time: 20 minutes
Cooking Time: 25 minutes
Serve: 1
Ingredients:
- 2 ½ pounds boneless beef chuck roast
- salt and ground black pepper to taste
- 2 tablespoons vegetable oil
- 2 onions, chopped
- 2 teaspoons olive oil
- ½ teaspoon salt
- 2 tablespoons Hungarian paprika
- 2 teaspoons caraway seeds, crushed
- 1 teaspoon freshly ground black pepper
- 1 teaspoon dried marjoram
- ½ teaspoon ground thyme
- ½ teaspoon cayenne pepper
- 4 cups chicken broth, divided
- ¼ cup tomato paste
- 3 cloves garlic, crushed
- 2 tablespoons balsamic vinegar
- 1 teaspoon white sugar
- ½ teaspoon salt, or to taste
- 1 bay leaf

Directions:
- Season the meat with salt and pepper. Heat the vegetable oil in a large pan over high heat; cook and stir the beef in batches until browned on both sides, about 5 minutes per batch. Transfer to a large stockpot, leaving the drippings in the skillet.
- Return skillet to medium heat; toss onions into saved drippings, sprinkle olive oil over onions, season with 1/2 teaspoon salt, and cook for 5 minutes, or until onion has softened. Add to the stockpot with the meat.
- In a pan, toast the paprika, caraway seeds, black pepper, marjoram, thyme, and cayenne pepper until aromatic, approximately 3 minutes. Stir in 1 cup chicken stock before adding to the meat and onion combination.
- 3 cups of the chicken broth should be added to the beef mixture. Bring tomato paste, garlic, vinegar, sugar, 1/2 teaspoon salt, and bay leaf to a boil in a stockpot over high heat. Reduce the heat to low and simmer for 1 1/2 to 2 hours, or until a fork easily inserts into the meat.

Slow Cooker Roast Beef
Preparation Time: 15 minutes
Cooking Time: 20 minutes
Serve: 1
Ingredients:
- ⅓ cup soy sauce
- 1 package dry onion soup mix
- 3 pounds beef chuck roast
- 2 teaspoons freshly ground black pepper

Directions:
- Mix the soy sauce and dry onion soup in the slow cooker. Insert the chuck roast into the slow cooker. Pour in enough water to cover the top 1/2 inch of the roast. Season with ground pepper to taste.

- Cook on low for 22 hours, covered.

Beef Kebabs with Pomegranate Couscous
Preparation Time: 15 minutes
Cooking Time: 18 minutes
Serve: 1
Ingredients:
- 2 ounces feta cheese, crumbled
- ¼ cup whole-milk plain Greek yogurt
- 1 teaspoon lemon juice
- ½ teaspoon lemon zest
- 1 tablespoon water, or more as needed
- 12 ounces beef top sirloin, cut into 1-inch cubes
- 1 tablespoon Baharat (Middle Eastern spice mix)
- 1 red bell pepper
- 1 cup cherry tomatoes
- 1 small red onion, cut into 1/2-inch wedges
- 2 portobello mushrooms, stem and ribs removed, cut into 1-inch pieces
- 2 cups reduced-sodium chicken broth
- 1 ½ cups Israeli (large pearl) couscous
- ⅓ cup pomegranate seeds
- ¼ cup chopped pistachios
- 1 tablespoon chopped fresh mint
- 1 teaspoon Baharat (Middle Eastern spice mix)

Directions:
- In a small mixing bowl, combine the feta, yogurt, lemon juice, and zest to make the feta sauce. Thin with water to achieve the required consistency.
- In a medium saucepan, bring broth to a boil to prepare the couscous. Mix in the couscous. Reduce heat to low and cover for 8 to 10 minutes, or until couscous is cooked and liquid is absorbed. Using a fork, fluff the rice. Pomegranate seeds, pistachios, mint, and Baharat are optional. To mix, toss everything together.
- Preheat an outside grill to medium (325 to 375 degrees Fahrenheit (160 to 190 degrees Celsius)). Toss the meat cubes in the Baharat to coat. Thread eight 10-inch metal skewers with steak, bell pepper, tomatoes, onion, and mushrooms.
- Grill the kebabs, turning once or twice until the veggies are soft and the meat is slightly pink in the center, 8 to 12 minutes. Kebabs should be served with couscous and feta sauce on the side.

Patsy's Best Barbeque Beef
Preparation Time: 15 minutes
Cooking Time: 22 minutes
Serve: 1
Ingredients:
- ⅛ teaspoon hot pepper sauce
- 1 bunch celery, chopped
- 3 large onions, chopped
- 3 tablespoons cider vinegar
- 6 pounds boneless beef chuck roast
- 1 teaspoon pepper
- 2 teaspoons chili powder
- 1 medium green bell pepper, chopped
- 2 tablespoons salt
- 1 ¼ cups ketchup
- ½ cup water

- 3 tablespoons barbeque sauce

Directions:

- In a large mixing basin, combine the celery, onions, green pepper, ketchup, water, barbeque sauce, vinegar, and hot pepper sauce. Chili powder, salt, and pepper to taste.
- Cover the roast with the sauce mixture in a slow cooker. Cook, covered, on low for about 12 hours.
- Using a fork, shred the meat. Increase the heat to high and continue to cook until most of the liquid has been reduced.

Easy Ginger Beef

Preparation Time: 10 minutes
Cooking Time: 18 minutes
Serve: 1
Ingredients:

- 1 pound round steak, thinly sliced
- 1 tablespoon soy sauce
- 1 teaspoon butter
- 1 red bell pepper
- 1 (1 inch) piece fresh ginger root
- 1 onion
- 12 mushrooms
- ¼ cup sweet and sour sauce
- 4 cups cooked rice

Directions:

- Combine the steak, ginger, and soy sauce, flip to coat. Marinate in the refrigerator for at least 30 minutes and up to overnight.
- Heat a wok over high heat and add the meat mixture. Cook, covered, for 5 minutes, or until meat is browned. Remove the meat from the wok.
- Melt the butter over high heat; add the bell pepper, onion, mushrooms, and sweet and sour sauce. Cook, covered, for 3 minutes, or until the veggies soften. Cook until heated through, about 2 minutes, after adding cooked meat to vegetable mixture. Serve with hot cooked rice.

Glazed Corned Beef

Preparation Time: 18 minutes
Cooking Time: 20 minutes
Serve: 1
Ingredients:

- 4 ½ pounds corned beef, rinsed
- 1 cup water
- 1 cup apricot preserves
- ¼ cup brown sugar
- 2 tablespoons soy sauce

Directions:

- Preheat the oven carefully to 350°F (175 degrees C).
- Spray a big skillet with nonstick cooking spray. Fill a dish halfway with water and add the corned meat. Bake for 2 hours, carefully wrapped in aluminum foil; drain liquid.
- Combine the apricot preserves, brown sugar, and soy sauce in a small mixing dish. Evenly distribute the apricot mixture over the corned meat.
- Bake uncovered at 350°F (175°C) for 25–30 minutes, or until the meat is cooked, basting periodically with pan drippings.
- Serve corned beef slices against the grain.

DSF's Shredded Beef

Preparation Time: 15 minutes
Cooking Time: 25 minutes
Serve: 1
Ingredients:

- 1 ½ pounds rump roast
- 1 ¼ cups water
- garlic powder, or to taste
- salt and ground black pepper to taste

Directions:

- Season the rump roast well with garlic powder, salt, and pepper before placing it in the crock of a slow cooker. Fill the crock with water.
- Cook for 5 hours on high. Transfer the roast to a chopping board and shred it with two forks.

Lengua (Beef Tongue)

Preparation Time: 20 minutes
Cooking Time: 20 minutes
Serve: 1
Ingredients:

- 1 beef tongue
- 1 large onion, chopped, divided
- 2 cloves garlic
- 3 tablespoons salt
- 1 whole jalapeno pepper, stemmed
- 3 whole tomatoes
- 2 whole jalapeno peppers, stemmed
- 2 tablespoons vegetable oil

Directions:

- In a large saucepan, combine the tongue, half of the chopped onion, garlic cloves, 3 tablespoons salt, and 1 jalapeño pepper. Fill with enough water to cover the tongue by a few inches, then bring to a boil over high heat. Reduce heat to medium-low; cover and simmer for 3 to 4 hours, or until very tender. Allow the tongue to cool after removing it from the water. Keep the liquid aside. Peel off the rough outer skin of the tongue once it has cooled, then shred the flesh with two forks.
- Over high heat, bring a large pot of water to a boil. Boil until the veggies are soft, then add the entire tomatoes and 2 jalapeño peppers. Put the veggies in a blender and purée them until smooth. In a large skillet over medium heat, heat the vegetable oil. Cook, often stirring, until the onion has softened and turned translucent about 5 minutes.
- Stir in the shredded beef tongue and tomato salsa once the onion has softened. Bring to a boil, stirring regularly, and then add 2 cups of the saved cooking liquid. Cook and stir for 20 minutes, or until the liquid evaporates, leaving juicy, delicious meat.

Bibimbap with Beef

Preparation Time: 15 minutes
Cooking Time: 25 minutes
Serve: 1
Ingredients:

- ½ pound beef top sirloin steak
- 2 tablespoons soy sauce
- 1 tablespoon sesame oil
- 2 teaspoons honey
- 2 teaspoons dry sherry

- 4 cups hot cooked rice
- 2 teaspoons vegetable oil
- 1 carrot, thinly sliced
- 1 ½ cups bean sprouts
- ½ cup peeled and matchstick-cut daikon radish
- ¼ teaspoon salt
- ground black pepper to taste
- ⅛ teaspoon cayenne pepper, or to taste
- 1 cup fresh spinach

Directions:
- Cut the steak into 2-inch-long, 1/4-inch-wide slices across the grain. Stack the slices and cut them into 1/4-inch strips lengthwise.
- Combine soy sauce, sesame oil, honey, and sherry in a mixing bowl. Toss in the meat strips. Stir. Marinate for 15 minutes at room temperature.
- Over high heat, heat a nonstick wok. Cook and stir the steak and marinate for approximately 2 minutes, or until the beef is slightly browned.
- Divide the rice among four individual serving dishes. Distribute the meat mixture over the rice. Maintain your body temperature.
- In the same wok, heat the oil over medium-high heat. Combine carrot, bean sprouts, daikon, salt, black pepper, and cayenne pepper in a mixing bowl. Cook and stir for 1 minute or until slightly tender. Mix in the spinach. Cook for 1 minute or until wilted. Distribute the vegetable mixture on top of the meat and rice.

Beef Martini
Preparation Time: 15 minutes
Cooking Time: 20 minutes
Serve: 1
Ingredients:
- ½ onion, chopped
- 2 cloves garlic, crushed
- 1 cup barbecue sauce
- ¼ cup gin
- 1 tablespoon dry vermouth
- 1 tablespoon green olive brine
- 1 teaspoon dried basil
- 4 (1/2 pound) beef sirloin steaks
- salt and pepper to taste

Directions:
- Combine the onion, garlic, barbecue sauce, gin, vermouth, olive brine, and basil in a medium mixing bowl.
- Place each steak in a resealable sandwich bag and season with salt and pepper. Divide the marinade evenly among the bags and seal. Make certain that the marinade is well dispersed across the steaks. Refrigerate for at least 2 hours and up to 24 hours.
- Preheat the grill to medium-high heat and liberally oil the grill grate.
- Remove the steaks from the bags and discard the marinade. Grill steaks for 7 to 8 minutes per side, or until done to preference.

Hawaiian Beef Stew
Preparation Time: 20 minutes
Cooking Time: 25 minutes
Serve: 1
Ingredients:

- 1 tablespoon vegetable oil
- 5 stalks celery
- 4 pounds stew beef
- 5 cloves garlic, minced
- ½ cup red wine
- 1 onion, cut into chunks
- 10 cups water
- 1 (6 ounces) can tomato paste
- 1 teaspoon ground black pepper
- 4 carrots
- 3 potatoes
- 2 tablespoons salt, or to taste
- 2 tablespoons white sugar
- 3 bay leaves
- ¼ cup cornstarch
- ¼ cup water

Directions:
- In a medium-high-heat saucepan, heat the oil. Cook and stir the meat for approximately 10 minutes or until browned. Cook for 2 to 3 minutes, or until the garlic is fragrant. Cook until the alcohol has cooked off, about 5 minutes. Cook until the celery and onions are soft, approximately 5 minutes.
- Fill the saucepan with 10 glasses of water. Combine tomato paste, salt, sugar, bay leaves, and pepper in a mixing bowl. Bring the water to a boil. Reduce the heat to medium-low. Cook, covered, for 1 hour, or until meat is tender.
- Cook until the carrots are slightly soft, about 10 minutes. Cook for 10 to 15 minutes, or until potatoes are soft.
- Combine the cornstarch and 1/4 cup water; add to the stew. Allow thickening for about 3 minutes.

Slow Cooker Beef Barbacoa
Preparation Time: 15 minutes
Cooking Time: 20 minutes
Serve: 1
Ingredients:
- 3 pounds boneless beef chuck roast
- 1 onion, chopped
- 3 bay leaves
- ½ teaspoon ground black pepper, or to taste
- 2 tablespoons garlic powder
- ¼ cup distilled white vinegar
- 1 (14 ounces) can tomato sauce
- ¼ cup chili powder
- salt to taste

Directions:
- In a slow cooker, combine the roast, onion, bay leaves, black pepper, garlic powder, and vinegar, cover with water fully. Cook, covered, on High for 4 hours, or until the flesh is extremely soft and falling apart.
- Take the meat out of the slow cooker and discard the juices. Return the meat to the slow cooker and shred with a fork and knife. Combine the shredded meat, tomato sauce, chili powder, and salt in a mixing bowl. Cook the beef and sauce for 2 hours on High, covered.

Greek-Style Beef Pita
Preparation Time: 15 minutes
Cooking Time: 18 minutes
Serve: 1

Ingredients:

- 1 pound beef sirloin tip steaks, cut 1/8 to 1/4-inch thick
- 1 tablespoon lemon pepper
- 3 teaspoons vegetable oil, divided
- ¾ cup plain or seasoned hummus
- 4 each whole-wheat pita bread, cut crosswise in half

Directions:

- Stack beef steaks and cut them half lengthwise, then crosswise into 1-inch broad strips. In a medium mixing dish, combine the beef and lemon pepper.
- In a large nonstick pan, heat 2 teaspoons oil over medium-high heat until hot. Stir-fry 1/2 of the meat for 1 to 3 minutes, or until the outer surface of the beef is no longer pink. (Avoid overcooking.) Take out of the skillet. Repeat with the entire meat, adding the remaining 1 teaspoon oil to the skillet as needed.
- Fill pita pockets equally with hummus. Fill with equal parts steak and preferred toppings.

Backyard Bourbon Beef Marinade

Preparation Time: 15 minutes
Cooking Time: 22 minutes
Serve: 1
Ingredients:

- 1 cup Kikkoman Soy Sauce
- ¾ cup water
- 3 tablespoons bourbon
- 2 tablespoons sugar
- 1 teaspoon crushed garlic clove
- 1 tablespoon confectioners' sugar
- 2 pounds beef flank steak

Directions:

- Except for the beef flank steak, combine all ingredients in a mixing bowl. Marinate the beef* in the marinade for 12 to 24 hours in the refrigerator. Grill using your preferred manner.

Asian Beef with Snow Peas

Preparation Time: 10 minutes
Cooking Time: 18 minutes
Serve: 1
Ingredients:

- 3 tablespoons soy sauce
- 2 tablespoons rice wine
- 1 tablespoon brown sugar
- ½ teaspoon cornstarch
- 1 tablespoon vegetable oil
- 1 tablespoon minced garlic
- 1 pound beef round steak
- 1 tablespoon minced fresh ginger root
- 8 ounces snow peas

Directions:

- Combine the soy sauce, rice wine, brown sugar, and cornstarch in a small bowl. Place aside.
- In a wok or pan, heat the oil over medium-high heat. For 30 seconds, stir-fry the ginger and garlic. Stir-fry the steak for 2 minutes, or until evenly browned. Stir in the snow peas for a further 3 minutes. Bring the soy sauce mixture to a boil while continually stirring. Reduce the heat to low and cook until the sauce is thick and smooth. Serve right away.

Grilled Beef Fajitas

Preparation Time: 18 minutes
Cooking Time: 20 minutes
Serve: 1
Ingredients:

- 1 (1 ounces) package fajita seasoning mix
- 1-pound boneless beef top round steak
- Reynolds Wrap® Heavy Duty Aluminum Foil
- 1 medium red or yellow bell pepper
- 1 medium green bell pepper, cut into strips
- 1 medium onion
- 1 tablespoon vegetable oil
- 8 (8 inches) flour tortillas
- Salsa

Directions:

- Prepare the fajita spice mix according to the package recommendations and pour over the meat. Marinate the steak for 1 to 2 hours in Reynolds Wrap® Heavy Duty Aluminum Foil.
- Form two layers of foil around the outside of a 13x9x2inch baking pan to make a grill pan. Remove the foil and crimp the edges to make a tight rim, resulting in a pan with 1-inch sides. Place on a baking sheet.
- Preheat the grill to high heat. Remove the steak from the marinade and discard the marinade. In a foil pan, combine the peppers, onion, and oil. Slide the foil pan from the cookie sheet onto the grill and set the steak next to it.
- Grill on high for 8 to 10 minutes in a covered grill. After 5 minutes, stir the veggies and flip the steak. Remove the foil pan from the grill and place it on a cookie sheet. Thinly slice the grilled steak.
- Wrap tortillas in foil and place them on the grill while carving meat. Wrap meat, peppers, and onions in warm tortillas and serve with salsa.

Butter Beef

Preparation Time: 15 minutes
Cooking Time: 25 minutes
Serve: 1
Ingredients:

- 3 pounds cubed beef stew meat
- ½ cup butter
- 1 (1 ounces) envelope dry onion soup mix

Directions:

- In a slow cooker, combine the meat and butter. Sprinkle with the onion soup mix. Cook on low for 8 hours or High for 4 to 5 hours, covered. Once or twice, stir the mixture.

Beef Bourguignon Without the Burgundy

Preparation Time: 20 minutes
Cooking Time: 20 minutes
Serve: 1
Ingredients:

- 1 (2 1/2 pound) boneless beef chuck roast
- salt and freshly ground black pepper
- 2 tablespoons vegetable oil
- 1 onion, chopped
- 1 tablespoon butter
- 2 tablespoons flour
- 2 cups Merlot wine

- 2 cups beef broth
- 2 carrots, cut into 1-inch pieces
- 2 stalks celery
- 4 sprigs of fresh thyme
- 1 bay leaf

Directions:

- Season the meat well with salt and pepper.
- In a large Dutch oven, heat the oil over high heat. Cook and stir beef cubes in heated oil for 10 to 15 minutes or browned on both sides. Place the meat on a platter.
- In a Dutch oven, cook and stir onion, butter, and a bit of salt until the onion begins to sweat. Next, cook and whisk the flour into the onion mixture for 3 to 4 minutes or until the onion softens.
- Pour wine into the onion mixture; bring to a boil and cook for 10 minutes, or until wine is reduced by half. Return the steak to the Dutch oven, along with any collected juices. Combine the beef broth, carrots, celery, thyme sprigs, bay leaf, and salt in a large pot. Bring to a simmer, cover with a lid, and cook for 1 1/2 hours on low or until the meat is almost tender.
- Remove the lid from the Dutch oven and continue to cook until the beef is cooked, and the stew is thick, about 30 minutes more. Season with salt and pepper to taste.

Baked Spanish Rice and Beef

Preparation Time: 15 minutes
Cooking Time: 25 minutes
Serve: 1
Ingredients:

- 1 (16 ounces) package ground beef
- 1 (28 ounces) can diced tomatoes
- 1 cup uncooked long-grain rice
- 1 cup chopped onion
- 1 cup chopped green bell pepper
- 1 teaspoon browning sauce
- 1 teaspoon salt
- 1 teaspoon chili powder
- ½ teaspoon ground black pepper
- ½ teaspoon dried thyme

Directions:

- Preheat the oven carefully to 350 degrees Fahrenheit (175 degrees C).
- Preheat a 4- to 6-quart Dutch oven on medium-high. Cook and stir the beef in the heated skillet for 5 to 7 minutes, or until it is browned and crumbly. Remove and discard the grease. Combine the tomatoes, rice, onion, green bell pepper, browning sauce, salt, chili powder, pepper, and thyme in a mixing bowl. Cover.
- Cook, tossing every 20 minutes until the rice is cooked, about 1 hour 10 minutes in a preheated oven.

Beef and Cheese Ball

Preparation Time: 15 minutes
Cooking Time: 20 minutes
Serve: 1
Ingredients:

- 1 (8 ounces) package cream cheese, softened
- 5 ounces dried beef
- 1 small white onion, chopped
- 1 small finely chopped green bell pepper

- 1 tablespoon Worcestershire sauce
- 1 teaspoon onion juice

Directions:

- Combine cream cheese, 2/3 of the meat, onion, green bell pepper, Worcestershire sauce, and onion juice in a medium mixing bowl. Mix well and roll the mixture into a ball. Coat the rest of the ball with the saved meat.

Simple Beef Stroganoff

Preparation Time: 20 minutes
Cooking Time: 25 minutes
Serve: 1
Ingredients:

- 1 (8 ounces) package egg noodles
- 1 pound ground beef
- 1 (10.75 ounces) can fat-free condensed cream of mushroom soup
- 1 tablespoon garlic powder
- ½ cup sour cream
- salt and pepper to taste

Directions:

- Set aside the egg noodles after cooking them according to package guidelines.
- Sauté the ground beef in a separate large pan over medium heat for 5 to 10 minutes or browned. After draining the fat, add the soup and garlic powder. Simmer, stirring periodically, for 10 minutes.
- Remove from the heat and toss in the meat mixture and egg noodles. Stir in the sour cream and season with salt and pepper to taste.

Corned Beef and Cabbage

Preparation Time: 15 minutes
Cooking Time: 20 minutes
Serve: 1
Ingredients:

- 1 pound kosher salt
- 2 gallons water, divided
- 8 pounds beef brisket
- 6 bay leaves
- 8 black peppercorns
- 1 onion, chopped
- 1 medium head cabbage, quartered
- 1-pound carrots, sliced
- 1 turnip, chopped
- 1 teaspoon chopped fresh cilantro
- 8 potatoes - peeled and cubed

Directions:

- Combine the salt, water, and beef in big stainless steel or cast-iron kettle. Allow it remains in the refrigerator for 7 days, covered. (Be aware that the brisket must be immersed, so increase the salt and water as needed.)
- Drain the brine after 7 days and replace it with 1 gallon of freshwater, bay leaves, and peppercorns. Bring to a boil, then lower to a low/medium-low heat and continue to cook for 3 to 3 1/2 hours.
- Add the onion, cabbage, carrots, turnip, cilantro, and potatoes during the last 45 minutes of simmering. Continue to cook until all of the veggies are soft.

Corned Beef and Cabbage
Preparation Time: 15 minutes
Cooking Time: 18 minutes
Serve: 1
Ingredients:
- 1 pound kosher salt
- 2 gallons water, divided
- 8 pounds beef brisket
- 6 bay leaves
- 8 black peppercorns
- 1 onion, chopped
- 1 medium head cabbage, quartered
- 1-pound carrots, sliced
- 1 turnip, chopped
- 1 teaspoon chopped fresh cilantro
- 8 potatoes - peeled and cubed

Directions:
- Add salt, water, and beef in big stainless steel or cast-iron saucepan. Refrigerate for 7 days, covered. (Note: Brisket must be totally immersed, so increase the salt and water if required.)
- After 7 days, remove the brine and replace it with 1 gallon of freshwater, bay leaves, and peppercorns. Bring to a boil, then lower to a low/medium-low heat and simmer for 3 to 3 1/2 hours.
- Add the onion, cabbage, carrots, turnip, cilantro, and potatoes in the last 45 minutes of simmering. Continue to boil until all of the veggies are soft.

Easy Vegetable Beef Soup
Preparation Time: 15 minutes
Cooking Time: 22 minutes
Serve: 1
Ingredients:
- 1 pound ground beef
- 2 quarts water
- 1 (14.5 ounces) can diced tomatoes
- 1 onion, chopped
- 4 potatoes, peeled and cubed
- 1 (16 ounces) package frozen mixed vegetables
- 8 cubes beef bouillon, crumbled
- ½ teaspoon ground black pepper

Directions:
- Cook beef until brown in a large saucepan over medium heat; drain.
- Cooked meat, water, tomatoes, onion, potatoes, mixed veggies, bouillon, and pepper in a large saucepan over medium heat. Bring to a boil, lower to low heat, and cook for 45 minutes.

Roasted Lamb Breast
Preparation Time: 10 minutes
Cooking Time: 18 minutes
Serve: 1
Ingredients:
- 2 tablespoons olive oil
- 2 teaspoons salt
- 2 teaspoons ground cumin
- 1 teaspoon freshly ground black pepper
- 1 teaspoon dried Italian herb seasoning
- 1 teaspoon ground cinnamon
- 1 teaspoon ground coriander
- 1 teaspoon paprika
- 4 pounds lamb breast, separated into two pieces
- ½ cup chopped Italian flat-leaf parsley
- ⅓ cup white wine vinegar, more as needed
- 1 lemon, juiced
- 2 cloves garlic, crushed
- 1 teaspoon honey
- ½ teaspoon red pepper flakes
- 1 pinch salt

Directions:
- Preheat the oven carefully to 300°F (150 degrees C).
- In a large mixing bowl, combine chopped parsley, vinegar, fresh lemon juice, garlic, honey, red pepper flakes, and salt. Set aside after thoroughly mixing.
- Add olive oil, salt, cumin, black pepper, dried Italian herbs, cinnamon, coriander, and paprika in a large mixing bowl.
- Coat each lamb breast in the olive oil and spice mixture and place fat side up in a roasting pan.
- Cover the roasting pan tightly with aluminum foil and bake for 2 hours, or until the flesh is tender when probed with a fork.
- Take the lamb out of the oven and chop it into four pieces.
- Raise the oven temperature to 450°F (230 degrees C).
- Place the lamb on a baking sheet lined with aluminum foil. Brush the tops of each piece with the roasting pan fat drippings.
- Bake, the lamb for 20 minutes, or until the flesh is browned and the edges are crispy.
- Turn the broiler too high and brown the lamb for 4 minutes. Then, take it out of the oven.
- Serve the lamb with parsley and vinegar sauce on the side.

Simple Grilled Lamb Chops
Preparation Time: 18 minutes
Cooking Time: 20 minutes
Serve: 2
Ingredients:
- ¼ cup distilled white vinegar
- 2 teaspoons salt
- ½ teaspoon black pepper
- 1 tablespoon minced garlic
- 1 onion, thinly sliced
- 2 tablespoons olive oil
- 2 pounds lamb chops

Directions:
- In a large resealable bag, combine the vinegar, salt, pepper, garlic, onion, and olive oil until the salt is dissolved. Add the lamb, stir to coat, and place in the refrigerator for 2 hours to marinade.
- Preheat the grill to medium-high heat.
- Remove the lamb from the marinade, leaving any onions stuck to the flesh. Any leftover marinade should be discarded. To protect the exposed ends of the bones from burning, wrap them with aluminum foil. Grill until done to preference, roughly 3 minutes per side for medium. The chops can also be grilled in the oven for about 5 minutes per side on medium heat.

Stuffed Greek Leg of Lamb

Preparation Time: 15 minutes
Cooking Time: 25 minutes
Serve: 1
Ingredients:

- 1 (3 1/2) pound leg of lamb
- olive oil
- 1 (12 ounces) jar marinated artichoke hearts
- 2 tablespoons chopped fresh oregano
- 2 tablespoons chopped fresh basil
- 1 (8 ounces) package crumbled feta cheese
- 1 (6 ounces) jar sun-dried tomatoes packed in oil, drained, and chopped
- 3 cloves garlic, minced
- salt and ground black pepper to taste

Directions:

- Preheat the oven carefully to 350°F (175 degrees C).
- Place the leg of lamb on a chopping board, with the interior facing you. Drizzle olive oil over the lamb in an equal layer. Season the lamb with oregano and basil. Season the lamb with salt and pepper and top with artichoke hearts, feta cheese, sun-dried tomatoes, and garlic.
- Wrap the lamb with the filling. To keep the lamb from unrolling, wrap it in kitchen twine. Next, wrap the lamb in foil and lay it in a baking dish.
- Roast in a preheated oven for 90 minutes, or until done to your liking, or an internal temperature of 150 degrees F (70 degrees C) for medium. Set aside for 10 minutes in a warm place before slicing. Keep the pan juices aside for dishing.

Chef John's Grilled Lamb with Mint Orange Sauce

Preparation Time: 20 minutes
Cooking Time: 20 minutes
Serve: 1
Ingredients:

- 2 pounds lamb loin chops
- 2 tablespoons olive oil
- 3 cloves garlic, minced
- 1 tablespoon cumin
- 1 teaspoon mixed herbs - Italian, Greek, or French blend
- ½ teaspoon black pepper
- ½ teaspoon ground coriander
- ¼ teaspoon cinnamon
- 1 pinch cayenne pepper
- salt as needed
- ¼ cup orange marmalade
- 1 pinch hot chili flakes
- ½ tablespoon rice vinegar
- 1 tablespoon chopped fresh mint

Directions:

- In a large mixing basin, combine the lamb chops. Season with the following ingredients: olive oil, garlic, cumin, mixed herbs, pepper, coriander, cinnamon, cayenne pepper, and salt. Toss until the oil and spices are well distributed. Refrigerate, covered. Allow at least 4 hours to marinate.
- Preheat an outside grill to high heat and brush the grate gently with oil. Place the lamb chops on the grill. Season the chops with salt and pepper. Grill until the first side is seared, 4 to 7 minutes, depending on the size of the chops. Before rotating the chops, give them a half-turn on the grill for about a minute. Next, turn and grill the other side until done, 4 to 7 minutes more. An instant-read thermometer put into the middle should read 125 to 130 degrees F for medium-rare (54 degrees C). Cover loosely with foil and transfer to a serving dish.
- Put the marmalade in a basin. Mix in the chili flakes, mint, and rice vinegar. Stir everything together completely.
- Serve with the sauce brushed over the chops.

Jinx-Proof Braised Lamb Shanks

Preparation Time: 15 minutes
Cooking Time: 25 minutes
Serve: 1
Ingredients:

- 5 ½ pounds lamb shanks
- 2 tablespoons olive oil
- salt and freshly ground black pepper
- ½ teaspoon dried rosemary
- ½ teaspoon dried thyme
- 1 tablespoon butter
- 1 onion, diced
- 1 rib celery, diced
- 1 large carrot, diced
- 1 ½ tablespoon all-purpose flour
- 4 cloves garlic, minced
- ½ cup red wine
- 1 cup chicken broth
- 1 cup water
- 1 tablespoon balsamic vinegar
- ⅛ teaspoon ground cinnamon
- 1 teaspoon minced fresh rosemary leaves

Directions:

- Preheat the oven carefully to 450°F (230 degrees C).
- Drizzle olive oil over lamb shanks in a roasting pan; season with salt, black pepper, dried rosemary, and thyme. Toss the lamb shanks in the oil and spices to coat.
- Cook until the lamb is browned, about 30 minutes in a preheated oven.
- Reduce the oven temperature to 325°F (165 degrees C).
- Melt butter in a saucepan over medium-high heat; cook and stir onion, celery, and carrot in the hot butter for 10 minutes, or until onion is browned. Combine flour and veggies in a mixing bowl; stir in garlic. Cook and stir for 1 minute more.
- Pour red wine into vegetable mixture and whisk to incorporate. Add chicken stock, water, balsamic vinegar, and cinnamon and stir to combine. In the roasting pan, pour the sauce over the lamb shanks. Cover the roasting pan with aluminum foil, loosely closing the foil to allow the sauce to decrease somewhat while it cooks.
- Bake the lamb shanks for 1 hour; turn the lamb shanks and replace the foil on the dish. Continue baking for another hour, or until a fork easily inserts into the flesh. Place the lamb shanks in a large mixing basin, cover with foil, and set aside for 10 minutes.
- Pour braising liquid into a saucepan and bring to a boil over high heat for 10 minutes, scraping fat as it reduces and thickens slightly. Stir in the rosemary, taste for salt and pepper, and serve the lamb shanks with the pan sauce.

Chile Pork

Preparation Time: 15 minutes
Cooking Time: 20 minutes

Serve: 1
Ingredients:
- 2 tablespoons chili powder
- 1 teaspoon salt
- 2 ½ teaspoons ground cumin
- 2 teaspoons minced garlic
- 1 tablespoon fresh cilantro
- 2 pounds pork tenderloin, cubed
- 1 dash ground black pepper

Directions:
- Chili powder, salt, cumin, garlic, cilantro, and pepper should be combined. Refrigerate pork cubes for 45 minutes after coating with the mixture.
- Preheat the oven carefully to 225°F (107 degrees C).
- Bake for 2 hours, or until crispy.

Pork Marinade
Preparation Time: 20 minutes
Cooking Time: 25 minutes
Serve: 1
Ingredients:
- ¼ cup dry mustard
- 1 ½ cups brown sugar
- ¾ cup chili sauce
- ¾ cup pineapple juice
- 2 teaspoons white sugar

Directions:
- Chill dry mustard, brown sugar, chili sauce, pineapple juice, and sugar.

Basic Pork Brine
Preparation Time: 15 minutes
Cooking Time: 20 minutes
Serve: 1
Ingredients:
- 2 cups water, more if needed
- 1 cup brown sugar
- 2 tablespoons kosher salt
- 3 cloves garlic, gently crushed
- 3 slices fresh ginger, gently crushed

Directions:
- In a mixing dish, combine water, brown sugar, and salt until the sugar is dissolved. Mix in the garlic and ginger.

Honey-Grilled Pork Chops
Preparation Time: 15 minutes
Cooking Time: 18 minutes
Serve: 1
Ingredients:
- ½ cup honey
- 6 tablespoons soy sauce
- 3 tablespoons lemon juice
- 2 teaspoons minced garlic
- 6 pork chops

Directions:
- Combine the honey, soy sauce, lemon juice, and garlic in a mixing dish until the marinade is smooth. Pour the marinade into a resealable plastic bag, keeping about 1/4 cup in a bowl for basting. Then add the pork chops to the bag, coat with the marinade, compress the bag to remove excess air, and

close the bag; marinate for at least 5 hours in the refrigerator.
- Preheat the grill to medium-high heat and liberally oil the grill grate. Shake off any excess marinade from the pork chops. Discard any leftover marinade.
- Grill the pork chops on a hot grill for 15 to 20 minutes, basting with the remaining marinade in the final few minutes, or until cooked through. In the center, an instant-read thermometer should register 145 degrees F. (63 degrees C). Allow 3 minutes for the pork chops to rest before serving.

Tim's Smoked Pork Butt
Preparation Time: 15 minutes
Cooking Time: 22 minutes
Serve: 1
Ingredients:
- ⅔ cup brown sugar substitute (such as Sukrin® Gold)
- 3 tablespoons applewood rub seasoning (such as McCormick® Grill Mates®)
- 2 tablespoons onion powder
- 2 tablespoons smoked paprika
- 1 tablespoon garlic powder
- 1 tablespoon salt
- 1 tablespoon ground black pepper
- 8 pounds boneless pork butt
- 2 (12 fluid ounces) cans or bottles of stout beer, divided
- 2 (12 fluid ounces) bottles of hard apple cider, divided

Directions:
- Season with brown sugar replacement, applewood rub, onion powder, smoked paprika, garlic powder, salt, and pepper in a mixing bowl.
- Trim the butt of the pig but leave a layer of fat on one side. 1/2 cup seasoning blend should be applied to the entire pork butt. Refrigerate for three days, covered with plastic wrap. Set aside any leftover spice blend for another use.
- Preheat, the smoker to 230°F (110 degrees C). Fill the smoker with your preferred wood chips or pellets.
- Place the pork butt onto the center rack, fat side up. In a drip pan, combine 12 ounces of stout and 12 ounces of cider.
- Pork should be smoked for 4 hours. Add the rest of the stout and cider to the drip pan, along with more wood chips or pellets. Continue to smoke for another 3 hours. Remove the drip pan and save the drippings in a basin.
- Continue to smoke the pork for 1 to 3 hours more, or until a meat thermometer reads 196 degrees F (91 degrees C). Then, allow for an hour of relaxation.
- Using two forks, pull the pork apart. Pour as much of the conserved drippings as you like over the pulled pork. Serve.

Simply the Easiest Beef Brisket
Preparation Time: 10 minutes
Cooking Time: 18 minutes
Serve: 1
Ingredients:
- 1 (3 pounds) beef brisket, trimmed of fat
- 1 medium onion, thinly sliced
- salt and pepper to taste
- 1 (12 fluid ounces) can of beer
- 1 (12 ounces) bottle tomato-based chili sauce
- ¾ cup packed brown sugar

Directions:

- Preheat the oven carefully to 325 degrees Fahrenheit (165 degrees C).
- Season the brisket with salt and pepper on all sides and set it in a glass baking dish. Add a layer of sliced onions on top. Combine the beer, chili sauce, and brown sugar in a medium mixing bowl. Pour the sauce over the roast. Wrap the dish in aluminum foil securely.
- In a preheated oven, bake for 3 hours. Bake for a further 30 minutes after removing the aluminum foil. Allow the brisket to rest for a few minutes before slicing and returning to the dish. Reheat in the oven, spooning the sauce over the cut meat.

Best Ever Beef Marinade
Preparation Time: 18 minutes

Cooking Time: 20 minutes
Serve: 1
Ingredients:

- 1 cup vegetable oil
- ¾ cup soy sauce
- ½ cup lemon juice
- ¼ cup Worcestershire sauce
- ¼ cup Dijon mustard
- 1 clove garlic, minced
- salt and ground black pepper to taste

Directions:

- Combine the vegetable oil, soy sauce, lemon juice, Worcestershire sauce, Dijon mustard, and garlic in a mixing bowl. Season with salt and pepper to taste.

CHAPTER 6:

Fish & Seafood

Tender & Flaky Salmon
Preparation Time: 10 minutes
Cooking Time: 8 minutes
Serve: 2
Ingredients:
- 2 salmon fillets
- ¼ tsp lemon pepper seasoning
- 2 tsp olive oil
- 1/8 tsp garlic powder
- 2 tsp brown sugar
- Pepper
- Salt

Directions:
- Preheat the air fryer to 400 F.
- In a small bowl, mix together lemon pepper seasoning, garlic powder, sugar, pepper, and salt.
- Brush salmon fillets with oil and rub with spice mixture.
- Place salmon fillets into the air fryer basket and cook for 6-8 minutes.
- Serve and enjoy.

Spicy Prawns
Preparation Time: 10 minutes
Cooking Time: 8 minutes
Serve: 2
Ingredients:
- 6 prawns
- 1/4 tsp pepper
- 1 tsp chili powder
- 1 tsp chili flakes, crushed
- 1/4 tsp salt

Directions:
- Preheat the air fryer to 350 F.
- In a bowl, toss shrimp with remaining ingredients.
- Transfer prawns into the air fryer basket and cook for 6-8 minutes.
- Serve and enjoy.

Shrimp Skewers
Preparation Time: 10 minutes
Cooking Time: 8 minutes
Serve: 2
Ingredients:
- 1 cup raw shrimp
- 1 garlic clove, minced
- ¼ tsp paprika
- 1 tbsp parsley, minced

- 1 fresh lime juice
- Pepper
- Salt

Directions:
- Preheat the air fryer to 350 F.
- In a bowl, mix shrimp with remaining ingredients.
- Thread shrimp onto the skewers and place skewers into the air fryer basket and cook for 8 minutes.
- Serve and enjoy.

Chipotle Lime Shrimp
Preparation Time: 10 minutes
Cooking Time: 8 minutes
Serve: 4
Ingredients:
- 1 1/2 lbs. shrimp, peeled and deveined
- 4 tbsp fresh lime juice
- 1/4 tsp ground cumin
- 2 tsp chipotle in adobo
- 2 tbsp canola oil
- Pepper
- Salt

Directions:
- Preheat the air fryer to 350 F.
- Add shrimp and remaining ingredients in a zip-lock bag. Seal bag and place in the refrigerator for 30 minutes.
- Thread marinated shrimp onto skewers and place skewers into the air fryer basket and cook for 8 minutes. Turn halfway through.
- Serve and enjoy.

Lemon Garlic Shrimp
Preparation Time: 10 minutes
Cooking Time: 6 minutes
Serve: 4
Ingredients:
- 1 lb. shrimp
- 1 tbsp parsley, chopped
- 2 tsp fresh lemon juice
- 2 tsp Canola oil
- 1 tsp lemon zest, grated
- 1 tsp steak seasoning
- 1/4 tsp red pepper flakes
- 1 tsp garlic, minced
- Pepper
- Salt

Directions:
- Preheat the air fryer to 400 F.

- Add shrimp and remaining ingredients into the bowl and toss well.
- Transfer shrimp into the air fryer basket and cook for 6 minutes.
- Serve and enjoy.

Creole Shrimp
Preparation Time: 10 minutes
Cooking Time: 7 minutes
Serve: 2
Ingredients:
- 1/2 lb. shrimp, deveined and shelled
- 1 tsp Creole seasoning
- 1/4 tsp paprika
- 1 tbsp canola oil
- 1 tsp vinegar
- 1/8 tsp cayenne
- Pepper
- Salt

Directions:
- Preheat the air fryer to 400 F.
- Add shrimp and remaining ingredients into the bowl and mix well.
- Add marinated shrimp into the air fryer basket and cook for 5-7 minutes.
- Serve and enjoy.

Lemon Scallops
Preparation Time: 10 minutes
Cooking Time: 12 minutes
Serve: 2
Ingredients:
- 8 scallops, cleaned and pat dry
- 2 tbsp parsley, chopped
- 1/4 cup canola oil
- 1/2 tsp garlic, chopped
- 1 tsp lemon zest, grated
- 2 tsp capers, chopped
- 1/4 tsp pepper
- 1/8 tsp salt

Directions:
- Preheat the air fryer to 400 F.
- Add scallops and remaining ingredients into the bowl and mix well.
- Add scallops into the air fryer basket and cook for 12 minutes. Turn halfway through.
- Serve and enjoy.

Asian Salmon
Preparation Time: 10 minutes
Cooking Time: 8 minutes
Serve: 4
Ingredients:
- 4 salmon fillets
- 2 tsp soy sauce
- 1 tsp sesame seeds, toasted
- 1 tbsp honey
- Pepper
- Salt

Directions:
- Preheat the air fryer to 375 F.
- Brush salmon with soy sauce and season with pepper and salt.
- Place salmon into the air fryer basket and cook for 8 minutes.
- Brush salmon with honey and sprinkle with sesame seeds.
- Serve and enjoy.

Herb Salmon
Preparation Time: 10 minutes
Cooking Time: 15 minutes
Serve: 4
Ingredients:
- 1 lb. salmon fillets
- 1/4 tsp dried basil
- 1 tbsp dried chives
- 1 tbsp canola oil
- 1/2 tbsp dried rosemary
- Pepper
- Salt

Directions:
- Preheat the air fryer to 400 F.
- In a small bowl, mix oil, basil, rosemary, and chives and brush over salmon.
- Place salmon fillets into the air fryer basket and cook for 15 minutes. Turn halfway through.
- Serve and enjoy.

Honey Garlic Salmon
Preparation Time: 10 minutes
Cooking Time: 20 minutes
Serve: 2
Ingredients:
- 2 salmon fillets
- 1 fresh lime juice
- 1/4 cup butter, melted
- 1/2 tbsp garlic, minced
- 2 tbsp honey
- Pepper
- Salt

Directions:
- Preheat the air fryer to 350 F.
- In a small bowl, mix honey, garlic, pepper, lime juice, butter, and salt.
- Brush salmon with honey mixture and place into the air fryer basket and cook for 12-15 minutes.
- Serve and enjoy.

Wonderful Fried Fish Tacos
Preparation Time: 15 minutes
Cooking Time: 25 minutes
Serve: 1
Ingredients:
- 1 cup dark beer
- 1 cup all-purpose flour
- ½ teaspoon salt
- 1 ½ pounds cod fillets, cubed
- 1-quart vegetable oil for frying

- 20 (6 inches) corn tortillas
- 5 cups shredded cabbage
- 1 cup mayonnaise
- ¼ cup salsa
- 1 lime, cut into wedges

Directions:

- Whisk together the beer, flour, and salt in a small basin.
- Rinse and pat dry the fish. Cut each piece into ten equal pieces.
- 1-inch oil, heated to 360 degrees F in a big saucepan (168 degrees C). Coat the fish in batter with a fork. Drop coated fish into heated oil; adjust heat to maintain oil temperature. Fry for about 2 minutes, or until golden. Remove with a slotted spoon and quickly drain on paper towels; keep heated. Fry the remaining fish in the same manner.
- 2 tortillas stacked Fill the tortillas with a salmon and 1/2 cup cabbage. Garnish with mayonnaise, lime wedges, and salsa if desired.

Marinated Fried Fish

Preparation Time: 20 minutes
Cooking Time: 20 minutes
Serve: 1
Ingredients:

- 2 (4 ounces) fillets flounder
- 2 tablespoons lemon juice
- 2 tablespoons chopped garlic
- 2 teaspoons ground cumin
- 1 teaspoon paprika
- ½ cup all-purpose flour
- 1 teaspoon dried dill weed
- ¼ teaspoon cayenne pepper, or to taste
- 1 egg, beaten
- 1 tablespoon water
- 1 cup vegetable oil for frying

Directions:

- Fillets of flounder should be placed in a small glass dish. Combine lemon juice, garlic, cumin, and paprika; pour over flounder fillets. Cover the dish with plastic wrap and place the flounder in the refrigerator for 2 hours to marinade.
- On a piece of waxed paper, combine the flour, dill weed, and cayenne pepper.
- In a large mixing basin, combine the egg and water.
- In a large skillet over medium heat, heat the oil.
- To coat the flounder fillets, gently press them into the flour mixture; shake to remove excess flour. Dip into the beaten egg to coat, then back into the flour mixture to coat.
- Fry flounder in heated oil for 5 minutes per side, or until the fish flakes readily with a fork.

Baked Fish Fillets

Preparation Time: 15 minutes
Cooking Time: 25 minutes
Serve: 1
Ingredients:

- 1 tablespoon vegetable oil, or to taste
- 2 pounds mackerel fillets
- 1 teaspoon salt
- ⅛ teaspoon ground black pepper
- ¼ cup butter, melted
- 2 tablespoons lemon juice

- ⅛ teaspoon ground paprika

Directions:

- Preheat the oven carefully to 350°F (175 degrees C). Vegetable oil should be used to grease a baking pan.
- Season the mackerel fillets in the baking pan with salt and pepper.
- Combine the butter, lemon juice, and paprika in a mixing dish. Serve with mackerel fillets.
- Cook in a preheated oven for 20 to 25 minutes or until the mackerel flakes easily with a fork.

Easy Baked Fish with Lemon

Preparation Time: 15 minutes
Cooking Time: 20 minutes
Serve: 1
Ingredients:

- 1 serving cooking spray
- 2 pounds tilapia fillets, cut into serving-sized pieces
- 1 cup dry seasoned breadcrumbs
- 2 tablespoons dried parsley
- 2 teaspoons lemon zest
- ½ teaspoon garlic powder
- ¼ cup melted butter

Directions:

- Preheat the oven carefully to 350 degrees Fahrenheit (175 degrees C). Coat a baking dish with nonstick cooking spray.
- Place the fish in the prepared baking dish. Combine breadcrumbs, parsley, lemon zest, and garlic powder in a small mixing bowl. Mix in the melted butter and sprinkle over the fish fillets.
- Bake for 15 minutes in a preheated oven or until the tilapia flakes easily with a fork.

Air Fryer Blackened Fish Tacos

Preparation Time: 20 minutes
Cooking Time: 25 minutes
Serve: 1
Ingredients:

- 1 (15 ounces) can seasoned black beans, rinsed, and drained
- 2 ears corn, kernels cut it from the cob
- 1 tablespoon olive oil
- 1 tablespoon lime juice
- ½ teaspoon salt
- 1 pound tilapia fillets
- cooking spray
- ¼ cup blackened seasoning
- 4 (6 inches) corn tortillas
- 1 lime, cut into wedges
- 1 teaspoon Louisiana-style hot sauce (Optional)

Directions:

- Preheat the oven carefully to 400 degrees Fahrenheit (200 degrees C).
- Combine black beans, corn, olive oil, lime juice, and salt in a mixing dish. Set aside after gently stirring until the beans and corn are uniformly covered.
- Place the fish fillets on a clean work area and pat with paper towels to dry. Spray each fillet lightly with cooking spray and sprinkle with 1/2 of the blackened seasoning. Turn the fillets over, spray with cooking spray, and season with the rest of the spice.

- Place the fish in the air fryer basket in a single layer, working in batches if required. 2 minutes in the oven, cook for 2 minutes more on the other side before transferring to a platter.
- Cook for 10 minutes, stirring halfway through, in the bean and corn mixture, in the air fryer basket.
- Fill corn tortillas with fish and top with bean and corn mixture. Serve with lime wedges and spicy sauce on the side.

Tamarind Sauce Fish Curry

Preparation Time: 15 minutes
Cooking Time: 20 minutes
Serve: 1
Ingredients:

- 2 pounds white carp
- 1 cup warm water
- ¼ cup oil
- 1 tablespoon vegetable oil
- 1 tablespoon red chili powder
- 1 tablespoon ground turmeric
- 1 ½ teaspoons salt
- ¼ cup tamarind pulp
- ½ teaspoon cumin seeds
- 1 large onion, minced
- 1 ½ tablespoon garlic paste
- 1 pinch salt to taste
- 2 tablespoons red chili powder
- 2 tablespoons ground coriander
- 1 tablespoon chopped fresh coriander

Directions:

- Place the fish in a bowl and toss with 1 tablespoon vegetable oil, 1 tablespoon chili powder, turmeric, and 1 1/2 teaspoons salt for about 10 minutes.
- Pour warm water over the tamarind pulp in a dish. To obtain the juice from the tamarind, squeeze it.
- In a pan over medium heat, heat 1/4 cup oil; add cumin seeds and stir. Cook, constantly stirring, until the onion is transparent, 5 to 10 minutes. Cook for 3 minutes after adding the garlic paste. Cover the skillet and cook the carp for 5 minutes.
- Bring the fish mixture to a boil with the tamarind juice. Turn the carp pieces over and season with 2 teaspoons red chili powder, coriander, and salt. Cook over low heat for 10 minutes or until the sauce thickens and the oil separates. Garnish with coriander leaves if desired.

Poached Fish with Cucumbers

Preparation Time: 15 minutes
Cooking Time: 18 minutes
Serve: 1
Ingredients:

- 1 teaspoon salt
- 2 cucumbers, peeled, halved lengthwise, seeded, and chopped
- 1 cup whipping cream
- 2 tablespoons prepared mustard
- 2 teaspoons chopped fresh tarragon
- 2 cups white wine
- salt to taste
- 1 bay leaf
- 2 (3 ounces) fresh tilapia fillets

Directions:

- Allow the cucumber chunks to rest for 1 hour after sprinkling with salt. Cucumber liquid should be strained.
- In a saucepan over medium heat, combine the whipping cream, mustard, and tarragon; add the cucumbers and cook for 8 minutes.
- In a large skillet over medium heat, pour in the wine. Season with salt and pepper, then add the bay leaf. Bring the wine to a boil in a saucepan. Place the tilapia in the skillet, decrease the heat to medium-low, and cook for 8 to 10 minutes, or until the fish flakes easily with a fork. Cucumbers should be served on the side with the fish.

Air-Fried Crumbed Fish

Preparation Time: 15 minutes
Cooking Time: 22 minutes
Serve: 1
Ingredients:

- 1 cup dry breadcrumbs
- ¼ cup vegetable oil
- 4 flounder fillets
- 1 egg, beaten
- 1 lemon, sliced

Directions:

- Preheat an air fryer to 350°F (180 degrees C).
- In a mixing dish, combine breadcrumbs and oil. Stir until the mixture is loose and crumbly.
- Shake off any excess egg before dipping the fish fillets. Then, coat the fillets evenly and completely in the bread crumb mixture.
- Place the coated fillets in the preheated air fryer. Cook for 12 minutes, or until the salmon flakes easily with a fork. Garnish with lemon slices if desired.

Seasoned Swai Fish Fillet

Preparation Time: 10 minutes
Cooking Time: 18 minutes
Serve: 1
Ingredients:

- cooking spray
- 4 (4 ounces) fillets swai fish
- 2 tablespoons margarine
- ¼ cup dry white wine
- 1 tablespoon lemon juice
- 1 tablespoon chopped fresh cilantro (optional)
- 1 teaspoon minced garlic
- 1 teaspoon salt
- 1 teaspoon ground black pepper
- 1 teaspoon paprika

Directions:

- Preheat the oven carefully to 350°F (175 degrees C). Coat a shallow baking dish or baking sheet with cooking spray.
- Fillets of fish should be placed in the preheated pan.
- In a saucepan over medium heat, melt the margarine. In a small saucepan, combine the melted margarine, white wine, lemon juice, cilantro, garlic, salt, and black pepper; cook for 2 minutes. Spoon sauce generously over fish fillets. Season the fillets with paprika.
- Bake for 10 to 12 minutes, or until the salmon flakes easily with a fork.

Whole Fish Fried with Basil and Chiles
Preparation Time: 18 minutes
Cooking Time: 20 minutes
Serve: 1
Ingredients:

- 1 whole (10 ounces) tilapia, or more as desired
- oil for deep frying
- 1 tablespoon vegetable oil, or as desired
- 1 yellow onion, chopped
- 5 large red chili peppers, sliced
- 5 cloves garlic, chopped
- 2 tablespoons fish sauce
- 2 tablespoons light soy sauce
- ¼ cup Thai basil leaves, or to taste
- ¼ cup chopped fresh cilantro, or to taste

Directions:

- Make multiple angled incisions down the fish's body, all the way to the rib bones. Next, cut two lateral slits down the fish's back, one on each side of the dorsal fin, from head to tail. These slices are designed to cook quickly and crisply.
- Heat the frying oil to 350 degrees F. (175 degrees C) in a deep-fryer or big saucepan.
- Place the fish in the heated oil and cook until crispy, about 3 to 4 minutes on each side. Remove the fish from the oil and drain it on a dish lined with paper towels.
- In a wok or large pan, heat 1 tablespoon vegetable oil over medium heat; sauté and stir onion, red chili peppers and garlic until gently browned, 5 to 10 minutes. Remove the wok from the heat and add the fish sauce and soy sauce. Stir basil and cilantro into sauce quickly.
- Place the fish on a large serving plate and drizzle with the sauce.

Baja Sauce for Fish or Shrimp Tacos
Preparation Time: 15 minutes
Cooking Time: 25 minutes
Serve: 1
Ingredients:

- ¼ cup sour cream
- ¼ cup mayonnaise
- 1 teaspoon lime juice
- 1 teaspoon finely chopped fresh cilantro
- ¾ teaspoon seafood seasoning (such as Old Bay®)
- ¼ teaspoon ground ancho chili pepper

Directions:

- Combine the sour cream, mayonnaise, lime juice, cilantro, seafood seasoning, and ancho chili pepper in a mixing bowl.
- Refrigerate for at least 1 hour, covered with plastic wrap.

Indian Fish Curry
Preparation Time: 20 minutes
Cooking Time: 20 minutes
Serve: 1
Ingredients:

- 2 teaspoons Dijon mustard
- 1 teaspoon ground black pepper
- ½ teaspoon salt
- 2 tablespoons canola oil
- 4 white fish fillets
- 1 onion, coarsely chopped
- 4 cloves garlic, roughly chopped
- 1 (1 inch) piece fresh ginger root
- 5 cashew halves
- 1 tablespoon canola oil
- 2 teaspoons cayenne pepper, or to taste
- ½ teaspoon ground turmeric
- 1 teaspoon ground cumin
- 1 teaspoon ground coriander
- 1 teaspoon salt
- 1 teaspoon white sugar
- ½ cup chopped tomato
- ¼ cup vegetable broth
- ¼ cup chopped fresh cilantro

Directions:

- Combine the mustard, pepper, 1/2 teaspoon salt, and 2 tablespoons canola oil in a small dish. Pour in the fish fillets and flip to coat. Refrigerate the salmon for 30 minutes to allow it to marinate.
- In a blender or food processor, combine the onion, garlic, ginger, and cashews and pulse until the mixture forms a paste.
- Preheat the oven carefully to 350°F (175 degrees C).
- In a skillet over medium-low heat, heat 1 tablespoon canola oil. Cook and stir for a minute or two after adding the prepared paste. Combine the cayenne pepper, turmeric, cumin, coriander, 1 teaspoon salt, and sugar in a mixing bowl. Cook and stir for another five minutes. Combine the chopped tomato and vegetable broth in a mixing bowl.
- Place the fish fillets in a baking tray and discard any excess marinade. Top the fish with the sauce, cover the baking dish, and bake for 30 minutes, or until the fish flakes easily with a fork. Garnish with cilantro, if desired.

Portuguese Cod Fish Casserole
Preparation Time: 15 minutes
Cooking Time: 25 minutes
Serve: 1
Ingredients:

- 2 pounds salted codfish
- 5 large potatoes, peeled and sliced
- 3 large onions, sliced
- ¾ cup olive oil
- 2 cloves garlic, minced
- 1 tablespoon chopped fresh parsley
- 1 ½ teaspoon crushed red pepper flakes
- 1 teaspoon paprika
- 3 tablespoons tomato sauce

Directions:

- Soak salted fish in cold water for several hours or overnight. Drain the water and repeat. Bring a big saucepan of water to a boil. Cook the fish for 5 minutes before draining and cooling it in big slices. Place aside.
- Preheat the oven carefully to 375°F (190 degrees C).
- Layer half of the potato pieces, the fish, and all of the onions in an 8x11 casserole dish. Finish with the remaining potato slices. Combine the olive oil, garlic, parsley, pepper flakes, paprika, and tomato sauce in a small mixing bowl. Distribute evenly over casserole.
- Bake for 45 minutes, or until potatoes are cooked, in a preheated oven.

Crispy Beer Batter Fish & Chips

Preparation Time: 15 minutes
Cooking Time: 20 minutes
Serve: 1
Ingredients:

- 1 cup self-rising flour
- 2 tablespoons rice flour
- ¼ teaspoon baking powder
- 2 tablespoons rice flour, or as needed
- salt to taste
- 4 (6 ounces) cod fillets
- 1 cup lager-style beer
- vegetable oil for frying

Directions:

- Combine self-rising flour, rice flour, and baking powder in a mixing bowl. Place in the freezer until ready to use.
- Pat the fish dry as much as possible. Cut each piece lengthwise to make eight 1-inch-thick strips. Season rice flour with salt and spread it out on a platter. Shake off any excess mixture before gently dusting the fish. Cover a dish with crinkled foil to create a rapid drying rack, then set the fish on top.
- Heat the oil in a deep fryer to 375°F (190 degrees C).
- Pour the beer into the flour mixture and stir until the batter is the consistency of the thick pancake batter. Dip the fish pieces into the batter to coat them, pull them out and allow the excess drip off.
- Fry the fish in batches until golden brown, 3 to 4 minutes, dipping periodically if necessary. Using paper towels, drain. Serve right away.

Parchment-Cooked Fish with Morels, Spring Garlic, and Thyme

Preparation Time: 20 minutes
Cooking Time: 25 minutes
Serve: 1
Ingredients:

- 1-pound fresh morel mushrooms
- salt and ground black pepper to taste
- 4 (6 ounces) Pacific halibut fillets
- 1 ½ teaspoons butter
- ½ cup chopped garlic scapes
- 5 sprigs fresh thyme, leaves stripped
- 1 tablespoon canola oil
- 4 12x20-inch pieces of parchment paper

Directions:

- Preheat the oven carefully to 350°F (175 degrees C).
- In a dry skillet over medium heat, season morel mushrooms with salt and black pepper. Cook, often stirring, for 5 minutes, or until the mushrooms release their juice and the liquid evaporates.
- Season both sides of the halibut fillets with salt and black pepper.
- Cook the halibut fillets in a large pan with butter over medium-low heat until golden brown on the exterior, about 2 minutes on each side. Remove the fish from the skillet and put it aside.
- In the same skillet used to cook the fish, sauté, and stir garlic scapes until fragrant, about 1 minute. Remove the pan from the heat and add the morel mushrooms, thyme, and garlic scapes.

- Crosswise fold a piece of parchment paper in half. Cut a giant valentine-like heart form out of the folded paper with scissors, as large as possible. Rep with the remaining sheet to create four huge heart shapes.
- Brush the right sides of the hearts with canola oil after opening the heart forms.
- 1/4 morel mushroom combination should be placed on each heart's left (unoiled) side. Arrange a halibut fillet on top of the mushroom mixture. Season the fish with salt and black pepper to taste.
- Fold the right side of the slippery heart over the fish. Starting at the rounded end, fold about 1/4 inch of parchment paper over and work your way down to the tip, folding as you go. Fold the edge over a second time to surround the fish and mushrooms in a double-folded, sealed bundle. Allow roughly a quarter inch of the bottom point to be unfurled.
- Blow air into the bundle using a straw put into the open bottom to make it puff out like a little balloon. Twist the bottom shut to seal in the air.
- Place the parchment bundles on two baking pans, ensuring they don't touch.
- Bake in a preheated oven for 15 minutes or until the fish is no longer transparent in the center.
- To serve, gently rip apart the paper and plate each slice to reveal the fish, mushrooms, and liquids. When the bundle is opened, heated steam will be released.

Smoked Fish Dip

Preparation Time: 15 minutes
Cooking Time: 20 minutes
Serve: 1
Ingredients:

- 2 cups flaked smoked whitefish
- 2 tablespoons fat-free mayonnaise
- 4 tablespoons fat-free sour cream
- 1 pinch Old Bay (TM) Seasoning
- 4 drops hot pepper sauce
- 3 drops Worcestershire sauce, or to taste
- 3 drops liquid smoke flavoring (optional)
- cracked black pepper to taste

Directions:

- Combine the whitefish, mayonnaise, and sour cream in a food processor. Old Bay TM seasoning, spicy pepper sauce, Worcestershire sauce, liquid smoke, and crushed black pepper Blend all ingredients together until the consistency resembles a spread.

Easy Elegant Baked Fish

Preparation Time: 15 minutes
Cooking Time: 18 minutes
Serve: 1
Ingredients:

- 2 pounds swai fish
- ¼ cup butter, melted
- ¼ teaspoon garlic powder, or to taste
- ¼ teaspoon garlic pepper seasoning, or to taste
- salt to taste
- 1 lemon, thinly sliced
- 1 tablespoon capers

Directions:

- Preheat the oven carefully to 350°F (175 degrees C).

- Place the fish in a baking dish and sprinkle with melted butter, season with garlic powder, garlic pepper spice, and salt. Garnish the fish with lemon wedges and capers.
- Bake for 15 to 20 minutes, or until the salmon flakes easily with a fork.

Crunchy Fish Tacos
Preparation Time: 15 minutes
Cooking Time: 22 minutes
Serve: 1
Ingredients:
- 9 each Old El Paso® taco shells
- 1 pound tilapia fillets
- 2 teaspoons Old El Paso
- 8 (6 inches) Old El Paso
- 1 cup Pico de Gallo salsa
- ½ cup sour cream

Directions:
- Preheat the oven carefully to 425°F. Line a cookie sheet with aluminum foil.
- Fill a 1-gallon resealable food-storage plastic bag halfway with taco shells. Seal the bag and crush the shells with a rolling pin. Shake in taco seasoning mix until thoroughly combined.
- Tilapia fillets, cut into 3x1-inch chunks. Place the fillet pieces in the bag and press the crumbs onto them to coat. Place on a baking sheet. Bake for 15 minutes, flipping halfway through. Place two slices of each on a tortilla. Toppings are optional. Roll the tortillas up.

Beth's Baked Fish
Preparation Time: 10 minutes
Cooking Time: 18 minutes
Serve: 1
Ingredients:
- ¼ cup unsalted butter, melted
- ½ teaspoon seasoned salt
- ½ teaspoon dried dill weed
- ¼ teaspoon garlic powder
- 2 (4 ounces) fillets cod fillets

Directions:
- Preheat the oven carefully to 350°F (175 degrees C).
- Combine the melted butter, seasoned salt, dill weed, and garlic powder in a small mixing bowl. Fill a large baking dish halfway with the mixture. Turn the fish fillets to cover both sides.
- Cook in a preheated oven for 20 to 30 minutes or until the cod flakes easily with a fork.

Chicken-Cheese-Fish
Preparation Time: 18 minutes
Cooking Time: 20 minutes
Serve: 1
Ingredients:
- 2 pounds skinless, boneless chicken breast halves
- 4 cups shredded Cheddar cheese
- 1 cup shredded Swiss cheese
- 4 (3 ounces) cans of tuna packed in olive oil
- 2 (16 ounces) cans pink salmon, drained
- 2 cups heavy whipping cream

- 4 eggs, beaten
- 2 cups crumbled feta
- 1 cup shredded mozzarella cheese
- 2 cups ricotta cheese
- 1 (8 ounces) package cream cheese, softened
- 2 eggs, beaten
- 3 cups Italian seasoned breadcrumbs
- 2 tablespoons butter, cut into small pieces

Directions:
- Preheat the oven carefully to 350°F (175 degrees C).
- Fill a large baking dish halfway with chicken breasts. Sprinkle with Cheddar and Swiss cheeses. Layer the tuna and salmon on the cheese in an equal layer. In a mixing bowl, combine the whipped cream and the 4 beaten eggs; pour over the top of the dish.
- In a mixing dish, combine the feta, mozzarella, and ricotta cheeses; distribute over the fish. Next, combine the cream cheese, 2 beaten eggs, and breadcrumbs; spread evenly over the cheese. Finally, arrange little slices of butter evenly throughout the entire dish. Wrap with aluminum foil.
- Bake for 1 1/2 hours, or until cooked through and golden brown on top, in a preheated oven.

Mexican Baked Fish
Preparation Time: 15 minutes
Cooking Time: 25 minutes
Serve: 1
Ingredients:
- 1 ½ pounds cod
- 1 cup salsa
- 1 cup shredded sharp Cheddar cheese
- ½ cup coarsely crushed corn chips
- 1 avocado - peeled, pitted, and sliced
- ¼ cup sour cream

Directions:
- Preheat the oven carefully to 400°F (200 degrees C). Grease one 8x12 inch baking dish lightly.
- Fish fillets should be rinsed under cold water and patted dry with paper towels. Place the fillets in the prepared baking dish side by side. Pour the salsa over the top, then equally sprinkle with the shredded cheese. Crush the corn chips on top.
- Bake for 15 minutes, uncovered, in a preheated oven, or until the fish is opaque and flakes with a fork. Serve with sliced avocado and sour cream on top.

Classic Fish and Chips
Preparation Time: 20 minutes
Cooking Time: 20 minutes
Serve: 1
Ingredients:
- 4 large potatoes, peeled and cut into strips
- 1 teaspoon baking powder
- 1 cup all-purpose flour
- 1 teaspoon ground black pepper
- 1 teaspoon salt
- 1 cup milk
- 1 egg
- 1-quart vegetable oil for frying
- 1 ½ pounds cod fillets

Directions:

- Place the potatoes in a medium dish of cool water. In a medium-sized mixing basin, combine the flour, baking powder, salt, and pepper separately. Whisk in the milk and egg and continue to stir until the mixture is smooth. Allow the mixture to stand for 20 minutes.
- Preheat the oil to 350°F in a big pot or electric skillet (175 degrees C).
- Fry the potatoes until they are soft in heated oil. They should be drained on paper towels.
- Dredge the fish in the batter, one piece at a time, and fry in heated oil. Fry the fish till golden brown. Increase the heat as needed to keep the temperature at 350 degrees F (175 degrees C). Drain well on paper towels.
- Fry the potatoes for another 1 to 2 minutes to enhance crispness.

Fish and Things Teriyaki Marinade
Preparation Time: 15 minutes
Cooking Time: 25 minutes
Serve: 1
Ingredients:

- 2 cups soy sauce
- ¾ cup brown sugar, divided
- ¾ cup white sugar, divided
- 8 green onions
- 1 clove garlic, chopped
- 4 slices fresh ginger root
- 1 cup honey

Directions:

- In a 2-quart saucepan, combine soy sauce, 1/2 cup brown sugar, 1/2 cup white sugar, green onions, ginger, and garlic. Bring the mixture to a simmer. Reduce the heat to low and continue to cook for 15 minutes.
- Pour in the remaining whites and brown sugar, as well as the honey. Bring the water to a boil. When the mixture rises and foams and doubles in size, take it from the fire and set it aside to cool.

Fish Tacos from Reynolds Wrap
Preparation Time: 15 minutes
Cooking Time: 20 minutes
Serve: 1
Ingredients:

- Reynolds Wrap® Non-Stick Aluminum Foil
- 4 (4 ounces) tilapia fillets, fresh or frozen (thawed)
- 1 tablespoon fresh lime juice
- 1 teaspoon olive oil
- 1 teaspoon seafood seasoning
- 1 clove garlic, minced
- ½ teaspoon salt
- ⅛ teaspoon red pepper flakes
- 8 (8 inches) flour tortillas
- Shredded lettuce
- Mango salsa
- Sliced avocado

Directions:

- Preheat the oven carefully to 400°F. Line a 13x9x2-inch baking sheet with Reynolds Wrap® Nonstick Foil, nonstick (dull) side up.
- Place the tilapia in a pan lined with foil.

- Combine lime juice, olive oil, seafood seasoning, garlic, salt, and red pepper flakes in a medium mixing bowl. Pour over the fish.
- Bake for 18 to 20 minutes, or until the salmon flakes easily with a fork. Fill each tortilla with 1/2 fillet, lettuce, salsa, and avocado.

Cerveza and Lime Marinade for Shrimp and Fish
Preparation Time: 20 minutes
Cooking Time: 25 minutes
Serve: 1
Ingredients:

- 2 cups minced onion
- ½ cup chopped fresh cilantro
- ½ cup seeded, minced jalapeno pepper
- ¼ cup minced garlic
- 1 cup oil
- ¾ cup fresh lime juice
- ½ cup Mexican beer
- 2 tablespoons tequila
- 1 tablespoon ground black pepper
- ½ tablespoon ground cumin

Directions:

- In a blender, combine the onion, cilantro, jalapeño pepper, garlic, oil, lime juice, beer, tequila, black pepper, and cumin until smooth. Marinate fish or shrimp in this marinade in the refrigerator for up to 2 hours before cooking.

Corn Crusted Red Fish
Preparation Time: 15 minutes
Cooking Time: 20 minutes
Serve: 1
Ingredients:

- 1 ½ cups fresh corn kernels
- 1 tablespoon red bell pepper, chopped
- 1 tablespoon red onion, chopped
- 1 tablespoon cornstarch
- 4 (5 ounces) red snapper fillets
- 1 teaspoon Creole seasoning, or to taste
- 1 cup all-purpose flour
- 3 egg whites, lightly beaten
- 1 tablespoon vegetable oil

Directions:

- Preheat the oven carefully to 350°F (175 degrees C). In a mixing dish, combine corn kernels, bell pepper, onion, and cornstarch; put aside.
- Season the red snapper with the Creole seasoning. Dip the fish in the flour, then in the egg whites. Coat both sides of the fish with the corn mixture by pushing it into the egg whites.
- In an oven-safe skillet, heat the vegetable oil over medium-high heat. Fry the fillets in the pan until brown, about 5 minutes per side. Place the pan in the preheated oven and cook for another 5 minutes, or until the fish flakes easily with a fork.

Halibut Fish Tacos
Preparation Time: 15 minutes
Cooking Time: 18 minutes

Serve: 1
Ingredients:

- 1 lime, juiced
- ¼ cup olive oil
- ¼ cup chopped cilantro
- 1 jalapeno pepper, diced
- 1 tablespoon ground ancho chili powder
- ¼ teaspoon ground cumin
- salt and ground black pepper to taste
- ½ pound halibut fillets
- 8 corn tortillas
- 2 cups shredded cabbage
- 1 (8 ounces) jar salsa
- 1 cup shredded pepper Jack cheese
- 1 avocado, sliced

Directions:

- In a large mixing bowl or resealable zip-top bag, combine lime juice, olive oil, cilantro, jalapeño, chili powder, cumin, salt, and pepper. Marinade the halibut for 20 to 25 minutes. Do not over marinate the fish since the lime juice will begin to 'cook' it.
- Preheat an outside grill to medium heat and brush the grate gently with oil. Drain marinade and cook fillets for 5 minutes on each side. Cook for another 2 minutes, or until the salmon flakes easily with a fork.
- Warm the tortillas on the grill or in the oven. Top tortillas with fish, cabbage, salsa, pepper Jack cheese, and avocado.

Beer Batter for Fish
Preparation Time: 15 minutes
Cooking Time: 22 minutes
Serve: 1
Ingredients:

- 3 eggs, ¾ cup beer
- 1 ½ cups milk
- 4 cups pastry flour
- 1 tablespoon baking powder
- ½ teaspoon baking soda
- 2 tablespoons cornstarch
- salt to taste
- ground black pepper to taste
- .063 teaspoon garlic powder
- 1 ½ pounds cod fillets
- 2 quarts of vegetable oil for frying

Directions:

- Combine flour, baking powder, baking soda, and cornstarch in a medium mixing basin.
- In a large mixing basin, combine eggs and milk. Pour in the beer. Mix in the flour mixture. Season with salt, pepper, and garlic powder to taste.
- Heat the oil to 375 degrees F in an electric deep fryer or a heavy saucepan (190 degrees C).
- Coat the fish with batter and place it in the heated oil. Fry for 4 to 5 minutes, or until golden brown. Serve.

Twice Fried Fish
Preparation Time: 10 minutes
Cooking Time: 18 minutes
Serve: 1
Ingredients:

- 1 tablespoon hoisin sauce

- 1 tablespoon canned tomato sauce
- 1 tablespoon dry sherry
- 1 teaspoon ground black pepper
- 2 tablespoons dark soy sauce
- 1 teaspoon white sugar
- 1 teaspoon salt
- 1 ½ pounds cod fillets
- 3 tablespoons vegetable oil
- 1 tablespoon lard
- 1 teaspoon cornstarch
- 4 tablespoons water

Directions:

- Mix hoisin sauce, tomato sauce, sherry, pepper, soy sauce, sugar, and salt in a mixing bowl. Allow for a 20-minute resting period.
- 1 tablespoon of oil should be rubbed into the filets of fish. Heat the remaining 2 tablespoons of oil in a large pan. Fry the fish for 2 minutes on both sides, then drain on paper towels.
- Remove the skillet's oil and replace it with 1 tablespoon of lard. Melt over medium heat and toss in the soy sauce mixture. Dissolve the cornstarch in the water and pour it into the skillet, continually swirling. Cook until the sauce thickens.
- Return the fish to the skillet and cook for another minute on each side.

Quick and Easy Baked Fish Fillet
Preparation Time: 18 minutes
Cooking Time: 20 minutes
Serve: 1
Ingredients:

- 1 pound flounder fillets
- ½ teaspoon salt
- ground black pepper to taste
- 1 tablespoon lemon juice
- 2 teaspoons melted butter
- 1 teaspoon minced onion

Directions:

- Preheat the oven carefully to 400°F (200 degrees C).
- Season the flounder in a baking dish with salt and pepper. Combine lemon juice, butter, and onion; pour over flounder.
- 25 to 30 minutes in a preheated oven until the salmon is opaque and flakes readily with a fork.

Baked Fish Croquettes
Preparation Time: 15 minutes
Cooking Time: 25 minutes
Serve: 1
Ingredients:

- 2 cups leftover cooked steelhead trout
- 1 cup soft breadcrumbs
- ½ sweet onion, minced
- ½ cup mayonnaise
- ½ cup sour cream
- ½ lemon, juiced
- ½ teaspoon Worcestershire sauce
- ½ teaspoon seasoned salt, or more to taste
- ½ teaspoon garlic powder
- ground black pepper to taste

- ½ cup panko breadcrumbs, or as needed

Directions:

- Preheat the oven carefully to 425°F (220 degrees C). Then, using parchment paper or aluminum foil, line a baking pan.
- Remove the skin, bones, and crust from the trout and flake it with a fork. In a mixing bowl, combine flaked fish, soft breadcrumbs, onion, mayonnaise, sour cream, lemon juice, Worcestershire sauce, salt, garlic powder, and black pepper. Form the mixture into balls, then roll each one in the panko. Place the balls on the baking sheet that has been prepared.
- Bake for 15 to 20 minutes, or until the croquettes are gently browned and crispy.

Grilled Tuna Fish Steaks
Preparation Time: 20 minutes
Cooking Time: 20 minutes
Serve: 1
Ingredients:

- 8 (3 ounces) fillets fresh tuna steaks, 1 inch thick
- ½ cup soy sauce
- ⅓ cup sherry
- ¼ cup vegetable oil
- 1 tablespoon fresh lime juice
- 1 clove garlic, minced

Directions:

- In a shallow baking dish, place the tuna steaks. Combine the soy sauce, sherry, vegetable oil, fresh lime juice, and garlic in a medium mixing bowl. Turn the tuna steaks in the soy sauce mixture to coat. Refrigerate for at least one hour, covered.
- Preheat the grill to high.
- Grease the grill grate lightly. Place the tuna steaks on the grill and discard the marinade. Grill for 3 to 6 minutes per side, or until done to preference.

Fish Batter with Newcastle™ Brown Ale
Preparation Time: 15 minutes
Cooking Time: 25 minutes
Serve: 1
Ingredients:

- 1-quart vegetable oil for frying
- ½ cup flour
- ½ cup cornmeal
- 1 teaspoon garlic salt
- ½ teaspoon garlic powder
- ½ teaspoon ground cinnamon
- 1 cup brown ale (such as Newcastle™ brown ale)
- 1 pound cod fillets, cut into pieces

Directions:

- Heat the oil in a deep fryer to 325°F (165 degrees C).
- Combine the flour, cornmeal, garlic salt, garlic powder, and cinnamon in a large mixing bowl. Mix in the beer until there are no dry lumps left. Dip the fish into the batter, allowing some of the excess to run out before gently placing it in the deep fryer. Cook for 8 minutes, or until the fish is golden brown and crispy on the exterior and easily flaked. To prevent overcrowding the deep fryer, cook the fish in batches.

Accidental Fish
Preparation Time: 15 minutes

Cooking Time: 20 minutes
Serve: 1
Ingredients:

- 2 (4 ounces) fillets Mahi Mahi
- ½ cup salted butter
- 2 teaspoons olive oil
- 2 drops Louisiana-style hot sauce
- 1 tablespoon lemon juice
- 1 Roma tomato, seeded and chopped
- 1 clove garlic, minced
- 1 green onion, chopped

Directions:

- Preheat the oven carefully to 450°F (230 degrees C).
- Place the mahi-mahi fillets on a baking dish and brush with olive oil.
- Bake for 20 minutes in a preheated oven or until the fish flakes easily with a fork.
- Melt the butter in a skillet over medium heat while the mahi-mahi bakes.
- Simmer the garlic, lemon juice, and spicy sauce in the melted butter for 1 minute. Cook and stir the tomato and green onion into the butter mixture until heated. To serve, spoon the sauce over the cooked fish.

Easy-Bake Fish
Preparation Time: 20 minutes
Cooking Time: 25 minutes
Serve: 1
Ingredients:

- 3 tablespoons honey
- 3 tablespoons Dijon mustard
- 1 teaspoon lemon juice
- 4 (6 ounces) salmon steaks
- ½ teaspoon pepper

Directions:

- Preheat the oven carefully to 325°F (165 degrees C).
- Combine the honey, mustard, and lemon juice in a small bowl. Distribute the mixture evenly over the salmon steaks. Season with pepper to taste. In a medium baking dish, arrange the ingredients.
- Bake for 20 minutes in a preheated oven or until the fish flakes easily with a fork.

Coconut Fish Curry
Preparation Time: 15 minutes
Cooking Time: 20 minutes
Serve: 1
Ingredients:

- 1 ½ teaspoon curry powder
- ½ teaspoon ground ginger
- ¼ teaspoon ground turmeric
- ¼ teaspoon olive oil
- 3 cloves garlic, minced
- 1 onion, chopped
- 4 ¼ ounces coconut milk, divided
- 4 ¼ ounces water, divided
- 3 ½ ounces cod, cut into bite-size pieces
- 1 large tomato, diced

Directions:

- Combine the curry powder, powdered ginger, and ground turmeric; roast the spices over medium heat until browned, about 5 minutes. Stir the olive oil and garlic into the spice mixture to produce a paste.

- Cook and toss the onion into the spice mixture for 5 to 7 minutes, or until it is soft. Stir in half of the coconut milk and half of the water to the onion mixture; cook for 5 minutes. Cook until the fish is firm, about 5 minutes, after adding it to the mixture. Cook until the tomato is softened, approximately 5 minutes, with the remaining coconut milk and water in the pan.

Lemony Steamed Fish
Preparation Time: 15 minutes
Cooking Time: 18 minutes
Serve: 1
Ingredients:
- 6 (6 ounces) halibut fillets
- 1 tablespoon dried dill weed
- 1 tablespoon onion powder
- 2 teaspoons dried parsley
- ¼ teaspoon paprika
- 1 seasoned pinch salt, or more to taste
- 1 pinch lemon pepper
- 1 pinch garlic powder
- 2 tablespoons lemon juice

Directions:
- Preheat the oven carefully to 375°F (190 degrees C).
- Make 6 foil squares, one for each fillet.
- Sprinkle dill weed, onion powder, parsley, paprika, seasoned salt, lemon pepper, and garlic powder on top of the fillets. Each fillet should be sprayed with lemon juice. Fold the foil over the fillets to form a pocket, then fold the edges close. Spread the wrapped packages out on a baking sheet.
- Bake for 30 minutes in a preheated oven or until the fish flakes easily with a fork.

Freda's Fabulous Fish
Preparation Time: 15 minutes
Cooking Time: 22 minutes
Serve: 1
Ingredients:
- 1 pound cod fillets
- ½ cup butter, melted
- ¼ cup soy-based steak marinade
- 1 teaspoon salt
- 1 teaspoon ground black pepper
- 1 teaspoon cayenne pepper
- 1 lemon, quartered
- 2 small tomatoes, thinly sliced

Directions:
- Preheat the oven carefully to 375°F (190 degrees C).
- Put the fish in a 13x9 baking dish or pan.
- Spread the butter, marinade, salt, and pepper all over the fish. Squeeze the lemon juice over the fish. Place tomato slices on top of the fish.
- 30 minutes in the oven, or until the fish is flaky.

Fiery Fish Tacos with Crunchy Corn Salsa
Preparation Time: 10 minutes
Cooking Time: 18 minutes
Serve: 1

Ingredients:
- 2 cups cooked corn kernels
- ½ cup diced red onion
- 1 cup peeled, diced jicama
- ½ cup diced red bell pepper, 1 cup fresh cilantro leaves, chopped
- 1 lime, juiced, and zested
- 2 tablespoons cayenne pepper, or to taste
- 1 tablespoon ground black pepper
- 2 tablespoons salt, or to taste
- 6 (4 ounces) fillets of tilapia
- 2 tablespoons olive oil
- 12 corn tortillas, warmed
- 2 tablespoons sour cream, or to taste

Directions:
- Preheat the grill to high.
- Combine corn, red onion, jicama, red bell pepper, and cilantro in a medium mixing bowl. Mix in the lime juice and zest.
- Combine cayenne pepper, ground black pepper, and salt in a small bowl.
- Brush each fillet with olive oil and season with salt and pepper to taste.
- Place the fillets on the grill grate and cook for 3 minutes on each side. Top two corn tortillas with fish, sour cream, and corn salsa for each spicy fish taco.

Spicy Fish Soup
Preparation Time: 18 minutes
Cooking Time: 20 minutes
Serve: 1
Ingredients:
- ½ onion, chopped
- 1 clove garlic, minced
- 1 tablespoon chili powder
- 1 ½ cups chicken broth
- 1 (4 ounces) can canned green chili peppers, chopped
- 1 teaspoon ground cumin
- 1 ½ cups canned peeled and diced tomatoes
- ½ cup chopped green bell pepper
- ½ cup shrimp
- ½ pound cod fillets
- ¾ cup plain nonfat yogurt

Directions:
- Over medium-high heat, coat a large pot with vegetable cooking spray. Sauté the onions for about 5 minutes, stirring often. Cook for 2 minutes more after adding the garlic and chili powder.
- Then, add the chicken broth, chili peppers, and cumin while stirring constantly. Bring to a boil, then lower to low heat, cover, and leave to simmer for 20 minutes.
- Add the tomatoes, green bell pepper, prawns, and fish next. Return to a boil, lower to low heat, cover, and continue cooking for 5 minutes. Stir in the yogurt gradually until it is cooked completely.

Air Fryer Fish Sticks
Preparation Time: 15 minutes
Cooking Time: 25 minutes
Serve: 1
Ingredients:

- 1 pound cod fillets
- ¼ cup all-purpose flour, 1 egg
- ½ cup panko breadcrumbs
- ¼ cup grated Parmesan cheese
- 1 tablespoon parsley flakes
- 1 teaspoon paprika
- ½ teaspoon black pepper
- cooking spray

Directions:

- Preheat an air fryer to 400°F (200 degrees C).
- Pat the fish dry using paper towels before slicing it into 1x3-inch pieces.
- In a small bowl, combine the flour and salt. In a separate shallow dish, beat the egg. In a third shallow dish, combine panko, Parmesan cheese, parsley, paprika, and pepper.
- Each fish stick should be coated in flour, then dipped in beaten egg, and then coated in seasoned panko mixture.
- Spray the air fryer basket with nonstick cooking spray. Arrange half of the sticks in the basket, ensuring none of them is a contact. Cooking spray should be sprayed on the top of each stick.
- Cook for 5 minutes in a hot air fryer. Cook for a further 5 minutes after flipping the fish sticks. Rep with the rest of the fish sticks.

Easy Baked Fish

Preparation Time: 20 minutes
Cooking Time: 20 minutes
Serve: 1
Ingredients:

- cooking spray
- ½ cup chicken broth
- ¼ cup butter
- 2 tablespoons dry white wine
- 1 tablespoon fresh lemon juice
- ½ teaspoon dried basil
- ½ teaspoon salt
- ¼ teaspoon ground black pepper
- 1 ⅓ cups instant rice
- 1 red onion, chopped
- 1 red bell pepper, chopped
- 1 cup frozen peas
- 2 cloves garlic, chopped
- 1-pound sole fillets
- 2 plum (Roma) tomatoes, thinly sliced
- 1 lemon, quartered

Directions:

- Preheat the oven carefully to 450°F (230 degrees C). Coat a 9x13-inch baking dish with nonstick cooking spray.
- In a saucepan over medium heat, combine the chicken broth, butter, wine, lemon juice, basil, salt, and black pepper until the butter has melted, about 5 minutes.
- Combine rice, onion, bell pepper, peas, and garlic in a prepared baking dish. Arrange sole fillets on the rice mixture, followed by tomato slices. Distribute the butter mixture over the fish, rice, and veggies. Wrap aluminum foil around the baking dish.
- Cook in a preheated oven for 20 to 25 minutes, or until the fish flakes easily with a fork and soft rice. With lemon slices, serve.

Fish on a Plank

Preparation Time: 15 minutes
Cooking Time: 25 minutes
Serve: 1
Ingredients:

- 1 cedar plank
- 6 (5 ounces) mahi-mahi fillets
- 1 cup bottled teriyaki sauce
- 2 mangos - peeled, seeded, and diced
- ½ red bell pepper, seeded and chopped
- 4 green onions, chopped
- 1 tablespoon chopped fresh cilantro
- 1 jalapeno pepper, seeded and chopped
- salt and pepper to taste
- ½ teaspoon garlic powder
- 1 teaspoon fresh lime juice
- 1 teaspoon lemon juice
- 2 teaspoons olive oil
- 1 teaspoon chipotle seasoning
- 1 teaspoon red pepper flakes
- 1 teaspoon hot-pepper sauce

Directions:

- Combine the mangos, green onion, cilantro bell pepper, and jalapeño pepper in a medium mixing bowl. Season with garlic powder, salt & pepper, and lime juice to taste. Stir together, then cover and chill until ready to serve to mix the flavors.
- Soak the plank in water for at least 2 hours, preferably longer. In a shallow dish, coat the mahi-mahi fillets with teriyaki sauce. Cover and set aside for at least 1 hour to marinate.
- Prepare an indirect-heat grill. Arrange and fire the coals beneath one-half of the grill if using charcoal. Season the fish fillets with lemon juice, chipotle spice, red pepper flakes, and hot pepper sauce. Lay the fillets out on the plank.
- Place the board over direct heat on the grill. Cook for 10 minutes, covered. Cook for 10 minutes more, or until the fish can be flaked with a fork, on the plank with the fish over indirect heat (the colder area of the grill). Serve the fillets with mango salsa on the side.

Pretzel Coated Fried Fish1-quart oil for frying

Preparation Time: 15 minutes
Cooking Time: 20 minutes
Serve: 1
Ingredients:

- 1-quart oil for frying
- ¾ cup all-purpose flour
- 1 teaspoon salt
- ½ teaspoon ground black pepper
- 1-pound frozen cod fillets, thawed
- 2 eggs
- ¾ cup crushed pretzels

Directions:

- Heat the oil in a deep fryer to 350°F (175 degrees C).
- In a large resealable plastic bag, combine the flour, salt, and pepper. Place the cod in the bag and shake gently to coat. Separate the eggs and crumbled pretzels into two small bowls. Coat the fish in eggs, then with broken pretzels.

- Fry coated fish in hot oil for 10 minutes, rotating once, until golden brown and readily flaked with a fork.

Easy Mediterranean Fish

Preparation Time: 20 minutes
Cooking Time: 25 minutes
Serve: 1
Ingredients:

- 4 (6 ounces) fillets of halibut
- 1 tablespoon Greek seasoning (such as Cavender's®)
- 1 large tomato, chopped
- 1 onion, chopped
- 1 (5 ounces) jar pitted kalamata olives
- ¼ cup capers
- ¼ cup olive oil
- 1 tablespoon lemon juice
- salt and pepper to taste

Directions:

- Preheat the oven carefully to 350°F (175 degrees C).
- Season the halibut fillets with Greek seasoning and place them on a wide piece of aluminum foil. Combine the tomato, onion, olives, capers, olive oil, lemon juice, salt, and pepper in a mixing bowl. Distribute the tomato mixture over the halibut. To make a huge packet, carefully seal all of the foil's edges. Spread the package out on a baking sheet.
- 30 to 40 minutes in a preheated oven until the salmon flakes easily with a fork.

Homemade Fish Stock

Preparation Time: 15 minutes
Cooking Time: 20 minutes
Serve: 1
Ingredients:

- 3 pounds fish heads, bones, and trimmings
- 2 tablespoons unsalted butter
- 2 leeks, white part only, thinly sliced
- 1 carrot, chopped
- 1 rib celery, chopped
- 1 cup dry white wine
- 2 ½ quarts water
- 1 bouquet garni
- 10 whole black peppercorns
- 3 thick slices of lemon

Directions:

- Fish should be washed in cold water and thoroughly drained.
- Melt the butter in a saucepan over low heat. Cook until the leeks, carrots, and celery are cooked, 5 to 7 minutes. Bring the fish portions, wine, and water to a boil for about 5 minutes. Residuum should be skimmed and discarded. After adding the bouquet garni, peppercorns, and lemon, return to a boil. Reduce heat to low and cook, uncovered, for 30 minutes, skimming and discarding residue as needed.
- Fill a colander lined with cheesecloth with water and strain the stock into a basin. Allow cooling before keeping in the fridge for up to a week or freezing for up to 3 months.

Sexy Fish Stew

Preparation Time: 15 minutes
Cooking Time: 18 minutes

Serve: 1
Ingredients:

- 2 tablespoons butter
- 1 large leek, cleaned and thinly sliced
- ½ cup sliced shallots
- salt
- ¾ cup white wine
- 1 ¼ cups chicken broth
- ½ cup thinly sliced fennel bulb
- 1 pound baby red potatoes, trimmed
- salt and freshly ground pepper to taste
- 1 pinch cayenne pepper
- ½ cup heavy whipping cream
- 1-pound boneless rockfish filets, cut into 1-inch pieces
- 1 tablespoon chopped fresh tarragon

Directions:

- In a large saucepan over medium-low heat, melt the butter. Cook and stir the leek, shallots, and 1/2 teaspoon salt in the melted butter for 10 to 15 minutes, or until softened.
- Stir the wine into the leek mixture, turn the heat up to medium and cook for 2 minutes. Bring the chicken broth to a boil.
- Stir in the fennel and potatoes and cook, occasionally turning, until the potatoes are nearly cooked about 10 minutes. Season with salt, pepper, and cayenne pepper to taste. Stir in the cream to mix.
- Cover and heat for 3 minutes after adding the fish and tarragon to the soup. Reduce heat to medium-low, stir gently, and cook until fish flakes easily with a fork, about 6 minutes. Season with salt and black pepper to taste.

Fish and Chips Sliders

Preparation Time: 15 minutes
Cooking Time: 22 minutes
Serve: 1
Ingredients:

- cooking spray
- 1 (8.5 ounces) bag malt vinegar-and-sea salt chips
- 3 egg whites
- 1 tablespoon apple cider vinegar
- ½ teaspoon celery seed
- 1 pound cod fillets
- ⅓ cup plain Greek yogurt
- 3 cups coleslaw mix
- 2 green onions, chopped
- 2 tablespoons honey mustard
- 1 pinch salt and ground black pepper
- 8 slider buns

Directions:

- Preheat the oven carefully to 450 degrees Fahrenheit (230 degrees C). Spray a wire rack with cooking spray and place it on a rimmed baking sheet.
- Blend the chips in batches until they have the consistency of breadcrumbs. Place the chips on a flat platter.
- In a mixing basin, combine egg whites. Place a piece of fish on the prepared rack after dipping it in egg white and coating it with chip crumbs. Rep with the leftover fish. Coat the fish with frying spray.
- Bake for 15 minutes in a preheated oven. Turn on the broiler and broil the salmon for 5 minutes, or until it is golden and crispy.

- In a large mixing bowl, combine coleslaw mix and green onions while the fish is cooking. Combine the yogurt, honey mustard, vinegar, celery seed, salt, and pepper in a separate dish. Toss the coleslaw mix with the dressing to blend.
- Top each slider bread with a slice of fish and a dollop of coleslaw.

Fort Worth Fish Tacos

Preparation Time: 10 minutes
Cooking Time: 18 minutes
Serve: 1
Ingredients:

- 8 (3 ounces) fillets tilapia
- 2 teaspoons salt
- 2 teaspoons hot pepper sauce
- 4 ounces cream cheese, softened
- 2 tablespoons chopped fresh cilantro
- ½ cup mayonnaise
- 1 (5.3 ounces) container plain Greek yogurt
- 1 tablespoon lime juice
- 1 cup flour
- 1 teaspoon salt
- 1 teaspoon garlic powder
- cayenne pepper to taste
- ¼ teaspoon ground black pepper
- 1 cup dark beer
- 3 cups peanut oil for frying
- 8 (8 inches) flour tortillas
- ¼ medium head cabbage, finely shredded
- 1 (8 ounces) jar prepared salsa
- ¼ cup chopped fresh cilantro
- 2 small limes, quartered

Directions:

- Place the tilapia fillets on a platter and season with salt and spicy sauce; cover and chill while creating the cilantro cream sauce.
- In a small or large measuring cup, combine cream cheese, 2 tablespoons cilantro, mayonnaise, and yogurt; stir well. Mix the lime juice into the cream sauce. Refrigerate, covered.
- In a mixing basin, add flour, salt, garlic powder, cayenne pepper, and pepper; stir in beer to produce a smooth batter.
- Heat the oil in a big, deep-frying pan to 375°F (190 degrees C).

- Remove the fish from the refrigerator, dip it in the beer batter, and cook it three times in the heated oil, flipping it until golden (approximately 2 minutes on each side, depending on the thickness). Drain the fish on paper towels and place it on a covered platter to keep warm. Rep with the remaining fillets.
- Wrap tortillas in a clean kitchen towel and microwave for 20 seconds or warm. Assemble tacos by laying a heated tortilla on top of a fish fillet. Shredded cabbage properly, a dollop of cilantro cream sauce, a teaspoon of salsa, and a sprinkling of chopped cilantro complete the dish. Each taco should be served with a lime quarter for squeezing.

Cod Fish Cakes

Preparation Time: 18 minutes
Cooking Time: 20 minutes
Serve: 1
Ingredients:

- 2 large potatoes, peeled and halved
- 1 pound cod fillets, cubed
- 1 tablespoon butter
- 1 tablespoon grated onion
- 1 tablespoon chopped fresh parsley
- 1 egg
- 3 tablespoons oil for frying

Directions:

- Put the potatoes in a large saucepan of water and bring to a boil. Allow the potatoes to simmer until almost tender.
- Add the fish to the saucepan and boil until both the fish and the potatoes are tender. Drain well and place the potatoes and fish in a large mixing dish.
- Mash together the butter, onion, parsley, and egg in a mixing dish. Make patties out of the mixture.
- In a large skillet over medium-high heat, heat the oil. Fry the patties until golden brown on both sides. Before serving, pat dry with paper towels.

Nutritional Value (Amount per Serving):

- Calories 277
- Fat 14.4 g
- Carbohydrates 0.3 g
- Sugar 0.3 g
- Protein 47.1 g
- Cholesterol 125 mg

CHAPTER 7:

Rice & Grains

Rice Stuffed Peppers
Preparation Time: 10 minutes
Cooking Time: 15 minutes
Serve: 4
Ingredients:
- 4 bell peppers, cut the tops & remove seeds
- 2 cups Colby jack cheese, shredded
- 1 tsp garlic powder
- 1 tbsp Italian seasoning
- 2 cups cooked rice
- 8 oz tomato sauce
- 15 oz can tomato, diced
- 1 lb. ground beef
- 1 tbsp canola oil
- 1 small onion, diced
- Pepper
- Salt

Directions:
- Heat oil in a pan over medium-high heat.
- Add onion and sauté until softened.
- Add meat and cook until meat is no longer pink.
- Add garlic powder, Italian seasoning, rice, tomato sauce, tomatoes, pepper, and salt and stir until well combined.
- Stuff rice mixture into the peppers and cook at 360 F for 10 minutes.
- Top with cheese and cook for 2 minutes more.
- Serve and enjoy.

Apple Oats
Preparation Time: 10 minutes
Cooking Time: 15 minutes
Serve: 1
Ingredients:
- ½ cup gluten-free oats
- 1 tbsp Greek yogurt
- ½ cup unsweetened almond milk
- 2 tbsp date spread
- ½ tsp cream of tartar
- ½ tsp baking powder
- 1 tbsp protein powder
- ¼ cup apple, chopped

Directions:
- In a mixing bowl, mix together oats, baking powder, and protein powder.
- Add yogurt, milk, date spread, and cream of tartar and mix until well combined.
- Add apple and fold well.
- Pour oat mixture into the greased air fryer baking dish.

- Place baking dish into the air fryer basket and cook at 330 F for 15 minutes.
- Serve and enjoy.

Peanut Butter Oatmeal
Preparation Time: 10 minutes
Cooking Time: 15 minutes
Serve: 1
Ingredients:
- ½ cup rolled oats
- 1 tsp maple syrup
- ¼ tsp vanilla
- ½ tsp baking powder
- ½ tbsp peanut butter
- 1/3 cup unsweetened almond milk
- ½ banana
- 1/8 tsp salt

Directions:
- Preheat the air fryer to 350 F.
- Add oats into the food processor and process until get flour like consistency.
- Add remaining ingredients and process until well combined.
- Pour batter into the greased ramekin.
- Place ramekin in air fryer basket and cook for 15-20 minutes.
- Serve and enjoy.

Oats Granola
Preparation Time: 10 minutes
Cooking Time: 30 minutes
Serve: 8
Ingredients:
- 3 cups old-fashioned oats
- 1 tsp vanilla
- 1 tsp cinnamon
- 3 tbsp brown sugar
- 3 tbsp coconut oil, melted
- ½ cup maple syrup
- ½ tsp salt

Directions:
- In a mixing bowl, mix together oats, vanilla, cinnamon, brown sugar, oil, maple syrup, and salt until well combined.
- Spread oats mixture into the parchment-lined air fryer basket and cook at 250 F for 30 minutes. Stir after every 10 minutes.
- Serve and enjoy.

Berry Oatmeal

Preparation Time: 10 minutes
Cooking Time: 8 minutes
Serve: 4
Ingredients:

- 2 eggs
- 7 oz banana
- 5 tbsp unsweetened almond milk
- 2 tbsp Greek yogurt
- 2 tbsp honey
- 1 tbsp vanilla
- 4.5 oz quick oats
- 2 tbsp mixed berries

Directions:

- In a mixing bowl, add banana and mash using the fork.
- Add oats, vanilla, honey, yogurt, milk, and eggs and mix until well combined.
- Add berries and fold well.
- Spoon mixture into the four greased ramekins.
- Place ramekins into the air fryer basket and cook at 400 F for 8 minutes.
- Serve and enjoy.

Chocolate Oats

Preparation Time: 10 minutes
Cooking Time: 15 minutes
Serve: 2
Ingredients:

- 1 egg
- 1 tbsp cocoa powder
- ½ tsp cinnamon
- ¼ cup unsweetened almond milk
- ½ tsp baking powder
- 1 tsp vanilla
- 1 tbsp maple syrup
- ½ cup rolled oats
- ½ banana
- Pinch of salt

Directions:

- Add oats and remaining ingredients into the blender and blend until smooth.
- Pour blended oat mixture into the greased ramekins.
- Place ramekins into the air fryer basket and cook at 330 F for 13-15 minutes.
- Serve and enjoy.

Curried Chickpeas

Preparation Time: 10 minutes
Cooking Time: 18 minutes
Serve: 4
Ingredients:

- 30 oz can chickpeas, drained & rinsed
- ½ tsp chili powder
- ½ tbsp parsley, chopped
- 2 tbsp curry powder
- 2 tbsp canola oil
- Salt

Directions:

- Add chickpeas and remaining ingredients into the mixing bowl and toss until well coated.
- Spread chickpeas into the air fryer basket and cook at 375 F for 15-18 minutes. Stir after every 5 minutes.
- Serve and enjoy.

Chocolate Chip Oats

Preparation Time: 10 minutes
Cooking Time: 18 minutes
Serve: 2
Ingredients:

- 1 egg
- 1 cup rolled oats
- ¼ cup chocolate chips
- ½ tsp vanilla
- ½ tsp baking powder
- 1 tbsp maple syrup
- 1 ripe banana
- ½ cup unsweetened almond milk
- Pinch of salt

Directions:

- Preheat the air fryer to 350 F.
- Add oats, egg, vanilla, baking powder, maple syrup, banana, milk, and salt into the blender and blend until smooth.
- Add chocolate chips and mix well.
- Pour oat mixture into the two greased ramekins.
- Place ramekins into the air fryer basket and cook for 18-20 minutes.
- Serve and enjoy.

Ranch Chickpeas

Preparation Time: 10 minutes
Cooking Time: 17 minutes
Serve: 8
Ingredients:

- 15 oz can chickpeas, drained & rinsed
- 1 tbsp fresh lemon juice
- 2 tsp onion powder
- 1 tbsp olive oil
- 2 tsp garlic powder
- 4 tsp dried dill
- Pepper
- Salt

Directions:

- Add chickpeas into the air fryer basket and cook at 400 F for 12 minutes.
- Transfer chickpeas into the mixing bowl. Add lemon juice, onion powder, garlic powder, dill, oil, pepper, and salt and toss until well coated.
- Return chickpeas into the air fryer basket and cook at 350 F for 5 minutes more.
- Serve and enjoy.

Coconut Oats

Preparation Time: 10 minutes
Cooking Time: 18 minutes
Serve: 2
Ingredients:

- 1 ripe banana

- 3 tbsp chocolate chips
- 2 tbsp unsweetened shredded coconut
- ½ tsp vanilla
- ½ tsp baking powder
- 1 tbsp maple syrup
- ½ cup unsweetened almond milk
- 1 cup rolled oats
- Pinch of salt

Directions:
- Preheat the air fryer to 350 F.
- Add banana, vanilla, baking powder, maple syrup, milk, oats, and salt into the blender and blend until smooth.
- Add shredded coconut and chocolate chips and mix well.
- Pour oat mixture into the two greased ramekins.
- Place ramekins into the air fryer basket and cook for 18-20 minutes.
- Serve and enjoy.

Mango Ginger Rice

Preparation Time: 15 minutes
Cooking Time: 25 minutes
Serve: 1
Ingredients:
- 2 tablespoons canola oil
- ¼ cup chopped dried mango
- 2 teaspoons minced fresh ginger root
- 1 cup uncooked jasmine rice
- 2 cups water
- ½ teaspoon salt
- ¼ cup chopped green onions
- 2 tablespoons chopped fresh cilantro (optional)

Directions:
- In a saucepan over medium-low heat, heat the oil. Cook for 2 to 3 minutes, or until the mango and ginger are aromatic. Cook, often stirring, until the rice is transparent, about 5 minutes. Bring the water and salt to a boil. Reduce heat to low and cover; simmer for 20 minutes or water absorbed.
- Place the heated rice on a serving dish and garnish it with green onions and cilantro.

Carrot Rice

Preparation Time: 20 minutes
Cooking Time: 20 minutes
Serve: 1
Ingredients:
- 1 cup basmati rice
- 2 cups water
- ¼ cup roasted peanuts
- 1 tablespoon margarine
- 1 onion, sliced
- 1 teaspoon minced fresh ginger root
- ¾ cup grated carrots
- salt to taste
- cayenne pepper to taste
- chopped fresh cilantro

Directions:
- In a medium saucepan, combine rice and water. Bring the water to a boil over high heat. Reduce the heat to low, cover with a lid, and steam for 20 minutes, or until the vegetables are soft.

- While the rice cooks, mix the peanuts in a blender and put them aside. In a pan over medium heat, melt the margarine. Cook and stir for 10 minutes, or until the onion has softened and turned golden brown. Stir in the ginger, carrots, and salt & pepper to taste. Reduce the heat to low and cover for 5 minutes to steam. Add the cayenne pepper and peanuts and mix well. Add it to the skillet and gently toss to blend with the other ingredients when the rice is done. Garnish with cilantro, if desired.

Persian Rice with Potato Tahdig

Preparation Time: 15 minutes
Cooking Time: 25 minutes
Serve: 1
Ingredients:
- 2 cups basmati rice
- 1 teaspoon salt
- 2 tablespoons cooking oil
- 1 potato, sliced into 1/4-inch rounds

Directions:
- Rice should be rinsed and drained twice.
- A big pot of water should be brought to a boil. Cook for 6 minutes after adding the rice and salt. Drain through a colander. Rinse and re-drain the rice.
- Place the potato slices in a single layer on top of the oil in the bottom of the saucepan. Pour prepared rice over potato slices, cover, and simmer for 20 to 30 minutes, or until soft rice and potatoes.
- Carefully invert onto a serving platter to make the sliced potatoes on top of the rice.

Easy Cilantro-Lime Rice

Preparation Time: 15 minutes
Cooking Time: 20 minutes
Serve: 1
Ingredients:
- 1 tablespoon olive oil
- 1 cup basmati rice
- 2 cloves garlic, minced
- 1 ½ cups chicken broth
- 2 tablespoons fresh lime juice
- 1 teaspoon salt
- ½ cup chopped cilantro
- ¼ cup whole-kernel corn
- 2 teaspoons green onions, chopped
- 1 lime, zested

Directions:
- In a saucepan over medium heat, heat the olive oil. Cook and stir rice and garlic in heated oil for 2 minutes or fragrant. Stir in the chicken broth, lime juice, and salt; bring to a boil, lower to medium-low heat, cover with a lid, and cook for 15 minutes, or until the rice is soft and the liquid has been absorbed.
- Cilantro, corn, green onions, and lime zest until well combined.

Jasmine Rice

Preparation Time: 20 minutes
Cooking Time: 25 minutes
Serve: 1
Ingredients:

- 2 tablespoons olive oil
- 2 tablespoons chopped onion
- ¼ cup green peas
- 1 bay leaf
- 1 ½ cups dry jasmine rice
- 3 cups water
- salt to taste

Directions:

- Warm the oil in a large saucepan over medium-low heat. Sauté the onion for 3 to 5 minutes. Next, incorporate the green peas, bay leaf, and jasmine rice. To coat the rice, give it a good stir.
- Pour in 3 cups of water and season with salt in a pot. Increase the heat to medium and bring the rice to a rapid boil. Reduce the heat to low and let the rice gently simmer, uncovered until all of the liquid has been absorbed. Remove the rice from the heat and cover it with a lid. Allow for a 40-minute resting period.

Better Spanish Rice

Preparation Time: 15 minutes
Cooking Time: 20 minutes
Serve: 1
Ingredients:

- 1 tablespoon vegetable oil
- ½ onion, chopped
- 1 ¼ cups uncooked instant rice
- 1 (14.5 ounces) can diced tomatoes
- ½ cup chopped fresh cilantro
- 1 cup chicken broth

Directions:

- In a pan over medium-high heat, heat the oil and sauté and toss the chopped onion until browned, approximately 8 minutes.
- Bring the rice, tomatoes, cilantro, and chicken stock to a boil. Reduce the heat to medium-low and continue to cook for approximately 10 minutes, or until the rice is tender and most of the liquid has been absorbed.

Black Rice

Preparation Time: 15 minutes
Cooking Time: 18 minutes
Serve: 1
Ingredients:

- 2 tablespoons butter
- 1 cup black rice
- ¼ cup diced onion
- ¼ cup slivered almonds
- 1 ¾ cups water
- 1 cube chicken bouillon

Directions:

- In a saucepan over medium heat, melt the butter. Cook and stir for 5 to 10 minutes, or until the black rice, onion, and almonds are gently toasted. Bring the water and bouillon cube to a boil.
- Reduce the heat to low, cover, and simmer for 25 to 30 minutes, or until the rice is cooked and the liquid has been absorbed.

Dirty Rice

Preparation Time: 15 minutes
Cooking Time: 22 minutes
Serve: 1
Ingredients:

- 1 tablespoon vegetable oil
- 6 ounces boneless pork shoulder, diced
- 1 yellow onion, diced
- ½ cup diced celery
- ½ cup diced green bell pepper
- 1 tablespoon paprika
- 2 teaspoons ground cumin
- 2 teaspoons freshly ground black pepper
- ½ teaspoon cayenne pepper
- ½ teaspoon garlic powder
- ¼ teaspoon dried oregano
- ¼ teaspoon dried thyme
- 1 andouille sausage, diced, or to taste
- 8 ounces chicken livers, minced
- 2 cups long-grain rice
- 2 teaspoons kosher salt, or to taste
- 4 cups chicken broth
- 1 bay leaf
- 1 dash Worcestershire sauce
- ¼ cup sliced green onions
- ¼ cup chopped Italian parsley

Directions:

- In a high-sided pan over medium-high heat, heat the oil. 5 to 7 minutes, cook and stir meat until thoroughly browned and fat is released. Cook until the onion, celery, and bell pepper are transparent, about 5 minutes. In a mixing bowl, combine paprika, cumin, black pepper, cayenne pepper, garlic powder, oregano, and thyme. Cook, stirring regularly, for 5 minutes, or until veggies continue to soften.
- Reduce the heat to medium and stir in the andouille sausage. Cook and stir for 2 to 3 minutes to release some flavor. Stir in the chicken livers and rice until thoroughly coated. Season with salt, add stock and bring to a boil over medium-high heat. Combine the bay leaf and Worcestershire sauce in a mixing bowl. Reduce the heat to medium-low and cover securely. Cook, without stirring, for approximately 25 minutes, or until most of the liquid has been absorbed and the rice is starting to become soft.
- Mix in the green onions and parsley. Cook for another 10 minutes over low to medium-low heat until the rice is tender. Before serving, taste for seasoning and discard the bay leaf.

Yellow Rice with Vegetables1 teaspoon vegetable oil

Preparation Time: 10 minutes
Cooking Time: 18 minutes
Serve: 1
Ingredients:

- 1 teaspoon vegetable oil
- 1 small onion, chopped
- 1 carrot, diced
- ½ cup chopped broccoli florets
- ¼ cup diced red bell pepper
- 1 clove garlic, minced
- 3 cups vegetable broth

- 1 ½ cups rice
- 1 (1.41 ounces) package sazon seasoning with coriander and achiote (such as Goya®)
- 1 dash adobo seasoning with pepper (such as Goya®)

Directions:
- In a saucepan over medium heat, heat the oil. Cook and stir onion, carrot, broccoli, red bell pepper, and garlic in heated oil for 5 minutes, or until garlic just begins to brown.
- Pour the vegetable broth into the saucepan, whisk in the rice, season spice, and adobo seasoning. Bring the liquid to a boil, then lower to low heat and simmer for 25 minutes, or until the liquid is absorbed and the rice is soft. To serve, fluff the rice with a fork.

Almond Wild Rice
Preparation Time: 18 minutes
Cooking Time: 20 minutes
Serve: 1
Ingredients:
- cooking spray
- 2 ½ cups chicken broth
- 1 ½ cups brown and wild rice mix
- 3 tablespoons butter
- 1 cup slivered almonds
- 2 tablespoons dried parsley
- 1 cup sweetened dried cranberries
- ¼ teaspoon salt
- ¼ teaspoon ground black pepper

Directions:
- Preheat the oven carefully to 375°F (190 degrees C). Coat an 8-inch square baking dish with nonstick cooking spray.
- In a saucepan, bring chicken broth to a boil.
- Place the rice mixture in the prepared baking dish. Pour the boiling chicken stock over the rice with care. Wrap the dish with aluminum foil.
- Bake it in a preheated oven for 1 hour or until the rice is soft.
- In a pan over medium heat, melt the butter. Cook and stir almonds in heated butter for 3 to 5 minutes, or until they brown. Continue to simmer and stir until the almonds are lightly toasted, about 3 to 5 minutes more.
- In a large mixing basin, combine the baked rice, almond mixture, cranberries, salt, and pepper; toss to combine.

Basmati Rice
Preparation Time: 15 minutes
Cooking Time: 25 minutes
Serve: 1
Ingredients:
- 1 ¾ cups water
- 1 cup basmati rice
- ¼ cup frozen green peas
- 1 teaspoon cumin seeds

Directions:
- Bring water to a boil in a saucepan. Stir in the rice. Reduce the heat to low, cover, and leave to simmer for 20 minutes.
- When the rice is done, add the peas and cumin. Allow to stand for 5 minutes, covered.

Thai Fried Rice
Preparation Time: 20 minutes
Cooking Time: 20 minutes
Serve: 1
Ingredients:
- 6 slices bacon, sliced crosswise into 1/2-inch pieces
- 2 cloves garlic, minced
- 1 onion, finely chopped
- 1 large tomato, cubed
- ½ cup chopped fresh pineapple
- 5 cups cooked jasmine rice, cooled
- 2 tablespoons ketchup
- 2 tablespoons light soy sauce
- 1 tablespoon white sugar
- ¼ teaspoon freshly ground white pepper
- 3 eggs, beaten
- ½ cucumber, sliced
- 2 green onions, chopped
- ¼ cup chopped fresh cilantro
- 1 lime, cut into wedges
- 4 green Thai chili peppers

Directions:
- Cook the bacon in a large pan or wok over medium heat until it is browned and crisp, about 5 minutes. Drain, saving the bacon fat in a separate basin. Return 2 tablespoons of the fat to the skillet.
- Increase the heat to medium-high and sauté the garlic for 30 seconds, or until fragrant. Cook often turns until the onion is softened, 2 to 3 minutes. Stir in the tomato and pineapple and cook for 2 minutes, or until heated through.
- 1 cup bacon grease 1 tablespoon bacon grease 1 tablespoon bacon grease 1 tablespoon bacon grease 1 Stir in the rice, breaking it up with a spatula so that it is fully covered with the bacon oil. Cook for approximately 3 minutes. Ketchup, soy sauce, sugar, and white pepper to taste.
- Place the rice mixture on one side of the skillet or wok and pour the beaten eggs on the other. Stir-fry for 2 to 3 minutes, or until the eggs are almost set. Combine eggs and rice mixture. Fold in the bacon pieces. Cucumber, green onions, cilantro, lemon wedges, and chili peppers

Brown Rice Pudding
Preparation Time: 15 minutes
Cooking Time: 25 minutes
Serve: 1
Ingredients:
- 1 ½ cups heavy cream
- 1 ¼ cups water
- ½ cup short-grain brown rice
- ¼ teaspoon salt
- ½ cup raisins (Optional)
- 3 egg yolks
- ¼ cup white sugar
- ½ teaspoon ground cinnamon
- 1 tablespoon butter, softened
- 2 teaspoons vanilla extract

Directions:
- In a saucepan, bring the heavy cream, water, brown rice, and salt to a boil; decrease the heat to low, cover, and simmer for 80 minutes, or until the liquid is entirely absorbed. Fold

SARAH JONES

the raisins into the mixture and simmer for another 10 minutes, or until the raisins are plump.

- In a mixing dish, combine the egg yolks, sugar, and cinnamon; gently pour into the saucepan with the rice while stirring. Cook and stir for 6 minutes, or until the mixture thickens. Take the pan off the heat and whisk in the butter and vanilla extract.

Cherry Wild Rice
Preparation Time: 15 minutes
Cooking Time: 20 minutes
Serve: 1
Ingredients:
- 2 ½ cups water, divided
- ½ cup wild rice
- ¼ cup brown rice, 1 cup pitted and sliced cherries
- ½ cup brown sugar
- ¼ cup sliced almonds
- ½ cup sliced celery
- ⅓ cup fresh orange juice
- 2 tablespoons red wine vinegar
- 1 teaspoon grated orange zest

Directions:
- In a saucepan, bring 2 cups of water and wild rice to a boil. Reduce the heat to medium-low, cover, and cook for 30 to 45 minutes, or until the rice is soft. Drain excess liquid, fluff rice with a fork, and cook for another 5 minutes, uncovered.
- In a saucepan, bring 1/2 cup water and brown rice to a boil. Reduce the heat to medium-low, cover, and simmer for 45 minutes, or until the rice is cooked and the liquid has been absorbed.
- In a large nonstick pan, combine cherries, brown sugar, and almonds; cook and stir over medium heat until brown sugar melts and coats cherries and almonds, about 6 minutes. Combine the brown rice, wild rice, celery, orange juice, red wine vinegar, and orange zest in a mixing bowl. Cook, stirring regularly, until well heated, approximately 5 minutes.

The Perfect Egyptian Rice with Vermicelli
Preparation Time: 20 minutes
Cooking Time: 25 minutes
Serve: 1
Ingredients:
- 1 ½ tablespoon olive oil
- ¼ cup 1/2-inch-long vermicelli
- 1 cup Egyptian rice (short-grain rice)
- salt to taste
- 1 ¾ cups water

Directions:
- In a saucepan over medium heat, heat the oil. Cook, stirring regularly until the vermicelli is golden brown, 3 to 5 minutes. Turn off the heat. Pour in the rice and salt, stirring until evenly covered with oil.
- Turn down the heat to low. Cook the rice mixture, stirring regularly, for 3 to 5 minutes, or until the rice turns pasty white.
- In a saucepan, bring water to a boil.
- Incorporate water into the rice mixture. Cook, covered, for 10 to 15 minutes, or until most of the water has been absorbed. Turn off the heat and set it aside for 5 minutes to allow the remaining water to soak. With a fork, fluff the rice.

Baked "Fried" Rice
Preparation Time: 15 minutes
Cooking Time: 20 minutes
Serve: 1
Ingredients:
- 2 cups long-grain white rice
- 2 tablespoons canola oil
- 1 tablespoon sesame oil, or to taste
- 3 cloves garlic, crushed
- ½ cup sliced green onions
- ½ cup diced red bell peppers
- ½ cup diced carrots
- ½ cup green peas
- 1 cup diced ham
- 1 pinch salt to taste (Optional)
- 3 cups chicken broth
- 3 tablespoons soy sauce
- 2 teaspoons chili paste (Optional)

Directions:
- Preheat the oven carefully to 400 degrees Fahrenheit (200 degrees C).
- In a large baking dish, place the rice. Drizzle canola and sesame oils over rice and toss to cover fully. Combine the garlic, green onions, bell peppers, carrots, peas, and ham in a mixing bowl. Season with salt and pepper. Stir until everything is completely blended.
- Combine the chicken broth, soy sauce, and chili paste in a saucepan over high heat. Bring to a boil, stirring constantly. Pour over the rice and give it a quick swirl. Wrap the top securely in heavy-duty aluminum foil.
- Bake for 32 minutes in a preheated oven. Remove from the oven and set aside for 10 minutes. Remove the lid and fluff the rice with a fork. Seasoning should be tasted and adjusted.
- Raise the oven temperature to 475°F (245 degrees C). Return to the oven for 10 minutes or until the rice is toasted and crusted.

Rice Patties
Preparation Time: 15 minutes
Cooking Time: 18 minutes
Serve: 1
Ingredients:
- 1 cup cooked rice
- ¼ cup shredded Cheddar cheese
- ½ small onion, chopped
- 1 egg, beaten
- ¼ teaspoon ground black pepper, or more to taste
- 1 teaspoon minced garlic
- ¼ teaspoon salt
- ¼ teaspoon chopped fresh parsley
- 1 tablespoon vegetable oil, or more to taste

Directions:
- In a mixing bowl, combine rice, onion, Cheddar cheese, egg, garlic, salt, red pepper flakes, black pepper, parsley, and onion powder by hand.
- Refrigerate for at least 30 minutes, covered with plastic wrap.
- Make four tiny patties out of the rice mixture.
- In a large skillet over medium-high heat, heat the vegetable oil. Fry patties in heated oil for 5 minutes per side or lightly browned.

THE COMPLETE AIR FRYER COOKBOOK

Mushroom Rice

Preparation Time: 15 minutes
Cooking Time: 22 minutes
Serve: 1
Ingredients:

- 2 teaspoons butter
- 6 mushrooms, coarsely chopped
- 1 clove garlic, minced
- 1 green onion, finely chopped
- 2 cups chicken broth
- 1 cup uncooked white rice
- ½ teaspoon chopped fresh parsley
- salt and pepper to taste

Directions:

- In a saucepan over medium heat, melt the butter. Cook the mushrooms, garlic, and green onion until the liquid has evaporated and the mushrooms are tender. Combine the chicken broth and rice in a mixing bowl. Season with parsley, salt, and pepper to taste. Reduce the heat to low, cover, and leave to simmer for 20 minutes.

Sarah's Rice Pilaf

Preparation Time: 10 minutes
Cooking Time: 18 minutes
Serve: 1
Ingredients:

- 2 tablespoons butter
- ½ cup orzo pasta
- ½ cup diced onion
- 2 cloves garlic, minced
- ½ cup uncooked white rice
- 2 cups chicken broth

Directions:

- In a covered skillet over medium-low heat, melt the butter. Orzo pasta should be cooked and stirred until golden brown. Sauté until the onion becomes transparent, add the garlic, and cook for 1 minute. Combine the rice and chicken broth in a mixing bowl. Turn the heat up to high and bring it to a boil. Reduce the heat to medium-low, cover, and cook for 20 to 25 minutes, or until the rice is soft and the liquid has been absorbed. Remove from the heat and set aside for 5 minutes before fluffing with a fork.

Island-Style Fried Rice

Preparation Time: 18 minutes
Cooking Time: 20 minutes
Serve: 1
Ingredients:

- 1 ½ cups uncooked jasmine rice
- 3 cups water
- 2 teaspoons canola oil
- 1 (12 ounces) can fully cook luncheon meat (such as SPAM®), cubed
- ½ cup sliced Chinese sweet pork sausage (lap Cheong)
- 3 eggs, beaten
- 2 tablespoons canola oil
- 1 (8 ounces) can pineapple chunks, drained
- ½ cup chopped green onion
- 3 tablespoons oyster sauce
- ½ teaspoon garlic powder

Directions:

- In a saucepan over high heat, bring the rice and water to a boil. Reduce the heat to medium-low, cover, and cook for 20 to 25 minutes, or until the rice is soft and the liquid has been absorbed. Allow the rice to cool fully.
- Brown the luncheon meat and sausage in a pan with 2 tablespoons of oil over medium heat. Set aside the beaten eggs and pour them into the heated skillet. Set aside the scrambled eggs.
- In a large nonstick pan over normal heat, heat 2 tablespoons of oil and toss in the rice. Toss the rice in the hot oil for approximately 2 minutes, or until cooked through and beginning to brown. Toss the rice for 1 minute longer to enhance the garlic flavor, then add the luncheon meat, sausage, scrambled eggs, pineapple, and oyster sauce. Cook and stir for 2 to 3 minutes, or until the oyster sauce covers the rice and other ingredients. Stir in the green onions and serve.

Vegan Korean Kimchi Fried Rice

Preparation Time: 15 minutes
Cooking Time: 25 minutes
Serve: 1
Ingredients:

- 1 tablespoon vegetable oil
- ¼ cup diced red onion
- 1 tablespoon minced garlic
- 1 ½ teaspoon minced ginger (optional)
- ½ cup finely chopped kimchi
- 1 tablespoon rice wine vinegar
- 1 cup day-old cooked white rice
- 2 tablespoons white sugar
- 2 tablespoons reduced-sodium soy sauce
- 2 tablespoons kimchi brine
- ½ tablespoon sesame oil
- salt to taste
- ground black pepper to taste

Directions:

- In a large nonstick skillet over medium heat, heat the oil. Mix in the red onion, garlic, and ginger. Cook, stirring periodically, for 3 minutes, or until the onion softens. Turn the heat up to high and add the kimchi and vinegar. Cooked rice, soy sauce, sugar, soy sauce, kimchi brine, and sesame oil should all be combined. Cook and stir for 5 minutes, or until heated through; scrape the bottom of the skillet to prevent sticking. Season with salt and pepper to taste.

Garlic Rice

Preparation Time: 20 minutes
Cooking Time: 20 minutes
Serve: 1
Ingredients:

- 2 tablespoons vegetable oil
- 1 ½ tablespoons chopped garlic
- 2 tablespoons ground pork
- 4 cups cooked white rice
- 1 ½ teaspoon garlic salt
- ground black pepper to taste

Directions:

- In a large skillet over medium-high heat, heat the oil. Add the garlic and ground pork after the oil is heated. Cook, constantly stirring until the garlic is golden brown. This is

110 | P a g.

the hue you want for optimum taste; the flavor will be bitter if it burns.

- Season with garlic, salt, and pepper and stir in the white rice. Cook and stir for 3 minutes, or until well cooked and well combined. Serve immediately and enjoy.

Cindy's Yellow Rice

Preparation Time: 15 minutes
Cooking Time: 25 minutes
Serve: 1
Ingredients:

- 2 cups water
- 1 cup white rice
- ¼ cup dried minced onion
- 2 tablespoons olive oil
- 1 teaspoon ground turmeric
- 1 teaspoon garlic powder
- 1 teaspoon ground black pepper
- 1 teaspoon salt

Directions:

- In a saucepan, bring water to a boil. Combine the rice, onion, olive oil, turmeric, garlic powder, black pepper, and salt in a mixing bowl. Cover the pot, decrease the heat to low, and simmer for 20 minutes, or until the water is absorbed and the rice is tender. With a fork, fluff the rice.

Sweet Coconut Rice

Preparation Time: 15 minutes
Cooking Time: 20 minutes
Serve: 1
Ingredients:

- 1 ½ cups long-grain white rice
- 1 ¼ cups water
- 1 teaspoon white sugar
- 1 (14 ounces) can of coconut milk
- 1 tablespoon shredded coconut

Directions:

- In a saucepan, combine rice, coconut milk, and water. Sugar should be dissolved in the liquid.
- Bring the mixture to a simmer, then decrease the heat to medium-low, cover the pot, and cook for 15 to 20 minutes, or until the bulk of the liquid has been absorbed by the rice. Turn off the heat and leave the pot on the fire for another 5 to 10 minutes to allow the rice to simmer until sticky. Garnish with shredded coconut if desired.

Quinoa Fried Rice

Preparation Time: 20 minutes
Cooking Time: 25 minutes
Serve: 1
Ingredients:

- 1 ½ cups water
- 1 cup quinoa
- salt to taste
- 2 ½ tablespoons soy sauce
- 1 ½ tablespoons teriyaki sauce
- ¾ teaspoon sesame oil
- 1 tablespoon olive oil, divided
- 2 carrots, peeled and chopped
- ¼ onion, chopped

- 3 scallions, chopped, divided
- 3 cloves garlic, minced
- ½ teaspoon minced fresh ginger
- 2 eggs, beaten
- ½ cup frozen peas

Directions:

- Bring the quinoa and water to a boil, season with salt. Reduce the heat to medium-low, cover, and cook for 15 to 20 minutes, or until the quinoa is tender and the water is absorbed. Turn off the heat and put aside for 5 minutes before fluffing the quinoa with a fork. Refrigerate for at least 8 hours and up to overnight.
- In a mixing bowl, combine soy sauce, teriyaki sauce, and sesame oil until equally combined.
- Heat 1 1/2 tsp oil and sauté carrots and onion in a large pan over high heat for 2 minutes. Sauté the remaining 2 scallions, garlic, and ginger for 2 minutes, or until aromatic. Cook until heated through, approximately 2 minutes, with the remaining 1 1/2 tablespoons oil and quinoa.
- Cook and swirl the sauce into the quinoa mixture for 2 minutes or evenly covered.
- In the center of the quinoa mixture, make a well. Pour the eggs into the well; heat and stir for 2 to 3 minutes, or until the eggs are scrambled and cooked through. Cook for 2 to 3 minutes, or until peas are cooked through. Stir in the remaining scallions.

One-Pot Rice and Beef Pilaf

Preparation Time: 15 minutes
Cooking Time: 20 minutes
Serve: 1
Ingredients:

- ½ cup olive oil
- 2 cups uncooked white rice
- 2 pounds bone-in beef pot roast, boned and cubed
- 1 onion, peeled, halved, and thinly sliced
- 4 carrots, peeled and cut into matchsticks
- 2 teaspoons ground cumin
- 2 fresh red chili peppers
- 1 head garlic, unpeeled (optional)
- salt to taste
- hot water to cover

Directions:

- Place the rice in a bowl and cover with warm water to soak while the meat cooks.
- Heat the olive oil in a saucepan over medium-high heat and sauté the bones for 5 minutes, or until gently browned. Place the bones on a platter. Cook until the onion is tender and translucent, about 5 minutes, in the same saucepan. Brown the meat on both sides, 5 to 10 minutes.
- Return the bones to the pan and add the carrots. Garnish with cumin. Stir in the entire chili peppers and garlic, then season with salt. Fill the container halfway with boiling water. Bring to a boil, then lower to low heat and continue to cook for 35 to 40 minutes, or until the flavors are fully integrated.
- With kitchen tongs, remove the bones and add the rice. Pour in 2 cups hot water and level out the rice to sit flat on top, but do not stir. Cook, covered, over low heat for 20 to 25 minutes, or until tender rice. Before serving, mix everything.

Cinnamon Rice

Preparation Time: 15 minutes
Cooking Time: 18 minutes
Serve: 1
Ingredients:

- 1 cup uncooked rice
- 2 cups water
- 2 tablespoons nonfat milk
- 5 tablespoons raisins
- 2 teaspoons margarine
- ½ teaspoon ground cinnamon
- 1 teaspoon sugar

Directions:

- In a saucepan over medium-high heat, bring rice, water, milk, raisins, and margarine to a boil, stirring periodically. Reduce the heat to low, cover, and simmer for 15 minutes, or until the liquid has been absorbed and the rice is soft. To serve, combine cinnamon and sugar and sprinkle over rice.

Cauliflower Rice (Biryani-Style)

Preparation Time: 15 minutes
Cooking Time: 22 minutes
Serve: 1
Ingredients:

- 1 head cauliflower, broken into florets
- 3 tablespoons butter
- 1 clove garlic, minced, or to taste
- ½ teaspoon cumin
- ½ teaspoon ground coriander
- ½ teaspoon garam masala
- ½ teaspoon ground turmeric
- ¼ teaspoon minced fresh ginger, or to taste
- 1 pinch cayenne pepper
- salt and ground black pepper to taste
- 1 lime, cut into wedges
- ¼ cup chopped fresh cilantro, or to taste

Directions:

- In a blender or food processor, break cauliflower florets into little pieces the size of rice.
- Melt the butter in a pan over medium-high heat and add the cauliflower rice, garlic, cumin, coriander, garam masala, turmeric, ginger, cayenne pepper, salt, and black pepper. Cook, stirring periodically, for approximately 10 minutes, or until cauliflower is softened.
- Remove the skillet from the heat and stir in the lime wedges and cilantro.

Morel Mushroom and Wild Rice Risotto

Preparation Time: 10 minutes
Cooking Time: 18 minutes
Serve: 1
Ingredients:

- 6 cups chicken broth
- 1 teaspoon dried thyme
- ¼ cup heavy cream
- 3 cups water
- 2 carrots, diced
- 2 stalks celery, diced
- 1 onion, diced
- 2 tablespoons olive oil
- 2 tablespoons unsalted butter
- 1 cup brown rice
- 1 cup wild rice
- ½ pound fresh morel mushrooms
- 2 cloves garlic, minced
- ½ cup dry white wine
- salt and ground black pepper to taste

Directions:

- In a large stockpot, combine chicken broth and water. Bring to a boil over medium-high heat; lower to low heat and keep warm.
- Heat 1 tablespoon butter and 1 tablespoon olive oil over medium heat until the butter melts in a large Dutch oven. Cook, stirring regularly, until the brown rice is toasted, about 5 minutes. Stir in the wild rice, carrots, celery, onion, and garlic, as well as half of the morel mushrooms. Cook, stirring regularly, for 3 to 5 minutes, or until onions are transparent. Pour in the white wine and heat for 2 to 3 minutes, or until it has evaporated.
- 1/2 of the chicken broth mixture should be mixed into the rice; toss to incorporate. Cook, covered, over medium heat for 30 minutes, stirring every 5 minutes, until thickened. Pour in the rest of the chicken broth mixture, morel mushrooms, and thyme. Cook, covered, over medium heat for 30 to 40 minutes, stirring every 5 minutes, until wild rice is soft.
- Combine the remaining 1 tablespoon butter and heavy cream in a mixing bowl. Cook for 1 minute more, or until the butter has melted. Season with salt and pepper to taste. Serve with Pecorino Romano cheese on top.

Classic Fried Rice

Preparation Time: 18 minutes
Cooking Time: 20 minutes
Serve: 1
Ingredients:

- 6 strips bacon, cut into 1/2-inch pieces
- 1 egg, beaten
- 8 green onions and tops, sliced
- 4 cups cold, cooked rice
- 1 tablespoon minced garlic
- 3 tablespoons Kikkoman Soy Sauce

Directions:

- In a large pan over medium heat, cook bacon until crisp. Transfer the bacon to the side of the pan; add the egg and scramble it. Move the egg to the skillet, add the green onions, cook for approximately a minute. Next, stir in the rice, followed by the garlic and soy sauce. Toss until the mixture is properly combined and thoroughly cooked.

Parmesan Asparagus Rice

Preparation Time: 15 minutes
Cooking Time: 25 minutes
Serve: 1
Ingredients:

- 1 cup UNCLE BEN'S® Basmati Rice - cooks in 10 minutes
- 2 cups vegetable stock
- 1 small, sweet onion, diced
- 1 clove garlic, minced
- 3 tablespoons butter, divided
- 2 tablespoons freshly grated Parmesan cheese

- 1 cup chopped fresh asparagus
- 1 pinch salt and ground black pepper

Directions:

- In a 3-quart saucepan over medium heat, melt 2 tablespoons of butter. Cook and stir onion for 1 minute or until softened and translucent. Cook for another minute after adding the garlic. Combine the rice, asparagus, and stock in a mixing bowl. Reduce the heat to medium-low and cover.
- Stir the rice occasionally to keep it from sticking to the bottom of the pan. Cook for another 10 minutes, or until the rice is soft.
- Remove from the heat and whisk in the Parmesan cheese and remaining butter. Serve right away.

Easy Oven Brown Rice

Preparation Time: 20 minutes
Cooking Time: 20 minutes
Serve: 1
Ingredients:

- 1 ½ cups brown rice
- 1 teaspoon salt
- 2 tablespoons butter
- 3 cups boiling water

Directions:

- Preheat the oven carefully to 400°F (200 degrees C).
- Combine the rice, salt, and butter in a casserole dish with a lid. Pour boiling water over the rice and toss to combine.
- Cover and bake in a preheated oven for 1 hour, or until liquid is absorbed and rice is soft. Remove from the oven, fluff with a fork, and serve immediately.

Yellow Rice with Meat

Preparation Time: 15 minutes
Cooking Time: 25 minutes
Serve: 1
Ingredients:

- 1 tablespoon olive oil
- 2 pork chops
- 2 boneless, skinless chicken thighs
- 2 green bell peppers, seeded
- 1 onion, diced
- 2 cloves garlic, finely chopped
- 1 sprig of fresh rosemary
- 4 sprigs of fresh thyme
- 2 teaspoons cloves
- 3 bay leaves
- 1 (10 ounces) package yellow rice
- 1 cup peas
- 1 lemon, cut into wedges
- 1 fresh jalapeno pepper, diced
- chili sauce

Directions:

- In a skillet over medium heat, heat the olive oil. Cook until the pork chops and chicken thighs are browned on both sides, the chicken juices run clear, and the pork chops are done. Set aside after removing from skillet.
- Cook until the bell peppers are cooked in the pan, then put aside. Mix in the onion and garlic. Combine rosemary, thyme, cloves, and bay leaves in a mixing bowl. Add rice to the pan, along with the amount of water specified on the rice bag. Cook for another 10 minutes.

- Combine the pork chops, chicken, rice, peppers, and peas in a pan. Cook for another 10 minutes, or until the rice is soft. Remove the rosemary, thyme, and bay leaves. To serve, pour lemon juice over the meats and rice, then top with chopped jalapeño and chili sauce.

Perfect White Rice

Preparation Time: 15 minutes
Cooking Time: 20 minutes
Serve: 1
Ingredients:

- 2 teaspoons unsalted butter
- 1 cup uncooked long-grain white rice
- 2 cups water
- ½ teaspoon salt

Directions:

- In a medium saucepan over medium heat, melt the butter. Stir in the rice to coat it. Cook for 1 to 2 minutes, or until the rice grains become opaque; do not brown. Pour in the water and salt.
- Bring to a boil, then lower to low heat. Allow boiling for 15 minutes, covered. Do not remove the cover.
- Remove from the heat and set aside for 5 minutes, covered. Before serving, fluff with a fork.

Jeera Rice

Preparation Time: 20 minutes
Cooking Time: 25 minutes
Serve: 1
Ingredients:

- 1 cup basmati rice
- 2 teaspoons vegetable oil
- 1 teaspoon cumin seeds
- 4 whole cloves
- 4 whole black peppercorns
- 2 cardamom pods
- 1 bay leaf
- 1 ½ cups water
- salt to taste

Directions:

- Rinse rice three to four times before placing it in a bowl; cover with water and soak for at least 30 minutes.
- Cook and swirl cumin in a pan over medium heat until it begins to pop, 2 to 4 minutes. Cook and stir for 1 1/2 minutes, or until the cloves, peppercorns, cardamom pods, and bay leaf are aromatic.
- Drain the rice and combine with spice mixture; add 1 1/2 cups water and salt to taste. Cook for 5 minutes, covered, over high heat. Reduce the heat to medium and cook for another 10 minutes. Reduce the heat to low and continue to cook for 15 minutes. Remove skillet from heat and set aside for 15 minutes with the lid on.
- Remove the lid and fluff the rice with a fork. Remove the bay leaf, cardamom pods, cloves, and peppercorns from the mixture.

South Indian-Style Lemon Rice

Preparation Time: 15 minutes
Cooking Time: 20 minutes
Serve: 1
Ingredients:

- 4 cups water
- 2 cups uncooked white rice
- 6 tablespoons vegetable oil
- ¼ cup raw peanuts
- ½ teaspoon ground turmeric
- ½ teaspoon mustard seeds
- 4 green chili peppers, chopped
- ¼ cup lemon juice
- 15 fresh curry leaves (Optional)
- 1 ½ teaspoons salt

Directions:

- Bring water and rice to a boil in a saucepan. Reduce to medium-low heat, cover, and simmer for 20 to 25 minutes, or until the rice is mushy and the water has been absorbed.
- In a large skillet over medium heat, heat the oil. Cook and stir the peanuts, turmeric, and mustard seeds for 2 to 3 minutes, or until the peanuts are browned. Combine the green chili peppers, lemon juice, curry leaves, and salt in a mixing bowl.
- Fold the cooked rice into the lemon juice mixture.

Cajun Wild Rice

Preparation Time: 15 minutes
Cooking Time: 18 minutes
Serve: 1
Ingredients:

- 1 cup uncooked wild rice
- 1 (14 ounces) can of chicken broth
- ¼ cup water
- ½ pound andouille sausage, diced
- ½ cup diced sweet onion
- 1 cup chopped fresh mushrooms
- 1 tablespoon minced garlic
- 1 (10.75 ounces) can condense cream of mushroom soup

Directions:

- Combine the wild rice, chicken broth, water, sausage, onion, mushrooms, and garlic in a saucepan. Bring to a boil, lower to low heat, cover, and leave to cook for 25 to 30 minutes, or until the rice is tender. Next, take the pan off the heat and whisk in the cream of mushroom soup. It's just that simple !

Linnie's Spanish Rice

Preparation Time: 15 minutes
Cooking Time: 22 minutes
Serve: 1
Ingredients:

- 1 cup uncooked white rice
- 1 teaspoon minced garlic
- 2 cups water
- 1 (16 ounces) jar salsa

Directions:

- In a large pot, combine the rice and garlic. Pour the rice mixture with the water and salsa.
- Bring the water to a full boil before lowering the heat to a simmer.
- Cook, occasionally stirring, for 20 minutes, or until the rice is tender. When the rice is done, fluff it with a fork.

Kheer (Rice Pudding)

Preparation Time: 10 minutes

Cooking Time: 18 minutes
Serve: 1
Ingredients:

- 2 cups coconut milk
- 2 cups milk
- 3 tablespoons white sugar
- ½ cup Basmati rice
- ¼ cup raisins
- ½ teaspoon ground cardamom
- ½ teaspoon rose water (Optional)
- ¼ cup sliced almonds, toasted
- ¼ cup chopped pistachio nuts

Directions:

- In a large saucepan, bring the coconut milk, milk, and sugar to a boil. Cook, occasionally stirring, until the stew thickens, and the rice is cooked for about 20 minutes.
- Cook for a few minutes more after adding the raisins, cardamom, and rose water. Garnish with almonds and pistachios before ladling into serving dishes.

Delicate Jasmine Rice

Preparation Time: 18 minutes
Cooking Time: 20 minutes
Serve: 1
Ingredients:

- 3 cups water
- 1 jasmine herbal tea bag
- 1 cube vegetable bouillon
- 1 ½ cups uncooked brown rice
- 1 tablespoon butter
- 2 tablespoons chopped fresh cilantro

Directions:

- In a large saucepan, bring 3 cups of water and the tea bag to a boil. Take the teabag out of the boiling water. Return the flavored water to a boil after stirring the rice and bouillon cube. Reduce heat carefully to low and cover the pan. Allow rice to steam for 45 minutes or until the water has been absorbed and the rice is soft. Remove from the heat and set aside for 5 minutes. With a fork, fluff the cooked rice and whisk in the butter. Garnish the rice with chopped cilantro.

Spent Grain Wheat Bread

Preparation Time: 15 minutes
Cooking Time: 25 minutes
Serve: 1
Ingredients:

- 1 ¼ cups water
- 3 tablespoons honey
- 3 tablespoons butter, softened
- ¼ cup spent grain
- 1 ½ tablespoons powdered milk
- 1 teaspoon white sugar
- 1 teaspoon salt
- ½ cup rye flour
- 1 ½ cups whole wheat flour
- 1 ½ cups bread flour
- ¼ cup vital wheat gluten
- 1 teaspoon active dry yeast

Directions:

- Place the ingredients in the bread machine's pan in the sequence indicated by the manufacturer. Choose the complete wheat cycle and hit the Start button. Reduce the water by 1 tablespoon if using the delay timer.

Chicken and Multi-Grain Stir Fry

Preparation Time: 20 minutes
Cooking Time: 20 minutes
Serve: 1
Ingredients:

- 1 bag Minute® Multi-Grain Medley, uncooked
- 1 cup chicken broth
- 2 large eggs, lightly beaten
- ½ teaspoon sesame oil
- 2 tablespoons olive oil, divided
- 2 cloves garlic, chopped
- ½ cup red onion, thinly sliced
- ½ cup snap peas
- ½ cup broccoli florets
- ½ cup red bell pepper, sliced
- ½ teaspoon Chinese five-spice powder (Optional)
- 2 cups cooked chicken, shredded

Directions:

- Make Multi-Grain Medley according to package directions but use broth instead of water. Whisk together the eggs and sesame oil in a small bowl.
- 12 tbsp olive oil, heated in a large pan at medium-low heat
- Soft scrambled eggs in a hurry. Remove from skillet and set aside to stay heated. Heat the remaining olive oil in a medium saucepan over medium heat. Sauté for 3 minutes with the garlic, onions, peas, broccoli, bell peppers, and five-spice powder.
- Cook for 2 minutes more, or until the chicken, Multi-Grain Medley, and eggs are crisp-tender.

Cranberry Pecan Multi-Grain Stuffing

Preparation Time: 15 minutes
Cooking Time: 25 minutes
Serve: 1
Ingredients:

- 1 tablespoon olive oil
- ½ cup chopped onion
- ¼ cup chopped fresh celery
- ¼ teaspoon poultry seasoning
- ½ cup dried cranberries
- 1 cup chicken broth
- 1 bag Minute® Multi-Grain Medley, uncooked
- ½ cup chopped pecans, toasted
- 1 pinch salt and ground black pepper

Directions:

- In a medium saucepan, heat the oil over medium heat. Cook for 2 minutes after adding the onion and celery. Combine the chicken seasoning, cranberries, and broth in a mixing bowl.
- Bring to a boil, then add the Multi-Grain Medley. Cover, decrease the heat to low and cook for 5 minutes.
- Remove from the heat and set aside for 5 minutes. Season with salt and pepper, if preferred, and stir in the pecans.

Whole Grain Pancakes with Fresh Fruit

Preparation Time: 15 minutes
Cooking Time: 20 minutes

Serve: 1
Ingredients:

- 1 cup whole wheat flour
- ¼ cup quick cooking rolled oats
- 2 tablespoons firmly packed brown sugar
- 1 ½ teaspoons baking powder
- ½ teaspoon salt
- ¾ cup fat-free milk
- ½ cup Egg Beaters® Original
- ¼ cup plain nonfat yogurt
- 1 tablespoon Pure Wesson® Canola Oil
- ½ teaspoon vanilla extract
- PAM® Organic Canola Oil No-Stick Cooking Spray
- ¼ cup honey
- 2 medium bananas, peeled and sliced
- ½ cup fresh blueberries
- 1 tablespoon Reddi-wip® Fat-Free Dairy Whipped Topping

Directions:

- In a large mixing basin, combine the flour, oats, sugar, baking powder, and salt; set aside. Next, combine the milk, Egg Beaters, yogurt, oil, and vanilla extract in a small mixing bowl. Add to the flour mixture and whisk just until combined. (Avoid overmixing.) The batter should still be a little lumpy.)
- Coat the skillet with frying spray. Heat over medium heat until hot, or preheat an electric skillet to 400°F. For each pancake, pour roughly 1/4 cup batter onto a heated griddle. Cook for 2 to 3 minutes, or until bubbles appear on the surface and the bottom is golden brown. Cook until golden brown on the other side. Rep with the remaining batter.
- Drizzle 1 tablespoon honey over each serving and top with fresh fruit. Serve right away.

Whole Grain Pancakes

Preparation Time: 20 minutes
Cooking Time: 25 minutes
Serve: 1
Ingredients:

- 1 cup whole wheat flour
- ½ cup rolled oats
- ¼ cup cornmeal
- 3 tablespoons flaxseed meal
- 3 tablespoons brown sugar
- 1 teaspoon baking powder
- ½ teaspoon baking soda
- 1 egg, beaten
- 2 cups buttermilk
- cooking spray

Directions:

- Combine the whole wheat flour, oats, cornmeal, flaxseed meal, brown sugar, baking powder, and baking soda in a large mixing basin. Pour in the buttermilk and the egg. Only stir until smooth.
- Melt butter in a large pan or skillet over medium heat. Coat with nonstick cooking spray. Drop batter onto the griddle in large spoonsful and heat until bubbles form, and the sides are dry. Cook, flipping once until the opposite side is browned. Rep with the remaining batter.

Easter Grain Pie

Preparation Time: 15 minutes

Cooking Time: 20 minutes
Serve: 1
Ingredients:

- 5 cups water
- ½ cup whole wheat berries
- 6 eggs
- 1 cup white sugar
- 1 (8 ounces) package mixed candied fruit
- 1 ½ pound ricotta cheese
- 1 teaspoon vanilla extract
- ½ teaspoon ground cinnamon
- 1 teaspoon grated lemon zest
- 2 teaspoons grated orange zest
- 1 tablespoon shortening
- 1 teaspoon salt
- 2 pastries for 9-inch lattice-top pies
- 2 tablespoons confectioners' sugar for dusting

Directions:

- In a big saucepan, bring water to a boil. Allow wheat to boiling for 40 minutes. While the wheat is cooking, beat the eggs in a large mixing basin while gradually adding 1 cup sugar. Combine the fruit, ricotta, vanilla essence, cinnamon, lemon rind, and orange rind in a mixing bowl.
- When the wheat is done, strain it in a strainer and rinse it with warm water. Combine 3/4 cup cooked wheat, shortening, and salt in a small bowl. Stir until the shortening is melted, then fold in the wheat mixture and the remaining cooked wheat berries.
- Preheat the oven carefully to 375°F (190 degrees C).
- Fill two 9-inch pie tins halfway with pastry. Cut the leftover pastry into strips for the pies' tops. Half of the filling should be placed in each pan. To make lattice tops, cover with pastry strips. Crimp the edges.
- Bake for 45 minutes, or until the crust is golden brown, in a preheated oven. Allow each pie to cool at room temperature before sprinkling with 1 tablespoon sugar. Allow chilling overnight before serving. Any leftovers should be refrigerated.

Grain and Nut Whole Wheat Pancakes

Preparation Time: 15 minutes
Cooking Time: 18 minutes
Serve: 1
Ingredients:

- 1 ½ cups old-fashioned oatmeal
- 1 ½ cups whole wheat flour
- 2 teaspoons baking soda
- 1 teaspoon baking powder
- ½ teaspoon salt
- 1 ½ cups buttermilk
- 1 cup milk
- ¼ cup vegetable oil
- 1 egg
- ⅓ cup sugar
- 3 tablespoons chopped walnuts (optional)

Directions:

- In a blender or food processor, grind the oats until fine. Combine ground oats, whole wheat flour, baking soda, baking powder, and salt in a large mixing basin.
- In a separate dish, whisk together the buttermilk, milk, oil, egg, and sugar with an electric mixer until smooth. Then, combine the wet and dry components with a few quick strokes. If using nuts, toss them in at the end.

- Preheat a pan or skillet to medium heat and lightly oil it. Spoon 1/3 cup batter into a heated skillet; cook the pancakes for 2 to 4 minutes per side, or until golden.

Rustic Grain Cereal

Preparation Time: 15 minutes
Cooking Time: 22 minutes
Serve: 1
Ingredients:

- ½ cup water
- ⅓ cup wheat berries
- 1 teaspoon butter
- 1 cup steel-cut oats
- ⅓ cup chopped pecans
- ⅓ cup slivered almonds
- 3 cups boiling water
- 1 cup chopped dried apples
- ⅓ cup white sugar, or to taste
- 1 ½ tablespoon ground cinnamon
- 1 teaspoon salt

Directions:

- In a small saucepan, combine 1/2 cup water and the wheat berries; bring to a boil. Cover saucepan, remove from heat and leave aside for 10 minutes to allow wheat berries to soak.
- Melt butter in a 2-quart saucepan over low heat; cook and stir oats, pecans, and almonds in melted butter for 5 minutes, or until brown and aromatic. Pour boiling water into the nut mixture, add the wheat berries and dried apples. Cook, covered, over low heat for 25 minutes, or until wheat berries are soft; mix in sugar, cinnamon, and salt.

Whole Grain Carrot Peach Muffins

Preparation Time: 10 minutes
Cooking Time: 18 minutes
Serve: 1
Ingredients:

- 2 tablespoons butter, slightly softened
- ¼ cup rolled oats
- 1 tablespoon dark brown sugar
- 1 tablespoon all-purpose flour
- ¼ teaspoon ground cinnamon
- ½ cup all-purpose flour
- ½ cup white whole-wheat flour
- ½ cup oat flour
- 1 ½ teaspoons baking powder
- 1 teaspoon ground cinnamon
- ½ teaspoon baking soda
- ½ cup canola oil
- ½ cup white sugar
- 2 large eggs
- 1 teaspoon vanilla extract
- 1 ½ cups diced peaches
- 1 cup grated carrots

Directions:

- Preheat the oven carefully to 350°F (175 degrees C). Prepare a muffin tin by lining it with paper liners.
- Combine the butter, rolled oats, dark brown sugar, 1 tablespoon all-purpose flour, and 1/4 teaspoon cinnamon in a mixing dish. Mix with a fork or your fingertips until the mixture is crumbly.

- In a large mixing bowl, combine 1/2 cup all-purpose flour, white whole-wheat flour, oat flour, baking powder, 1 teaspoon cinnamon, and baking soda.
- Combine the oil, sugar, eggs, and vanilla essence in a separate dish. Pour into the flour mixture and fold until barely mixed. Next, gently fold in the peaches and carrots.
- Fill prepared muffin tins about 2/3 full of batter. Garnish with oat topping.
- Bake for 15 minutes, or until a toothpick inserted into the center comes out clean. Cool for 5 to 10 minutes in the pan before transferring muffins to a wire rack to cool fully.

Zucchini Banana Multi-Grain Bread

Preparation Time: 18 minutes
Cooking Time: 20 minutes
Serve: 1
Ingredients:

- 1 bag Minute® Multi-Grain Medley, uncooked
- 1 serving Nonstick cooking spray
- 3 large eggs, lightly beaten
- ½ cup sugar
- 1 ripe banana, mashed
- 3 tablespoons vegetable oil, ¼ cup milk
- 1 teaspoon vanilla extract
- 1 medium zucchini, grated
- ½ cup walnuts, chopped
- 2 cups baking mix

Directions:

- Preheat the oven carefully to 400°F. Follow the package directions to make the Multi-Grain Medley. Using nonstick cooking spray, coat a loaf pan.
- In a large mixing basin, combine the eggs, sugar, and banana. Stir in the rice, oil, milk, vanilla, zucchini (approximately 1 1/2 cups shredded), and walnuts. Stir in the baking mix until all of the ingredients are mixed. Pour the mixture into the prepared pan.
- 45 minutes in the oven, or until a toothpick inserted into the middle comes out clean.
- Allow to cool for 10 minutes before removing from pan and cooling on a rack.

CHAPTER 8:

Vegan

Vegetable Skewers

Preparation Time: 10 minutes
Cooking Time: 10 minutes
Serve: 4
Ingredients:

- 1 eggplant, cut into 1-inch pieces
- 1/2 onion, cut into 1-inch pieces
- 2 bell peppers, cut into 1-inch pieces
- 1 zucchini, cut into 1-inch pieces
- 1 tbsp olive oil
- 1 tsp garlic powder
- ¼ tsp paprika
- Pepper, Salt

Directions:

- Preheat the air fryer to 390 F.
- In a mixing bowl, toss veggies with oil, garlic powder, paprika, pepper, and salt until well coated.
- Thread vegetables onto the soaked wooden skewers.
- Place vegetable skewers into the air fryer basket and cook for 10 minutes. Turn halfway through.
- Serve and enjoy.

Healthy Jicama & Green Beans

Preparation Time: 10 minutes
Cooking Time: 45 minutes
Serve: 6
Ingredients:

- 12 oz green beans, sliced in half
- 1 medium jicama, cubed
- 1 tsp dried thyme
- 3 tbsp canola oil
- 3 garlic cloves, minced
- 1 tsp dried rosemary
- 1/2 tsp salt

Directions:

- Preheat the air fryer to 400 F.
- Add green beans, jicama, and remaining ingredients into the mixing bowl and toss well.
- Spread green beans and jicama mixture into the air fryer basket and cook for 45 minutes. Stir halfway through.
- Serve and enjoy.

Crispy Brussels Sprouts

Preparation Time: 10 minutes
Cooking Time: 15 minutes
Serve: 4
Ingredients:

- 2 cups Brussels sprouts

- 2 tbsp canola oil
- 1/4 cup almonds, crushed
- 2 tbsp everything bagel seasoning
- Pepper
- Salt

Directions:

- Preheat the air fryer to 375 F.
- Add Brussels sprouts into the saucepan with 2 cups of water. Cover and cook for 10 minutes. Drain well and let it cool completely.
- Cut each Brussels sprouts in half.
- Add Brussels sprouts and remaining ingredients into the bowl and toss to coat.
- Add Brussels sprouts into the air fryer basket and cook for 15 minutes. Stir halfway through.
- Serve and enjoy.

Flavorful Green Beans

Preparation Time: 5 minutes
Cooking Time: 10 minutes
Serve: 2
Ingredients:

- 2 cups green beans
- 1/2 tsp dried oregano
- 1/8 tsp cayenne pepper
- 1/8 tsp ground allspice
- 2 tbsp canola oil
- 1/4 tsp ground coriander
- 1/4 tsp ground cumin
- 1/4 tsp ground cinnamon
- 1/2 tsp salt

Directions:

- Preheat the air fryer to 370 F.
- Add green beans and remaining ingredients into the mixing bowl and toss well.
- Add green beans into the air fryer basket and cook for 8-10 minutes. Stir halfway through.
- Serve and enjoy.

Easy Ratatouille

Preparation Time: 10 minutes
Cooking Time: 15 minutes
Serve: 6
Ingredients:

- 1 eggplant, diced
- 2 bell peppers, diced
- 1 1/2 tbsp olive oil
- 2 tbsp herb de Provence
- 1 tbsp vinegar

- 1 onion, diced
- 3 tomatoes, diced
- 2 garlic cloves, chopped
- Pepper
- Salt

Directions:
- Preheat the air fryer to 400 F.
- Add all ingredients into the bowl and toss well and transfer into the air fryer baking dish.
- Place baking dish into the air fryer basket and cook for 15 minutes.
- Serve and enjoy.

Tasty Zucchini Chips
Preparation Time: 10 minutes
Cooking Time: 12 minutes
Serve: 3
Ingredients:
- 1 large zucchini, cut into slices
- 3 tbsp roasted pecans, crushed
- 3 tbsp almond flour
- 1 tbsp olive oil
- 1 tbsp Bagel seasoning

Directions:
- Preheat the air fryer to 350 F.
- Add zucchini slices, crushed pecans, almond flour, oil, and bagel seasoning into the mixing bowl and toss until well coated.
- Arrange zucchini slices into the air fryer basket and cook for 12 minutes. Turn halfway through.
- Serve and enjoy.

Crispy Cauliflower Tots
Preparation Time: 10 minutes
Cooking Time: 12 minutes
Serve: 4
Ingredients:
- 1 large cauliflower head, cut into florets
- 1/4 cup extra-virgin olive oil
- 2 tbsp arrowroot
- 3 tbsp hot sauce
- 1 tbsp olive oil
- Pepper
- Salt

Directions:
- Preheat the air fryer to 380 F.
- Toss cauliflower florets with oil and coat with arrowroot.
- Add cauliflower florets into the air fryer basket and cook for 6 minutes.
- Meanwhile, in a mixing bowl, mix together hot sauce and extra-virgin olive oil.
- Once cauliflower florets are cooked then transfer them into the sauce and toss well.
- Return cauliflower florets into the air fryer basket and cook for 6 minutes more.
- Serve and enjoy.

Crispy Tofu Cubes
Preparation Time: 10 minutes

Cooking Time: 15 minutes
Serve: 4
Ingredients:
- 15 oz extra-firm tofu, pressed and cut into cubes
- 1 tbsp rice vinegar
- 1 tsp sesame oil
- 2 tbsp soy sauce

Directions:
- Preheat the air fryer to 400 F.
- In a mixing bowl, mix together tofu, vinegar, sesame oil, and soy sauce. Allow to sit for 20 minutes.
- Add tofu into the air fryer basket and cook for 12-15 minutes. Stir halfway through.
- Serve and enjoy.

Tasty Carrots Chips
Preparation Time: 10 minutes
Cooking Time: 12 minutes
Serve: 4
Ingredients:
- 12 oz carrot chips
- 1/4 tsp pepper
- ¼ tsp chili powder
- 1/2 tsp garlic powder
- 1 tbsp canola oil
- 1/4 tsp paprika
- 1/2 tsp salt

Directions:
- Preheat the air fryer to 375 F.
- Add carrot chips and remaining ingredients into the bowl and toss well.
- Add carrot chips into the air fryer basket and cook for 12 minutes. Stir halfway through.
- Serve and enjoy.

Herb Olives
Preparation Time: 10 minutes
Cooking Time: 5 minutes
Serve: 4
Ingredients:
- 2 cups olives
- 1/2 tsp red pepper flakes, crushed
- 2 tbsp canola oil
- 1/2 tsp dried fennel seeds
- 2 tsp garlic, minced
- 1/2 tsp dried oregano
- Pepper
- Salt

Directions:
- Preheat the air fryer to 300 F.
- Add olives and remaining ingredients into the bowl and toss to coat well.
- Add olives into the air fryer basket and cook for 5 minutes.
- Serve and enjoy.

Air Fryer Burgers
Preparation Time: 15 minutes
Cooking Time: 25 minutes
Serve: 1

Ingredients:

- 1 (16 ounces) package ground beef
- ½ red onion, diced
- 1 teaspoon minced garlic
- 1 teaspoon salt
- 1 teaspoon ground black pepper
- 1 teaspoon Worcestershire sauce
- 1 teaspoon hot English mustard

Directions:

- Preheat an air fryer carefully to 350°F (175 degrees C).
- Combine the meat, red onion, garlic, salt, pepper, Worcestershire sauce, and English mustard in a mixing bowl.
- Patties may be made by flattening a ball of ground beef with your hand and rounding the sides to the appropriate size.
- Cook the burgers in the preheated air fryer for about 10 minutes, or until firm and no longer pink in the middle. In the middle, an instant-read thermometer should read at least 160 degrees F. (70 degrees C).

Air Fryer Vegan Buffalo Tofu Bites

Preparation Time: 20 minutes
Cooking Time: 20 minutes
Serve: 1
Ingredients:

- 1 (8 ounces) container extra-firm tofu
- 4 tablespoons cornstarch
- 4 tablespoons unsweetened rice milk
- ¾ cup panko breadcrumbs
- ⅛ teaspoon garlic powder
- ⅛ teaspoon paprika
- ⅛ teaspoon onion powder
- ⅛ teaspoon freshly ground black pepper
- ⅔ cup vegan Buffalo wing sauce (such as Frank's®)

Directions:

- Take the tofu block out of the packaging and discard the liquid. Wrap tofu in cheesecloth, set on a platter, and cover with a heavy saucepan for 10 minutes to press out any residual liquid. Remove the cheesecloth from the tofu and chop it into 20 1-inch bite-sized pieces. Place in a freezer-safe container and place in the freezer for 8 hours overnight.
- Remove the frozen tofu from the freezer and defrost it on paper towels or a dry cheesecloth. Allow airing to dry.
- Fill a resealable plastic bag halfway with cornstarch while the tofu is thawing. Fill a small bowl halfway with rice milk.
- Preheat an air fryer carefully to 375°F (190 degrees C).
- Place the tofu in the bag with the cornstarch, close, and shake to cover the tofu pieces fully. Remove the tofu and coat each piece with rice milk.
- In a resealable plastic bag, combine the breadcrumbs, garlic powder, paprika, onion powder, and pepper with the cornstarch residue; shake until thoroughly combined. Return each piece of tofu to the bag with the breadcrumbs, one at a time. Shake the bag until the tofu is thoroughly covered, then gently shake off the excess and lay the tofu on a wire rack while you repeat with the other tofu pieces.
- Cook for 10 minutes in the air fryer basket with covered tofu. To loosen the fragments, shake the basket. Cook for 3 minutes more, or until browned.
- Toss fried tofu bits in a basin with 1/3 cup buffalo sauce to coat. Drizzle the remaining buffalo sauce over the tofu and toss to cover. Serve right away.

Air Fryer Vegan Buffalo Cauliflower

Preparation Time: 15 minutes
Cooking Time: 25 minutes
Serve: 1
Ingredients:

- 1 ½ pound cauliflower florets
- 4 tablespoons Egg substitute, liquid
- ¾ cup all-purpose flour
- 1 teaspoon garlic powder
- 1 teaspoon paprika
- ½ teaspoon salt
- ¼ teaspoon ground black pepper
- nonstick cooking spray
- ½ cup vegan Buffalo wing sauce (such as Frank's®)

Directions:

- Preheat the air fryer carefully to 400°F (200 degrees C).
- In a large mixing basin, combine cauliflower florets. Stir the egg replacement into the florets to coat.
- Combine the flour, garlic powder, paprika, salt, and pepper in a large plastic resealable bag. Shake and zip until evenly blended.
- 1/2 of the florets should be dipped in seasoned flour. Zip it up and shake it to coat. Fill the air fryer basket with florets. Nonstick cooking spray should be sprayed on the tops.
- 5 minutes in the air fryer. Cook for 5 minutes more after flipping the cauliflower and spraying any powdery places. Repeat with the rest of the cauliflower florets.
- Meanwhile, prepare the buffalo wing sauce in a skillet over medium heat. Place the cauliflower in a large mixing basin. Toss the top with the wing sauce until uniformly covered. Serve right away.

Air Fryer Vegan Sweet Potato Fritters

Preparation Time: 15 minutes
Cooking Time: 20 minutes
Serve: 1
Ingredients:

- 1 ½ cups shredded sweet potato
- ½ cup almond flour
- ¼ cup finely diced onions
- ½ tablespoon olive oil
- ½ teaspoon salt
- ½ teaspoon freshly ground black pepper
- ¼ teaspoon ground turmeric
- avocado oil cooking spray

Directions:

- Preheat an air fryer carefully to 350°F (175 degrees C).
- Combine the shredded sweet potato, almond flour, onions, olive oil, salt, pepper, and turmeric in a mixing bowl. Using a large cookie scoop, divide the mixture into 9 balls and shape it into patties. Place the patties in the air fryer basket, ensuring they don't touch. Coat the tops with cooking spray.
- Cook in a preheated air fryer for 10 to 12 minutes, or until the cakes begin to brown on the edges. Flip the patties over, coat with cooking spray, and continue to air fry for 6 to 8 minutes. Allow for a 1-minute rest before removing from the air fryer basket.

Vegan Air Fryer Taquitos

Preparation Time: 20 minutes

Cooking Time: 25 minutes
Serve: 1
Ingredients:

- 1 large russet potato, peeled
- 1 teaspoon plant-based butter (such as Country Crock®)
- 2 tablespoons diced onions
- 1 clove garlic, minced
- ¼ cup plant-based butter (such as Country Crock®)
- 2 tablespoons unsweetened, plain almond milk
- salt and ground black pepper to taste
- 6 corn tortillas
- avocado oil cooking spray

Directions:

- Fill a saucepan halfway with salted water and bring to a boil. Reduce the heat to medium-low and cook until the vegetables are soft, about 20 minutes.
- While the potato is boiling, heat 1 teaspoon plant-based butter in a pan and sauté onions for 3 to 5 minutes, or until tender and translucent. Cook until the garlic is aromatic, approximately 1 minute. Set aside some time
- Drain the potato and place it in a bowl. Mash in 1/4 cup plant-based butter and almond milk, season with salt and pepper. Combine the onion and garlic in a mixing bowl.
- Heat tortillas in a pan or directly on the gas stove grates till warm and flexible. Place 3 teaspoons of the potato mixture down the middle of each tortilla, fold it over, and roll it up.
- Preheat an air fryer carefully to 400°F (200 degrees C).
- Place the taquitos in the air fryer basket without touching and spritz with avocado oil. If necessary, cook in batches.
- 6 to 9 minutes in the air fryer until the taquitos are golden brown and crispy. Turn the taquitos over, spray with avocado oil, and continue to air fry for 3 to 5 minutes.

Vegan Jalapeno Cornbread in the Air Fryer

Preparation Time: 15 minutes
Cooking Time: 18 minutes
Serve: 1
Ingredients:

- 1 tablespoon flaxseed meal
- ⅔ cup all-purpose flour
- 3 tablespoons water
- cooking spray
- 1 cup stone-ground yellow cornmeal
- ¼ cup nutritional yeast
- 2 tablespoons white sugar
- 1 cup unsweetened almond milk
- 2 ¼ teaspoons baking powder
- 1 teaspoon kosher salt
- ½ teaspoon ground black pepper
- ⅓ cup vegetable oil
- 1 large jalapeno pepper, seeded and minced

Directions:

- In a small dish, combine water and flaxseed meal and let aside for 10 minutes.
- Meanwhile, prepare an air fryer to 350°F (175°C) according to the manufacturer's recommendations. Coat a 6-inch heat-resistant inner pot with cooking spray.
- Combine cornmeal, sugar, baking powder, flour, nutritional yeast, salt, and pepper in a medium mixing bowl. Stir in the flaxseed and water combination, almond milk, and oil until

it barely comes together and there are no lumps. Pour into the prepared pot and set in the air fryer; stir in the jalapeno.

- Cook for 15 minutes in a preheated air fryer. Remove the inner pot with tongs, turn the cornbread, and continue to air fry for another 5 minutes, or until a toothpick inserted into the middle comes out clean. Serve hot.

Air Fryer Donut Sticks

Preparation Time: 15 minutes
Cooking Time: 18 minutes
Serve: 1
Ingredients:

- 1 package refrigerated crescent roll dough
- ¼ cup butter, melted
- ½ cup white sugar
- 2 teaspoons ground cinnamon
- ½ cup any flavor fruit jam

Directions:

- Roll out the crescent roll dough sheet to an 8x12-inch rectangle. With a pizza cutter, cut the dough in half lengthwise, then crosswise into 1/2-inch broad "sticks." Dip doughnut sticks in melted butter and arrange them in an air fryer basket in a single layer.
- Cook for 4 to 5 minutes in an air fryer at 380°F (195°C) until nicely browned.
- In a pie dish or shallow basin, combine the sugar and cinnamon. Take the doughnut sticks out of the air fryer and roll them in the cinnamon-sugar mixture. Rep with the remaining dough.
- Serve doughnut sticks with jam.

Air Fryer Root Vegetables with Vegan Aioli

Preparation Time: 15 minutes
Cooking Time: 22 minutes
Serve: 1
Ingredients:

- 1 clove garlic, minced
- ½ cup vegan mayonnaise
- ½ teaspoon fresh lemon juice
- salt and ground black pepper to taste
- 1 tablespoon minced fresh rosemary
- 4 tablespoons extra virgin olive oil
- 3 cloves garlic, finely minced
- ½ teaspoon ground black pepper
- 1 teaspoon kosher salt
- 1-pound parsnips, peeled and cut vertically into uniform pieces
- ½ pound baby carrots split lengthwise
- 1 pound baby red potatoes, cut lengthwise into 4 or 6 pieces
- ½ red onion cut lengthwise into 1/2-inch slices
- ½ teaspoon grated lemon zest (Optional)

Directions:

- In a small bowl, combine mayonnaise, garlic, lemon juice, salt, and pepper to make the garlic aioli; refrigerate until ready to serve.
- If your air fryer manufacturer suggests preheating, preheat it to 400 degrees F (200 degrees C).
- In a small bowl, combine the olive oil, rosemary, garlic, salt, and pepper; leave aside to blend the flavors. Next, combine the parsnips, potatoes, carrots, and onion in a large mixing dish. Stir in the olive oil-rosemary mixture until the veggies are well covered. Place a part of the veggies in the air fryer

- basket in a single layer, then properly add a rack and another layer of vegetables.
- Cook for 15 minutes in an air fryer.
- When the timer goes off, serve the vegetables, and keep warm, or continue cooking in 5-minute intervals until the vegetables are done and browning to your liking.
- Place the remaining veggies in the air fryer basket and cook for 15 minutes, monitoring doneness as required. Use the rack again if you have more veggies than fit in a single layer. When all veggies are cooked, serve with garlic aioli and lemon zest on top.

Air Fryer Apple Dumplings
Preparation Time: 10 minutes
Cooking Time: 18 minutes
Serve: 1
Ingredients:
- 2 tablespoons sultana raisins
- 1 tablespoon brown sugar
- 2 sheets puff pastry
- 2 small apples, peeled and cored
- 2 tablespoons butter, melted

Directions:
- Preheat an air fryer carefully to 320°F (180 degrees C). Aluminum foil should be used to line the air fryer basket.
- In a mixing dish, combine sultanas and brown sugar.
- Place a sheet of puff pastry on a clean work surface. Fill the core of an apple with the sultana mixture and place it on the crust. Fold the dough around the apple to cover it completely. Repeat with the rest of the pastry, apple, and filling.
- Brush the dumplings with melted butter and place them in the prepared basket.
- Cook the dumplings for 25 minutes, or until golden brown and the apples are tender.

Air Fryer Egg Rolls
Preparation Time: 18 minutes
Cooking Time: 20 minutes
Serve: 1
Ingredients:
- 2 cups frozen corn, thawed
- 1 ½ cups shredded jalapeno Jack cheese
- 1 cup sharp Cheddar cheese
- 1 (4 ounces) can dice green chiles
- 4 green onions, sliced
- 1 teaspoon salt
- 1 (15 ounces) can of black beans
- 1 (13.5 ounces) can spinach, drained
- 1 teaspoon ground cumin
- 1 teaspoon chili powder
- 1 (16 ounces) package egg roll wrappers
- cooking spray

Directions:
- In a large mixing bowl, combine corn, beans, spinach, jalapeño Jack cheese, Cheddar cheese, green chiles, green onions, salt, cumin, and chili powder for the filling.
- An egg roll wrapper should be placed at an angle. Wet your finger and lightly wet all four sides. Fill the middle of the wrapper with about 1/4 cup of the filling. Fold one corner over the filling and tuck in the edges to construct a roll. Repeat with the remaining wrappers, misting each egg roll with cooking spray as you go.

- Preheat an air fryer carefully to 390°F (199 degrees C). Place the egg rolls in the basket, making sure they don't touch; cook in batches as needed. Fry for 8 minutes, then turn and cook for another 4 minutes, or until the crispy skins.

Air Fryer Pakoras
Preparation Time: 15 minutes
Cooking Time: 25 minutes
Serve: 1
Ingredients:
- 2 cups chopped cauliflower
- 1 cup diced yellow potatoes
- 1 ¼ cups chickpea flour (bean)
- ¾ cup water
- ½ red onion, chopped
- 1 tablespoon salt
- 1 clove garlic, minced
- 1 teaspoon curry powder
- 1 teaspoon coriander
- ½ teaspoon ground cayenne pepper
- ½ teaspoon cumin
- 1 serving cooking spray

Directions:
- In a large mixing bowl, combine cauliflower, potatoes, chickpea flour, water, red onion, salt, garlic, curry powder, coriander, cayenne pepper, and cumin. Set aside for 10 minutes to relax.
- Preheat the air fryer carefully to 350°F (175 degrees C).
- Coat the air fryer basket with cooking spray. 2 tablespoons cauliflower mixture, flattened in the basket Repeat as many times as the space in your basket permits without the pakoras touching. Spray the tops of each pakora with nonstick cooking spray.
- 8 minutes in the oven Cook for an additional 8 minutes on the other side. Transfer to a plate lined with paper towels. Rep with the remaining batter.

Air Fryer Steak for Fajitas
Preparation Time: 20 minutes
Cooking Time: 20 minutes
Serve: 1
Ingredients:
- 2 tablespoons olive oil
- ½ teaspoon ground cumin
- 2 teaspoons salt
- ½ teaspoon garlic powder
- ½ teaspoon jalapeno chili powder (Optional)
- ¼ teaspoon chili powder (Optional)
- 1 onion, sliced into strips
- ¼ teaspoon ground coriander
- 1 pound skirt steak, sliced into strips against the grain
- 1 bell pepper, seeded and sliced into strips

Directions:
- In a resealable plastic bag, combine olive oil, salt, garlic powder, cumin, jalapeño chili powder, chili powder, and coriander. Add the steak, onion, and bell pepper to the bag, cover with the marinade, push out extra air, and close. Marinate for 8 hours to overnight in the refrigerator.
- Line the air fryer basket with perforated parchment paper. Mix in the marinated onions, peppers, and beef.

- Cook for 5 minutes at 400°F in an air fryer (200 degrees C). Shake the air fryer basket to ensure consistent cooking. Cook until the steak is cooked through, about 4 minutes more.

Hasselback Air Fryer Potatoes

Preparation Time: 15 minutes
Cooking Time: 25 minutes
Serve: 1
Ingredients:

- 4 (6 ounces) russet potatoes, scrubbed and dried
- 2 chopsticks
- 4 tablespoons olive oil, or as needed
- salt and ground black pepper to taste
- ½ teaspoon chopped fresh chives (Optional)

Directions:

- Preheat the air fryer carefully to 350°F (180 degrees C).
- 1 potato, cut a very thin slice lengthwise from the flattest side. Place the potato cut side down on a chopping board to lay uniformly without rolling. Place chopsticks along the top and bottom sides of the potato lengthwise. Slice the potato evenly across the length to form 1/4-inch slices, ensuring sure the knife comes to rest on the chopsticks each time to keep the bottom of the potato intact. Rep with the remaining potatoes. Brush oil on the outsides and between the slices. Season with salt and pepper to taste.
- Place the potatoes in the air fryer dish and cook for 15 minutes. Brush with oil and cook for another 15 minutes until the edges are crispy and the centers are soft. Serve garnished with chives.

Air Fryer Salmon Nuggets

Preparation Time: 15 minutes
Cooking Time: 20 minutes
Serve: 1
Ingredients:

- ⅓ cup maple syrup
- ¼ teaspoon ground dried chipotle pepper, 1 pinch sea salt
- 1 ½ cups butter- and garlic-flavored croutons
- 1 large egg
- 1 (1 pound) skinless, center-cut salmon fillet, cut into 1 1/2-inch chunk
- cooking spray

Directions:

- Combine the maple syrup, chipotle powder, and salt in a saucepan and bring to a simmer over medium heat. To keep warm, turn the heat down to low.
- Place the croutons in a tiny food processor bowl and pulse until fine crumbs form. Place in a small basin. In a separate dish, whisk the egg.
- Preheat the air fryer carefully to 390°F (200 degrees C).
- Lightly season the fish with sea salt. Dip fish in egg mixture lightly, allowing excess to fall out. Coat fish with crouton breading, shaking off excess. Place on a dish and lightly coat with cooking spray.
- Coat the air fryer basket with cooking spray. Place salmon nuggets within, working in batches as necessary to minimize congestion.
- Cook for 3 minutes in a hot air fryer. Turn the salmon pieces gently, spritz generously with oil, and cook until the salmon is cooked through, 3 to 4 minutes more. Drizzle with heated chipotle-maple syrup and arrange on a serving plate. Serve right away.

Air Fryer Mini Meatloaves

Preparation Time: 20 minutes
Cooking Time: 25 minutes
Serve: 1
Ingredients:

- 1 serving cooking spray
- 2 pounds ground chuck
- 1 egg
- ¼ cup seasoned breadcrumbs
- 2 tablespoons mayonnaise
- 2 teaspoons onion powder
- 1 teaspoon salt
- 6 tablespoons ketchup

Directions:

- Preheat the air fryer carefully basket to 390 degrees F and spray with oil (200 degrees C).
- Combine the chuck, egg, breadcrumbs, mayonnaise, onion powder, and salt in a large mixing basin. Make 6 little loaves out of the dough.
- Place the meatloaves in the prepared basket, careful not to overlap them. Cook for 30 minutes for a well-done product. Cook for 3 minutes more after smearing ketchup over each meatloaf.

Air Fryer Tofu Milanese

Preparation Time: 15 minutes
Cooking Time: 20 minutes
Serve: 1
Ingredients:

- 1 (8 ounces) container firm tofu, drained and pressed
- ⅓ cup dry breadcrumbs
- 1 tablespoon taco seasoning mix
- 2 eggs
- cooking spray

Directions:

- Tofu should be cut into two slabs lengthwise. Each slab should be cut into two triangles.
- In a small skillet or dish, combine breadcrumbs and taco spice. In a separate shallow pan or dish, lightly beat the eggs.
- Preheat the air fryer carefully to 375°F (190 degrees C).
- Each tofu triangle should be dipped into the beaten eggs. Using a fork, dredge them in the bread crumb mixture. Gently push down on either side to coat. Arrange on a platter in a single layer. Lightly spray with cooking spray.
- Cook for 15 minutes on one side of the air fryer. Each triangle should be flipped and lightly sprayed with cooking spray. Cook for another 10 minutes, or until browned. Depending on the size of your air fryer basket, you may need to cook in batches.

Spicy Air Fryer Salmon

Preparation Time: 15 minutes
Cooking Time: 18 minutes
Serve: 1
Ingredients:

- 2 tablespoons grill seasoning (such as Montreal Steak Seasoning)

- 1 tablespoon brown sugar
- ¾ teaspoon ground cumin
- ½ teaspoon ground coriander
- ¼ teaspoon cayenne pepper
- 2 pounds salmon fillets, skin on

Directions:

- Preheat the air fryer carefully to the fish setting of 330°F (165°C) for 2 minutes.
- Combine steak seasoning, brown sugar, cumin, coriander, and cayenne pepper in a small bowl. Season each salmon fillet with about 2 tablespoons of the spice mix (or more, if preferred). Arrange the salmon in a single layer in the air fryer basket.
- Cook the salmon in the air fryer, in batches if required, until it flakes easily with a fork, about 18 minutes. Place the cooked fish on a platter and keep warm in an oven set to the lowest temperature. Rep with the rest of the salmon fillets. Serve right away.

Air Fryer Shrimp and Polenta

Preparation Time: 15 minutes
Cooking Time: 22 minutes
Serve: 1
Ingredients:

- ½ (16 ounces) tube polenta, sliced into 6 rounds
- 2 teaspoons extra-virgin olive oil, divided
- salt and ground black pepper to taste
- 8 ounces thawed frozen jumbo shrimp - drained, peeled, and deveined
- 12 grape tomatoes
- 2 tablespoons unsalted butter, softened
- 2 teaspoons chopped fresh parsley
- 1 teaspoon hot pepper sauce
- ½ teaspoon lemon-pepper seasoning

Directions:

- Preheat an air fryer carefully to 400°F (200 degrees C).
- Arrange the polenta rounds on a clean work surface. Set aside after brushing both sides with 1 teaspoon olive oil and seasoning with salt and pepper.
- In a mixing dish, combine the shrimp and tomatoes. Toss in the remaining 1 teaspoon olive oil to coat. Transfer the tomatoes to the air fryer basket with tongs.
- Cook the tomatoes in the preheated air fryer for about 2 minutes or until blistered. Transfer the tomatoes to a large mixing basin and mash them with a wooden spoon.
- Cook the shrimp in the air fryer basket for 10 minutes. Place the shrimp in the basin with the mashed tomatoes.
- Cook the polenta rounds in the air fryer basket for 15 minutes. Cook until golden brown on the other side, about 15 minutes more.
- While the polenta rounds are cooking, add the butter, parsley, hot pepper sauce, and lemon-pepper seasoning in a mixing dish and stir well.
- Divide the polenta cakes between two plates. Serve with seasoned butter on top of the tomato-shrimp combination.

Air Fryer Turkey Fajitas

Preparation Time: 10 minutes
Cooking Time: 18 minutes
Serve: 1
Ingredients:

- ½ teaspoon onion powder
- 2 limes, divided

- 1 tablespoon chili powder
- 1 large red onion, halved and sliced into strips
- ½ tablespoon dried Mexican oregano
- 1-pound skinless, boneless turkey breast
- 1 teaspoon freshly ground black pepper
- 1 ½ tablespoon vegetable oil, divided
- 1 large red bell pepper, sliced into strips
- 1 tablespoon ground cumin
- ½ tablespoon paprika
- 1 jalapeno pepper
- 1 teaspoon garlic powder
- 1 medium yellow bell pepper
- ¼ cup chopped fresh cilantro

Directions:

- Combine chili powder, cumin, paprika, oregano, pepper, garlic powder, and onion powder in a small bowl. 1 lime juice squeezed over the turkey breast Season the meat with the spice combination. 1 tablespoon of oil Set aside after tossing to coat.
- Cover the bell peppers and onion with the remaining oil in a bowl. To coat, toss everything together.
- The manufacturer's instructions preheat an air fryer carefully to 375°F (190°C).
- In a preheated air fryer, cook the bell peppers and onion for 8 minutes. Cook for another 5 minutes after shaking. Add the jalapenos. 5 minutes in the oven Shake the basket and arrange the turkey strips in a single layer on top of the veggies. Cook for 7 to 8 minutes with the basket closed. Open the basket, shake it to disperse the mixture, and cook for another 5 minutes, or until the turkey strips are crispy and no longer pink in the middle and the peppers are soft.
- Remove the fajitas from the basket and set them in a dish or on a tray. Garnish with cilantro and squeeze the remaining lime juice over the top.

Air Fryer Salmon for One

Preparation Time: 18 minutes
Cooking Time: 20 minutes
Serve: 1
Ingredients:

- 1 (6 ounces) salmon fillet
- ½ teaspoon salt
- ½ teaspoon Greek seasoning (such as Cavender's®)
- ¼ teaspoon ground black pepper
- 1 pinch dried dill weed

Directions:

- Preheat the air fryer carefully for 5 minutes at 370 degrees F (190 degrees C).
- Season the salmon fillet with salt, Greek seasoning, pepper, and dill in the meantime.
- Line the air fryer's interior basket with a perforated parchment circle. Place the salmon skin-side down on the parchment paper.
- Air fried the fish for about 15 minutes, or until it is cooked through.

Air Fryer Broiled Grapefruit

Preparation Time: 15 minutes
Cooking Time: 25 minutes
Serve: 1
Ingredients:

- 1 red grapefruit, refrigerated
- 1 tablespoon softened butter
- 1 tablespoon brown sugar
- 2 teaspoons brown sugar
- aluminum foil
- ½ teaspoon ground cinnamon

Directions:

- Preheat the air fryer carefully to 400°F (200 degrees C).
- If the grapefruit isn't lying flat, cut it in half crosswise and slice a tiny sliver from the bottom of each side. Next, cut along the outside edge of the grapefruit and between each segment with a sharp paring knife to make the fruit easier to consume once cooked.
- Combine melted butter and 1 tablespoon brown sugar in a small mixing dish. Distribute the mixture evenly over each grapefruit half. Finish with the remaining brown sugar.
- Place each grapefruit half on one 5-inch square of aluminum foil and fold up the edges to capture any juices. Then, place the air fryer basket in the air fryer.
- Broil in the air fryer for 6 to 7 minutes, or until the sugar mixture is bubbling. Before serving, sprinkle the fruit with cinnamon.

Air Fryer Turkey Fajitas

Preparation Time: 20 minutes
Cooking Time: 20 minutes
Serve: 1
Ingredients:

- ½ tablespoon dried Mexican oregano
- 1 tablespoon chili powder
- ½ tablespoon paprika
- 1 medium yellow bell pepper, sliced into strips
- 1 large red onion, halved and sliced into strips
- 1 teaspoon freshly ground black pepper
- 1 teaspoon garlic powder
- ½ teaspoon onion powder
- 1 tablespoon ground cumin
- 2 limes, divided
- 1-pound skinless, boneless turkey breast
- 1 ½ tablespoon vegetable oil, divided
- 1 jalapeno pepper, seeded and chopped
- 1 large red bell pepper, sliced into strips
- ¼ cup chopped fresh cilantro

Directions:

- Combine chili powder, cumin, paprika, oregano, pepper, garlic powder, and onion powder in a small bowl. 1 lime juice squeezed over the turkey breast Season the meat with the spice combination. 1 tablespoon of oil Set aside after tossing to coat.
- Cover the bell peppers and onion with the remaining oil in a bowl. To coat, toss everything together.
- The manufacturer's instructions preheat an air fryer carefully to 375°F (190°C).
- In a preheated air fryer, cook the bell peppers and onion for 8 minutes. Cook for another 5 minutes after shaking. Add the jalapenos. 5 minutes in the oven Shake the basket and arrange the turkey strips in a single layer on top of the veggies. Cook for 7 to 8 minutes with the basket closed. Open the basket, shake it to disperse the mixture, and cook for another 5 minutes, or until the turkey strips are crispy and no longer pink in the middle and the peppers are soft.

- Remove the fajitas from the basket and set them in a dish or on a tray. Garnish with cilantro and squeeze the remaining lime juice over the top.

Air Fryer Latkes

Preparation Time: 15 minutes
Cooking Time: 25 minutes
Serve: 1
Ingredients:

- 1 (16 ounces) package frozen shredded hash brown potatoes
- 2 tablespoons matzo meal
- 1 egg
- ½ cup shredded onion
- kosher salt and ground black pepper to taste
- avocado oil cooking spray

Directions:

- The manufacturer's instructions preheat an air fryer carefully to 375°F (190°C). Next, prepare a piece of parchment or waxed paper.
- Place the thawed potatoes and shredded onion between layers of paper towels. Cover with extra paper towels and wring out as much liquid as possible.
- Combine the egg, salt, and pepper in a large mixing bowl. With a fork, mix in the potatoes and onion. Stir in the matzo meal until the ingredients are uniformly distributed. Form the mixture into ten 3- to 4-inch broad patties with your hands. Place the patties on a sheet of parchment or waxed paper.
- Cooking spray should be sprayed on the air fryer basket. Place half of the patties properly in the basket and coat with cooking spray generously.
- Air-fry for 10 to 12 minutes, or until the exterior is crispy and dark golden brown. (If you like a softer latke, check for doneness at 8 minutes.) Transfer the latkes to a plate. In the same manner, cook the remaining patties and coat them with cooking spray before cooking.

Spicy Air Fryer Salmon

Preparation Time: 15 minutes
Cooking Time: 20 minutes
Serve: 1
Ingredients:

- 2 tablespoons grill seasoning (such as Montreal Steak Seasoning)
- 1 tablespoon brown sugar
- ¾ teaspoon ground cumin
- ½ teaspoon ground coriander
- ¼ teaspoon cayenne pepper
- 2 pounds salmon fillets, skin on

Directions:

- Preheat the air fryer carefully to the fish setting of 330°F (165°C) for 2 minutes.
- Combine steak seasoning, brown sugar, cumin, coriander, and cayenne pepper in a small bowl. Season each salmon fillet with about 2 tablespoons of the spice mix (or more, if preferred). Arrange the salmon in a single layer in the air fryer basket.
- Cook the salmon in the air fryer, in batches if required, until it flakes easily with a fork, about 18 minutes. Place the cooked fish on a platter and keep warm in an oven set to the lowest temperature. Rep with the rest of the salmon fillets. Serve right away.

Air Fryer Salmon Patties

Preparation Time: 20 minutes
Cooking Time: 25 minutes
Serve: 1
Ingredients:

- ½ cup mayonnaise
- 1 teaspoon finely minced garlic
- ½ teaspoon fresh lemon juice
- 2 pinches Cajun seasoning
- 12 ounces salmon, minced
- 1 tablespoon snipped fresh chives
- 1 teaspoon dried parsley
- 1 teaspoon finely minced garlic
- ½ teaspoon salt
- 1 tablespoon all-purpose flour
- cooking spray

Directions:

- Combine mayonnaise, garlic, lemon juice, and Cajun spice in a small bowl. Refrigerate dipping sauce until required.
- Combine the salmon, chives, parsley, garlic, and salt in a medium mixing dish. Mix in the flour well. Divide into four equal amounts and shape into patties.
- Preheat the air fryer carefully to 350°F (175 degrees C). Cut the lemon into four pieces.
- Place lemon slices in the bottom of the air fryer basket, then top with salmon patties. Spray the patties lightly with cooking spray.
- Place the basket in the hot fryer and reduce the temperature to 275 degrees F. (135 degrees C).
- Cook in the air fryer for 10 to 15 minutes, or until an instant-read thermometer is put into the middle of a patty registers 145 degrees F (63 degrees C). Serve with your favorite sauce.

Air Fryer Stuffed Mushrooms

Preparation Time: 15 minutes
Cooking Time: 20 minutes
Serve: 1
Ingredients:

- 1 (16 ounces) package whole white button mushrooms
- 2 scallions
- 4 ounces cream cheese, softened
- ¼ cup finely shredded sharp Cheddar cheese
- ¼ teaspoon ground paprika
- 1 pinch salt
- cooking spray

Directions:

- Gently clean the mushrooms with a moist towel. Remove and discard the stems.
- Separate the white and green sections of the scallions.
- Preheat an air fryer carefully to 360°F (182 degrees C).
- In a small mixing dish, combine cream cheese, Cheddar cheese, the white sections of the scallions, paprika, and salt. Stuff the filling into the mushrooms, pushing it in with the back of a small spoon to fill the cavity.
- Cooking sprays the air fryer basket and place the mushrooms inside. You may need to perform two batches depending on the size of your air fryer.
- Cook for 8 minutes or until the filling is gently browned. Rep with the remaining mushrooms.

- Allow mushrooms to cool for 5 minutes before serving, then top with scallion greens.

Air Fryer Corn on The Cob

Preparation Time: 15 minutes
Cooking Time: 18 minutes
Serve: 1
Ingredients:

- ¼ cup mayonnaise
- 2 teaspoons crumbled cotija cheese
- 1 teaspoon lime juice
- ¼ teaspoon chili powder
- 2 ears corn, shucked and halved
- 4 sprigs of fresh cilantro (Optional)

Directions:

- Preheat an air fryer carefully to 400°F (200 degrees C).
- In a shallow bowl, combine mayonnaise, cotija cheese, lime juice, and chili powder.
- Roll each piece of corn in the mayonnaise mixture until it is evenly coated on both sides.
- Cook for 8 minutes with all four pieces of corn in the air fryer basket. Garnish with cilantro if desired.

Air Fryer Frittata

Preparation Time: 15 minutes
Cooking Time: 22 minutes
Serve: 1
Ingredients:

- cooking spray
- 2 teaspoons butter (Optional)
- ⅓ cup diced bell pepper
- ⅓ cup chopped onion
- ½ cup breakfast sausage crumbles
- ½ cup shredded Colby Jack cheese
- 6 eggs
- salt and ground black pepper to taste
- ½ teaspoon hot pepper sauce (Optional)
- ¼ cup salsa, or more to taste (Optional)

Directions:

- According to the manufacturer's recommendations, pre-heat a 5.8-quart or larger air fryer to 350°F (175°C).
- Spray cooking spray over the bottom and sides of a tiny metal container, about 6 inches round and 4 inches high, meant to be an inner pot.
- Insert the inner pot into the air fryer and melt the butter for 45 seconds. Fry the bell pepper and onion for 2 minutes.
- Remove the inner pot with care and toss in the sausage crumbs. Set aside and sprinkle with Colby Jack cheese.
- In a mixing dish, combine the yolks and whites of the eggs. Season with salt, pepper, and spicy sauce to taste. Pour the egg mixture over the remaining ingredients in the inner saucepan and gently combine everything.
- Return the inner pot to the air fryer basket and cook for 12 minutes, or until the top of the frittata is lightly browned and a toothpick inserted into the middle comes out clean. Continue to air fry in 30-second increments until the frittata has set. Serve with salsa, heated or at room temperature.

Air Fryer Fingerling Potatoes

Preparation Time: 10 minutes

Cooking Time: 18 minutes
Serve: 1
Ingredients:

- 1 pound fingerling potatoes, halved lengthwise
- 1 tablespoon olive oil
- ½ teaspoon ground paprika
- ½ teaspoon parsley flakes
- ½ teaspoon garlic powder
- salt and ground black pepper to taste

Directions:

- Preheat an air fryer carefully to 400°F (200 degrees C).
- In a large mixing dish, combine potato halves. Stir in olive oil, paprika, parsley, garlic powder, salt, and pepper until evenly covered.
- Cook the potatoes in the prepared air fryer basket for 10 minutes. Cook, often stirring until the desired crispness is obtained, about 5 minutes more.

Air Fryer Baked Potatoes

Preparation Time: 18 minutes
Cooking Time: 20 minutes
Serve: 1
Ingredients:

- 2 large russet potatoes, scrubbed
- 1 tablespoon peanut oil
- ½ teaspoon coarse sea salt

Directions:

- Preheat the air fryer carefully to 400°F (200 degrees C).
- Potatoes should be brushed with peanut oil and seasoned with salt. Place them in the air fryer basket, then in the air fryer.
- Cook until potatoes are tender, about 1 hour. Prick them with a fork to see whether they're done.

Air Fryer Eggplant Fries

Preparation Time: 15 minutes
Cooking Time: 25 minutes
Serve: 1
Ingredients:

- 1 medium eggplant
- ½ cup Italian breadcrumbs
- ¼ cup freshly grated Parmesan cheese
- 1 teaspoon Italian seasoning
- 1 teaspoon salt
- ½ teaspoon dried basil
- ½ teaspoon garlic powder
- ½ teaspoon onion powder
- ½ teaspoon ground black pepper
- ¼ cup all-purpose flour
- 2 eggs

Directions:

- Cut the eggplant into 1/2-inch circles, then into 1/4-inch sticks. Allow airing to dry.
- In a shallow bowl, combine breadcrumbs, Parmesan cheese, Italian seasoning, onion powder, salt, basil, garlic powder, and black pepper. Fill a second small basin halfway with flour. In a third dish, whisk together the eggs.
- Dip eggplant sticks in flour, then in beaten eggs, and last in breadcrumbs. Place on a platter and set aside for 5 minutes to rest.
- Preheat an air fryer carefully to 370°F (185 degrees C).

- Place the eggplant sticks in the basket, ensuring they don't touch; cook in batches if required.
- Cook for 8 to 10 minutes in a preheated air fryer. Shake the basket and cook for another 4 to 6 minutes, or until the desired crispiness is reached.

Air Fryer Mushrooms

Preparation Time: 20 minutes
Cooking Time: 20 minutes
Serve: 1
Ingredients:

- 1 (8 ounces) package cremini mushrooms, halved or quartered
- 2 tablespoons avocado oil
- 1 teaspoon low-sodium soy sauce
- ½ teaspoon garlic granules
- salt and ground black pepper to taste

Directions:

- Preheat the air fryer carefully to 375°F (190 degrees C).
- In a mixing bowl, combine the mushrooms, avocado oil, soy sauce, garlic granules, salt, and pepper; toss to coat. Place in the air fryer bowl.
- Cook the mushrooms for 10 minutes in the air fryer, shaking periodically.

Air Fryer Turkey Breast

Preparation Time: 15 minutes
Cooking Time: 25 minutes
Serve: 1
Ingredients:

- 1 tablespoon finely chopped fresh rosemary
- 1 teaspoon finely chopped fresh chives
- 1 teaspoon finely minced fresh garlic
- ½ teaspoon salt
- ¼ teaspoon ground black pepper
- 2 tablespoons cold unsalted butter
- 2 ¾ pounds skin-on, bone-in split turkey breast

Directions:

- Preheat the air fryer carefully to 350°F (175 degrees C).
- Combine the rosemary, chives, garlic, salt, and pepper on a chopping board. Place thin slices of butter on the herbs and spices and mash until thoroughly combined.
- Pat the turkey breast dry and massage it on both sides and beneath the skin with herbed butter.
- Place the turkey in the air fryer basket, skin side down, and cook for 20 minutes.
- Turn the turkey skin-side up and fry for another 18 minutes, or until an instant-read thermometer placed near the bone registers 165 degrees F (74 degrees C). Transfer to a dish and tent with aluminum foil for 10 minutes to rest. Serve heated, sliced.

Air Fryer French Fries

Preparation Time: 15 minutes
Cooking Time: 20 minutes
Serve: 1
Ingredients:

- 1 pound russet potatoes, peeled
- 2 teaspoons vegetable oil
- 1 pinch cayenne pepper

- ½ teaspoon kosher salt

Directions:

- Each potato should be cut lengthwise into 3/8-inch-thick slices. Sections should be cut into 3/8-inch-wide sticks as well.
- Cover potatoes with water and soak for 5 minutes to allow extra starches to be released. Drain and cover with a few inches of boiling water (or place in a bowl of boiling water). Allow for a 10-minute resting period.
- Drain the potatoes and pat them dry with paper towels. Blot out any excess water and set it aside for at least 10 minutes to cool fully. Drizzle with oil, season with cayenne pepper, and toss to coat in a mixing bowl.
- Preheat the air fryer carefully to 375°F (190 degrees C). In the fryer basket, stack potatoes in a double layer. The cooking time is 15 minutes. Slide the basket out, toss the fries, cook until golden brown, approximately 10 minutes longer. In a mixing dish, toss the fries with salt. Serve right away.

Air Fryer Baba Ghanoush

Preparation Time: 20 minutes
Cooking Time: 25 minutes
Serve: 1
Ingredients:

- 5 ½ tablespoons olive oil, divided
- 1 medium eggplant, halved lengthwise
- ½ teaspoon kosher salt
- 1 tablespoon chopped fresh parsley
- 1 bulb garlic
- ¼ cup tahini (sesame seed paste)
- ¼ teaspoon ground cumin
- ⅛ teaspoon smoked paprika
- 2 tablespoons lemon juice, or more to taste
- 2 tablespoons crumbled feta cheese
- ½ teaspoon lemon zest

Directions:

- Season the cut sides of the eggplant with salt. Allow for a 20- to 30-minute resting period. Then, using paper towels, blot dry.
- Preheat an air fryer carefully to 400°F (200 degrees C).
- 1 tablespoon olive oil on the sliced sides of the eggplant. Remove the top 1/4 inch of the garlic bulb to expose the cloves. Wrap the bulb in aluminum foil after brushing it with 1/2 tablespoon olive oil. In the air fryer basket, combine the eggplant and garlic.
- Cook in a preheated air fryer for 15 to 20 minutes, or until the eggplant and garlic are soft, and the eggplant is a deep golden-brown color. Allow cooling for about 10 minutes after removing from the oven.
- Scoop out the flesh of the eggplant and place it in the bowl of a food processor. Pulse in tahini, lemon juice, 4 cloves, roasted garlic, remaining 4 tablespoons of olive oil, cumin, and paprika until smooth. Serve with feta cheese, parsley, and lemon zest on top.

Air Fryer Roasted Garlic

Preparation Time: 15 minutes
Cooking Time: 20 minutes
Serve: 1
Ingredients:

- 1 head garlic
- aluminum foil
- 1 teaspoon extra-virgin olive oil
- ¼ teaspoon salt
- ¼ teaspoon ground black pepper

Directions:

- Preheat the air fryer carefully to 380°F (190 degrees C).
- Remove the top of the garlic head and set it on a square piece of aluminum foil. Wrap the foil around the garlic. Season with salt and pepper and drizzle with olive oil. Fold the ends of the foil over the garlic to form a pouch.
- 16 to 20 minutes in the air fryer until the garlic is tender. Open the foil package with extreme caution, as hot steam will escape.

Air Fryer Eggplant Parmesan

Preparation Time: 15 minutes
Cooking Time: 18 minutes
Serve: 1
Ingredients:

- ½ cup Italian breadcrumbs
- ¼ cup freshly grated Parmesan cheese
- 1 teaspoon Italian seasoning
- 1 teaspoon salt
- ½ teaspoon dried basil
- ½ teaspoon garlic powder
- ½ teaspoon onion powder
- ½ teaspoon freshly ground black pepper
- ¼ cup flour
- 2 large eggs, beaten
- 1 cup marinara sauce, or more to taste
- 1 medium eggplant, sliced into 1/2-inch rounds
- 8 slices mozzarella cheese

Directions:

- Combine breadcrumbs, basil, garlic powder, onion powder, Parmesan cheese, Italian seasoning, salt, and black pepper in a shallow bowl. In a separate shallow dish, place the flour, and in a third shallow bowl, place the beaten eggs.
- Dip sliced eggplant in flour, then in whisked eggs, and then in bread crumb mixture. Place the coated eggplant on a platter and set aside for 5 minutes to rest.
- Preheat an air fryer carefully to 370°F (185 degrees C).
- Place the breaded eggplant rounds in the air fryer basket, not touching; work in batches if required. Cook for 8 to 10 minutes, then turn each round and cook for another 4 to 6 minutes until desired crispiness. Top each eggplant circle with 1 slice of mozzarella cheese and marinara sauce. Return the basket to the air fryer and cook for 1 to 2 minutes, or until the cheese begins to melt. If necessary, repeat with the remaining eggplant.

Air Fryer Popcorn Shrimp

Preparation Time: 15 minutes
Cooking Time: 22 minutes
Serve: 1
Ingredients:

- 12 ounces large shrimp, peeled and deveined
- ¼ cup all-purpose flour
- 1 egg
- 1 cup panko breadcrumbs
- ½ teaspoon paprika
- ½ teaspoon onion powder

- ¼ teaspoon salt
- ⅛ teaspoon ground black pepper
- nonstick cooking spray

Directions:

- In a large mixing bowl, combine the shrimp. Sprinkle flour over the top and toss until the shrimp are equally coated. In a separate dish, beat the egg. Combine the panko breadcrumbs, paprika, onion powder, salt, and pepper in a third bowl.
- Each flour-coated shrimp is dipped in an egg, tossed in the panko mixture, and placed on a baking sheet. Allow for a 5-minute break while the air fryer heats up.
- Preheat the air fryer carefully for 5 minutes at 400 degrees F (200 degrees C).
- Coat the air fryer basket with cooking spray. Place half of the shrimp in the basket. Cooking spray should be sprayed on the top of each shrimp.
- 4 minutes in the oven, Flip each shrimp over with tongs and spritz any chalky places with cooking spray. Cook for another 4 minutes. Rep with the remaining shrimp.

Air Fryer Shrimp Fajitas

Preparation Time: 10 minutes
Cooking Time: 18 minutes
Serve: 1
Ingredients:

- 1 red bell pepper
- 1 green bell pepper, sliced into thin strips
- 1 red onion, sliced into thin strips
- 1-pound uncooked medium shrimp
- 1 (1.12 ounces) package fajita seasoning mix, divided
- 3 tablespoons olive oil, divided
- 4 (10 inches) flour tortillas, toasted

Directions:

- Preheat the air fryer carefully to 400°F (200 degrees C).
- In a large mixing basin, combine the bell peppers and onion. Set aside the shrimp in a separate dish. 2 tablespoons of fajita seasoning on top of the shrimp Season the veggies with the remaining seasoning. Drizzle 2 tablespoons olive oil over the veggies and toss to coat evenly. Stir in the remaining 1 tablespoon olive oil with the shrimp.
- Place the veggies in the preheated air fryer basket and cook for 12 minutes, shaking halfway through. Transfer the mixture to a large mixing basin.
- Cook the shrimp in the air fryer basket for 5 minutes. Cook for 3 minutes more on the other side. Distribute the veggies among the tortillas and top with the prawns.

Air Fryer Potato Wedges

Preparation Time: 18 minutes
Cooking Time: 20 minutes
Serve: 1
Ingredients:

- 2 medium Russet potatoes, cut into wedges
- 1 ½ tablespoon olive oil
- ½ teaspoon paprika
- ½ teaspoon parsley flakes
- ½ teaspoon chili powder
- ½ teaspoon sea salt
- ⅛ teaspoon ground black pepper

Directions:

- Preheat the air fryer carefully to 400°F (200 degrees C).

- In a large mixing basin, combine the potato wedges. Next, mix olive oil, paprika, parsley, chili, salt, and pepper until completely combined.
- Cook for 10 minutes with 8 wedges in the air fryer basket.
- Cook for an additional 5 minutes after flipping the wedges with tongs. Rep with the remaining 8 wedges.

Air Fryer Scotch Eggs

Preparation Time: 15 minutes
Cooking Time: 25 minutes
Serve: 1
Ingredients:

- 3 tablespoons Greek yogurt
- 2 tablespoons mango chutney (such as Patak's®)
- 1 tablespoon mayonnaise
- ⅛ teaspoon salt
- ⅛ teaspoon pepper
- ⅛ teaspoon curry powder
- ⅛ teaspoon cayenne pepper (Optional)
- 1 pound pork sausage (such as Jimmy Dean®)
- 6 eggs, hard-boiled and shelled
- ⅓ cup flour
- 2 eggs, lightly beaten
- 1 cup panko breadcrumbs
- cooking spray

Directions:

- In a small mixing dish, combine the yogurt, chutney, mayonnaise, salt, pepper, curry powder, and cayenne. Place in the refrigerator until ready to use.
- Make 6 equal servings of pork sausage. Make a thin patty out of each part. Put one egg in the center and wrap the sausage around it, sealing all edges. Place the eggs on a platter.
- Preheat the air fryer carefully to 390°F (200 degrees C).
- In one small bowl, combine the flour and the beaten eggs. On a dish, spread out the panko breadcrumbs. Each sausage-wrapped egg should be dipped in flour, then into a beaten egg, allowing excess to drip off. Place on a platter and roll in breadcrumbs.
- Spray the air fryer basket with cooking spray and lay the eggs inside. Cook in batches if required; do not overcrowd. Cook for 12 minutes, flipping the eggs halfway through. Rep with the remaining eggs. With dipping sauce, serve.

Air-Fryer Fries

Preparation Time: 20 minutes
Cooking Time: 20 minutes
Serve: 1
Ingredients:

- 1-pound potatoes
- ¼ teaspoon salt
- 1 teaspoon vegetable oil
- 1/4 teaspoon seasoning

Directions:

- Allow potatoes to soak in water for 30 minutes. Using paper towels, drain and wipe dry. Drizzle oil over the vegetables and toss to coat.
- Preheat the air fryer carefully to 400°F (200 degrees C).
- Arrange the potatoes in the fryer basket in a double layer. Cook, tossing every 5 minutes, for 15 to 20 minutes, or until golden brown. Season with salt and pepper to taste.

Air Fryer Blueberry Chimichangas
Preparation Time: 15 minutes
Cooking Time: 25 minutes
Serve: 1
Ingredients:
- ½ (8 ounces) package Neufchatel cheese, softened
- 2 tablespoons sour cream
- 1 ½ tablespoon white sugar
- 1 teaspoon vanilla extract
- 1 (6 ounces) container blueberries
- 5 (7 inches) flour tortillas
- avocado oil cooking spray
- 2 ½ tablespoons white sugar
- ½ tablespoon ground cinnamon

Directions:
- Combine Neufchatel cheese, sour cream, sugar, and vanilla extract in a mixing bowl and whisk with an electric hand mixer. Fold in the blueberries with care.
- Heat tortillas until soft and malleable in a big pan or directly on the grates of a gas burner. 1/4 cup blueberry mixture should be placed down the center of each tortilla. Fold the top and bottom of the tortillas over the filling, then wrap each tortilla into a burrito form. Mist with avocado oil and set in an air fryer basket.
- Cook the chimichangas in the air fryer at 400 degrees F (200 degrees C) for 4 to 6 minutes, or until golden brown. 1 to 2 minutes more, flip each chimichanga over, spritz with cooking spray, and air fry until golden brown. Allow cooling slightly.
- In a small dish, combine the sugar and cinnamon. Each chimichanga should be sprayed with avocado oil and rolled with cinnamon sugar.

Cajun Air Fryer Salmon
Preparation Time: 15 minutes
Cooking Time: 20 minutes
Serve: 1
Ingredients:
- 2 (6 ounces) skin-on salmon fillets
- cooking spray
- 1 tablespoon Cajun seasoning
- 1 teaspoon brown sugar

Directions:
- Preheat the air fryer carefully to 390°F (200 degrees C).
- Using a paper towel, rinse and dry the salmon fillets. Cooking spray should be sprayed on the fillets. In a small bowl, combine the Cajun spice and brown sugar. Distribute on a dish. Season the flesh sides of the fillets with the seasoning mixture.
- Spray the air fryer basket with cooking spray and insert the salmon fillets skin-side down. Cooking spray should be sprayed sparingly on the fish once more.
- 8 minutes in the oven Remove from the air fryer and set aside 2 minutes to rest before serving.

Air Fryer Falafel
Preparation Time: 20 minutes
Cooking Time: 25 minutes
Serve: 1
Ingredients:

- 1 cup dry garbanzo beans
- 1 ½ cups fresh cilantro, stems removed
- ¾ cup fresh flat-leafed parsley stems removed
- 1 small red onion, quartered
- 1 clove garlic
- 2 tablespoons chickpea flour
- 1 tablespoon ground coriander
- 1 tablespoon ground cumin
- 1 tablespoon sriracha sauce
- salt and ground black pepper to taste
- ½ teaspoon baking powder
- ¼ teaspoon baking soda
- cooking spray

Directions:
- Soak chickpeas for 24 hours in a large amount of cold water. Rub your fingers through the wet chickpeas to help loosen and remove the skins. Rinse and drain well. To dry, spread chickpeas on a wide clean dish towel.
- In a food processor, combine chickpeas, cilantro, parsley, onion, and garlic until rough paste forms. Transfer the mixture to a large mixing basin. Chickpea flour, coriander, cumin, sriracha, salt, and pepper. Allow the mixture to rest for 1 hour, covered.
- Preheat an air fryer carefully to 375°F (190 degrees C).
- To the chickpea mixture, add the baking powder and baking soda. Using your hands, mix until just blended. Create 15 equal-sized balls and softly press them to form patties. Cooking spray should be sprayed on the falafel patties.
- Cook for 10 minutes in a preheated air fryer with 7 falafel patties. Cook for 10 to 12 minutes, transfer cooked falafel to a platter and repeat with the remaining 8 falafel.

Air Fryer Roasted Okra
Preparation Time: 15 minutes
Cooking Time: 20 minutes
Serve: 1
Ingredients:
- ½ pound okra ends trimmed, and pods sliced
- 1 teaspoon olive oil
- ¼ teaspoon salt
- ⅛ teaspoon ground black pepper

Directions:
- Preheat an air fryer carefully to 350°F (175 degrees C).
- Combine the okra, olive oil, salt, and pepper in a mixing dish. Place in the air fryer basket in a single layer.
- Cook for 5 minutes in the air fryer. Cook for 5 minutes more after tossing. Cook for 2 minutes more after tossing. Serve right away.

Air Fryer Arancini
Preparation Time: 15 minutes
Cooking Time: 18 minutes
Serve: 1
Ingredients:
- 3 eggs, divided
- 1/2 teaspoon Highlands Italian cheese sprinkle
- 2 ounces fresh mozzarella cheese, cubed
- 1 cup panko breadcrumbs
- 2 ½ cups cooked rice
- ½ teaspoon salt
- ¼ teaspoon ground black pepper
- ⅔ cup grated Parmesan cheese

- ⅓ cup butter, melted
- ½ teaspoon Italian seasoning
- 1 pinch salt
- 1 pinch ground black pepper
- nonstick cooking spray

Directions:

- In a large mixing basin, gently beat 2 eggs. Mix rice, Parmesan cheese, butter, cheese sprinkle, 1/2 teaspoon salt, and 1/4 teaspoon pepper. Refrigerate the mixture for 20 minutes, covered.
- According to the manufacturer's instructions, preheat an air fryer carefully to 370°F (187°C).
- Make 1 1/2-inch ball out of the mixture. Reshape each ball by pressing a mozzarella cube into the middle.
- In a shallow dish, combine panko breadcrumbs, salt, Italian seasoning, and pepper. Then, in a separate dish, softly beat the remaining egg. Each rice ball should be dipped in egg first, then the panko mixture. Next, spray the air fryer basket with cooking spray and place the rice balls in it.
- Cook for 6 minutes in a hot air fryer. Increase the temperature to 400 degrees F (200 degrees C) and air fry for 3 minutes.

Air Fryer Roasted Pineapple

Preparation Time: 15 minutes
Cooking Time: 22 minutes
Serve: 1
Ingredients:

- 1 fresh pineapple

Directions:

- Preheat the air fryer carefully to 375°F (190 degrees C). Then, using parchment paper, line the air fryer basket.
- Using a pineapple core or slicer, core the pineapple and cut it into rings. Fill the prepared basket with pineapple rings.
- 8 to 10 minutes in the air fryer until the slices roast. Flip the slices over and continue to air fry for 3 to 5 minutes.

Air Fryer Bison Burgers

Preparation Time: 10 minutes

Cooking Time: 18 minutes
Serve: 1
Ingredients:

- 1 pound ground bison
- ½ cup finely chopped onion
- 1 egg, beaten
- 2 tablespoons dry breadcrumbs
- 1 tablespoon Worcestershire sauce
- ½ teaspoon liquid smoke
- 1 pinch salt and ground black pepper
- 4 roll (blank)s hamburger buns

Directions:

- Preheat the air fryer carefully to 380°F (190 degrees C).
- Combine the ground bison, onion, egg, breadcrumbs, Worcestershire sauce, liquid smoke, salt, and pepper in a mixing bowl. Make four equal-sized patties.
- Set the timer for 8 minutes and carefully insert it in the bottom of the preheated air fryer. Open the air fryer, carefully turn the patties, and cook for another 4 to 5 minutes, or until the juices run clear. Place one patty on each bun.

Air Fryer Polenta Fries

Preparation Time: 18 minutes
Cooking Time: 20 minutes
Serve: 1
Ingredients:

- 1 (16 ounces) package prepared polenta
- nonstick olive oil cooking spray
- salt and ground black pepper to taste

Directions:

- Preheat an air fryer carefully to 350°F (175 degrees C).
- Cut the polenta into long, thin slices that resemble French fries.
- Cooking spray should be sprayed on the bottom of the basket. Place half of the polenta fries in the basket and spritz the tops gently with cooking spray. Season with salt and pepper to taste.
- Cook for 10 minutes in a preheated air fryer. Flip the fries with a spatula and cook for another 5 minutes, or until crispy. Place the fries on a dish lined with paper towels. Repeat with the other half of the fries.

CHAPTER 9:

Special Events

Flavorful Chicken Skewers

Preparation Time: 10 minutes
Cooking Time: 20 minutes
Serve: 4
Ingredients:

- 1 1/2 lbs. chicken breast, cut into 1-inch cubes
- **For marinade:**
- 2 tbsp dried oregano
- 1 tbsp red wine vinegar
- 1/2 cup low-fat yogurt
- 2 tbsp fresh rosemary, chopped
- 1/4 cup fresh mint leaves
- 1 cup olive oil
- 4 garlic cloves
- 1/2 cup lemon juice
- 1/4 tsp cayenne
- Pepper
- Salt

Directions:

- Add all marinade ingredients into the blender and blend until smooth.
- Pour marinade into a mixing bowl.
- Add chicken and coat well, cover and place in the refrigerator for 1 hour.
- Thread marinated chicken onto the soaked wooden skewers.
- Place chicken skewers into the air fryer basket and cook at 400 F for 15-20 minutes.
- Serve and enjoy.

Turkey Meatballs

Preparation Time: 10 minutes
Cooking Time: 18 minutes
Serve: 6
Ingredients:

- 1 lb. ground turkey
- 1 tbsp garlic, minced
- 1 tsp cumin
- 1 tbsp dried onion flakes
- 2 eggs, lightly beaten
- 1/3 cup almond flour
- 2 cups zucchini, grated
- 1 tsp dried oregano
- 1 tbsp basil, chopped
- Pepper
- Salt

Directions:

- Preheat the air fryer to 400 F.

- Add turkey and remaining ingredients into the mixing bowl and mix until well combined.
- Make small balls from the turkey mixture and place into the air fryer basket and cook for 15-18 minutes. Turn halfway through.
- Serve and enjoy.

Tandoori Chicken Drumsticks

Preparation Time: 10 minutes
Cooking Time: 15 minutes
Serve: 4
Ingredients:

- 4 chicken drumsticks
- **For marinade:**
- 1/2 tsp garam masala
- 1 tbsp fresh lime juice
- 1 tsp ground cumin
- 1/2 tsp turmeric
- 1 tsp chili powder
- 1 tbsp ginger garlic paste
- 1/4 cup yogurt
- 1 tsp salt

Directions:

- Preheat the air fryer to 360 F.
- In a mixing bowl, add marinade ingredients and mix until well combined.
- Add chicken in marinade and mix until well coated. Cover and place in the refrigerator for overnight.
- Place marinated chicken drumsticks into the air fryer basket and cook for 15 minutes. Turn halfway through.
- Serve and enjoy.

Chicken Burger Patties

Preparation Time: 10 minutes
Cooking Time: 18 minutes
Serve: 4
Ingredients:

- 1 lb. ground chicken
- 2 oz mozzarella cheese, shredded
- 3 oz almond flour
- 1 tbsp oregano
- Pepper
- Salt

Directions:

- Preheat the air fryer to 360 F.
- Add chicken and remaining ingredients into the mixing bowl and mix until well combined.
- Make four patties from the chicken mixture.

- Place chicken patties into the air fryer basket and cook for 18 minutes. Turn halfway through.
- Serve and enjoy.

Flavorful Stew Meat
Preparation Time: 10 minutes
Cooking Time: 25 minutes
Serve: 4
Ingredients:
- 1 lb. beef stew meat, cut into strips
- 1 tbsp garlic powder
- 1/2 tsp onion powder
- 1/2 fresh lime juice
- 1 tbsp olive oil
- 1/2 tbsp ground cumin
- Pepper
- Salt

Directions:
- Preheat the air fryer to 380 F.
- Add stew meat and remaining ingredients into the mixing bowl and mix well.
- Add stew meat into the air fryer basket and cook for 25 minutes. Stir halfway through
- Serve and enjoy.

Cheesy Lamb Patties
Preparation Time: 10 minutes
Cooking Time: 8 minutes
Serve: 4
Ingredients:
- 1 lb. ground lamb
- 1/4 cup mint leaves, minced
- 1/4 cup fresh parsley, chopped
- 1 tsp dried oregano
- 1 cup goat cheese, crumbled
- 1 tbsp garlic, minced
- 8 basil leaves, minced
- 1 tsp chili powder
- 1/4 tsp pepper
- 1/2 tsp kosher salt

Directions:
- Preheat the air fryer to 400 F.
- Add ground lamb and remaining ingredients into the mixing bowl and mix until well combined.
- Make four equal shape patties from the lamb mixture.
- Place patties into the air fryer basket and cook for 8 minutes. Turn halfway through.
- Serve and enjoy.

Chipotle Rib-eye Steak
Preparation Time: 10 minutes
Cooking Time: 10 minutes
Serve: 3
Ingredients:
- 1 lb. rib-eye steak
- 1/2 tsp coffee powder
- 1/8 tsp cocoa powder
- 1/8 tsp coriander powder

- 1/4 tsp onion powder
- 1/4 tsp garlic powder
- 1/4 tsp chili powder
- 1/4 tsp chipotle powder
- 1/4 tsp paprika
- Pepper
- Salt

Directions:
- Preheat the air fryer to 390 F.
- In a small bowl, mix together all ingredients except steak.
- Rub spice mixture all over the steak and allow to sit steak for 30 minutes.
- Place steak into the air fryer basket and cook for 10 minutes. Turn halfway through.
- Serve and enjoy.

Yogurt Beef Kebabs
Preparation Time: 10 minutes
Cooking Time: 15 minutes
Serve: 8
Ingredients:
- 1 1/2 lbs. beef, cut into 1-inch pieces
- 2 bell pepper, cut into chunks
- 1/4 cup Greek yogurt
- 1 tsp garlic, minced
- 1 onion, cut into chunks
- pepper
- Salt

Directions:
- Preheat the air fryer to 350 F.
- Add meat and remaining ingredients into the mixing bowl and mix well. Cover and place in refrigerator for 30 minutes.
- Thread marinated beef pieces, bell pepper, and onion pieces onto the skewers.
- Place meat skewers into the air fryer basket and cook for 15 minutes. Turn halfway through.
- Serve and enjoy.

Asian Pork Chops
Preparation Time: 10 minutes
Cooking Time: 12 minutes
Serve: 2
Ingredients:
- 2 pork chops, boneless
- 1 tsp liquid stevia
- 1 tbsp sesame oil
- 3 tbsp lemongrass, chopped
- 1 tbsp shallot, chopped
- 1 tbsp garlic, chopped
- 1 tbsp fish sauce
- 1 tsp soy sauce

Directions:
- Preheat the air fryer to 400 F.
- Add pork chops and remaining ingredients into the mixing bowl and mix well. Cover and place in refrigerator for 2 hours.
- Place marinated pork chops into the air fryer basket and cook for 12 minutes. Turn halfway through.
- Serve and enjoy.

Cheese Balls

Preparation Time: 10 minutes
Cooking Time: 12 minutes
Serve: 8
Ingredients:

- 2 eggs
- 1/2 cup almond flour
- 1/4 cup parmesan cheese, shredded
- 1/4 cup mozzarella cheese, shredded
- 1/2 tsp baking powder
- 1/2 cup cheddar cheese, shredded
- Pepper
- Salt

Directions:

- Preheat the air fryer to 400 F.
- In a mixing bowl, whisk eggs. Add almond flour, parmesan cheese, mozzarella cheese, baking powder, cheddar cheese, pepper, and salt and mix until well combined.
- Make 8 equal shapes of balls from the cheese mixture and place into the air fryer basket and cook for 12 minutes.
- Serve and enjoy.

Crumbed Chicken Tenderloins

Preparation Time: 15 minutes
Cooking Time: 25 minutes
Serve: 1
Ingredients:

- 1 egg
- ½ cup dry breadcrumbs
- 2 tablespoons vegetable oil
- 8 chicken tenderloins

Directions:

- Preheat an air fryer carefully to 350°F (175 degrees C).
- In a small bowl, whisk the egg.
- Combine breadcrumbs and oil in a separate dish until the mixture is loose and crumbly.
- Dip each chicken tenderloin into the egg, then shake off any excess. Dip the chicken into the crumb mixture, coating it evenly and completely. Place the chicken tenderloins in the air fryer basket. Cook until the center is no longer pink, approximately 12 minutes. In the middle, an instant-read thermometer should read at least 162 degrees F. (74 degrees C).

Air-Fried Sweet and Sour Chicken Wings

Preparation Time: 20 minutes
Cooking Time: 20 minutes
Serve: 1
Ingredients:

- 2 pounds party chicken wings
- 1 tablespoon extra-virgin olive oil
- ½ teaspoon salt
- ¾ cup white sugar
- ⅔ cup distilled white vinegar
- ⅓ cup water
- 2 tablespoons reduced-sodium soy sauce
- 2 tablespoons cornstarch
- 1 tablespoon ketchup

Directions:

- Preheat the air fryer carefully to 380°F (190 degrees C).

- Place the wings in a large mixing basin. Drizzle the oil over the top, then sprinkle with the salt and mix until evenly blended. Place half of the wings, skin side down, in the air fryer basket.
- 10 minutes in the air fryer. Cook for 10 minutes longer after flipping the wings with tongs. Raise the temperature to 400°F (200 degrees C). Cook until the wings are crispy on the other side, about 5 minutes more. Rep with the remaining wings.
- Meanwhile, add sugar, vinegar, water, soy sauce, cornstarch, and ketchup in a saucepan over medium-high heat. For 3 to 5 minutes, whisk until sauce has thickened. Turn off the heat and set it aside to cool somewhat.
- Place the wings in a large mixing basin. Pour the sauce over the top, mix to coat, and serve right away.

Amazing Buttermilk Air Fried Chicken

Preparation Time: 15 minutes
Cooking Time: 25 minutes
Serve: 1
Ingredients:

- 1 cup buttermilk
- ½ teaspoon hot sauce
- ⅓ cup tapioca flour
- ½ teaspoon garlic salt
- ⅛ teaspoon ground black pepper
- 1 egg
- ½ cup all-purpose flour
- 2 teaspoons salt
- 1 ½ teaspoons brown sugar
- 1 teaspoon garlic powder
- ½ teaspoon paprika
- ½ teaspoon onion powder
- ¼ teaspoon oregano
- ¼ teaspoon black pepper
- 1-pound skinless, boneless chicken thighs

Directions:

- Add buttermilk and spicy sauce; stir to blend.
- Shake together tapioca flour, garlic salt, and 1/8 teaspoon black pepper in a resealable plastic bag.
- In a small dish, beat the egg.
- In a gallon-sized resealable bag, add flour, salt, brown sugar, garlic powder, paprika, onion powder, oregano, and 1/4 teaspoon black pepper.
- Dip the chicken thighs in the following order: buttermilk mixture, tapioca mixture, egg mixture, and flour mixture, brushing off the excess after each dipping.
- Preheat an air fryer carefully to 380°F (190 degrees C). Then, using parchment paper, line the air fryer basket.
- Fry the coated chicken thighs in batches for 10 minutes in the air fryer basket. Fry the chicken thighs for a further 10 minutes, or until the chicken is no longer pink in the middle and the juices flow clear.

Air-Fried Peruvian Chicken Drumsticks with Green Crema

Preparation Time: 15 minutes
Cooking Time: 20 minutes
Serve: 1
Ingredients:

- olive oil for brushing

- 2 cloves garlic, grated
- 1 tablespoon honey
- 1 tablespoon olive oil
- 1 teaspoon salt
- 1 teaspoon ground cumin
- ½ teaspoon smoked paprika
- ½ teaspoon dried oregano
- ¼ teaspoon ground black pepper
- 6 (4 ounces) chicken drumsticks
- 1 cup baby spinach leaves, stems removed
- ¾ cup sour cream
- ¼ cup cilantro leaves
- 2 tablespoons fresh lime juice
- 1 clove garlic, smashed
- ½ jalapeno pepper, seeded
- ¼ teaspoon salt
- ¼ teaspoon ground black pepper

Directions:
- Brush olive oil into an air fryer basket.
- In a large mixing bowl, combine garlic, honey, 1 tablespoon olive oil, salt, cumin, paprika, oregano, and pepper. Toss in the drumsticks to coat. Arrange the drumsticks in the prepared basket vertically, resting against the basket wall and one another.
- Cook in the air fryer at 400 degrees F (200 degrees C) for 15 to 20 minutes, or until an instant-read thermometer placed into the thickest section of the drumstick registers 175 degrees F (80 degrees C). To ensure consistent cooking, rearrange the drumsticks using kitchen tongs halfway through.
- Meanwhile, mix spinach, sour cream, cilantro, lime juice, garlic, jalapeño pepper, salt, and pepper; process until crème is smooth. Drizzle some cream sauce over the drumsticks and serve the rest of the crema.

Dry-Rub Air-Fried Chicken Wings
Preparation Time: 20 minutes
Cooking Time: 25 minutes
Serve: 1
Ingredients:
- 1 tablespoon dark brown sugar
- 1 tablespoon sweet paprika
- ½ tablespoon kosher salt
- 1 teaspoon garlic powder
- 1 teaspoon onion powder
- 1 teaspoon poultry seasoning
- ½ teaspoon mustard powder
- ½ teaspoon freshly ground black pepper
- 8 chicken wings, or more as needed

Directions:
- Preheat the air fryer carefully to 350°F (175 degrees C).
- In a large mixing bowl, combine brown sugar, paprika, salt, garlic powder, onion powder, poultry seasoning, mustard powder, and pepper. Toss in the chicken wings and work the spices into them with your hands until they are well covered.
- Arrange the wings in the preheated air fryer basket, standing up on their ends and resting against each other and the basket wall.
- Cook for 35 minutes, or until the wings are soft on the inside and golden brown and crisp on the exterior. Place the wings on a dish and serve immediately.

Mustard Fried Chicken
Preparation Time: 15 minutes
Cooking Time: 20 minutes
Serve: 1
Ingredients:
- 5 pounds chicken wings, separated at joints, tips discarded
- 2 tablespoons onion powder
- 2 tablespoons ground black pepper
- 1 tablespoon seasoned salt
- 2 tablespoons garlic powder
- 3 tablespoons prepared yellow mustard
- 3 cups all-purpose flour
- 1-quart oil for frying, or as needed

Directions:
- Season both sides of the chicken wings with seasoned salt, garlic powder, onion powder, pepper, and MSG. I prefer to spread everything out on a large plastic bag for simpler cleanup. Apply a little coating of mustard on each slice. You may use a basting brush or your fingers to apply the sauce. Fill a plastic bag halfway with flour, add the chicken, and shake to coat.
- Heat the oil in a deep-fryer or heavy skillet to 350°F (175 degrees C). Cook the chicken for 6 minutes on each side, or until the juices run clear after the oil is heated. Cool for 5 minutes on paper towels before serving.

Beer Can Chicken Texas Style
Preparation Time: 15 minutes
Cooking Time: 18 minutes
Serve: 1
Ingredients:
- 1 (3 pounds) whole fryer chicken
- 2 lemons, quartered
- 2 limes, quartered
- ½ teaspoon garlic salt
- ¼ teaspoon ground allspice
- salt and ground black pepper to taste
- 6 tablespoons minced garlic, divided
- ¾ (12 ounces) can beer
- 4 cups water
- 1 (12 fluid ounces) can or bottle beer
- 1 cup vinegar
- 6 tablespoons Worcestershire sauce
- 1 red onion, chopped
- 1 red bell pepper, chopped
- 3 tablespoons minced garlic
- 1 tablespoon salt
- 1 tablespoon ground black pepper

Directions:
- Rinse and pat dry the chicken with paper towels. Squeeze the quarters of lemon and lime over the chicken. In a mixing bowl, combine garlic salt, allspice, salt, and black pepper to taste, massage the spices over the chicken skin, insert squeezed lemon and lime quarters into the chicken cavity. Fill the cavity with 3 teaspoons of minced garlic. Wrap the chicken in plastic wrap and place it in the refrigerator for 6 to 8 hours.
- Preheat the grill to medium-low heat; a grill thermometer should read 275°F (135°C) with the lid closed.
- Place the remaining 3 tablespoons garlic into the partially filled can of beer and place the chicken upright atop the beer

can, careful not to spill any lemon and lime quarters or garlic.

- In a saucepan over medium heat, combine water, 1 12-ounces can of beer, vinegar, and Worcestershire sauce; toss in red onion, red bell pepper, 3 tablespoons minced garlic, salt, and black pepper. Bring the mopping sauce to a boil, then reduce to low heat and leave to simmer for 10 minutes. Set aside the sauce.
- Cook until the skin is browned, and the flesh is no longer pink inside, about 2 hours, over a hot grill with the chicken standing erect with the beer can. Inserting an instant-read meat thermometer into the thickest breast section should yield a temperature of at least 160 degrees F. (70 degrees C). As the chicken cooks, use a brush to sprinkle mopping sauce on it every 30 minutes. Discard any remaining sauce.

Garlic and Parmesan Chicken Wings
Preparation Time: 15 minutes
Cooking Time: 22 minutes
Serve: 1
Ingredients:
- cooking spray
- 3 quarts cold water
- ⅓ cup balsamic vinegar
- ¼ cup salt
- 1 bay leaf
- 1 teaspoon dried thyme
- 1 teaspoon dried oregano
- 1 teaspoon dried rosemary
- 8 cloves garlic, minced
- 1 pinch salt
- 3 tablespoons olive oil, or as needed
- 1 tablespoon freshly ground black pepper
- 2 teaspoons red pepper flakes
- 4 pounds chicken wings, separated at joints, tips discarded
- 2 tablespoons fine breadcrumbs
- 1 cup finely grated Parmigiano-Reggiano cheese, divided

Directions:
- Preheat the oven to 450°F (230 degrees C). Line a baking sheet with foil and spray with cooking spray.
- Bring water, vinegar, 1/4 cup salt, bay leaf, thyme, oregano, and rosemary to a boil in a large stockpot. Return to a boil and cook the chicken wings for 15 minutes. Transfer the chicken wings to a cooling rack and set aside for 15 minutes to dry.
- In a mortar and pestle, mash garlic with a pinch of salt until smooth.
- Combine the mashed garlic, olive oil, black pepper, and red pepper flakes in a large mixing bowl. Toss in the chicken wings and breadcrumbs to coat. Add 1/2 cup Parmigiano-Reggiano cheese on top. Sprinkle with the remaining 1/2 cup Parmigiano-Reggiano cheese and place on the prepared baking sheet.
- Cook in a preheated oven for 20 to 25 minutes or until browned.

Gluten-Free Almond Flour Chicken Nuggets
Preparation Time: 10 minutes
Cooking Time: 18 minutes
Serve: 1
Ingredients:

- 1 ¼ pounds ground chicken
- 2 teaspoons salt, divided
- 2 teaspoons ground black pepper, divided
- ½ teaspoon dry mustard
- ½ teaspoon paprika
- ½ teaspoon dried oregano
- 2 cups King Arthur Almond Flour
- ¼ cup cornstarch
- ¼ cup water
- 2 tablespoons olive oil

Directions:
- Preheat the oven to 375 degrees Fahrenheit. Set aside an oven-safe wire rack on top of a baking sheet.
- Combine the chicken, 1 teaspoon salt and pepper, and the other spices in a large mixing basin. Set aside after thoroughly mixing.
- Whisk the almond flour and the remaining salt and pepper in a separate basin. Set aside this dish as well.
- Combine the cornstarch and cold water in a third bowl to make a slurry.
- Take roughly 2 teaspoons of chicken and form it into a tiny disk with damp palms. Coat in almond flour first, then dip in the cornstarch slurry, coat again in almond flour, and place on a wire rack to cool (which is on top of your baking sheet).
- This technique should be repeated until no chicken remains.
- In a nonstick skillet, heat the 2 tablespoons olive oil. When the pan is heated, add half of the chicken nuggets. Cook for 1 minute or until the bottoms start to brown. Cook for another minute on the other side to brown. Return the nuggets to the wire rack.
- Continue frying until all of the nuggets are golden.
- Bake for 10 minutes with the full baking sheet (with the wire rack on top) on the middle rack of the oven.
- Remove the nuggets from the oven and place them on a cooling rack to cool.
- Toss with your favorite dipping sauce and serve. Enjoy!

Air-Fried Popcorn Chicken Gizzards
Preparation Time: 18 minutes
Cooking Time: 20 minutes
Serve: 1
Ingredients:
- 1 pound chicken gizzards
- ⅓ cup all-purpose flour
- 1 ½ teaspoon seasoned salt (such as LAWRY'S®)
- ½ teaspoon ground black pepper
- ½ teaspoon garlic powder
- ½ teaspoon paprika
- 1 pinch cayenne pepper (Optional)
- 1 large egg, beaten
- cooking spray

Directions:
- A big pot of water should be brought to a boil. Add the gizzards, cut into bite-sized pieces, to the boiling water. 30 minutes at a boil Drain.
- Combine the flour, seasoned salt, pepper, garlic powder, paprika, and cayenne in a flat plastic container. Put the lid on and shake until everything is mixed.
- Combine the seasoned flour with the gizzards. Replace the cover and shake until evenly coated.

- In a separate dish, beat the egg. Each gizzard piece should be dipped in the beaten egg and then into the seasoned flour. Snap the cover back on and give it one more shake. Allow resting for 5 minutes while the air fryer warms up.
- Preheat the air fryer carefully to 400°F (200 degrees C).
- Spray the tops of the gizzards with cooking spray and place them in the basket. For 4 minutes in the oven, Shake the basket, and re-spray any chalky areas with cooking spray. Cook for another 4 minutes.

Restaurant-Style Extra Crispy Chicken

Preparation Time: 15 minutes
Cooking Time: 25 minutes
Serve: 1
Ingredients:

- 4 cups water
- 1 tablespoon salt
- ½ teaspoon monosodium glutamate
- 1 (4 pounds) whole chicken
- 4 cups oil for deep frying
- 1 egg, beaten
- 1 cup milk
- 2 cups all-purpose flour
- 2 ½ teaspoons salt
- ¾ teaspoon ground black pepper
- ¾ teaspoon monosodium glutamate

Directions:

- Mix the water, salt, and monosodium glutamate in a big glass dish or basin. Cover and refrigerate for 20 minutes, flipping a couple of times to marinate the chicken.
- Combine the egg and milk in a shallow dish or bowl. Separately, combine the flour, salt, pepper, and monosodium glutamate in a shallow dish or basin. Drain the chicken after removing it from the marinade (discarding the excess marinade).
- Preheat the oil in a deep fryer to 350°F (175 degrees C).
- Dip chicken pieces one at a time into the flour mixture, then the egg/milk mixture, and finally the flour mixture, ensuring sure each piece is fully coated. Place the coated pieces on a dish or baking sheet.
- Place the chicken, one piece at a time, into the heated oil. Fry half of the chicken parts (4 pieces) for 12 to 15 minutes, or until golden brown, then repeat with the remaining pieces. (Note: Stir the chicken halfway through the frying time to ensure that each piece cooks evenly.) Before serving, drain the fried chicken for 5 minutes on paper towels or a wire cooling rack.

Airline Chicken Breast

Preparation Time: 20 minutes
Cooking Time: 20 minutes
Serve: 1
Ingredients:

- 1 whole chicken
- 1 drizzle olive oil
- kosher salt to taste
- ground black pepper to taste
- 2 pinches herb de Provence
- ¼ teaspoon cayenne pepper
- 1 tablespoon olive oil
- 3 tablespoons butter, divided

- 1 sprig of fresh rosemary
- 2 sprigs of fresh thyme
- ½ cup chicken stock

Directions:

- By cutting through the junction where the wing joins the drumette, take 1/2 of each chicken wing. Cut the flesh between the thighs and the breasts. To separate the breasts, make a shallow cut along the breastbone and two deep cuts on either side.
- Using the knife's point, cut each breast from the carcass, keeping the blade pushed against the bone. Then, remove the breast with the wing connected by cutting through the cartilage.
- Tenders should be removed and trimmed as needed. Season with olive oil, salt, pepper, herbs de Provence, and cayenne pepper to taste.
- To separate the skin from the flesh, carefully push your finger beneath the skin of each breast, exactly adjacent to the wing bone. Next, 1 tender should be slid beneath the skin, centered, and smoothed over the skin. Then, season the breasts with salt.
- In a pan over medium-high heat, heat 1 tablespoon olive oil. Place the chicken breasts, skin side down, in a baking dish. Cook for 6 to 7 minutes, or until the bottom is browned. Reduce heat to medium and cook until the interior is no longer pink, 7 to 10 minutes more. 1 tablespoon butter, rosemary, and thyme are all good additions. Baste the chicken with butter. Take the chicken out of the skillet.
- Pour in the stock and turn up the heat to high. Boil for about 2 minutes or until the required thickness is reached. Remove from heat and whisk in the remaining butter. Divide each chicken breast into thirds and cover with the pan sauce.

Crispy Flautas

Preparation Time: 15 minutes
Cooking Time: 25 minutes
Serve: 1
Ingredients:

- 1 teaspoon vegetable oil
- ½ green bell pepper, chopped
- ½ onion, finely diced
- 1-pound skinless, boneless chicken breast
- 1 (1 ounce) package taco seasoning mix
- ¾ cup water
- 1 (10 ounces) package corn tortillas (such as Ortega®)
- ½ cup shredded Cheddar cheese
- 1 cup salsa
- 24 toothpicks
- 2 cups vegetable oil for frying

Directions:

- In a pan over medium heat, heat 1 teaspoon vegetable oil. Stir in the bell pepper and onion; simmer and stir for 5 minutes, or until the onion has softened and turned translucent. Raise the heat to medium-high and add the chicken breast. Cook and stir for 10 minutes, or until the chicken breast is no longer pink in the middle. Using two forks, shred the chicken. Combine the taco seasoning and water in a mixing bowl. Simmer for 10 minutes, stirring regularly, until the liquid has evaporated. Remove from the pan and set aside the Cheddar cheese.
- Brush a thin coating of salsa onto each corn tortilla. Along the bottom border of the tortilla, place roughly 2 teaspoons of the chicken mixture. Roll the tortilla tightly into a

cylinder, then attach the ends with one or two toothpicks. Rep with the remaining tortillas.

- Heat 2 cups vegetable oil to 375 degrees F. (190 degrees C) in a large pan.
- Fry the flautas, no more than four at a time, in the hot oil until golden and crisp, about 4 minutes. Drain the flautas on a dish lined with paper towels. Remove toothpicks and top flautas with remaining salsa.

Crispy Baked Moroccan Chicken Wings with Yogurt Dip

Preparation Time: 15 minutes
Cooking Time: 20 minutes
Serve: 1
Ingredients:

- 2 ½ pounds chicken wings
- 1 ½ tablespoon vegetable oil
- 1 teaspoon paprika
- 1 teaspoon ground cumin
- ¼ teaspoon ground cinnamon
- ¼ teaspoon ground ginger
- ¼ teaspoon cayenne pepper
- ¼ teaspoon ground turmeric
- ½ teaspoon salt
- ¼ teaspoon pepper
- Reynolds Wrap® Non-Stick Aluminum Foil
- 1 cup plain Greek yogurt
- 2 tablespoons fresh lemon juice
- 1 tablespoon chopped fresh mint
- 1 tablespoon chopped fresh cilantro
- 1 ½ tablespoon honey
- ½ teaspoon salt
- ¼ teaspoon pepper

Directions:

- Preheat the oven to 400 degrees Fahrenheit. Reynolds Wrap® Nonstick Foil should be used to line a baking pan. Toss the chicken wings in a large mixing basin with the vegetable oil until they are fully covered.
- Combine the paprika, cumin, cinnamon, ginger, cayenne pepper, turmeric, salt, and pepper in a small mixing bowl. Toss the wings in the spice mixture until thoroughly covered. Arrange the wings on the baking sheet in a single layer, spreading them apart, so they don't touch.
- Bake the wings for 40 to 45 minutes, or until cooked through, before transferring them to a serving tray.
- Combine the yogurt, lemon juice, mint, cilantro, honey, salt, and pepper in a small mixing dish. Season the dip with extra salt and pepper to taste. With the yogurt dip, serve the wings.

Baked Panko-Crusted Chicken Tenders

Preparation Time: 20 minutes
Cooking Time: 25 minutes
Serve: 1
Ingredients:

- ½ cup plain fat-free Greek yogurt
- ¼ cup jarred roasted red peppers - drained, patted dry, and chopped
- 1 tablespoon balsamic vinegar
- ¼ teaspoon dried basil
- ⅛ teaspoon salt
- ⅛ teaspoon black pepper
- ⅛ teaspoon garlic powder
- ¼ teaspoon garlic powder
- ¼ teaspoon onion powder
- ¼ teaspoon salt
- ¼ teaspoon freshly ground black pepper
- 1 pound chicken tenders
- 1 cup Italian-seasoned panko (Japanese breadcrumbs)
- 1 large egg, lightly beaten

Directions:

- Preheat the oven to 400 degrees Fahrenheit (200 degrees C). Preheat the oven to 350°F. Line a baking sheet with parchment paper.
- In a tiny food processor, combine Greek yogurt, red peppers, balsamic vinegar, basil, salt, pepper, and 1/8 teaspoon garlic powder. Blend until smooth, then chill the dipping sauce until ready to use.
- Combine 1/4 teaspoon garlic powder, onion powder, salt, and pepper in a small bowl. Toss the chicken tenders in the seasoning mixture to coat evenly. Place aside.
- In a skillet over medium-high heat, toast panko crumbs until golden brown, 4 to 5 minutes. Put the panko in a shallow dish. Separately, crack one egg into a shallow dish. Dip chicken tenders into the egg, allowing excess to drop out, and then cover with panko. Place the tenders on the baking sheet that has been prepared.
- Bake it until the chicken is no longer pink in the center and the juices run clear, 12 to 15 minutes total, flipping halfway through. In the middle, an instant-read thermometer should read at least 160 degrees F. (74 degrees C). Serve it with the dipping sauce on the side.

Crispy Honey Sriracha Chicken Wings

Preparation Time: 15 minutes
Cooking Time: 20 minutes
Serve: 1
Ingredients:

- 2 tablespoons baking powder
- 1 tablespoon kosher salt
- 1 teaspoon freshly ground black pepper
- 1 teaspoon smoked paprika
- 2 ½ pounds chicken wing sections
- ⅓ cup honey
- ⅓ cup sriracha sauce
- 1 tablespoon seasoned rice vinegar
- ¼ teaspoon sesame oil
- 1 pinch sesame seeds, or as desired

Directions:

- Preheat the oven to 425°F (220 degrees C). Then line a baking sheet with aluminum foil and set an oven-safe wire rack on top.
- Combine the baking powder, salt, black pepper, and paprika in a small mixing bowl. In a large mixing basin, combine the chicken wings. Toss the wings in 1/2 of the baking powder mixture to coat. Toss the wings with the remaining baking powder mixture to coat. Place the wings on the rack of the baking sheet that has been prepared.
- Bake for 20 minutes in a preheated oven. Bake the wings for another 20 minutes. Bake for another 15 minutes, or until the wings are golden and crispy. Place the wings in a large mixing basin.
- Combine honey, sriracha sauce, rice vinegar, and sesame oil in a mixing bowl until smooth. Drizzle glaze over wings and

toss to coat evenly. Place the wings on a serving plate and garnish with sesame seeds.

Zesty Broiled Chicken Thighs

Preparation Time: 15 minutes
Cooking Time: 18 minutes
Serve: 1
Ingredients:

- 1 large onion, chopped
- ¼ cup lime juice
- ¼ cup orange juice
- 8 cloves garlic, peeled
- 2 tablespoons avocado oil
- 2 teaspoons ground coriander
- 2 teaspoons ground cumin
- 2 teaspoons Mexican oregano
- 1 teaspoon chipotle chili powder
- ½ teaspoon smoked paprika
- 1 pinch salt and ground black pepper
- 3 pounds boneless, skinless chicken thighs

Directions:

- In a blender or food processor, combine onion, lime juice, orange juice, garlic, avocado oil, coriander, cumin, Mexican oregano, chipotle chili powder, and smoky paprika. Pulse several times to combine, then puree for 1 minute, or until no visible chunks remain.
- Place the chicken thighs in a 1-gallon resealable bag and pour the marinade. Squeeze the majority of the air out and seal. Squeeze the contents of the bag gently until the chicken pieces are coated. Marinate for 30 minutes to 3 hours in the refrigerator.
- Preheat the oven's broiler and position an oven rack approximately 4 inches from the heat source. On a broiler pan, place the marinated chicken thighs.
- Broil the chicken thighs for 8 minutes or until they begin to brown. Broil for another 7 minutes, or until gently browned the second side. An instant-read thermometer put into the thickest section of the chicken thigh should register at least 165°F (74 degrees C).
- Transfer the chicken to a serving plate.

Paper-Wrapped Chicken

Preparation Time: 15 minutes
Cooking Time: 22 minutes
Serve: 1
Ingredients:

- ½ cup teriyaki sauce, 2 cloves garlic, minced
- 1 (1 inch) piece fresh ginger, grated
- ¼ teaspoon crushed red pepper flakes
- 1-pound skinless, boneless chicken breast halves - cut into bite-size pieces
- 30 4x4-inch squares aluminum foil, or as needed
- oil for deep frying

Directions:

- Combine the teriyaki sauce, garlic, ginger, and red pepper flakes; whisk in the chicken pieces until fully covered.
- Refrigerate the chicken for 3 to 4 hours or overnight in a covered bowl.
- Remove a piece of marinated chicken and lay it in the center of an aluminum square.
- Fold the square in a triangular shape over the chicken piece; fold up the open corners of the triangle several times and

press tightly together to seal the chicken inside the foil. Rep with the rest of the chicken pieces. Remove the used marinade.

- Heat the oil in a deep fryer or big saucepan to 350°F (175 degrees C).
- Add the wrapped foil packets to the heated oil and fry for 2 to 4 minutes, or until the chicken is tender and cooked through. Allow the packets to drain on paper towels and cool slightly.
- Tear apart the packages along the sealed edges to serve.

Chicken Fajita Egg Rolls

Preparation Time: 10 minutes
Cooking Time: 18 minutes
Serve: 1
Ingredients:

- vegetable oil for frying
- 2 eggs
- 2 tablespoons milk
- 2 tablespoons olive oil
- 1 red onion, minced
- 1 red bell pepper, chopped
- 1 green bell pepper, chopped
- 1 jalapeno pepper, seeded and minced (Optional)
- ½ cup finely chopped mushrooms (Optional)
- cayenne pepper
- 2 pounds skinless, boneless chicken breasts
- 2 (8 ounces) packages of shredded pepper Jack cheese
- 16 egg roll wrappers, or more as needed

Directions:

- Heat the oil in a deep fryer or big saucepan to 350°F (175 degrees C).
- To prepare egg wash, combine eggs and milk in a mixing bowl.
- In a sauté pan over medium heat, heat the olive oil. Cook and stir the onion, peppers, mushrooms, and cayenne for 5 minutes, or until slightly softened. Cook until the chicken is no longer pink, about 5 minutes. 1 to 2 minutes, mix in the pepper Jack cheese until fully incorporated and beginning to melt.
- Fill each egg roll wrapper with an equal amount of the filling mixture. Fold in the side corners and wrap up, using egg wash to seal the edges.
- Cook the egg rolls in the heated oil for 3 to 5 minutes, or until they float to the top and turn golden brown. To minimize overpopulation, work in bunches. Then, lay flat on paper towels to drain, standing on end to drain any excess oil.

Grandma Egan's Chicken Stock

Preparation Time: 18 minutes
Cooking Time: 20 minutes
Serve: 1
Ingredients:

- 1 (8 pounds) chicken
- 3 stalks celery, chopped
- 1 onion, quartered

Directions:

- In a large stockpot, combine the chicken, celery, and onion. Fill the container halfway with water. Bring the water to a boil.

- Remove any extra fat. Reduce the heat to a simmer and cook for 2 to 3 hours.
- Take out the chicken and veggies. Using a cheesecloth, strain the soup.

Smoked Chicken Drumsticks

Preparation Time: 15 minutes
Cooking Time: 25 minutes
Serve: 1
Ingredients:

- 12 chicken drumsticks
- ¼ cup vegetable oil
- ⅓ cup BBQ rub

Directions:

- Remove the drumsticks from the package and set them on a rack over a drip tray or baking sheet. Refrigerate for 8 hours to overnight to air dry.
- Preheat an electric smoker to 275°F (135 degrees C). Follow the manufacturer's directions for adding wood chips.
- Brush the drumsticks with a little vegetable oil. Put the drumsticks in a resealable plastic bag with the rub and shake to coat. To coat evenly, toss everything together.
- Place the drumsticks on the smoker rack. Smoke for 2 hours, or until the chicken reaches an internal temperature of 165°F (74°C).

Chicken and Waffle Sandwich

Preparation Time: 20 minutes
Cooking Time: 20 minutes
Serve: 1
Ingredients:

- 2 cups all-purpose flour
- 4 teaspoons baking powder
- 1 teaspoon salt
- ¼ teaspoon granulated garlic
- ¼ teaspoon Italian seasoning (such as Trader Joe's® 21 Seasoning Salute)
- 1 ½ cups warm milk
- 2 large eggs
- ⅓ cup salted butter, melted
- ⅓ cup shredded Cheddar cheese
- 1 (24 ounces) package frozen breaded chicken breast fillets (such as Kirkwood®)
- cooking spray
- 1 pinch salt

Directions:

- In a large mixing bowl, combine the salt, garlic, flour, baking powder, and seasoning; set aside. Combine the eggs, milk, and melted butter in a separate dish. Pour the milk mixture into the flour mixture and stir until combined. Mix in the Cheddar cheese.
- Preheat an air fryer carefully for 5 minutes at 400 degrees F (200 degrees C).
- 7 minutes in the air fryer. Cook for another 6 minutes after turning the chicken pieces.
- Meanwhile, preheat the oven to 200°F (95 degrees C). Preheat a waffle maker according to the manufacturer's directions. Coat the waffle maker with nonstick cooking spray.
- Pour 3 tablespoons batter onto the waffle maker. Cook for 5 minutes, or until the waffle is golden brown and the iron stops steaming. Place on a baking sheet lined with

parchment paper and keep heat in the oven. Rep with the remaining batter.

- Once all waffles are done, assemble the waffle and chicken sandwiches.

Hot Bean and Bacon Dip with Air Fryer Tortilla Chips

Preparation Time: 15 minutes
Cooking Time: 25 minutes
Serve: 1
Ingredients:

- avocado oil cooking spray
- ½ pound bacon
- ½ cup chopped onion
- 1 (4 ounces) can chop green chiles
- 2 cloves garlic, minced
- 1 (29 ounces) can pinto beans, undrained
- ½ cup chicken broth
- 1 teaspoon chili powder
- 2 tablespoons cream cheese
- salt and ground black pepper to taste
- 1 cup shredded sharp Cheddar cheese
- 1 cup shredded pepper Jack cheese
- 12 (6 inches) corn tortillas

Directions:

- Preheat the oven to 350 degrees Fahrenheit (175 degrees C). Spray an 8x8-inch baking dish lightly with cooking spray.
- Cook the bacon in a large pan over medium-high heat, stirring periodically, for approximately 10 minutes, or until uniformly browned. On paper towels, drain the bacon slices. Once cool, crumble.
- In the same skillet, cook the onion until transparent, about 4 to 5 minutes. Cook for 2 minutes more after adding the green chilies and garlic. Bring the pinto beans to a boil. Combine the chicken broth and chili powder in a mixing bowl. Reduce to low heat and mash the beans. Allow boiling for 5 to 6 minutes, or until slightly thickened. Next, stir in the cream cheese until it is melted. Simmer for 5 to 6 minutes, or until slightly thickened. Finally, stir in the bacon until completely mixed. Season with salt and pepper to taste.
- Layer 1/2 of the bean mixture, 1/2 cup pepper Jack, and 1/2 cup Cheddar cheese in the prepared baking dish. Layers should be repeated.
- Bake for 15 minutes, covered, in a preheated oven. Uncover and bake for 5 to 7 minutes more, or until the cheese is melted or lightly browned.
- Meanwhile, prepare an air fryer to 350°F (175°C) according to the manufacturer's recommendations.
- Each tortilla should be cut into fourths. Avocado oil should be sprayed on both sides of each tortilla. Place in a single layer in the air fryer basket. 4 to 6 minutes in the air fryer. Cook for another 2 to 3 minutes, or until crisp. Because they can burn fast, always keep an eye on your basket. Serve with a hot-dip and a sprinkle of salt.

Air Fryer Rotisserie Chicken

Preparation Time: 15 minutes
Cooking Time: 20 minutes
Serve: 1
Ingredients:

- 1 tablespoon sea salt
- 2 teaspoons ground paprika

- 1 teaspoon onion powder
- 1 teaspoon ground thyme
- 1 teaspoon ground white pepper
- ½ teaspoon ground black pepper
- ½ teaspoon cayenne pepper
- ½ teaspoon garlic powder
- 3 tablespoons vegetable oil
- 1 (4 pound) whole fryer chicken, giblets removed

Directions:
- According to the manufacturer's instructions, preheat an air fryer carefully to 350°F (175°C).
- In a small bowl, combine salt, paprika, onion powder, thyme, white pepper, black pepper, cayenne pepper, and garlic powder.
- Rub half of the oil and half of the spice mixture over the chicken.
- Cook for 30 minutes in a preheated air fryer. Remove the chicken from the frying with care.
- Turn the chicken over. Brush the opposite side with oil and sprinkle with the remaining spice mixture. Return to the air fryer and cook for another 30 minutes, or until the meat is no longer pink at the bone and the juices flow clear. An instant-read thermometer implanted near the bone into the thickest section of the thigh should register 165 degrees F. (74 degrees C).
- Remove from the fryer, cover with a double layer of aluminum foil, and set aside 10 minutes before slicing.

Air Fryer Stuffed Chicken Thighs
Preparation Time: 20 minutes
Cooking Time: 25 minutes
Serve: 1
Ingredients:
- 6 ounces Swiss cheese
- 1 cup panko breadcrumbs
- 1 tablespoon salon seasoning
- ½ cup flour, divided
- salt and freshly ground black pepper
- 2 large eggs
- 6 slices turkey lunch meat
- 6 medium boneless skinless chicken thighs
- nonstick cooking spray

Directions:
- Preheat an air fryer carefully to 400°F (200 degrees C).
- Swiss cheese should be cut into six 2 x 1/2 x 1/2-inch pieces.
- Set up a breading station by putting breadcrumbs, 2 teaspoon sounder spice, 1 tablespoon flour in one shallow dish, remaining flour and sounder seasoning in another shallow dish, and eggs in a third shallow dish. Whip the eggs until they are golden and foamy. Season the eggs with salt and pepper to taste.
- Place one piece of Swiss cheese on top of each piece of turkey meat. Wrap luncheon meat in a layer of Swiss cheese.
- Open the chicken thighs and insert the turkey cheese bundle in the center. Wrap the chicken thigh around the bundle. Place the chicken bundles in the air fryer, seam side down. Nonstick spray should be sprayed on the chicken bundles.
- Reduce the temperature of the air fryer to 380 degrees F (193 degrees C) and air-fried the chicken for 15 minutes. Turn the bundles over, coat with nonstick spray, and reduce the temperature of the air fryer to 370 degrees F. (187

degrees C). Cook until the chicken is cooked through, about 8 minutes more in the air fryer. Serve right away.

Air-Fried Breaded Chicken Thighs
Preparation Time: 15 minutes
Cooking Time: 20 minutes
Serve: 1
Ingredients:
- 4 medium bone-in, skin-on chicken thighs
- 1 cup buttermilk
- ¼ cup all-purpose flour
- ¼ cup plain breadcrumbs
- 2 tablespoons grated Parmesan cheese
- ½ teaspoon ground paprika
- 1 teaspoon garlic powder
- 1 teaspoon salt
- ½ teaspoon onion powder
- ½ teaspoon black pepper
- nonstick cooking spray

Directions:
- Combine the chicken thighs and buttermilk in a nonreactive container with a cover or a resealable plastic bag. Marinate for at least 1 hour or overnight in the refrigerator.
- Take the chicken out of the refrigerator. Pour out the buttermilk and let the chicken aside to rest while preparing the breading mixture.
- In a wide, shallow dish or pie plate, whisk or mix the flour, breadcrumbs, Parmesan cheese, paprika, garlic powder, salt, onion powder, and black pepper until equally blended.
- Preheat the air fryer carefully from 375°F to 380°F (190 to 195 degrees C). Lightly coat the air fryer basket with nonstick spray.
- Once the air fryer is heated, dip the chicken thighs, one at a time, into the breading mixture, making sure the breading adheres to both sides as much as possible. Then, place gently in the air fryer basket. Repeat until all thighs have been breaded and placed in the basket. They should not be stacked on top of one other.
- Set the timer for 25 minutes in the air fryer. When the timer goes off, use an instant-read thermometer to check the temperature. The inside temperature should be 180 degrees Fahrenheit (82 degrees C). If they aren't quite done but the breading is turning black, simply seal the basket and set them aside to rest or turn the air fryer back on for a few minutes and check again. Serve right away.

Air-Fried Chicken Calzone
Preparation Time: 15 minutes
Cooking Time: 18 minutes
Serve: 1
Ingredients:
- 1 teaspoon olive oil, ¼ cup finely chopped red onion
- 3 cups baby spinach leaves
- ⅓ cup low-sodium marinara sauce
- ⅓ cup shredded cooked chicken breast
- 6 ounces prepared pizza dough
- ⅓ cup shredded mozzarella cheese
- cooking spray

Directions:
- In a nonstick skillet, heat the oil over medium-high heat. Cook occasionally turns until the onion is soft, approximately 2 minutes. Cover and simmer until the

spinach is wilted, about 1 1/2 minutes. Remove from the heat and mix in the marinara and chicken.

- According to the manufacturer's instructions, preheat an air fryer carefully to 325°F (165°C).
- Cut the dough into four equal pieces. Roll each piece into a 6-inch circle on a lightly floured work surface. 1/4 of the spinach mixture should be spread over the bottom half of each dough round. Top with a quarter of the mozzarella cheese on each. Fold the dough over the filling to make half-moons, then crimp the edges to secure. Coat well with cooking spray.
- Place the calzone in the air fryer basket, 8 minutes in the oven. Cook until golden brown on the other side, about 4 minutes longer.

Crispy Chicken Salad with Yummy Honey Mustard Dressing
Preparation Time: 15 minutes
Cooking Time: 22 minutes
Serve: 1
Ingredients:

- 2 tablespoons olive oil
- 1 ½ cups panko breadcrumbs
- ¼ teaspoon garlic powder
- 2 tablespoons chopped fresh parsley
- cooking spray
- ½ cup all-purpose flour
- ¼ teaspoon salt
- ¼ teaspoon ground black pepper
- 2 large eggs
- 2 tablespoons water
- 1 ½ pound skinless, boneless chicken breast halves
- 8 cups mixed spring salad greens
- 2 large carrots, peeled and sliced diagonally
- 1 cup sliced radishes
- ¾ cup mayonnaise
- 3 tablespoons prepared yellow mustard
- 3 tablespoons honey
- 4 teaspoons Dijon mustard
- 1 tablespoon lemon juice

Directions:

- In an extra-large skillet, heat the oil over medium heat. Mix in the panko and garlic powder. Cook, constantly stirring, for 2 to 3 minutes, or until toasted. Allow cooling in a shallow dish for 2 to 3 minutes. Mix in the parsley.
- Preheat the air fryer carefully to 400°F and coat the air fryer basket with cooking spray (200 degrees C).
- Meanwhile, combine the flour, salt, and pepper in a separate shallow dish. Finally, whisk together the eggs and water in a third shallow dish.
- Cut chicken breasts into 1x3-inch strips lengthwise. To coat, dip the chicken strips in the flour mixture, then egg mixture, and finally the panko mixture.
- Add the chicken to the prepared air fryer in batches. Cook, rotating once, for 5 to 7 minutes, or until an instant-read thermometer inserted into the thickest sections registers 165°F (74°C). Transfer to a platter, cover with foil and keep warm.
- In a large mixing basin, combine salad leaves, carrots, and radishes.
- In a small mixing bowl, combine the mayonnaise, yellow mustard, honey, Dijon mustard, and lemon juice for the dressing.

- Salad should be divided among plates, topped with chicken, and drizzled with dressing.

Air Fryer Gluten-Free Fried Chicken
Preparation Time: 10 minutes
Cooking Time: 18 minutes
Serve: 1
Ingredients:

- 1 ¼ cups gluten-free flour
- 6 large eggs
- salt and freshly ground black pepper to taste
- 2 pounds boneless, skinless chicken breast
- 1 ¼ cups Gluten-free crackers
- ¼ cup vegetable oil

Directions:

- In a small dish, whisk together the eggs and season with salt and pepper. In a separate bowl, properly combine the flour and cracker crumbs.
- Dredge the chicken pieces in flour, then in eggs, and then in cracker crumbs. Next, place the pieces on an air fryer rack, ensuring they don't touch. Finally, brush the tops of the birds with oil.
- Air-fried chicken for 10 minutes at 375°F (190°C) until cooked through and crisp.

Air Fryer Chicken Thighs and Potatoes
Preparation Time: 18 minutes
Cooking Time: 20 minutes
Serve: 1
Ingredients:

- 1 tablespoon ground paprika
- 1 teaspoon granulated garlic
- 1 teaspoon onion powder
- 1 teaspoon Greek seasoning (such as Cavender's®)
- 1 teaspoon Goya Sanader Total
- 2 pounds bone-in, skin-on chicken thighs
- ¼ cup water
- salt and ground black pepper to taste
- 1 tablespoon vinegar
- 6 tablespoons olive oil, divided
- ½ pound baby red potatoes

Directions:

- Combine paprika, garlic, onion powder, Greek seasoning, Casado total, salt, and pepper in a small bowl. In a small dish, reserve 1 tablespoon seasoning; cover and keep away until required for the potatoes.
- Combine the remaining spice, water, 4 tablespoons olive oil, and vinegar in a 1-gallon resealable bag. Add the chicken thighs to the bag; massage to cover with spice, press excess air, and close. Marinate for 8 hours or overnight in the refrigerator.
- Preheat the air fryer carefully for 5 minutes at 400 degrees F (200 degrees C).
- Meanwhile, mix 1 tablespoon leftover seasoning with the remaining 2 tablespoons olive oil in a small dish; toss to blend. Toss in the potatoes and toss until thoroughly covered. In the air fryer basket, combine the potatoes and thighs.
- Cook in a preheated air fryer for 28 minutes, or until the potatoes are cooked, and the chicken is no longer pink at the bone, and the juices flow clear. A thermometer near the bone should read 165 degrees F. (74 degrees C).

Crispy Air-Fried Chicken
Preparation Time: 15 minutes
Cooking Time: 25 minutes
Serve: 1
Ingredients:
- 1 tablespoon ground paprika
- 1 teaspoon salt
- 1 teaspoon onion powder
- 1 teaspoon garlic powder
- ½ teaspoon dried marjoram
- ½ teaspoon ground sage
- ½ teaspoon ground black pepper
- ⅛ teaspoon ground nutmeg
- 2 (8 ounces) bone-in, skin-on chicken breast halves
- ¼ cup coconut oil, at room temperature
- 2 tablespoons dry sherry
- 2 tablespoons lime juice

Directions:
- In a small bowl, combine paprika, salt, onion powder, garlic powder, marjoram, sage, pepper, and nutmeg. Rub the spice rub all over the chicken breasts, including beneath the skin.
- According to the manufacturer's instructions, preheat an air fryer carefully to 400°F (200°C). In a small dish, combine the coconut oil, sherry, and lime juice; put aside.
- Cook for 15 minutes with the chicken breast side down in the air fryer basket. Brush the saved basting oil over the chicken. Cook for another 15 minutes after flipping the chicken and lowering the heat to 360 degrees F (182 degrees C). Cook until the chicken is no longer pink at the bone and the juices run clear, about 6 to 12 minutes more. A thermometer near the bone should read 165 degrees F. (74 degrees C).

Greek-inspired Air Fryer Cornish Hen
Preparation Time: 20 minutes
Cooking Time: 20 minutes
Serve: 1
Ingredients:
- 1 tablespoon olive oil
- ¼ teaspoon dried oregano
- ⅛ teaspoon dried dill weed
- ⅛ teaspoon garlic powder
- ⅛ teaspoon onion powder
- ⅛ teaspoon dried rosemary
- ⅛ teaspoon paprika
- 1 (2 pounds) Chicken, Cornish game hens, meat, and skin, raw

Directions:
- Preheat the air fryer carefully to 390°F (200 degrees C).
- Combine olive oil, oregano, dill, garlic powder, onion powder, rosemary, and paprika in a mixing bowl. Brush the mixture all over the hen, paying special attention to the wings and legs.
- Place the hen in the air fryer basket and cook for 30 minutes. Remove to a chopping board and set aside for 10 minutes before serving.

Air Fryer Cornish Hen
Preparation Time: 15 minutes
Cooking Time: 25 minutes

Serve: 1
Ingredients:
- 2 pounds Cornish hen, giblets removed
- salt and freshly ground black pepper
- nonstick cooking spray

Directions:
- Preheat an air fryer carefully to 390°F (200 degrees C).
- Dry the Cornish hen with paper towels and season with salt and pepper on both sides.
- Place the hen in the air fryer basket and cook for 15 minutes. Cook for 15 minutes more after spraying the top of the hen with nonstick cooking spray. A thermometer near the bone should read 165 degrees F. (74 degrees C).
- Place the hen on a chopping board and set aside for 10 minutes. Carve and serve the meat.

Crispy Smoked Chicken Wings
Preparation Time: 15 minutes
Cooking Time: 20 minutes
Serve: 1
Ingredients:
- 3 tablespoons whole black peppercorns
- 2 tablespoons coriander seeds
- 2 tablespoons mustard seeds
- 1 tablespoon fennel seeds
- 1 tablespoon cumin seeds
- 4 cups water
- 1 onion, diced
- 8 cloves garlic, smashed
- 1 (2 inches) piece fresh ginger, sliced
- 2 tablespoons dried rosemary
- 2 tablespoons dried thyme
- 6 bay leaves
- ½ cup white sugar
- ⅓ cup salt
- 3 pounds chicken wings, tips removed, and sections separated
- 2 lemons, zested and juiced
- 2 limes, zested and juiced
- 5 ice cubes
- 1 (64 fluid ounces) bottle apple juice
- applewood chips, soaked
- vegetable oil for frying

Directions:
- In a mortar and pestle, combine peppercorns, coriander, mustard, fennel, and cumin; smash until aromatic and slightly broken.
- In a saucepan, bring water to a boil. Bring back to a boil with the peppercorn-seed combination, onion, garlic, ginger, rosemary, thyme, and bay leaves. Reduce the heat to low and cook for about 25 minutes, or until the flavors have melded. Allow brine to cool for about 10 minutes.
- Fill a big 10-quart plastic container with a tight-fitting lid with 2 cups brine. Stir in the sugar and salt until completely dissolved. Combine the chicken wings, lemon zest and juice, and lime zest and juice in a mixing bowl.
- Add ice to the pot containing the remaining brine to chill the brine. Fill the plastic container halfway with water. Pour in enough apple juice to completely coat the wings. Refrigerate for 24 to 48 hours after thoroughly stirring and sealing the container.

- According to the manufacturer's instructions, preheat the smoker to 275 to 300 degrees Fahrenheit (135 to 150 degrees Celsius).
- Rinse wings under cold running water and dry on wire racks, unstacked. Set the racks in the smoker. Follow the manufacturer's instructions for adding the applewood chips. Smoke for approximately 25 minutes, or until the chicken has a smokey taste but is not cooked. Place the wings on a tray and pat them dry with paper towels.
- Heat the oil in a deep fryer or big saucepan to 350°F (175 degrees C). Fry 8 to 10 wings at a time for 60 to 90 seconds, or until golden brown and crispy.

Greek-inspired Air Fryer Cornish Hen

Preparation Time: 20 minutes
Cooking Time: 25 minutes
Serve: 1
Ingredients:

- 1 tablespoon olive oil
- ¼ teaspoon dried oregano
- ⅛ teaspoon dried dill weed
- ⅛ teaspoon garlic powder
- ⅛ teaspoon onion powder
- ⅛ teaspoon dried rosemary
- ⅛ teaspoon paprika
- 1 (2 pounds) Chicken, Cornish game hens, meat, and skin, raw

Directions:

- Preheat the air fryer carefully to 390°F (200 degrees C).
- Combine olive oil, oregano, dill, garlic powder, onion powder, rosemary, and paprika in a mixing bowl. Brush the mixture all over the hen, paying special attention to the wings and legs.
- Place the hen in the air fryer basket and cook for 30 minutes. Remove to a chopping board and set aside for 10 minutes before serving.

Air Fryer Chicken Piccata

Preparation Time: 15 minutes
Cooking Time: 20 minutes
Serve: 1
Ingredients:

- 2 large eggs, beaten
- 3 tablespoons lemon juice, divided
- 1 teaspoon garlic powder
- ½ cup all-purpose flour
- ½ cup grated Parmesan cheese
- 2 tablespoons dried parsley flakes
- 1 teaspoon salt
- 1-pound skinless, boneless chicken breast halves
- nonstick cooking spray
- 2 tablespoons butter
- ½ cup chicken broth
- 2 tablespoons capers with liquid, or more to taste

Directions:

- Set up your dredging station by whisking together the eggs, 1 tablespoon lemon juice, and garlic powder in a mixing basin.
- In a broad and shallow basin (or pie plate), combine the flour, Parmesan cheese, parsley, and salt and whisk with a fork until thoroughly combined.

- The manufacturer's instructions preheat an air fryer carefully to 375°F (190°C). Cooking sprays the bottom insert of the fryer.
- Pound your chicken fillets until consistent and thin (cover with plastic wrap beforehand and use a meat mallet).
- Dredge the chicken in flour, then in egg wash, then in flour again, and place it in the air fryer as you go, arranging it so that it doesn't overlap; if you have too many pieces of chicken, cook them in stages.
- Bake for 14 minutes in a preheated air fryer, or until the centers are no longer pink and an instant-read thermometer put into the middle registers 165 degrees F (74 degrees C).
- While the chicken is cooking, melt the butter in a small saucepan over medium heat, then whisk in the chicken broth, remaining lemon juice, and capers, beginning with 2 tablespoons and adding more capers to taste. While the chicken cooks, bring the sauce to a simmer and reduce it somewhat. The sauce will be runny.
- Drizzle the lemon butter sauce over the chicken before serving.

Air Fryer Chicken Piccata with Lemon-Caper Sauce

Preparation Time: 15 minutes
Cooking Time: 18 minutes
Serve: 1
Ingredients:

- 4 tablespoons unsalted butter
- 4 cloves garlic, minced
- 2 tablespoons all-purpose flour
- ½ cup chicken broth
- ½ cup dry white wine
- ¼ cup fresh lemon juice
- 2 tablespoons capers, drained
- 1 tablespoon finely chopped fresh parsley
- 1 teaspoon lemon zest
- ½ teaspoon kosher salt
- ¼ teaspoon black pepper
- nonstick cooking spray
- 2 (8 ounces) skinless
- ½ cup all-purpose flour
- 1 large egg
- 1 tablespoon fresh lemon juice
- 1 tablespoon freshly grated Parmesan cheese
- 1 tablespoon freshly grated Asiago cheese
- 1 tablespoon freshly grated Pecorino Romano cheese
- 1 cup seasoned breadcrumbs
- 1 ½ teaspoon ground black pepper
- 1 teaspoon kosher salt

Directions:

- Make the lemon-caper sauce: Melt the butter in a small saucepan over medium heat. Cook, stirring periodically, until the garlic is fragrant, approximately 1 minute. Cook, whisking continually, until the mixture is slightly thickened, about 2 minutes.
- Bring the chicken broth, white wine, and lemon juice to a boil. Remove from the fire and stir in the capers, parsley, lemon zest, salt, and pepper. Cover and keep heated until ready to use, then whisk gently before serving.
- Preparing the chicken: Preheat an air fryer carefully to 400 degrees F (200 degrees C) for 10 minutes, according to the

manufacturer's recommendations. Coat the air fryer basket lightly with nonstick spray.

- Each chicken breast should be cut in half crosswise. Then line a large cutting board with plastic wrap set the chicken breast halves on it, cover with plastic wrap. Using a meat mallet, pound each chicken breast half until it is 1/2-inch thick.

- In a medium mixing bowl, combine the flour and baking powder. In a second medium mixing bowl, combine the egg and lemon juice. In a third medium mixing dish, combine the breadcrumbs and cheeses. Finally, season both sides of the chicken breast halve equally with pepper and salt.

- Dredge a piece of chicken carefully in flour until fully coated, working in batches. Transfer it to the egg mixture and gently toss to coat, then toss again in the bread crumb mixture to coat. Place on a baking sheet. Repeat until all the chicken has been breaded.

- In the preheated fryer basket, place 2 pieces of breaded chicken. Cook for 8 to 10 minutes, or until golden brown and crispy, and a thermometer inserted into the thickest section registers 165 degrees F (74 degrees C). Halfway through the cooking time, turn the chicken pieces and re-spray the top. Cook the remaining chicken and transfer it to a plate.

- Serve immediately with the lemon-caper sauce.

Air Fryer Honey Chicken

Preparation Time: 15 minutes
Cooking Time: 22 minutes
Serve: 1
Ingredients:

- cooking spray
- 6 tablespoons honey
- 6 tablespoons olive oil
- 2 cups dry breadcrumbs
- 2 cups panko breadcrumbs
- 2 skinless, boneless chicken breast halves

Directions:

- Cooking spray should be sprayed on an air fryer basket.
- In a mixing dish, combine honey and oil. In a separate dish, combine the breadcrumbs and panko.
- Cut the chicken breasts in half lengthwise to make four thin cutlets. Dip the cutlets in the honey mixture until thoroughly coated, then in the bread crumb mixture.
- Place in the air fryer basket that has been preheated. Coat the tops in cooking spray.
- Air-fry for 5 minutes at 390 degrees F (199 degrees C) per manufacturer's directions. Cook until the center is no longer pink, and the juices run clear, approximately 7 minutes more. In the middle, an instant-read thermometer should read at least 160 degrees F. (74 degrees C).

Chicken Cordon in the Air Fryer

Preparation Time: 10 minutes
Cooking Time: 18 minutes
Serve: 1
Ingredients:

- 4 skinless, boneless chicken breast halves
- 2 slices deli ham
- 2 slices deli Swiss cheese
- ¼ cup all-purpose flour
- ½ teaspoon salt
- ¼ teaspoon ground black pepper

- 1 large egg, lightly beaten
- ⅔ cup plain dry breadcrumbs
- 3 tablespoons unsalted butter, melted

Directions:

- Place each chicken breast between two pieces of parchment paper on a chopping board. Then, using a mallet or a foil-wrapped block, flatten each breast to a thickness of 1/4 inch, being cautious not to pound all the way through.

- Cut the ham and Swiss cheese slices in half so that you have four pieces of each in the center of each flattened chicken breast; layer 1 piece ham and 1 piece cheese. Roll up the breast like a jelly roll, tucking the ham and cheese inside as you go. Secure the ends and sides with toothpicks to prevent the cheese from escaping. Refrigerate for at least 15 minutes, but no more than 4 hours.

- If the manufacturer recommends it, Preheat an air fryer carefully to 350°F (175°C).

- Combine the flour, salt, and pepper in a small mixing bowl. In the second bowl, beat the egg. Finally, in a third bowl, combine the breadcrumbs.

- To coat, dip each chicken bundle in the flour mixture, the egg, and breadcrumbs. If you see places that are only faintly covered in flour, softly pat them with a beaten egg and breadcrumbs. Place each bundle in the air fryer basket after gently patting it with melted butter.

- Air-fry for 20 minutes, or until the crust is well browned, and the chicken is no longer pink in the middle, and the juices flow clear. In the middle, an instant-read thermometer should read at least 160 degrees F. (74 degrees C).

Air-Fried Chicken Strips

Preparation Time: 18 minutes
Cooking Time: 20 minutes
Serve: 1
Ingredients:

- 1 ½ pounds chicken tenderloins
- 1 cup buttermilk
- 1 cup panko breadcrumbs
- ½ cup all-purpose flour
- 1 teaspoon adobo seasoning
- 1 teaspoon Mexican seasoning mix
- cooking spray

Directions:

- Each chicken tenderloin should have its membrane removed. Soak chicken tenderloins for 1 to 2 hours in buttermilk.

- According to the manufacturer's instructions, preheat an air fryer carefully to 400°F (200°C).

- Combine panko, flour, adobo spice, and Mexican seasoning in a mixing bowl. Combine thoroughly. Remove the tenderloins from the buttermilk and press them into the panko mixture.

- Cooking spray should be sprayed into the air fryer basket. Spray the tenderloins with cooking spray and place them in the air fryer basket. 8 minutes in the air fryer. Spray again after flipping each tenderloin. 8 minutes in the air fryer. Shake the basket and re-spray the tenderloins. 4 minutes longer in the air fryer.

Air Fryer Cornflake Chicken

Preparation Time: 15 minutes
Cooking Time: 25 minutes

Serve: 1

Ingredients:

- ½ pound skinless, boneless chicken breast
- ½ cup all-purpose flour
- 1 teaspoon adobo seasoning
- ½ teaspoon granulated garlic
- 2 cups corn flakes cereal
- 1 teaspoon taco seasoning mix
- 1 serving cooking spray

Directions:

- Remove any visible fat from the chicken breast and chop it into bite-sized pieces.
- Combine the flour, adobo spice, and garlic in a resealable plastic bag. Shake vigorously. Toss in the chicken pieces to coat. Refrigerate for at least 8 hours and up to overnight.
- Preheat the air fryer carefully for 5 minutes at 400 degrees F (200 degrees C).
- In a food processor, combine cornflakes and process for 20 seconds, or until the texture is like flour. Take out 1/2 cup. Mix Mexican spice into cornflake 'flour.' Add the seasoned chicken to a resealable plastic bag. Shake vigorously. Place the chicken pieces in the air fryer basket. Coat lightly with cooking spray.
- 5 minutes in the air fryer. Shake the basket and re-spray the chicken with cooking spray. 5 minutes longer in the air fryer. Serve right away.

Air Fryer Chicken Satay with Dipping Sauce

Preparation Time: 20 minutes
Cooking Time: 20 minutes
Serve: 1

Ingredients:

- ¼ cup full-fat coconut milk
- 3 tablespoons coconut aminos
- 1 tablespoon finely grated fresh ginger
- 1 tablespoon fish sauce
- 3 cloves garlic, minced
- 2 teaspoons curry powder
- 1 ½ teaspoon ground turmeric
- ½ teaspoon ground cumin
- ½ teaspoon ground coriander
- salt and ground black pepper to taste
- 2 ½ pounds boneless, skinless chicken thighs
- ½ cup teriyaki sauce
- ⅓ cup cashew butter
- 3 tablespoons orange juice
- 2 cloves garlic, minced
- 1 teaspoon cayenne pepper
- 2 tablespoons chopped raw cashews (Optional)
- 5 cups hot cooked rice
- ½ bunch cilantro sprigs

Directions:

- In a gallon-sized resealable bag, combine coconut milk, coconut aminos, ginger, fish sauce, garlic, curry powder, turmeric, cumin, coriander, salt, and pepper. Toss in the chicken pieces. Squeeze out most of the air, seal, and gently squeeze the chicken pieces until they are evenly coated in marinade. Refrigerate for at least 4 hours and up to 24 hours, turning the bag regularly.
- Prepare the dipping sauce 1 hour before cooking the chicken to allow the flavors to mix. Combine the teriyaki

sauce, cashew butter, orange juice, garlic, and cayenne pepper in a small mixing bowl. Refrigerate until ready to serve, well covered.

- According to the manufacturer's instructions, preheat an air fryer carefully to 400°F (200°C).
- Thread chicken chunks onto each skewer and arrange them on a skewer attachment rack.
- Place the rack in the air fryer basket and cook for 8 minutes on high. Cook for an additional 8 minutes after carefully turning each skewer. Rep with the remaining chicken. When an instant-read thermometer is put into the center of the chicken registers 165 degrees F, it is done (74 degrees C).
- Top the dipping sauce with chopped cashews. Serve the skewers with the dipping sauce on top of hot cooked rice. Garnish with cilantro sprigs if desired.

Air Fryer Chicken Fajitas for Two

Preparation Time: 15 minutes
Cooking Time: 25 minutes
Serve: 1

Ingredients:

- ½ teaspoon ground cumin
- ½ teaspoon smoked paprika
- ½ teaspoon ancho chili powder
- ½ teaspoon garlic powder
- ¼ teaspoon ground coriander
- salt and ground black pepper to taste
- ½ pound chicken breast tenderloins
- ½ medium green bell pepper, sliced into strips
- ½ medium onion, sliced into rings
- 2 tablespoons extra-virgin olive oil, divided
- ½ lime
- 4 (8 inches) flour tortillas

Directions:

- According to the manufacturer's instructions, preheat an air fryer carefully to 370°F (190°C).
- Combine cumin, smoked paprika, ancho chili powder, garlic powder, coriander, salt, and pepper in a mixing bowl. Tenderloins should be cut into 1/2-inch strips lengthwise.
- Combine the bell pepper strips and onion pieces in a large mixing bowl. Toss with 1 tablespoon olive oil, then sprinkle with half of the spice mixture. Toss until everything is equally covered. Fill the bottom of the air fryer basket with veggies.
- Toss tenderloin strips with the remaining 1 tablespoon olive oil in a mixing basin. Toss the chicken strips in the remaining spice mixture to coat evenly. Place the chicken strips in the air fryer basket on the veggies.
- Air-fried the chicken for about 10 minutes, or until it is well done. Squeeze the lime juice over everything. Serve with tortillas made from flour.

Air Fryer Fried Chicken

Preparation Time: 15 minutes
Cooking Time: 20 minutes
Serve: 1

Ingredients:

- 2 cups buttermilk
- 2 teaspoons hot pepper sauce
- 1 teaspoon salt
- 1 ½ pound bone-in chicken pieces, with skin
- 1 cup all-purpose flour

- 2 teaspoons sweet paprika
- 2 teaspoons smoked paprika
- 2 teaspoons garlic salt
- 2 teaspoons onion powder
- 1 ⅔ teaspoons salt
- 1 teaspoon ground black pepper
- 1 teaspoon ground cumin
- ½ teaspoon dried thyme
- ½ teaspoon dried basil
- ⅓ teaspoon dried oregano
- cooking spray

Directions:
- In a large gallon-sized resealable bag, combine buttermilk, spicy sauce, and salt. Add the chicken and knead it thoroughly to coat it with the marinade. Marinate the chicken in the refrigerator for 8 hours to overnight.
- In a second gallon-sized resealable bag, combine flour, sweet and smoked paprika, garlic salt, onion powder, salt, pepper, cumin, thyme, basil, and oregano. Shake well to mix. Remove the chicken from the buttermilk and add it to the dry ingredients. Shake well to coat.
- Preheat an air fryer carefully to 400°F (200 degrees C).
- Coat the chicken with frying spray. Air fry for 20 minutes, rotating halfway through.

Air Fryer BBQ Chicken Tenders
Preparation Time: 20 minutes
Cooking Time: 25 minutes
Serve: 1
Ingredients:
- 3 ½ ounces barbecue-flavored pork rinds
- 1 cup all-purpose flour
- 1 tablespoon barbecue seasoning
- 1 egg, beaten
- 1 ½ pounds chicken breast tenderloins
- cooking spray

Directions:
- Preheat an air fryer carefully to 370°F (190 degrees C).
- In a food processor, pulse pig rinds until they are the size of breadcrumbs. In a small bowl, combine all the ingredients. In a shallow bowl, combine the flour and barbecue spice. In a third shallow dish, beat the egg.
- Coat each chicken tender in the flour mixture first, the beaten egg, and the pork rind crumbs.
- Spray the air fryer basket with nonstick cooking spray. Place half of the chicken tenders in the air fryer basket, making sure none of them contact. Cooking spray should be sprayed on the top of each tender. Cook for 15 minutes, or until the chicken is cooked through and no longer pink in the center. Rep with the remaining tenders.

Golden Air-Fried Chicken Tenders
Preparation Time: 15 minutes
Cooking Time: 20 minutes
Serve: 1
Ingredients:
- 1 egg
- ½ teaspoon salt
- ⅛ teaspoon ground black pepper
- 2 cornbread muffins, crumbled
- ¼ cup panko breadcrumbs

- 2 teaspoons honey powder (such as Savory Spice®)
- 1 tablespoon tropical poultry rub (such as Savory Spice® Gold Coast Poultry Rub)
- 1 pound chicken tenders

Directions:
- Whisk the egg, salt, and pepper until thoroughly blended in a small dish. Combine cornbread crumbs, panko, honey powder, and poultry rub in a separate shallow dish.
- Each chicken tender should be dipped in the egg mixture. Dredge in cornmeal coating after shaking off excess.
- Preheat an air fryer carefully to 380°F (190 degrees C). The cooking time for chicken tenders is 6 minutes. Cook for another 6 minutes on the other side.

Air Fryer Cornish Hen
Preparation Time: 15 minutes
Cooking Time: 18 minutes
Serve: 1
Ingredients:
- 2 pounds Cornish hen, giblets removed
- salt and freshly ground black pepper
- nonstick cooking spray

Directions:
- Preheat an air fryer carefully to 390°F (200 degrees C).
- Dry the Cornish hen with paper towels and season with salt and pepper on both sides.
- Place the hen in the air fryer basket and cook for 15 minutes. Cook for 15 minutes more after spraying the top of the hen with nonstick cooking spray. A thermometer near the bone should read 165 degrees F. (74 degrees C).
- Place the hen on a chopping board and set aside for 10 minutes. Carve and serve the meat.

Air Fryer Chicken Piccata
Preparation Time: 15 minutes
Cooking Time: 22 minutes
Serve: 1
Ingredients:
- 2 large eggs, beaten
- 3 tablespoons lemon juice, divided
- 1 teaspoon garlic powder
- ½ cup all-purpose flour
- ½ cup grated Parmesan cheese
- 2 tablespoons dried parsley flakes
- 1 teaspoon salt
- 1-pound skinless, boneless chicken breast halves
- nonstick cooking spray
- 2 tablespoons butter
- ½ cup chicken broth
- 2 tablespoons capers with liquid, or more to taste

Directions:
- Set up your dredging station by whisking together the eggs, 1 tablespoon lemon juice, and garlic powder in a mixing basin.
- In a broad and shallow basin (or pie plate), combine the flour, Parmesan cheese, parsley, and salt and whisk with a fork until thoroughly combined.
- The manufacturer's instructions preheat an air fryer carefully to 375°F (190°C). Cooking sprays the bottom insert of the fryer.

- Pound your chicken fillets until consistent and thin (cover with plastic wrap beforehand and use a meat mallet).
- Dredge the chicken in flour, then in egg wash, then in flour again, and place it in the air fryer as you go, arranging it so that it doesn't overlap; if you have too many pieces of chicken, cook them in stages.
- Bake for 14 minutes in a preheated air fryer, or until the centers are no longer pink and an instant-read thermometer put into the middle registers 165 degrees F (74 degrees C).
- While the chicken is cooking, melt the butter in a small saucepan over medium heat, then whisk in the chicken broth, remaining lemon juice, and capers, beginning with 2 tablespoons and adding more capers to taste. While the chicken cooks, bring the sauce to a simmer and reduce it somewhat. The sauce will be runny.
- Drizzle the lemon butter sauce over the chicken before serving.

Chicken Cordon Bleu in the Air Fryer
Preparation Time: 10 minutes
Cooking Time: 18 minutes
Serve: 1
Ingredients:
- 4 skinless, boneless chicken breast halves
- 2 slices deli ham
- 2 slices deli Swiss cheese
- ¼ cup all-purpose flour
- ½ teaspoon salt
- ¼ teaspoon ground black pepper
- 1 large egg, lightly beaten
- ⅔ cup plain dry breadcrumbs
- 3 tablespoons unsalted butter, melted

Directions:
- Place each chicken breast between two pieces of parchment paper on a chopping board. Then, using a mallet or a foil-wrapped block, flatten each breast to a thickness of 1/4 inch, being cautious not to pound all the way through.
- Cut the ham and Swiss cheese slices in half so that you have four pieces of each in the center of each flattened chicken breast; layer 1 piece ham and 1 piece cheese. Roll up the breast like a jelly roll, tucking the ham and cheese inside as you go. Secure the ends and sides with toothpicks to prevent

the cheese from escaping. Refrigerate for at least 15 minutes, but no more than 4 hours.
- If the manufacturer recommends it, Preheat an air fryer carefully to 350°F (175°C).
- Combine the flour, salt, and pepper in a small mixing bowl. In the second bowl, beat the egg. Finally, in a third bowl, combine the breadcrumbs.
- To coat, dip each chicken bundle in the flour mixture, the egg, and breadcrumbs. If you see places that are only faintly covered in flour, softly pat them with a beaten egg and breadcrumbs. Place each bundle in the air fryer basket after gently patting it with melted butter.
- Air-fry for 20 minutes, or until the crust is well browned, and the chicken is no longer pink in the middle, and the juices flow clear. In the middle, an instant-read thermometer should read at least 160 degrees F. (74 degrees C).

Easy Air-Fried Chicken Breast
Preparation Time: 18 minutes
Cooking Time: 20 minutes
Serve: 1
Ingredients:
- 1 (8 ounces) chicken breast
- 2 teaspoons olive oil
- salt to taste
- freshly ground black pepper to taste
- garlic powder to taste

Directions:
- Preheat an air fryer carefully to 360°F (182 degrees C).
- Brush the chicken breast with olive oil on both sides and season with salt, pepper, and garlic powder on one side. Next, place the seasoned side of the chicken breast in the air fryer basket and season the other side with salt, pepper, and garlic powder.
- Air-fry for 9 minutes, then turn and cook for another 9 minutes, or until the chicken breast is no longer pink in the center and the juices run clear. In the middle, an instant-read thermometer should read at least 165 degrees F. (74 degrees C).
- Place the chicken breast on a platter and cover loosely with foil. Allow for a 5-minute pause before serving.

CHAPTER 10:

Desserts

Delicious Apple Crisps
Preparation Time: 10 minutes
Cooking Time: 25 minutes
Serve: 2
Ingredients:
- For filling:
- 1 apple, diced
- ½ tbsp fresh lime juice
- ½ tbsp maple syrup
- ½ tsp cinnamon
- For topping:
- ½ tsp cinnamon
- 1 tsp whole wheat flour
- 1 tbsp maple syrup
- 1 tbsp butter, melted
- 1/3 cup rolled oats

Directions:
- Mix together apple, lime juice, maple syrup, and cinnamon and divide into two ramekins.
- Mix together topping ingredients and spread on top of the apple mixture.
- Cover ramekin with foil and place into the air fryer basket and cook at 350 F for 15 minutes.
- Remove foil and cook for 10 minutes more.
- Serve and enjoy.

Moist Orange Muffins
Preparation Time: 10 minutes
Cooking Time: 15 minutes
Serve: 12
Ingredients:
- 4 eggs
- 3 cups almond flour
- 1 tsp baking soda
- 1 orange zest
- 1 orange juice
- 1/2 cup butter, melted

Directions:
- Preheat the air fryer to 350 F.
- Add all ingredients into the mixing bowl and mix until well combined.
- Spoon mixture into the silicone muffin molds.
- Place muffin molds into the air fryer basket and cook for 12-15 minutes.
- Serve and enjoy.

Sliced Apples
Preparation Time: 10 minutes
Cooking Time: 10 minutes
Serve: 6
Ingredients:
- 4 small apples, sliced
- 2 tbsp butter, melted
- 1 tsp apple pie spice
- 1/2 cup erythritol

Directions:
- Preheat the air fryer to 350 F.
- In a mixing bowl, toss apple slices with butter, apple pie spice, and sweetener.
- Transfer apple slices into the baking dish.
- Place baking dish into the air fryer basket and cook for 10 minutes.
- Serve and enjoy.

Baked Pears
Preparation Time: 10 minutes
Cooking Time: 10 minutes
Serve: 4
Ingredients:
- 2 medium pears, cut in half & cored
- 1 tbsp honey
- 2 tbsp butter, melted
- ½ tsp cinnamon
- 1 tbsp sugar

Directions:
- Mix together sugar and cinnamon and sprinkle over pears.
- Place pears into the air fryer basket and cook at 370 F for 10 minutes.
- Drizzle butter and honey over pears and serve.

Gooey Chocolate Cake
Preparation Time: 10 minutes
Cooking Time: 10 minutes
Serve: 4
Ingredients:
- 2 eggs
- 1 ½ tbsp self-rising flour
- 3 ½ tbsp sugar
- 1 cup dark chocolate chips
- 7 tbsp butter

Directions:
- Add butter and chocolate chips into the bowl and microwave for 30 seconds or until butter and chocolate chips melted. Stir well.

- In a separate bowl, whisk eggs and sugar.
- Add melted chocolate mixture and flour and stir until smooth.
- Spoon batter into the four greased ramekins.
- Place ramekins into the air fryer basket and cook at 370 F for 10 minutes.
- Serve and enjoy.

Chocolate Brownies
Preparation Time: 10 minutes
Cooking Time: 12 minutes
Serve: 4
Ingredients:
- 1 egg
- ¼ cup cocoa powder
- 6 tbsp flour
- ¼ cup butter, melted
- ½ tsp vanilla
- ½ cup sugar
- ¼ tsp salt

Directions:
- In a bowl, beat eggs with vanilla, sugar, and salt until light.
- Add butter and mix well.
- Add cocoa powder and flour and stir until well combined.
- Pour batter into the greased air fryer baking dish.
- Place baking dish into the air fryer basket and cook at 330 F for 12 minutes.
- Slice and serve.

Sweet Caramel Pineapple
Preparation Time: 10 minutes
Cooking Time: 12 minutes
Serve: 4
Ingredients:
- 2 cups pineapple slices
- 1 tsp cinnamon
- 2 tbsp maple syrup
- 1 tbsp butter, melted

Directions:
- Preheat the air fryer to 380 F.
- In a mixing bowl, mix together pineapple slices, butter, maple syrup, and cinnamon until well coated.
- Place pineapple slices into the air fryer basket and cook for 12 minutes. Turn halfway through.
- Serve and enjoy.

Blueberry Cobbler
Preparation Time: 10 minutes
Cooking Time: 15 minutes
Serve: 2
Ingredients:
- 6 oz blueberries
- 1 tbsp fresh lemon juice
- 1 tbsp sugar
- For topping:
- ¼ cup milk
- ½ tsp baking powder
- 2 tbsp sugar
- ¼ cup all-purpose flour

- ½ tsp salt

Directions:
- Add blueberries, sugar, and lemon juice into the two ramekins and mix well.
- In a bowl, mix together topping ingredients and pour over blueberry mixture.
- Place ramekins into the air fryer basket and cook at 320 F for 12-15 minutes.
- Serve and enjoy.

Apple Pecan Carrot Muffins
Preparation Time: 10 minutes
Cooking Time: 10 minutes
Serve: 12
Ingredients:
- 1 egg
- 1 ½ cups all-purpose flour
- ½ cup pecans, chopped
- ½ cup raisins
- 1 cup apples, shredded
- 1 cup carrots, shredded
- 2 tsp vanilla
- 2/3 cup honey
- ½ cup yogurt
- 1/3 cup applesauce
- ¼ tsp nutmeg
- ½ tsp ginger
- 2 tsp cinnamon
- 2 tsp baking powder
- ½ tsp salt

Directions:
- Preheat the air fryer to 350 F.
- In a mixing bowl, mix together flour, ginger, nutmeg, cinnamon, baking powder, and salt.
- Add egg, vanilla, honey, yogurt, and applesauce and mix until just combined.
- Add pecans, raisins, apples, and carrots and fold well.
- Spoon batter into the silicone muffin molds.
- Place muffin molds into the air fryer basket and cook for 10 minutes.
- Serve and enjoy.

Blueberry Muffins
Preparation Time: 10 minutes
Cooking Time: 12 minutes
Serve: 8
Ingredients:
- 1 egg
- ¾ cup blueberries
- 2 tsp vanilla
- 3 tbsp butter, melted
- 1/3 cup unsweetened almond milk
- ¼ tsp cinnamon
- ¼ cup sugar
- 1 cup self-rising flour

Directions:
- Preheat the air fryer to 340 F.
- In a mixing bowl, whisk egg with sugar, vanilla, butter, and almond milk.
- Add flour and cinnamon and stir until well combined.

- Add blueberries and fold well. Spoon batter into the silicone muffin molds.
- Place muffin molds into the air fryer basket and cook for 12-14 minutes.
- Serve and enjoy.

Air Fryer Kale Chips with Parmesan

Preparation Time: 15 minutes
Cooking Time: 25 minutes
Serve: 1
Ingredients:

- 1 bunch kale
- 1 tablespoon olive oil
- salt and ground black pepper to taste
- 1 ½ teaspoon chili-lime seasoning
- 2 tablespoons grated Parmesan cheese

Directions:

- Carefully to 280°F (138°C) according to the manufacturer's instructions.
- Wash the kale and separate the leaves from the ribs. Dry the kale leaves fully before tearing them into pieces. Ribs should be discarded.
- In a large mixing bowl, combine the kale leaves and olive oil; toss with your hands until the kale is uniformly and lightly coated. Season with salt and pepper to taste. Mix in the chili-lime seasoning until equally distributed.
- Place some kale in the hot air fryer in batches without overlapping. 5 minutes in the oven Shake the basket and continue to air-fry for 3 minutes. Sprinkle with Parmesan cheese to coat, shake, and air-fry for another 2 minutes, or until crispy. Repeat with the remaining batches, keeping an eye on the air fryer and keeping the temperature low.

Air Fryer Pear Crisp for Two

Preparation Time: 20 minutes
Cooking Time: 20 minutes
Serve: 1
Ingredients:

- 2 large pear (approx. 2 per lb.) spears - peeled, cored, and diced
- 1 teaspoon lemon juice
- ¾ teaspoon ground cinnamon, divided
- 2 tablespoons quick-cooking oats
- 1 tablespoon all-purpose flour
- 1 tablespoon brown sugar
- 1 tablespoon salted butter, softened

Directions:

- Preheat the air fryer carefully to 360°F (180 degrees C).
- Combine the pears, lemon juice, and 1/4 teaspoon cinnamon in a medium mixing dish. Toss to coat, then divide between two ramekins.
- Combine the oats, flour, brown sugar, and the remaining 1/2 tsp cinnamon in a small mixing bowl. Stir in the softened butter using a fork until the mixture is crumbly. Sprinkle on top of the pears.
- Place the ramekins in the air fryer basket and cook for 18 to 20 minutes, or until the pears are tender and bubbly.

Air Fryer Mini Blueberry Scones

Preparation Time: 15 minutes
Cooking Time: 25 minutes
Serve: 1
Ingredients:

- 1 cup all-purpose flour
- 4 tablespoons white sugar, divided
- 1 ½ teaspoons baking powder
- ⅛ teaspoon baking soda
- ⅛ teaspoon salt
- 2 tablespoons butter
- 1 egg
- ¼ cup buttermilk
- ½ teaspoon vanilla extract
- ¼ cup fresh blueberries
- 2 teaspoons orange zest

Directions:

- Preheat the air fryer carefully to 360°F (180 degrees C).
- In a medium mixing basin, combine the flour, 2 tablespoons sugar, baking powder, baking soda, and salt with 2 knives or a pastry blender. Cut in the butter until the mixture resembles coarse crumbs.
- In a small bowl, beat the egg with a fork. Set aside 2 tablespoons of the egg in a separate small dish. Whisk the remaining egg, buttermilk, and vanilla extract with a fork until incorporated. Stir until slightly moistened with the flour mixture. Stir in the blueberries gently.
- Place the dough on a lightly floured surface. Gently knead the dough for 8 to 10 strokes, or until it is no longer sticky. Make a 6-inch round out of the dough. Without separating, cut into 8 wedges, soaking the knife in flour between cuts.
- Combine the remaining 2 tablespoons of sugar and orange zest in a separate dish. Brush the top of the dough with the saved egg, then sprinkle with the sugar mixture. Separate the dough wedges and gently put them in a single layer in the fryer basket, in batches if required, using a little broad spatula.
- Cook the scones for 6 minutes, or until golden brown. Serve hot.

Air Fryer Turkey Breakfast Sausage Links

Preparation Time: 15 minutes
Cooking Time: 20 minutes
Serve: 1
Ingredients:

- 1 (9.6 ounces) package turkey breakfast sausage links

Directions:

- Preheat the air fryer carefully to 350°F (175 degrees C).
- Place all 12 links in the air fryer basket in a single layer.
- 6 minutes in the oven

Air Fryer Garlic and Parsley Baby Potatoes

Preparation Time: 20 minutes
Cooking Time: 25 minutes
Serve: 1
Ingredients:

- 1 pound baby potatoes, cut into quarters
- 1 tablespoon avocado oil
- ¼ teaspoon salt
- ½ teaspoon granulated garlic

- ½ teaspoon dried parsley

Directions:

- Carefully to 350°F (175 degrees C).
- Toss the potatoes in a basin with the oil to coat. Toss in 1/4 teaspoon granulated garlic and 1/4 teaspoon parsley to coat. Rep with the rest of the garlic and parsley. Place the potatoes in the air fryer basket.
- Place the basket in the air fryer and cook, stirring regularly, for 20 to 25 minutes, or until golden brown.

Air Fryer Salmon Cakes with Sriracha Mayo

Preparation Time: 15 minutes
Cooking Time: 20 minutes
Serve: 1
Ingredients:

- ¼ cup mayonnaise
- 1 tablespoon Sriracha
- 1-pound skinless salmon fillets
- 1 egg, lightly beaten
- ⅓ cup almond flour
- 1 ½ teaspoon seafood seasoning
- 1 green onion, coarsely chopped
- cooking spray
- 1 pinch seafood seasoning (such as Old Bay®) (Optional)

Directions:

- In a small mixing dish, combine mayonnaise and sriracha. 1 tablespoon Sriracha mayo in a food processor; chill the remainder until ready to use.
- To the Sriracha mayo, add the salmon, almond flour, egg, 1 1/2 teaspoons seafood spice, and green onion; pulse quickly for 4 to 5 seconds, or until ingredients are barely mixed but tiny bits of salmon remains. (Be careful not to overprocess the mixture, or it will turn mushy.)
- Line a plate with waxed paper and squirt cooking spray on your hands. Transfer the salmon mixture to a dish and shape it into 8 tiny patties. Refrigerate for 15 minutes or until cool and stiff.
- Preheat the air fryer carefully to 390°F (200 degrees C). Cooking spray should be sprayed on the air fryer basket.
- Take the salmon cakes out of the refrigerator. Spray both sides with frying spray and place in the air fryer basket, working in batches as required to minimize congestion.
- Cook for 6 to 8 minutes in a preheated air fryer. Serve with the remaining Sriracha mayo and a small dusting of Old Bay seasoning, if preferred, on a serving dish.

Air Fryer Spicy Dill Pickle Fries

Preparation Time: 15 minutes
Cooking Time: 18 minutes
Serve: 1
Ingredients:

- 1 ½ (16 ounces) jars spicy dill pickle spears
- 1 cup all-purpose flour
- ½ teaspoon paprika
- ¼ cup milk
- 1 egg, beaten
- 1 cup panko breadcrumbs
- cooking spray

Directions:

- Drain and pat dry the pickles.

- In a mixing dish, combine the flour and paprika. In a separate dish, whisk together the milk and the beaten egg. In a third bowl, combine the panko.
- Carefully to 400°F (200°C) according to the manufacturer's instructions.
- Place a pickle on a dish after dipping it in the flour mixture, then the egg mixture, and finally the breadcrumbs. Rep with the remaining pickles. Lightly spray the covered pickles with cooking spray.
- Place the pickles in the air fryer basket in a single layer; cook in batches if required to avoid overflowing the fryer. Set a timer for 14 minutes and flip the pickles halfway through.

Air Fryer Brown Sugar and Pecan Roasted Apples

Preparation Time: 15 minutes
Cooking Time: 22 minutes
Serve: 1
Ingredients:

- 2 tablespoons coarsely chopped pecans
- 1 tablespoon brown sugar
- 1 teaspoon all-purpose flour
- ¼ teaspoon apple pie spice
- 2 medium apples
- 1 tablespoon butter

Directions:

- Preheat the air fryer carefully to 360°F (180 degrees C).
- Combine pecans, brown sugar, flour, and apple pie spice in a small mixing bowl. In a medium mixing bowl, combine apple wedges and drizzle with butter, tossing to coat. Arrange the apples in the air fryer basket in a single layer and top with the pecan mixture.
- Cook in a hot air fryer for 10 to 15 minutes, or until apples are soft.

Air Fryer Hard-Boiled Eggs

Preparation Time: 10 minutes
Cooking Time: 18 minutes
Serve: 1
Ingredients:

- 6 eggs

Directions:

- Carefully to 250°F (120 degrees C).
- Fill the air fryer basket halfway with eggs.
- The cooking time for eggs is 15 minutes. Then, remove the eggs and immerse them in a cold-water bath for 8 to 10 minutes or completely cool.

Air Fryer Soy-Ginger Shishito Peppers

Preparation Time: 18 minutes
Cooking Time: 20 minutes
Serve: 1
Ingredients:

- 6 ounces shishito peppers
- 1 teaspoon vegetable oil
- 1 tablespoon reduced-sodium soy sauce
- 1 tablespoon fresh lime juice
- 1 teaspoon honey
- ½ teaspoon grated fresh ginger

Directions:

- Carefully to 390°F (199 degrees C).
- Tossing the peppers with the oil to coat in a medium mixing basin. Fill the air fryer basket halfway with peppers. 6 to 7 minutes, shaking the basket halfway through until blistered and tender.
- Meanwhile, add the soy sauce, lime juice, honey, and ginger to the medium bowl. Toss in the cooked peppers to coat. Serve hot.

Air Fryer Tilapia with Fresh Lemon Pepper
Preparation Time: 15 minutes
Cooking Time: 25 minutes
Serve: 1
Ingredients:

- 4 (6 ounces) tilapia fillets
- 2 tablespoons lemon zest
- 2 tablespoons olive oil
- 1 ½ teaspoon coarsely ground black peppercorns
- cooking spray, ½ teaspoon salt
- 2 cloves garlic, minced
- 1 pinch paprika
- 1 sprig parsley, chopped
- 4 wedges lemon

Directions:

- Preheat the air fryer carefully for 3 minutes at 400 degrees F (200 degrees C).
- While the fryer is heating up, rinse the tilapia fillets and blot them dry with a paper towel.
- Combine the lemon zest, olive oil, pepper, salt, and garlic in a mixing bowl. Rub the spice mixture on top of the fish. Lightly sprinkle the fillets with paprika. Coat the fillets with cooking spray and set them in the air fryer basket, coated side up.
- Air fried the fish for 7 to 10 minutes, or until it can be flaked with a fork. Do not overcrowd the fish filets; depending on the size of your air fryer, and you may need to fry a second batch.
- Transfer the tilapia to a platter and top with chopped parsley. Serve with lemon wedges.

Air Fryer Breaded Sea Scallops
Preparation Time: 20 minutes
Cooking Time: 20 minutes
Serve: 1
Ingredients:

- ½ cup finely crushed buttery crackers (such as Ritz®)
- ½ teaspoon garlic powder
- ½ teaspoon seafood seasoning (such as Old Bay®)
- 2 tablespoons butter, melted
- 1 pound sea scallops, patted dry
- 1 serving cooking spray

Directions:

- Preheat the air fryer carefully to 390°F (198 degrees C).
- Combine the cracker crumbs, garlic powder, and seafood seasoning in a small bowl. In a second shallow dish, place the melted butter.
- Dip each scallop in the melted butter, then roll in the breading until well covered. Place the scallops on a platter and repeat with the remaining scallops.

- Coat the air fryer basket lightly with cooking spray. Arrange the scallops in the prepared basket to don't touch; you may need to work in batches.
- Cook for 2 minutes in a preheated air fryer. Cook until the scallops are opaque, approximately 2 minutes more, using a small spatula.

Easy Air Fryer French Toast Sticks
Preparation Time: 15 minutes
Cooking Time: 25 minutes
Serve: 1
Ingredients:

- 4 slices of slightly stale thick bread, such as Texas toast
- parchment paper
- 2 eggs, lightly beaten
- ¼ cup milk
- 1 teaspoon vanilla extract
- 1 teaspoon cinnamon
- 1 pinch ground nutmeg (optional)

Directions:

- To make sticks, cut each slice of bread into thirds. Then, to fit the bottom of the air fryer basket cut a piece of parchment paper.
- Preheat the air fryer carefully to 360°F (180 degrees C).
- Combine the eggs, milk, vanilla extract, cinnamon, and nutmeg in a mixing dish until thoroughly blended. Dip each slice of bread into the egg mixture, ensuring sure it is well immersed. Shake each breadstick to remove extra liquid before placing it in the air fryer basket in a single layer. If necessary, cook in batches to avoid overflowing the fryer.
- Fry for 5 minutes, then flip the bread slices and cook for another 5 minutes.

Air Fryer Pull-Apart Pepperoni-Cheese Bread
Preparation Time: 15 minutes
Cooking Time: 20 minutes
Serve: 1
Ingredients:

- cooking spray
- 1 ½ pound fresh pizza dough
- 1-ounce sliced turkey pepperoni
- dried oregano to taste
- ground red pepper to taste
- garlic salt to taste
- 1 teaspoon melted butter
- 1 teaspoon grated Parmesan cheese
- ½ cup shredded mozzarella cheese

Directions:

- To fit the bottom of your air fryer, shape a big piece of aluminum foil into a pan with 2-inch-high edges. Coat the pan with nonstick cooking spray.
- Preheat the air fryer carefully to 390°F (200°C) for 15 minutes.
- Roll the pizza dough into 1-inch balls and set them in an aluminum foil pan in a single layer. Season with pepperoni, oregano, red pepper flakes, and garlic salt to taste. Brush with melted butter, then top with Parmesan cheese.
- Cook for 15 minutes with the pan at the bottom of the air fryer. Cook until the mozzarella cheese is melted and bubbling on the bread, about 2 minutes longer. Remove

from the air fryer by pulling the sides of the pan up and out of the machine using tongs.

Air Fryer Asian-Inspired Deviled Eggs

Preparation Time: 20 minutes
Cooking Time: 25 minutes
Serve: 1
Ingredients:

- 6 large eggs
- 2 tablespoons mayonnaise
- 1 ½ teaspoons sriracha sauce
- 1 ½ teaspoon sesame oil
- 1 teaspoon low-sodium soy sauce
- 1 teaspoon Dijon mustard
- 1 teaspoon finely grated ginger root
- 1 teaspoon rice vinegar
- toasted sesame seeds
- 1 green onion, thinly sliced

Directions:

- Place the eggs on an air fryer rack or trivet, leaving enough room between them for air to circulate. Set the air fryer to 260 degrees Fahrenheit (125 degrees Celsius) and the timer for 15 minutes. The air fryer should be closed.
- Place the eggs in a dish of cold water for 10 minutes after being removed from the air fryer. Then, remove the eggs from the water, peel them, and cut them half.
- Scoop out the yolks and set them in a tiny food processor. In a mixing bowl, combine the mayonnaise, sriracha, sesame oil, low-sodium soy sauce, Dijon mustard, ginger root, and rice vinegar. Process until the mixture is well blended and creamy, mousse-like consistency.
- Fill a piping bag halfway with the yolk mixture and evenly spread it into the egg white halves until they are overflowing full; you can also do this with a spoon. Garnish with sesame seeds and green onion, if desired.

Air Fryer Chocolate Chip Cookie Bites

Preparation Time: 15 minutes
Cooking Time: 20 minutes
Serve: 1
Ingredients:

- ½ cup butter softened
- ½ cup packed brown sugar
- ¼ cup white sugar
- ½ teaspoon baking soda
- ½ teaspoon salt, 1 egg
- 1 ½ teaspoons vanilla extract
- 1 ⅓ cups all-purpose flour
- 1 cup miniature semisweet chocolate chips
- ⅓ cup finely chopped pecans, toasted

Directions:

- To fit an air fryer basket, cut a piece of parchment paper.
- In a large mixing basin, beat the butter for 30 seconds on medium to high-speed using an electric mixer. Mix in the brown sugar, white sugar, baking soda, and salt for 2 minutes on medium speed, scraping the bowl regularly. Mix in the egg and vanilla essence until well mixed. Mix in as much flour as possible. Combine the remaining flour, chocolate chips, and pecans in a mixing bowl.
- Drop the dough by teaspoonfuls onto the parchment paper, 1 inch apart. Transfer the parchment paper to the air fryer basket with care.

- Preheat the air fryer carefully to 300°F (150°C) and cook until golden brown and firm, about 8 minutes. Cool the parchment paper on a wire rack. Repeat with the rest of the cookie dough.

Air Fryer Steak Tips and Portobello Mushrooms

Preparation Time: 15 minutes
Cooking Time: 18 minutes
Serve: 1
Ingredients:

- ¼ cup olive oil
- 1 tablespoon coconut aminos
- ½ teaspoon garlic powder
- 2 strip steaks
- 2 teaspoons Montreal steak seasoning
- 4 ounces portobello mushrooms, quartered

Directions:

- Combine the olive oil, coconut aminos, steak seasoning, and garlic powder in a small bowl. Mix well, then add the steak pieces and marinate for 15 minutes.
- Carefully to 390°F (200 degrees C). The perforated parchment paper should line the bottom of the air fryer basket.
- Remove the meat from the marinade. Fill the air fryer basket halfway with steak and quartered portobello mushrooms.
- Cook for 5 minutes in a hot air fryer. Remove the basket, stir the steak and mushrooms around, and cook for 4 minutes.

Crispy Air Fryer Cod

Preparation Time: 15 minutes
Cooking Time: 22 minutes
Serve: 1
Ingredients:

- 1 pound cod, about 1-inch thick
- ¼ cup all-purpose flour
- 1 ½ teaspoon seafood seasoning
- ¼ cup polenta
- 1 ½ teaspoon garlic salt
- 1 teaspoon onion powder
- ½ teaspoon ground black pepper
- ½ teaspoon paprika
- olive oil cooking spray

Directions:

- Carefully to 380°F (195 degrees C). Using paper towels, pat the codpieces dry.
- Combine the polenta, flour, seafood seasoning, garlic salt, onion powder, pepper, and paprika in a shallow dish. Coat each piece of cod with the breading mixture, pressing the breading into each side of the fish until well coated.
- Spray the air fryer basket with olive oil cooking spray. Arrange the cod in the basket, leaving enough space between each piece to allow air to flow. Cooking spray should be sprayed on the top of each piece of fish.
- 8 minutes in the oven cook for 4 minutes longer after turning each piece and spraying with cooking spray.

Air Fryer Fried Mushrooms

Preparation Time: 10 minutes

Cooking Time: 18 minutes
Serve: 1
Ingredients:

- 3 eggs
- 1 cup all-purpose flour
- ½ cup plain breadcrumbs
- ½ cup panko breadcrumbs
- ½ tablespoon kosher salt
- 1 teaspoon onion powder
- 1 teaspoon garlic powder
- 1 teaspoon ground black pepper
- 1 teaspoon paprika
- 1 teaspoon seafood seasoning (such as Old Bay®)
- 1-pound small cremini mushrooms
- 1 serving nonstick cooking spray

Directions:

- Preheat the air fryer carefully to 400°F (200 degrees C).
- In a mixing dish, whisk together the eggs. Then, combine the flour, breadcrumbs, kosher salt, onion powder, garlic powder, pepper, paprika, and seafood seasoning in a separate bowl.
- Dip the mushrooms in the eggs first, then in the seasoned flour. Dip into the eggs again, then into the seasoned flour. Serve on a platter.
- Place a batch of mushrooms in the air fryer basket, being careful not to overlap them. Coat the pan with nonstick cooking spray. 6 minutes in the oven Shake the basket and apply nonstick cooking spray on chalky places. Cook for another 6 minutes. Rep with the remaining mushrooms

Air Fryer One-Bite Roasted Potatoes

Preparation Time: 18 minutes
Cooking Time: 20 minutes
Serve: 1
Ingredients:

- ½ pound mini potatoes
- 2 teaspoons extra-virgin olive oil
- 2 teaspoons dry Italian-style salad dressing mix
- salt and ground black pepper to taste

Directions:

- Preheat the air fryer carefully to 400°F (200 degrees C).
- Wash and pat dry the potatoes. Trim the edges so that both ends have a level surface.
- Combine the extra-virgin olive oil and salad dressing mix in a large mixing bowl. Toss in the potatoes until they are completely covered. Fill the air fryer basket in a single layer. If necessary, cook in batches.
- 5 to 7 minutes in the air fryer until golden brown the potatoes. Flip the potatoes and continue to air fry for 2 to 3 minutes. Season with salt and pepper to taste.

Air Fryer Keto Garlic Cheese 'Bread.'

Preparation Time: 15 minutes
Cooking Time: 25 minutes
Serve: 1
Ingredients:

- 1 cup shredded mozzarella cheese
- ¼ cup grated Parmesan cheese
- 1 large egg
- ½ teaspoon garlic powder

Directions:

- Wrap a piece of parchment paper around the air fryer basket.
- In a mixing dish, combine mozzarella cheese, Parmesan cheese, egg, and garlic powder; stir well. Form a spherical circle on the parchment paper in the air fryer basket.
- Preheat the air fryer carefully to 350°F (175 degrees C). Toast the bread for 10 minutes. Remove. Warm, but not hot, garlic cheese bread

Chocolate Cake in an Air Fryer

Preparation Time: 20 minutes
Cooking Time: 20 minutes
Serve: 1
Ingredients:

- cooking spray
- ¼ cup white sugar
- 3 ½ tablespoons butter, softened
- 1 egg
- 1 tablespoon apricot jam
- 6 tablespoons all-purpose flour
- 1 tablespoon unsweetened cocoa powder
- salt to taste

Directions:

- Carefully to 320°F (160 degrees C). Coat a small, fluted tube pan with nonstick cooking spray.
- In a mixing bowl, beat the sugar and butter with an electric mixer until light and fluffy. Mix in the egg and jam until well mixed. Sift in the flour, cocoa powder, and salt and thoroughly combine. Pour the batter into the prepared baking dish. Using the back of a spoon, smooth down the batter's surface.
- Insert the pan into the air fryer basket. Cook for about 15 minutes, or until a toothpick inserted into the center of the cake comes out clean.

Air Fryer Italian Sausages, Peppers, and Onions

Preparation Time: 15 minutes
Cooking Time: 25 minutes
Serve: 1
Ingredients:

- 2 small onions
- 1 small red bell pepper, thinly sliced
- 1 small yellow bell pepper, thinly sliced
- 1 small orange bell pepper, thinly sliced
- 2 tablespoons olive oil
- 1 teaspoon Italian seasoning
- ¾ teaspoon salt
- ½ teaspoon ground black pepper
- 1-pound sweet Italian sausage links
- 4 each lightly toasted buns
- 4 slices provolone cheese

Directions:

- Preheat the air fryer carefully to 350°F (180 degrees C).
- Cut the onions in half from root to stem, then into thirds. In a medium mixing dish, combine the onions and bell peppers. Toss in the olive oil, Italian seasoning, salt, and pepper. Place the veggies in the air fryer basket and place the sausage links on top, not touching.
- Cook for 15 minutes in an air fryer. Air fried the sausages for another 10 minutes.

- Top each sausage with veggies and provolone cheese in a bun.

Air Fryer Shrimp a la Bang Bang

Preparation Time: 15 minutes
Cooking Time: 20 minutes
Serve: 1
Ingredients:

- ½ cup mayonnaise
- ¼ cup sweet chili sauce
- 1 tablespoon sriracha sauce
- ¼ cup all-purpose flour
- 1 cup panko breadcrumbs
- 1-pound raw shrimp, peeled and deveined
- 1 head loose-leaf lettuce
- 2 green onions, chopped

Directions:

- Carefully to 400°F (200 degrees C).
- In a mixing bowl, combine mayonnaise, chili sauce, and sriracha sauce until smooth. If preferred, keep some bang bang sauce in a separate dish for dipping.
- On a dish, spread out the flour. Then, on a separate plate, place the panko.
- Coat the shrimp with flour first, then with the mayonnaise mixture, and last with panko. Next, place the shrimp on a baking sheet that has been coated.
- Place the shrimp in the air fryer basket without crowding them.
- 12 minutes in the oven Rep with the remaining shrimp.
- Serve in lettuce wraps with green onions on top.

Air Fryer Fried Pickles

Preparation Time: 20 minutes
Cooking Time: 25 minutes
Serve: 1
Ingredients:

- ½ cup mayonnaise
- 2 tablespoons sriracha sauce
- 1 (16 ounces) jar dill pickle chips
- 1 egg
- 2 tablespoons milk
- ½ cup all-purpose flour
- ½ cup cornmeal
- ½ teaspoon seasoned salt
- ¼ teaspoon paprika
- ¼ teaspoon garlic powder
- ⅛ teaspoon ground black pepper
- cooking spray

Directions:

- In a small bowl, combine mayonnaise and sriracha sauce. Place in the refrigerator until ready to serve.
- Carefully to 400°F (200 degrees C).
- Drain the pickles and pat them dry with paper towels.
- In a mixing dish, combine the egg and milk. Next, combine the flour, cornmeal, seasoned salt, paprika, garlic powder, and black pepper in a separate bowl.
- Dip pickle chips first in the egg mixture, then in the flour mixture, coating both sides and lightly pushing the flour mixture into the chips.

- Cooking spray should be sprayed on the air fryer basket. Place pickle chips in a single layer in the basket; if required, divide them into two batches.
- Cook for 4 minutes before gently flipping the chips. Cook until the desired brownness is achieved, about 4 minutes more. Serve with sriracha mayonnaise.

Air Fryer Sweet Potato Tots

Preparation Time: 15 minutes
Cooking Time: 20 minutes
Serve: 1
Ingredients:

- 2 sweet potatoes, peeled
- ½ teaspoon Cajun seasoning
- olive oil cooking spray
- sea salt to taste

Directions:

- Bring a saucepan of water to a boil before adding the sweet potatoes. Boil for 15 minutes, or until potatoes can be pierced with a fork but are still firm. If you overcook them, they will be difficult to grate. Allow cooling after draining.
- Using a box grater, shred sweet potatoes into a bowl. Mix in the Cajun spice with care. Form the mixture into cylinders in the shape of tots.
- Use olive oil spray to coat the air fryer basket. Place the tots in the basket in a single row, not touching one other or the basket's sides. Toss tots in olive oil spray and season with sea salt.
- Preheat the air fryer carefully to 400°F (200°C) and cook the tots for 8 minutes. Turn, re-spray with olive oil spray, then top with additional sea salt. Cook for an additional 8 minutes.

Air Fryer Cauliflower Tots

Preparation Time: 15 minutes
Cooking Time: 18 minutes
Serve: 1
Ingredients:

- 1 serving nonstick cooking spray
- 1 (16 ounces) package frozen cauliflower tots (such as Green Giant® Cauliflower Veggie Tots)

Directions:

- Preheat the air fryer carefully to 400°F (200 degrees C). Nonstick cooking spray should be sprayed on the air fryer basket.
- Place as many cauliflower tots as you can in the basket, ensure they don't touch and cook in batches if required.
- Cook for 6 minutes in a hot air fryer. Remove the basket, flip the tots over, and cook for another 3 minutes, or until browned and cooked through.

Air Fryer Souffle Egg Cups

Preparation Time: 15 minutes
Cooking Time: 22 minutes
Serve: 1
Ingredients:

- 2 eggs
- ¼ cup frozen pepper and onion stir fry mix
- ¼ cup shredded mild Cheddar cheese
- ¼ teaspoon taco seasoning mix
- ⅛ teaspoon garlic salt

Directions:

- Preheat the air fryer carefully for 5 minutes at 370 degrees F (190 degrees C).
- In a mixing bowl, whisk the eggs until they are light and fluffy. Combine the Cheddar cheese, veggie mix, taco seasoning, and garlic salt in a mixing bowl. Fill silicone baking cups with the batter and place them in the air fryer basket.
- 5 minutes in the air fryer. Serve right away.

Air Fryer BBQ Baby Back Ribs
Preparation Time: 10 minutes
Cooking Time: 18 minutes
Serve: 1
Ingredients:

- 3 pounds baby back pork ribs
- 1 tablespoon brown sugar
- 1 tablespoon white sugar
- 1 teaspoon sweet paprika
- 1 teaspoon smoked paprika
- 1 teaspoon granulated garlic
- ½ teaspoon ground black pepper
- ½ teaspoon ground cumin
- ½ teaspoon granulated onion
- ¼ teaspoon Greek seasoning (Optional)
- ⅓ cup barbeque sauce

Directions:

- Preheat the air fryer carefully to 350°F (175 degrees C).
- Remove the membrane off the rear of the ribs and cut the ribs into four equal pieces.
- Combine brown sugar, white sugar, sweet paprika, smoked paprika, granulated garlic, pepper, cumin, onion, and Greek seasoning in a small mixing bowl. Rub the spice mixture all over the ribs before placing them in the air fryer basket.
- Cook the ribs for 30 minutes in the air fryer, flipping after 15 minutes. Brush with barbecue sauce and continue to air fry for 5 minutes.

Air Fryer Jerk Pork Skewers with Black Bean and Mango Salsa
Preparation Time: 18 minutes
Cooking Time: 20 minutes
Serve: 1
Ingredients:

- 2 tablespoons white sugar
- 4 ½ teaspoons onion powder
- 4 ½ teaspoons dried thyme, crushed
- 1 tablespoon ground allspice
- 1 tablespoon ground black pepper
- 1 ½ teaspoons cayenne pepper
- 1 ½ teaspoons salt
- ¾ teaspoon ground nutmeg
- ¼ teaspoon ground cloves
- ¼ cup shredded coconut
- 1 (1 pound) pork tenderloin, cut into 1 1/2-inch cube
- 4 each bamboo skewers, soaked in water for 30 minutes, drained
- 1 tablespoon vegetable oil
- 1 mango - peeled, seeded, and chopped
- ½ (15 ounces) can black beans

- ¼ cup finely chopped red onion
- 2 tablespoons fresh lime juice
- 1 tablespoon honey
- 1 tablespoon chopped fresh cilantro
- ¼ teaspoon salt
- ⅛ teaspoon ground black pepper

Directions:

- In a small bowl, combine the sugar, onion powder, thyme, allspice, black pepper, cayenne pepper, salt, nutmeg, and cloves for the seasoning mix. Transfer the rub to a small airtight container, leaving 1 tablespoon in a separate bowl for the pork. Stir in the coconut and the remaining 1 tablespoon spice.
- Preheat the air fryer carefully to 350°F (175 degrees C).
- Thread the skewers with the pork slices. Brush the pork with oil and spice combination on all sides before placing it in the air frying basket.
- Cook for 5 to 7 minutes in a preheated air fryer until an instant-read thermometer put into the thickest section of the meat reads 145 degrees F (63 degrees C).
- Meanwhile, in a medium mixing bowl, mash 1/3 of the mango. Add the remaining mango, black beans, red onion, lime juice, honey, cilantro, salt, and pepper to taste. Serve with pork skewers and salsa.

Air Fryer Peanut Butter & Jelly S'mores
Preparation Time: 15 minutes
Cooking Time: 25 minutes
Serve: 1
Ingredients:

- 1 chocolate-covered peanut butter cup
- 2 chocolate graham cracker squares, divided
- 1 teaspoon seedless raspberry jam
- 1 large marshmallow

Directions:

- Preheat the air fryer carefully to 400°F (200 degrees C).
- Place 1 graham cracker square on top of a peanut butter cup. Serve with jelly and marshmallows on top. Place in the air fryer basket with care.
- Cook for 1 minute in a hot air fryer until marshmallow is lightly browned and melted. Top with the remaining graham cracker square right away.

Air Fryer Mini Bean and Cheese Tacos
Preparation Time: 20 minutes
Cooking Time: 20 minutes
Serve: 1
Ingredients:

- 1 (16 ounces) can refried beans
- 1 (1 ounce) envelope taco seasoning mix
- 12 slices American cheese, cut in half
- 12 (6 inches) flour tortillas
- cooking spray

Directions:

- Preheat the air fryer carefully to 400°F (200 degrees C).
- In a bowl, combine the refried beans. Stir in taco seasoning until evenly blended.
- 1 slice of cheese in the center of a tortilla 1 spoonful of the bean mixture should be spooned over the cheese. On top of the beans, place another piece of cheese. To seal the taco, fold the tortilla over and press down. Continue with the remaining tortillas, beans, and cheese.

- Nonstick frying spray should be sprayed on all sides of the tacos. Place tacos in the air fryer basket, ensuring sure none overlap.
- 3 minutes in the oven cook for 3 minutes longer after flipping the tacos. Rep with the remaining tacos.

Sweet Potato Chips in the Air Fryer

Preparation Time: 15 minutes
Cooking Time: 25 minutes
Serve: 1
Ingredients:

- 1 teaspoon avocado oil
- 1 medium sweet potato, peeled and sliced crossways into 1/8-inch slices
- ½ teaspoon Creole seasoning

Directions:

- Preheat the air fryer carefully to 400°F (200 degrees C).
- In a large mixing basin, combine the sweet potato pieces. Mix with the avocado oil, covering each piece equally. Stir in the Creole seasoning until well combined. Spread the slices on the bottom of the air fryer basket in a thin layer.
- Cook for 7 minutes in a preheated air fryer. Shake and flip the slices to ensure consistent frying. Cook for another 6 minutes, or until the desired crispness is attained. Allow the potato slices to cool on a rack.

Skinny Air Fryer Funnel Cakes

Preparation Time: 15 minutes
Cooking Time: 20 minutes
Serve: 1
Ingredients:

- nonstick cooking spray
- 1 teaspoon vanilla extract
- 1 cup almond flour
- 4 tablespoons erythritol confectioners' sweetener
- 1 tablespoon almond flour
- 1 cup nonfat plain Greek yogurt
- 1 ½ teaspoons baking powder
- 1 teaspoon ground cinnamon
- ½ teaspoon salt

Directions:

- Carefully to 325°F (165°C) according to the manufacturer's instructions. Line the basket with parchment paper and sprinkle it with nonstick cooking spray.
- Combine almond flour, Greek yogurt, 2 tablespoons sweetener, baking powder, cinnamon, vanilla extract, and salt in a mixing dish. Make the dough come together by kneading it with your hands.
- Flour your work surface, divide the dough into four equal pieces, and form into balls. Using a bench scraper, cut each ball into 8 equal pieces. Roll each piece in flour and roll into a long, thin rope between your palms. Place all 8 ropes, one by one, into the preheated air fryer basket in a circular mound. Repeat with the rest of the dough balls. Cooking spray should be sprayed on each funnel cake.
- 5 to 6 minutes in the air fryer until golden brown. Flip each funnel cake over, coat with cooking spray, and continue to air fry for 3 to 4 minutes. Finish with the remaining 2 teaspoons of sweetener.

Air-Fried Jalapeno Poppers

Preparation Time: 20 minutes
Cooking Time: 25 minutes
Serve: 1
Ingredients:

- 6 medium jalapeno peppers, halved and seeded
- 6 ounces cream cheese, softened
- 1-ounce shredded Cheddar cheese
- 3 slices salami, dry or hard, pork, beef
- 6 slices bacon, cut in half lengthwise

Directions:

- Carefully to 390°F (199°C) according to the manufacturer's instructions.
- Fill each half of jalapeño with cream cheese and Cheddar cheese. If desired, place 1/2 a slice of salami on top of each pepper, wrap with bacon, and fasten with a toothpick.
- Layer the jalapeño poppers in the preheated air fryer and cook for 10 to 12 minutes, or until the bacon is browned and the cheese is melted.

Air Fryer Frog Legs

Preparation Time: 15 minutes
Cooking Time: 20 minutes
Serve: 1
Ingredients:

- 1 pound frog legs
- 2 cups milk
- 2 cups yellow cornmeal
- 1 cup all-purpose flour
- 2 tablespoons seafood seasoning (such as Old Bay®)
- cooking spray

Directions:

- Pour milk over the top of the frog legs in a dish. Refrigerate for 1 hour, covered.
- Carefully to 400°F (200°C) according to the manufacturer's instructions.
- Meanwhile, add cornmeal, flour, and seafood seasoning in a gallon-sized resealable plastic bag. To blend, seal the container and shake it vigorously.
- Remove 1 frog leg from the milk, allowing the excess to drip into the dish. Shake the bag with the seasoned cornmeal mixture to coat. Return the frog legs to the cornmeal mixture after dipping them back in the milk. Shake again to coat, then transfer to a dish. Rep with the remaining frog legs.
- Cooking sprays the air fryer basket and puts as many frog legs as you can without overlapping. Coat the tops in cooking spray. If necessary, work in bunches.
- 5 minutes in the air fryer. Cooking spray should be used to remove any chalky patches. Cook for another 3 minutes, or until the bacon is crispy. Repeat with the remaining batches on a platter.

Air Fryer Hush Puppies

Preparation Time: 15 minutes
Cooking Time: 18 minutes
Serve: 1
Ingredients:

- nonfat cooking spray
- 1 cup yellow cornmeal

- ¾ cup all-purpose flour
- 1 ½ teaspoons baking powder
- ½ teaspoon salt
- ¼ teaspoon cayenne pepper, or more to taste
- ¼ teaspoon garlic powder
- 2 tablespoons minced onion
- 2 tablespoons minced green bell pepper
- ¾ cup low-fat buttermilk
- 1 large egg

Directions:

- Carefully to 390°F (198°C) according to the manufacturer's instructions. Spray the bottom of the air fryer basket with nonfat cooking spray and line with aluminum foil.
- In a large mixing bowl, combine cornmeal, flour, baking powder, salt, cayenne pepper, and garlic powder. Next, combine the onion and bell pepper.
- In a separate dish, whisk together the buttermilk and egg. Mix into the cornmeal mixture. Allow the mixture to sit for 5 minutes.
- Using a 2-tablespoon cookie scoop, scoop the cornmeal mixture into the foil-lined basket, making sure not to overlap. Coat the pan with nonfat cooking spray.
- 9 to 10 minutes in a preheated air fryer, until golden brown, crispy, and cooked through. Serve immediately.

Air-Fried Ratatouille, Italian-Style
Preparation Time: 15 minutes
Cooking Time: 22 minutes
Serve: 1
Ingredients:

- ½ small eggplant, cut into cubes
- 1 zucchini, cut into cubes
- 1 medium tomato, cut into cubes
- ½ large yellow bell pepper, cut into cubes
- ½ large red bell pepper, cut into cubes
- ½ onion, cut into cubes
- 1 fresh cayenne pepper, diced
- 5 sprigs fresh basil, stemmed and chopped
- 2 sprigs of fresh oregano, stemmed and chopped
- 1 clove garlic, crushed
- salt and ground black pepper to taste
- 1 tablespoon olive oil
- 1 tablespoon white wine
- 1 teaspoon vinegar

Directions:

- Carefully to 400°F (200 degrees C).
- Combine the eggplant, zucchini, tomato, bell peppers, and onion in a mixing dish. Next, combine the cayenne pepper, basil, oregano, garlic, salt, and pepper in a mixing bowl. To ensure that everything is distributed equally, combine all ingredients in a mixing bowl. Drizzle in the oil, wine, and vinegar and toss to cover all veggies.
- Place the vegetable mixture in a baking dish and place it in the air fryer basket. 8 minutes in the oven cook for another 8 minutes, stirring occasionally. Stir once more and simmer until tender, 10 to 15 minutes more, stirring every 5 minutes. Turn off the air fryer but leave the dish inside. Allow for a 5-minute pause before serving.

Air Fryer Eggplant Parmesan Mini Pizzas
Preparation Time: 10 minutes

Cooking Time: 18 minutes
Serve: 1
Ingredients:

- 1 medium eggplant, sliced into 1/2- inch rounds
- salt to taste
- 1 egg, beaten
- 1 tablespoon water
- 1 cup Italian breadcrumbs
- ¼ cup freshly grated Parmesan cheese
- cooking spray
- 4 ounces pizza sauce
- 1 (2.25 ounces) can slice ripe olives, drained
- 8 ounces shredded mozzarella cheese
- 1 tablespoon chopped fresh basil for garnish

Directions:

- Arrange the eggplant rounds on a broad chopping board and season lightly on both sides. Allow for a 10-minute rest. Then, using paper towels, pat dry. Preheat the oven to 250 degrees Fahrenheit (120 degrees C).
- Meanwhile, in a mixing dish, combine the egg and water. On a flat dish, combine breadcrumbs and Parmesan cheese. Line a rimmed baking sheet with foil and set a cooling rack on top.
- Each eggplant round should be dipped in beaten egg and then coated in a bread crumb mixture.
- Carefully to 400°F (200 degrees C). Nonstick cooking spray should be sprayed on the basket.
- Fill your basket with as many eggplant rounds as space permits without overloading. Coat the tops in cooking spray. The cooking time is 10 minutes. Place the rounds on a cooling rack and keep warm in a preheated oven. Rep with the leftover eggplant.
- Spread pizza sauce on top of each eggplant circle. Cover with olive slices and mozzarella cheese.
- Preheat the oven's broiler to high and position the oven rack about 6 inches from the heat source.
- Broil the eggplant slice pizzas for 4 minutes or until the cheese melts. Garnish with basil if desired.

Air Fryer Corn Dogs
Preparation Time: 18 minutes
Cooking Time: 20 minutes
Serve: 1
Ingredients:

- parchment paper
- 6 bamboo skewers
- 1 (6.5 ounces) package cornbread mix
- ⅔ cup milk
- 1 egg
- 1 teaspoon white sugar
- 8 hot dogs, cut in half

Directions:

- Divide the soaking bamboo skewers into thirds. To properly fit the bottom of the air fryer basket, cut a piece of parchment paper.
- Preheat the air fryer carefully to 400°F (200 degrees C).
- In a mixing bowl, combine cornbread mix, milk, egg, and sugar until blended; pour into a tall glass.
- Insert a skewer into the center of each hot dog piece. Remove the air fryer basket and lay the cut parchment paper on the bottom of the basket. Dip four hot dogs in the batter and set them on top of the parchment paper, alternating the direction of the stick ends.

- Cook for 8 minutes in a preheated air fryer without turning, or until desired brownness. Repeat with the remaining hot dogs on a dish.

Air Fryer Mustard-Crusted Pork Tenderloin with Potatoes and Green Beans
Preparation Time: 15 minutes
Cooking Time: 25 minutes
Serve: 1
Ingredients:

- ¼ cup Dijon mustard
- 2 tablespoons brown sugar
- 1 teaspoon dried parsley flakes
- ½ teaspoon dried thyme
- ¼ teaspoon salt
- ¼ teaspoon ground black pepper
- 1 ¼ pound pork tenderloin
- ¾ pound small potatoes (such as The Little Potato® Company), halved
- 1 (12 ounces) package fresh green beans, trimmed
- 1 tablespoon olive oil
- salt and ground black pepper to taste

Directions:

- Carefully to 400°F (200°C) according to the manufacturer's instructions.
- Combine mustard, brown sugar, parsley, thyme, salt, and pepper in a large mixing bowl. Roll the tenderloin in the mustard mixture until uniformly coated on both sides.
- Combine the potatoes, green beans, and olive oil in a separate bowl. Season with salt and pepper to taste and mix well. Place aside.
- Place the tenderloin in the basket of a prepared air fryer and cook, undisturbed, for 20 minutes or until the middle is slightly pink. In the middle, an instant-read thermometer should read at least 145 degrees F. (63 degrees C). Transfer to a chopping board and set aside for 10 minutes to rest.
- Meanwhile, cook the green beans and potatoes in the air fryer basket for 10 minutes, shaking halfway through.
- Serve tenderloin with potatoes and green beans.

Chinese Five-Spice Air Fryer Butternut Squash Fries
Preparation Time: 20 minutes
Cooking Time: 20 minutes
Serve: 1
Ingredients:

- 1 large butternut squash
- 2 tablespoons olive oil
- 1 tablespoon Chinese five-spice powder
- 1 tablespoon minced garlic
- 2 teaspoons sea salt
- 2 teaspoons black pepper

Directions:

- Preheat the air fryer carefully to 400°F (200 degrees C).
- In a large mixing basin, combine the chopped squash. Toss in the oil, five-spice powder, garlic, salt, and black pepper to coat.
- Cook butternut squash fries in a preheated air fryer for 15 to 20 minutes, shaking every 5 minutes, until crisp. Remove the fries and season with sea salt to taste.

Air Fryer Churros
Preparation Time: 15 minutes
Cooking Time: 25 minutes
Serve: 1
Ingredients:

- ¼ cup butter
- ½ cup milk
- 1 pinch salt
- ½ cup all-purpose flour
- 2 eggs
- ¼ cup white sugar
- ½ teaspoon ground cinnamon

Directions:

- In a saucepan over medium-high heat, melt the butter. Pour in the milk and season with salt. Reduce the heat to medium and bring to a boil, constantly stirring with a wooden spoon. Add the flour all at once. Continue to whisk until the dough comes together.
- Remove from the fire and set aside for 5 to 7 minutes to cool. With a wooden spoon, mix the eggs until the pastry comes together. Fill a pastry bag with a big star tip with the dough. Pipe dough strips directly into the air fryer basket.
- For 5 minutes, air-fried churros at 340 degrees F (175 degrees C).
- Meanwhile, mix the sugar and cinnamon in a separate dish and spread it out on a shallow plate.
- Take the cooked churros out of the air fryer and roll them in the cinnamon-sugar mixture.

Air Fryer Salt and Vinegar Fries for One
Preparation Time: 15 minutes
Cooking Time: 20 minutes
Serve: 1
Ingredients:

- 1 large Yukon Gold potato
- 1 cup distilled white vinegar
- ½ tablespoon light vegetable oil
- salt and ground black pepper to taste

Directions:

- Peel the potato and cut it into 1/2-inch sticks lengthwise. For a few seconds, rinse the potato sticks under cold running water. Transfer to a large mixing bowl. Pour in just enough water to cover the potatoes with vinegar. Allow for a 30-minute soak.
- Preheat the air fryer carefully to 320°F (160 degrees C).
- Drain and pat dry the potatoes. Toss in a bowl with the oil, salt, and pepper and place in the air fryer basket.
- Cook for 16 minutes in a hot air fryer until soft but not browned. Shake the basket and heat it to 355 degrees Fahrenheit (180 degrees C). 6 minutes in the air fryer, shake, and check for doneness. Cook for another 6 minutes, or until the outsides of the fries are crispy and golden. Before serving, taste and adjust the salt.

Air-Fried Cauliflower with Almonds and Parmesan
Preparation Time: 20 minutes
Cooking Time: 25 minutes
Serve: 1
Ingredients:

- 3 cups cauliflower florets
- 3 teaspoons vegetable oil, divided
- 1 clove garlic, minced
- ⅓ cup finely shredded Parmesan cheese
- ¼ cup chopped almonds
- ¼ cup panko breadcrumbs
- ½ teaspoon dried thyme, crushed

Directions:

- In a medium mixing basin, combine cauliflower florets, 2 tablespoons oil, and garlic; toss to coat. Place in an air fryer basket in a single layer.
- Cook for 10 minutes in the air fryer at 360°F (180°C), shaking the basket halfway through.
- Toss the cauliflower with the remaining 1 teaspoon oil in the basin. Toss in the Parmesan cheese, almonds, breadcrumbs, and thyme to coat. Return cauliflower mixture to air fryer basket and cook for another 5 minutes, or until crisp and golden.

Air Fryer Breakfast Toad-in-the-Hole Tarts

Preparation Time: 15 minutes
Cooking Time: 20 minutes
Serve: 1
Ingredients:

- 1 sheet frozen puff pastry, thawed
- 4 tablespoons shredded Cheddar cheese
- 4 tablespoons diced cooked ham
- 4 eggs
- 1 tablespoon chopped fresh chives

Directions:

- Preheat the air fryer carefully to 400°F (200 degrees C).
- Unfold the pastry sheet and cut it into 4 squares on a level surface.
- Cook 6 to 8 minutes with 2 pastry squares in the air fryer basket.
- Remove the basket from the air fryer. To make an indentation, lightly push each square with a metal tablespoon. Fill each hole with 1 tablespoon Cheddar cheese and 1 tablespoon ham, then top with 1 egg.
- Return the basket to the air fryer. Cook until done, about 6 minutes more. Remove tarts from the basket and set them aside for 5 minutes to cool. Rep with the rest of the pastry squares, cheese, ham, and eggs.
- Tarts should be garnished with chives.

Air Fryer Roasted Brussels Sprouts with Maple-Mustard Mayo

Preparation Time: 15 minutes
Cooking Time: 18 minutes
Serve: 1
Ingredients:

- 2 tablespoons maple syrup, divided
- 1 tablespoon olive oil - ¼ teaspoon kosher salt
- ¼ teaspoon ground black pepper
- 1 pound Brussels sprouts, trimmed and halved
- ⅓ cup mayonnaise
- 1 tablespoon stone-ground mustard

Directions:

- Preheat the air fryer carefully to 400°F (200 degrees C).
- In a large mixing bowl, combine 1 tablespoon maple syrup, olive oil, salt, and pepper. Toss in the Brussels sprouts to

coat. Arrange Brussels sprouts in an air fryer basket in a single layer, without overcrowded; work in batches if required. 4 minutes in the oven cook until the sprouts are deep golden brown and tender, 4 to 6 minutes longer.

- Meanwhile, combine mayonnaise, the remaining 1 tablespoon maple syrup, and mustard in a small mixing dish. Toss the sprouts in a little sauce combination and serve as a dipping sauce.

Air Fryer Onion Bhaji

Preparation Time: 15 minutes
Cooking Time: 22 minutes
Serve: 1
Ingredients:

- 1 small red onion, thinly sliced
- 1 small yellow onion, thinly sliced
- 1 tablespoon salt
- 1 jalapeno pepper, seeded and minced
- 1 clove garlic, minced - 1 teaspoon coriander
- 1 teaspoon chili powder
- 1 teaspoon ground turmeric
- ½ teaspoon cumin - ⅔ cup chickpea flour (bean)
- 4 tablespoons water, or as needed
- cooking spray

Directions:

- In a large mixing bowl, combine red onion, yellow onion, salt, jalapeño, garlic, coriander, chili powder, turmeric, and cumin. Stir until everything is well blended. Mix in the chickpea flour and water. To make a thick batter, put all ingredients in a mixing bowl. If required, add extra water. Allow the mixture to settle for 10 minutes.
- Preheat the air fryer carefully to 350°F (175 degrees C).
- Nonstick cooking spray should be sprayed on the air fryer basket. Flatten 2 tablespoons of batter into the basket. Repeat as many times as your basket permits without touching the bhajis.
- Cook for 6 minutes in a hot air fryer. Cooking spray should be sprayed on the tops of each bhaji. Cook for 6 minutes more on the other side. Transfer to a plate lined with paper towels. Rep with the remaining batter.

Easy Spring Rolls (Air Fried)

Preparation Time: 10 minutes
Cooking Time: 18 minutes
Serve: 1
Ingredients:

- 2 ounces dried rice noodles
- 1 tablespoon sesame oil
- 7 ounces ground beef
- 1 cup frozen mixed vegetables
- 1 small onion, diced
- 3 cloves garlic, crushed
- 1 teaspoon soy sauce
- 1 (16 ounces) package egg roll wrappers
- 1 tablespoon vegetable oil

Directions:

- Soak noodles in a dish of boiling water for 5 minutes or until soft. Noodles should be cut into shorter strands.
- In a wok, heat the sesame oil over medium-high heat. Combine ground beef, mixed veggies, onion, and garlic in a mixing bowl. Cook for 6 minutes, or until the meat is almost completely browned. Turn off the heat. Stir in the noodles

and set aside until the juices have been absorbed. Soy sauce should be added to the filling.

- Preheat the air fryer carefully to 350°F (175 degrees C).
- 1 egg roll wrapper should be placed on a flat work surface; a diagonal strip of filling should be placed across the wrapper. Fold the top corner over the filling, then fold in the two side corners, brush the center with cold water, and roll the spring roll over to seal. Rep with the rest of the wrappers and filling.
- Brush the spring rolls' tops with vegetable oil. Place a batch of spring rolls in the air fryer basket and cook for 8 minutes, or until crisped and lightly browned. Repeat until all of the eggs are done.

Air-Fried Italian Stuffed Tomatoes

Preparation Time: 18 minutes
Cooking Time: 20 minutes
Serve: 1
Ingredients:

- 4 medium tomatoes
- ⅓ cup freshly grated Parmesan cheese
- olive oil, as needed
- 1 cup cooked brown rice
- ¼ cup crumbled goat cheese
- 2 tablespoons chopped fresh basil
- 2 cloves garlic, minced
- ¼ cup chopped toasted walnuts
- ¼ cup Italian-seasoned breadcrumbs
- 1 tablespoon olive oil

Directions:

- Remove the tops properly from the tomatoes and scoop out the meat with a melon baller, leaving 1/4- to 1/2-inch-thick sides and bottoms. Remove the tomato tops and flesh.
- Brush olive oil on the bottom of an air fryer basket.
- Combine cooked rice, walnuts, 1 tablespoon basil, Parmesan cheese, goat cheese, and garlic in a medium mixing bowl. In a small mixing bowl, combine breadcrumbs and 1 tablespoon olive oil. Fill tomatoes halfway with rice mixture, then top with bread crumb mixture. Place the filled tomatoes in the air fryer basket that has been preheated.
- Cook for 15 minutes in the air fryer at 370°F (188°C) until the tomatoes are soft, the filling is cooked through, and the topping is golden brown. Garnish with any leftover basil.

Conclusion

An air fryer is one of the versatile kitchen appliances that work like a convection oven. It comes in a compact size and easily fits on your kitchen countertop. As compared with the traditional deep frying method air fryer cooks your food by circulating hot air around the food basket. It requires 90% less fat and oil while air frying your favorite food. The air fryer makes your food crispy crunchy from the outside and juicy tenders from the inside.

This cookbook contains 100 healthy and delicious air fryer recipes that come from different categories like breakfast to desserts. The recipes written in this cookbook are simple to make and written into an easy and understandable format. All the recipes start with their preparation and cooking time information with the step-by-step instruction set. All the recipes written in this cookbook come with their nutritional values which will help you to keep track of daily calorie consumption.

Made in the USA
Middletown, DE
14 February 2022

61144364R00093